Symbolic Power in the World Trade Organization

Symbolic Power in the World Trade Organization

Matthew Eagleton-Pierce

OXFORD
UNIVERSITY PRESS

OXFORD
UNIVERSITY PRESS

Great Clarendon Street, Oxford, OX2 6DP,
United Kingdom

Oxford University Press is a department of the University of Oxford.
It furthers the University's objective of excellence in research, scholarship,
and education by publishing worldwide. Oxford is a registered trade mark of
Oxford University Press in the UK and in certain other countries

First Edition published in 2013

Impression: 1

British Library Cataloguing in Publication Data
Data available

Library of Congress Cataloging in Publication Data
Data available

ISBN 978–0–19–966264–7

Printed and bound by CPI Group (UK) Ltd, Croydon, CR0 4YY

Acknowledgements

There are many friends, family members, and colleagues who have been rich sources of advice, encouragement, and inspiration during the writing of this book, but certain individuals stand out. First and foremost, I need to pay respect to the brilliant supervisory skills of Kalypso Nicolaïdis during my time at the University of Oxford. At every stage of the process, her friendly criticism always tested and challenged my abilities and assumptions. I have learnt a great deal from her and could not imagine having a better supervisor. In terms of other colleagues, Andrew Hurrell, also at Oxford, and Rorden Wilkinson at the University of Manchester, deserve particular praise for their careful, critical reading of previous drafts and very helpful encouragement. Andrew Lang and Nicolas Lamp, both at the London School of Economics, also deserve a note of appreciation for offering advice on improving the manuscript. The book has also been enhanced in many ways by the excellent suggestions provided by the peer reviewers.

I also need to dearly thank both my parents, Mary Eagleton and David Pierce, for their multiple and enduring sources of support. I could not have accomplished this piece of work without both of them by my side. This book is also dedicated to Ammara Maqsood who has eased and clarified my mind on many occasions. She has proved to be a wonderful bedrock of support. I also need to express gratitude to each of the interview subjects who enlightened me on the issues contained in this book. On a financial note, I must thank the Economic and Social Research Council for providing me with the time and space needed to conduct the majority of the research. The other main institutional support was provided by St Antony's College, Oxford, a unique intellectual and social environment, which was a happy home for six years. On a final note, I want to express my gratitude to Dominic Byatt at OUP. He has been an excellent commissioning editor.

Chapter 4 features arguments that were contained in the following article published by Taylor & Francis: 'The Competing Kings of Cotton: (Re)framing the WTO African Cotton Initiative', *New Political Economy*, 17 (2012), 3: 313–37. I would like to thank the publisher for allowing me to reuse and expand upon material contained in this article.

For my parents, Mary Eagleton and David Pierce

Contents

List of figures

List of abbreviations

ACA	African Cotton Association
ACP	Africa, Caribbean, and Pacific countries/group
AGOA	Africa Growth and Opportunity Act
AMS	Aggregate measure of support
AoA	Agreement on Agriculture
AU	African Union
C4	Cotton Four (group of countries)
CAFOD	Catholic Agency for Overseas Development
CAP	Common Agricultural Policy
CBI	Caribbean Basin Initiative
CCFF	Compensatory and Contingency Financing Facility
CFA	Communauté financière d'Afrique
CFF	Compensatory Financing Facility
CMA/CWA	West- and central-African ministers of agriculture
COMTRADE	Commodity Trade database
CSI	Coalition of Service Industries
DG	Director general
DSB	Dispute Settlement Body
EC	European Communities
ECOWAS	Economic Community of West African States
ENDA	Environment and Development Action in the Third World
EU	European Union
EWG	Environmental Working Group
FAO	Food and Agriculture Organization of the United Nations
G10	Group of 10 (Northern countries)
G20	Group of 20 (Southern countries)
G33	Group of 33 (Southern countries)
G77	Group of 77 (Southern countries)
GATS	General Agreement on Trade in Services

GATT	General Agreement on Tariffs and Trade
HS	Harmonized Commodity Description and Coding System
ICAC	International Cotton Advisory Committee
ICTSD	International Centre for Trade and Sustainable Development
IF	Integrated Framework for Trade-Related Technical Assistance to Least-Developed Countries
IFSL	International Financial Services London
IMF	International Monetary Fund
IPE	International political economy
IR	International relations
ITO	International Trade Organization
LDCs	Least-developed countries
LMG	Like Minded Group
NCC	National Cotton Council
NGO	Non-governmental organization
OECD	Organisation for Economic Co-operation and Development
POs	Producer organizations
PSE	Producer subsidy equivalent
ROPPA	Le Réseau des Organisations Paysannes et de Producteurs de l'Afrique de l'Ouest
SDT	Special and differential treatment
SPs	Special products
SSG	Special Agricultural Safeguard
SSM	Special Safeguard Mechanism
STABEX	Système de Stabilisation des Recettes d'Exportation
TA	Technical asssistance
TRIPS	Agreement on Trade-Related Aspects of Intellectual Property Rights
TRQ	Tariff rate quota
UN	United Nations
UNCTAD	United Nations Conference on Trade and Development
UNDP	United Nations Development Programme
UK	United Kingdom
US	United States
USDA	US Department of Agriculture
USTR	US Trade Representative
WCA	West and central Africa
WTO	World Trade Organization

1

Introduction

On the last night of the ministerial conference of the World Trade Organization (WTO) in Doha, Qatar in 2001 the pressures were tremendous and the exchanges often fierce. Delegates from thirteen countries gathered in a small room to define the latest agenda of the global trading system. The director general (DG), as referee, had quietly informed all parties that only two representatives per country would be allowed in the room, but somehow the US delegation had five. Negotiation texts had been flying back and forth all day, covering a range of topics yet, in a kind of 'act of magic', the objections of many Southern countries did not appear to have been incorporated into the main text.[1] At key moments, phone calls were placed from Northern capitals to Southern capitals in an effort to build consensus. According to the most privileged actors, some Southern negotiators were behaving in a 'recalcitrant' manner. Their 'unreasonable obstructions', it was argued, would not be viewed in a favourable light, especially when considering preferential economic agreements and other political relations. Wisdom dictated that failure to sign a deal would inevitably send a 'poor signal' to those technicians working in 'the market', not to mention terrorists working in caves. Progressively, as the meeting dragged on until seven o'clock in the morning, the burden of proof shifted from those making new proposals to those not wanting them. Tensions were high, fatigue was setting in, and personal insults were registered. Outside, the other 130 countries that had come to the conference to defend their interests waited anxiously, unable to shape events. When the final text was revealed, many Southern countries were left with feelings of 'deep disappointment and betrayal'.[2] The declaration was much worse than all previous drafts. Yet the conference was over.

These quotes and insights into the process are gleaned from interviews conducted with delegates from Southern countries who attended that Fourth Ministerial Conference. This declaration became known as the 'Doha Development Agenda'. It has been commonly argued that its purpose was to 'rebalance' the multilateral trading system in order to serve the interests of Southern countries. When one tries to understand how this final meeting at Doha was conducted, including assessing who adjusted the agenda and why, it is clear that the role of power is important. Power is said to 'matter' in trading relations. The concept is integral to our efforts to explain how the structures of the WTO are conceived, how actions within them are enabled, and what distributional outcomes are achieved. Power is at work, according to the conventional definition, when one actor compels another to do something they would not have done otherwise. When the US team overrode the decision of DG Michael Moore to limit the number of negotiators or when the White House placed a phone call to Islamabad to secure Pakistan's acquiescence, it is usual to say that power is being exercised.[3] On reflection and through analysis, it can be argued that the most privileged WTO members draw upon a repertoire of methods in order to control other actors. For outsiders, however, these forms of power are not always directly observable. Some of these techniques may be viewed as 'underhand', 'silent', or 'gestural'. Behind the Doha Declaration thus stands a whole other 'declaration' of power relations, and it is the purpose of this book to explore this undisclosed 'declaration' in an effort to shed light on how the process informed the outcome.

As many political analysts have argued, there is nothing secondary or self-evident about the concept of power. There remains considerable disagreement among scholars over its definition and meaning, and little indication that an 'endpoint' or, at least, a partial resolution can be found. More than one scholar, for instance, will have felt Michel Foucault's exasperation: 'I understand who gains and who loses, it is power I do not understand'.[4] When reflecting upon the WTO system, theorists have tended to gravitate towards concepts of power that have emphasized either compulsory, institutional, or structural dimensions.[5] Power may be represented in terms of one member denying market access to another, or by indirect control over the rules and procedures of the WTO, or by shaping the macro belief systems and norms of the trade policy game. My argument is that each of these approaches has certain limitations which, in turn, have cut short or worked against the development of more critical notions of power and legitimacy. One limitation concerns an overemphasis on the dynamics of legalization and institutionalized cooperation, often at the expense of understanding the manifold sources and effects of power. Another is rooted in materialist perspectives that have tended to privilege the study of overt, decision-making actions in the study of power. This understanding, however, can also be problematic, especially if it contributes to a process of 'naturalizing' the relations and structures of the WTO system. Critical concepts of power would historicize the trading order so as to understand the roots of taxonomies and how their political meanings can, in turn, shape the interests and capacities of actors.

Instead, I argue in this book that one needs to think about power in the WTO system broadly rather than narrowly, to the extent that brute diplomatic moves or economic structures represent only one face of power. It seeks to show the analytical value of blending insights from the field of international political economy (IPE) with sociological perspectives on power in order to enhance our understanding of practices and outcomes. In particular, the book aims to examine critically how material power in this domain of capitalism cannot be conserved or transformed without substantial social labour, including the residual labour of past political struggles. In other words, I argue that the conceptual evaluation of power needs to be tightly paired with an analysis of forms of political legitimation in order to better understand patterns of stability and change in international trade relations. For any power in question to survive and prosper, to live beyond a single moment and replenish itself, it needs to be supported by forms of justification. How these representations of legitimacy are socially constructed and contested forms part of the *symbolic face* of power, the central focus of enquiry in this book.

The primary inspiration for this approach is the work of the sociologist Pierre Bourdieu, an important postwar intellectual who is widely cited in the social sciences, but has so far received very little attention within IPE. The notion of symbolic power is designed to focus on how language, as a key symbolic system of political value, both reflects and constitutes power.[6] In this way, as Bourdieu puts it, the concept aims to uncover how agents struggle to burnish or tarnish existing forms of power. Understanding how these complex, often socially draining processes of legitimation work is important for several reasons. In one crucial sense, it helps to explain how and why certain political interests, and the social practices that encompass them, become recognized as 'acceptable' or 'universal', rather than 'arbitrary' or 'particular'. Subsequently, with the privileging of certain interests over others, Bourdieu suggests that the contests over such power shape the material distribution of resources, an often uneven process with lasting effects over time and space. The struggle over symbolic power is, at the same time, also a struggle over groups and their capacity for mobilization. Thus, in short, Bourdieu depicts symbolic power as a kind of '*worldmaking* power' in the sense that it involves the ability to construct and impose the 'legitimate vision of the social world and of its divisions'.[7]

In the literature on the political economy of world trade, such critical theorizing on power has been underexplored. This book seeks to explain why such a deficiency is important to acknowledge and how a Bourdieusian account of power can be put to work in the study of WTO politics. The central question addressed is: how does symbolic power manifest itself in the WTO system? Three main arguments are advanced. First, I argue that while the effects of symbolic power frame the entire trade policy game, conditioning the historically specific experiences of agents, there are particular phases that matter more than others. In particular, this is witnessed in struggles over classifications and at points when certain interests are codified into law. Second, the argument probes the intricate ways in which symbolic power is nurtured, protected, and disputed, particularly around tensions to define legitimate 'orthodox' and 'heterodox' opinions on trade policy. All WTO members can potentially cultivate symbolic power—and this presents opportunities for actors who are historically marginalized—but at the same time, one often finds that the most privileged players are equally, if not more, adept at steering such forces to their advantage. Third, I argue that symbolic power should be understood as a relational concept in regards to both its internal properties and external dynamics. Rather than viewing power as purely concentrated in units or locations, I have tried to understand the concept here in terms of relations of forces, some of which operate with a subtle or latent quality. In particular, attention is given to how symbolic power is engaged in a complex relationship with compulsory power and institutional power.

In terms of the empirical application of these conceptual ideas, the book examines two Southern-led coalitions in agricultural trade that have emerged during the Doha Round. The first case study centres on a west- and central-African group that campaigned for the reform of international cotton trade, while the second case study addresses a larger coalition that has attempted to rethink food security and rural development concerns in relation to the WTO Agreement on Agriculture (AoA). These two cases present an informative comparative study between offensive and defensive Southern agendas in the WTO system and how each can be understood through the lens of symbolic power. In sum, therefore, the objective of the book is not to arrive at a single master category or theory of power, but to challenge IPE scholars, and WTO analysts in particular, to a more rigorous and, at the same time, flexible interrogation of this core concept.

The following introduction is designed to clarify the reasoning behind this research design. There are four main parts. First, I critically review some of the major literature on power analysis in reference to the trading regime and argue that different biases restrict the development of more critical appreciations of power. Second, I discuss in more detail the concept of symbolic power, its attributes, and what contribution it makes to the study of WTO negotiations. In this part I also provide a justification for focusing on agricultural trade and explain why the two cases studies have been selected. Third, a selection of relevant methodological considerations and problems are discussed. Fourth, the structure of the book is briefly outlined.

1.1 Power and the WTO system: conceptual conventions

When evaluating the existing literature on the role of power in the WTO system, it can be argued that in general two kinds of conceptual blind spots work to inhibit and narrow the possibilities for considering more critical understandings of power. These tendencies are found not only within IPE accounts of the WTO, but also within other disciplines including law and economics. The first bias is remarkable in a negative sense for its portrayal of a trading system that has largely moved *from*-power-*to*-law. Theorists within this tradition either do not grant, or reserve a limited role for, power analysis, preferring instead to focus on aspects of legalization and institutionalized cooperation. The second bias refers to those scholars who have argued that power 'matters' in explaining outcomes in WTO politics, but do so largely from a strict, materialist standpoint. While this second bias is an improvement compared to the former legalistic depiction, it is also deficient in important respects, placing too much emphasis on the study of overt, decision-making behaviour in the study of power. However, not all scholars of the WTO regime are prone to these conceptual orientations and predispositions. It is also important, therefore, to discuss how the notion of ideas, viewed from a constructivist perspective, can offer certain insights into the meaning of power in trade politics, including how power can be considered in a wider social context.

1.1.1 *Law and power*

The opinion that the multilateral trading system has evolved from a 'power-based' order of the General Agreement on Tariffs and Trade (GATT) to a 'rule-based' order of the WTO is a popular narrative, one found within policy-making circles as well as in the academy.[8] From this historical reading, the GATT is represented as a Western diplomatic 'club', one that mostly marginalized Southern countries.[9] Following the establishment of the WTO, references to the normatively appealing benefits of trade rules have been repeated *ad nauseam* by some of the chief defenders of the multilateral system. Often adopting views derived from utilitarianism or constitutional theory, such scholars have argued that a rule-based order is preferable because it helps to 'seal off' the field of international trade from the vagaries of domestic politics, as well as to guard against economic abuses and failures by representative governments.[10] For some, this development is not simply an historical fact, but a prescriptive, normative goal that all actors should be seeking. The WTO system facilitates international cooperation and institutionalizes rules of reciprocity, monitoring, and enforcement. As a consequence, it is argued that less-privileged agents are more likely to support rule-oriented systems than power-oriented ones. In short, many have argued that the trade 'legalists' have thus emerged victorious over the trade 'pragmatists'.[11] We are led to believe that this change should be welcomed by all Southern countries.

This view that trade rules can contain the negative consequences of power is, of course, not only restricted to legal theorists. In international relations (IR), within liberal institutionalism, there exists a similar tradition. According to Andrew Hurrell, these scholars have adopted a kind of 'optimistic Hobbesianism', believing that power can be moderated, if not bypassed, through rational bargaining and cooperation.[12] Power is thus acknowledged, but the emphasis is placed on how legalization can provide increased precision, delegation, and obligation in the management of trading relations.[13] From this reading, the WTO system serves important functions for all members, including facilitating information exchange and reducing transaction costs. The Secretariat-organized Trade Policy Review Mechanism, which generates data on members' trading practices, is often held up as one example of this activity. This instrument is said to be beneficial to all because it enables transparency and encourages public debate on trade issues.[14] According to some authors, such institutional designs lead to Pareto-enhancing contracts for all actors, even if disproportionate gains may be transferred to the most powerful members.[15] Thus, while there is an appreciation that the WTO may be an institution 'of the privileged, by the privileged, and all too often for the privileged... in the absence of such institutions, dictation by strong states would be even more direct, less encumbered by rules'.[16]

Although both these interpretations on the role of power in the WTO system may appear slightly formal, they can still be criticized in two important respects. First, the history of the trading regime is not marked by some 'graduation' from power to law. On the contrary, the relationship between politics and rule-making has always been dynamic and unstable. As E. H. Carr put it, 'politics and law are indissolubly intertwined... Law, like politics, is a meeting place for ethics and power.'[17] Scholars such as Robert Howse, Matthew Dunne, Joost Pauwellyn, and Joseph Conti have all argued that a more persuasive narrative of the trading system would examine the interdependent relationship between power and legalization.[18] The idea that laws are assumed to be 'natural' ordering principles 'driving' the system in a unidirectional manner is therefore strongly contested. Rather, the development of law, as constructivists and critical legal theorists have long argued, should always be considered as being a broad and deep social phenomenon focused on the classification and stabilization of meanings.[19] Thus, there is power in particular types of knowledge and expertise, which Southern countries often struggle to access, leading one theorist to question if the 'rule of law' in fact blends into the 'rule of lawyers'.[20]

The second criticism, which is related to the first, is that these scholars tend to be bound to logocentric assumptions of cultural cohesion among diverse populations, and this has consequences for which concepts of power are privileged. There always exists the temptation for WTO analysts to begin to 'naturalize' and 'objectify' the very classifications and principles that they seek to describe and explain. For example, the idea of North–South 'partnerships' on trade issues may indeed be a valuable focus of study, but not at the expense of homogenizing economic practices and histories. If the observer fails to account adequately for how the WTO is a product of historical struggle and an institution of its time, there remains a possibility that their analysis may reinforce the existing mechanisms of legitimation, which, I would argue, are deeply interwoven into power relations. Of equal importance for my purposes, when we lose sight of the role of symbolic power, there is a danger of neglecting or missing how the legitimation of certain interests and practices can shape the way actors are represented and, in turn, how this informs their ability to move through the organization.

1.1.2 *Materialism and power*

It can be seen that both legal and institutionalist scholars require an underlying concept of power in their analyses. Before addressing how WTO members manage the consequences of anarchy and self-help, these theorists need at least a tacit acknowledgement of what power is, even if it does not feature as a central category. For most of the time, the compulsory notion of power is adopted. This is said to represent the most 'intuitive' definition of power, the production of obedience to the preferences of others. In the study of trade relations, many scholars have tended to understand power in this way. Power-as-property, in terms of market capacity, is treated as the first approximation of bargaining strength in negotiations. Thus, the US and the EU clearly exercise authority in relation to other members by threatening to open or close their markets.[21] They are trade hegemons by virtue of the costs and adjustments they can force on to other actors. Similarly, other writers in the neo-Gramscian tradition have directly focused not only on the total aggregate of trade flows per member, but also on the specific corporate actors that benefit from the design of current rules. The material power structure of the WTO regime can therefore only be understood through examining how domestic and transnational firms contribute towards the drafting and promotion of WTO rules.[22]

In turn, it is commonly argued that attention to the material capabilities of states provides the context for understanding organizational behaviour in WTO talks. One can see, in this respect, how Robert Dahl's formulation of power—that 'A has power over B to the extent that he can get B to do something that B would not otherwise do'—continues to be a template and guiding principle for many scholars.[23] As David Baldwin has defined it, power is the capacity of one actor to compel another to do something they would not have done otherwise, not simply in respect to policy behaviour, but also in terms of the attitudes, values, and the inclination to act.[24] The researcher is expected to know when power is at work because it takes the form of direct, intentional, actor-to-actor (state) exercises. Historically, Northern countries have been able to adjust the preferences of others through their command of informational resources and their ability to successfully navigate the institutional mechanisms of the WTO system.[25] They not only challenge other members by using market access as a diplomatic weapon, but also threaten to litigate, shift to other forums, or deny political sympathy in other issue areas.[26] In sum, therefore, one must not forget how compulsory power can point to the power not only to make changes, but also to resist them.

The virtues of this theoretical convention appear clear and many WTO analysts stop at this point, assuming that they have 'captured the essence' of the concept of power. Yet this book argues that the compulsory power vision, while necessary, is also problematic in respect to what is analytically privileged. Rooted in a conservative and materialist understanding of behaviour, users of the concept tend to depict trade relations as rather resilient or, indeed, even fixed. If taken too far, such thinking can risk caricaturing the power of the powerful as pervasive or invulnerable. When considering how Southern groups in recent Doha Round negotiations have challenged the common wisdom on economic diplomacy, this orientation would seem in need of clarification as to what it can explain. Another related problem of overplaying the analysis of materialism concerns the focus on conflict and observable decision-making by privileged agents. As will be argued, such moves in many ways represent only one side of the coin. 'Non-decision-making' has always been important for the reproduction of power and the 'suppression or thwarting of a latent or manifest challenge to the values or interests of the decision-maker'.[27] As Elmer Eric Schattschneider once expressed it, '*organization is the mobilization of bias*. Some issues are organized into politics while others are organized out.'[28] In sum, therefore, what is arguably left out of common appraisals of world trade politics is a sense of the 'manufacturing' or legitimation processes bound to the exercise of power. Broadly speaking, this book advances a conceptual framework that addresses how power can be understood through struggles over the justification of political ideas, a perspective which also, inevitably, touches upon some existing thinking in the field.

1.1.3 *Ideas and power*

The study of how certain ideas matter in explaining international trade politics is an increasingly prominent scholarly agenda. Such work can be framed in light of the turn towards social constructivist theorizing in IPE, although such moves have been less advanced than in other areas of IR.[29] In one sense, coming out of the conventional trade literature which builds upon, and reacts to, rationalist perspectives, the attention to ideas as an analytical category is not a new concern. For instance, in reference to the postwar economic bargain, John Ruggie characterizes his notion of 'embedded liberalism' as a 'fusion between power and legitimate social purpose'.[30] A focus on the hegemonic power of the US is not enough to explain how and why the postwar international trading order took its form. Rather, Ruggie calls attention to how normative struggles, such as over the welfare state in many Western polities, were intertwined with appeals for safeguards in the GATT talks. Elsewhere, Judith Goldstein's work on the origins of US agricultural and industrial trade policies also uses ideas as an important explanatory factor, with those key ideas that inform policy 'carried by individuals or groups with political clout'.[31]

In recent scholarship on trade politics, the conceptual analysis of so-called 'ideational' structures has been further refined and rethought. Adopting a more critical legal approach to the international trade regime, Andrew Lang has developed one of the most sophisticated accounts of the links between law and knowledge in the making of trade policy.[32] Partly inspired by Ruggie and Bourdieu, among others, Lang argues that the trade system should be understood as a social space through which intersubjective meanings on the purpose of commerce are constructed, defended, and contested.[33] The point of such a perspective is to introduce a richer sociological sense of how trade law specifically and, more broadly, the 'background' beliefs in the system, can work to constitute certain forms of material power and not others. In this way, Lang is alert not only to how trade law generates its authority through appeals to objectivity, but also to the normative effects of such justifications, particularly when law appears to close the scope for deliberation on alternatives. For instance, the 'trade' versus 'non-trade' dichotomy for organizing issues, such as 'trade' versus 'labour rights', appears to be an innocent distinction, one that is part of the vocabulary of trade experts.[34] But Lang challenges this common view, arguing instead that the dichotomy has tended to legitimize and naturalize the *telos* of the liberal trade project via the privileging of those (commercial or political) values attached to 'free trade'. The division thus gives the appearance of subjecting the trade regime to political contestation but, in practice, such classifications typically work to 'reproduce and reconstitute' a conservative opinion, in the process blunting more profound critiques.[35] In short, Lang sees constructivism as playing a 'destabilizing' role in the trade literature, upsetting common analytical presumptions and norms.[36]

Lang's work stands as an exemplary body of constructivist theorizing in trade politics, but there are other contributions of significance. For instance, as alluded to, Joseph Conti, writing in reference to the WTO Dispute Settlement Body (DSB), argues that concentrating 'only on grand political games or structural trade issues misses how institutional dynamics, like legal capacity and experience, and interpersonal dynamics, like reputation, shame, and fear, shape processes of disputing'.[37] Importantly, Conti contends that 'power relationships do not disappear in legal contexts, but are instead reconfigured, authorizing new strategies and resources in the context of political and symbolic skirmishing'.[38] Similarly, in a study of the telecommunication and airline industries, Cornelia Woll sheds light on how trade conflicts are embedded in a deeper social and political fabric.[39] In particular, Woll shows how the preference formation of firms and governments is much more complex than rationalist-informed models of IPE would suggest, involving agents that not only form their interests intersubjectively, but are often unsure about the 'correct' strategy to pursue at different junctures. Thus, in short, Conti, Woll, and Lang all introduce a welcome sense of social contingency into explanatory frameworks on trade politics.

This book certainly shares conceptual affinities with this literature. However, it is important to note some concerns. First, in keeping with constructivism broadly, there still remains a risk that researchers will stray into forms of 'ideational essentialism' in which the concept of power, while acknowledged to play some role, remains submerged and underspecified.[40] I am not arguing that ideas do not create effects deemed 'powerful' but rather that such symbolic structures can only be adequately understood within a symbiotic relationship with material structures. In other words, constructivist analysis in this vein needs to be tightly paired with political economy, which includes, crucially, close attention to complex political tactics and empirical inequalities. Furthermore, the conception of 'ideas' itself can be problematic. One major notion, which fits into a modified rational-choice framework *à la* Goldstein, tends to depict ideas as commodity-like tools that are '"supplied" by "political entrepreneurs" on a "market-place" in response to "demands", and then "circulate" through that market-place to be "peddled" and "consumed"'.[41] Another main conception sees ideas being reproduced in more diffuse terms, as notions such as 'shared beliefs', 'ideologies', and 'worldviews' try to capture. The ideas-as-commodities vision has been criticized for its false compartmentalization by Lang and Woll. But I would argue that both conceptions should not be seen as irreconcilable in a larger research design. For instance, as will be explored in the case studies, some moments in trade talks feature policy-makers who appear to strategically manipulate certain ideas in a calculated manner. At the same time, however, one needs to understand how and why such ideas acquire a sense of legitimacy in the first place, a question that can only be addressed historically with attention to the relationship between systems of social representation and processes of political institutionalization.

1.2 The argument

This section provides an introduction and outline of the major arguments expressed in the book. From a critical sociological perspective, the thought of Bourdieu serves as the primary theoretical inspiration for exploring WTO negotiations in the context of the Doha Round. The discussion is divided into two subsections. Initially, I explain in more detail the justifications for advancing a framework on symbolic power and how such notions can be translated to a study of the WTO system. Subsequently, the discussion moves to introduce the major empirical backdrop of the book: Southern countries and agricultural trade. The choice of the two case studies is also outlined.

1.2.1 *Uncovering symbolic power*

In the broader study of international politics, the potential utility of Bourdieu as a practical and theoretical inspiration has sparked increased interest in recent years, mirroring the appropriation of his ideas elsewhere in the social sciences. In larger terms, Bourdieu has been framed in light of the so-called 'practice turn' in IR, which has sought to conceive of political action in ways not captured by pure instrumental rationality (logic of consequences), norms (logic of appropriateness), or communicative action (logic of arguing).[42] This interest has been particularly strong among scholars who address the politics of international security and diplomacy.[43] Indeed, the extent to which Bourdieu has now 'made it' in IR can be illustrated by special volumes dedicated to analysing his work and how it can inform international political explanations.[44] However, notwithstanding these developments, so far at least, Bourdieu's concepts have rarely been used for enhancing our understanding of the politics of the world economy, a neglect that this book aims to address.[45]

The application of Bourdieu's conceptual framework of symbolic power to the specific study of the WTO system is certainly not an automatic move. However, I argue that his ideas do have merit and, coupled with a sense of the strengths and deficiencies of conventional notions of power, can enrich our understanding of political practices in this particular institution. Bourdieu was a subtle and eclectic thinker, one who was preoccupied with explaining the complex movements of power in society, but we should refrain from rigidly adopting his concepts. He is treated here as an intellectual stimulus, not a prophet. Thus my argument draws back from overextending his theory by attempting to translate too many of his concepts at the same time. In this sense, the book does not concentrate on his tripartite 'species' of power (economic, cultural, and social), nor does it adopt his more amorphous idea of a higher 'field of power' connecting privileged actors within different social domains.[46] Equally, the argument does not engage explicitly with his 'habitus' and 'field' notions, although the related ideas of 'doxa' and social space are debated. For some, this may appear that one is 'talking up' Bourdieu, only to leave behind some of his other major concepts. This is not the intention; rather, I am approaching his theorizing on power fully conscious of the challenges and risks of translation but, at the same time, fully convinced of his relevance to the particular study of WTO politics.

Symbolic power should be interpreted here as a framework that houses a series of important sub-concepts. With an eye on relational analysis, these 'thinking tools' work together to form a larger theoretical design. In essence, with a brevity that potentially does violence to Bourdieu's imagination, symbolic power offers a way to conceptualize how existing forms of power acquire legitimacy or, as Bourdieu would put it, pass as (mis)recognized. It places particular attention on how language, as a pre-eminent symbolic system, both reflects and constitutes power, to the extent that the notion of 'power' is considered intertwined with the idea of 'legitimation'.[47]

There are four main contributions to this perspective that can be highlighted. First, such a framework offers new objects of analysis that are not present or are underplayed in common notions of power used to study the WTO system. Against the compulsory power vision, which tends either to discount the struggle over language or treat it as some 'ephemeral' or 'negligible' feature of power, the notion of symbolic power can be used to explore the properties of the 'linguistic market', a Bourdieu term for a bounded social space where only certain arguments acquire legitimacy. In turn, through applications to WTO politics, the book explores how the linguistic market in trade can be divided into three layers of abstraction:

(1) a macro-level focus on major classifications for organizing problems
(2) a meso-level struggle between 'orthodox' and 'heterodox' views on the 'conventional wisdom' in trade policy
(3) a micro-level contest over the symbolic power associated with particular social spaces and individuals.

To further refine the empirical application, the book also deploys two other separate sociological notions: framing and mimicry. In addition, the approach is also distinctive for highlighting how WTO policy-making features so-called 'taken-for-granted' presumptions between agents and the political world, referred to here as 'doxic relations'. Again, compared to common positivistic treatments of power that ignore the space occupied by the body, the notion of doxa addresses the internalization of power and, subsequently, its externalization in the form of 'durable dispositions' of diplomatic practice.[48]

Second, once power is understood to operate through language, the book advances a series of arguments on how the struggle over symbolic power produces significant political effects. In contrast to other notions of power that are often fixated on pure material forces orchestrated by privileged actors, symbolic power is designed to showcase how many other WTO players can potentially participate or become immersed in this complex of power. Thus, I suggest that this may help us to better understand how Southern countries, in particular, have increased their activism in trade politics in recent years. At the same time, however, the argument makes clear that symbolic power is unevenly distributed in the trade policy game. For Bourdieu, one needs to examine the historical genesis of dominant classifications and orthodox opinions, particularly in terms of legal definitions, in order to understand the more potent forms of 'objectified' symbolic power. When a certain set of interests have been codified into law, they tend to 'crystallize' and universalize, shaping—but in no way predetermining—the scope for subsequent deliberation. Moreover, this relational contest to impose the legitimately recognized meanings of trade problems also matters for the identity of actors. Thus it will be argued that symbolic power informs not only agendas, but also the capabilities of actors to get themselves recognized, often in the form of a group, and, ultimately, to win a place in the WTO order.

Third, connecting these particular processes, the book explores how a Bourdieusian perspective helps to excavate and plot the often-elaborate schemes of justification seen in WTO politics. The point is not to discount that brute arm-twisting takes place, but to explain the more common legitimation struggles surrounding such compulsory power episodes. In this way, Bourdieu follows, and enriches, Max Weber's argument that a power left unvarnished or naked is always vulnerable to critique and thus will tend to seek out ways to secure its own reproduction.[49] These methods of justification take a variety of forms in the WTO arena, including appeals to historical principles of political exchange, such as reciprocity; disciplinary systems of knowledge, such as neoclassical trade theory; as well as references to specific rules and codes of conduct. Such methods are, indeed, debated in scholarship that has explored how agents draw upon WTO institutional power resources. However, the symbolic power framework can be distinguished in two senses:

(1) by drawing attention to the complex social labour engaged in these practices, within and beyond the social environment of Geneva

(2) by thoroughly politicizing the examination of interests which includes, notably, interests concealed or distorted not only through rigorously defended laws, but also more subtle euphemisms and sleights of hand.

In this sense, the book explores how the nurturing, transmission, and consolidation of symbolic power is not a predetermined process but, rather, is often beset by setbacks and disturbances, as well as more fundamental contradictions and crises.

Finally, at a higher level of abstraction, in a manner reminiscent of Bourdieu's metatheory, the book aims to critique and dissolve what I view as unhelpful conceptual dichotomies, which surround the analysis of power. Most notably, this includes efforts to transcend the opposition between 'power' versus 'legitimation' and 'materialism' versus 'symbolism', which are, in turn, reflective of master dichotomies between 'structure' versus 'agency' or 'objectivism' versus 'subjectivism'. The point is to explore how the political economy of practices in the WTO environment cannot be reduced to purely materialistic forces. Rather, the evolution of the system rests upon the interdependence between symbolic structures and material structures. In particular, the book aims to explore the ways in which the three forms of power—compulsory, institutional, and symbolic—relate to each other, rather than setting up a 'gladiatorial' battle between them for intellectual supremacy.[50] Thus, I would argue that we need a framework on symbolic power to more effectively understand when and under what conditions the other modes of power acquire added analytical meaning. For instance, actions of compulsory power are sometimes used to quickly meet a challenge that cannot be accomplished by more arduous processes of symbolic power. The coercive move may be used to cut short a rival strategy of legitimation, but one would need to examine the content of such symbolic power to understand why compulsory power was being exercised at that point in time. In short, therefore, symbolic power matters because it has the potential to define the political world through the visions and divisions that agents both conceptualize and materially construct.[51]

1.2.2 *Empirical context and framework*

The book takes seriously the difficult task of trying to put concepts into action. To divorce theoretical knowledge from practical knowledge would be to miss how each body can potentially inform the other and thus enhance our overall understanding. This subsection provides the empirical backdrop for the main arguments and illustrations, focused on introducing a Southern-centric viewpoint, the significance of agricultural concerns, before outlining the constitution of the case studies. However, before tackling these points, an initial qualification is necessary here: the non-completion of the Doha Round at the time of writing. It is true that examining contemporary events that are still evolving presents difficulties, particularly in respect to major political projects. Yet, in regards to both case studies, the argument covers a substantial period of events over the past decade when Southern countries have engaged in power struggles and institutional adaptation. In addition, the negotiations on agriculture are arguably very close to the 'endgame' in the sense that debates are now focused on technical 'modalities' rather than any radically new propositions.[52] In this respect, key turning points in the process of negotiations require serious analysis and such work can be conducted now. It is also worth noting in passing that significant books dedicated to examining the Doha Round have also been published in recent years.[53]

SOUTHERN-CENTRIC PERSPECTIVE

The examination of Southern country experiences in the multilateral trading system has become an increasingly important field of enquiry in trade scholarship. Such work is particularly noticeable given the general paucity of relevant studies conducted during the postwar GATT period.[54] Following the founding of the WTO in 1995, a new wave of literature has sought to explain the changing political and economic fortunes of Southern countries. Different enquiries have been pursued, covering a range of trade problems and actors. For instance, one prominent set of studies, epitomized by the work of John S. Odell and Amrita Narlikar, has explored the making of coalitions and negotiation analysis, including assessment of the factors that have historically led to effective policy outcomes.[55] Other book-length enquiries have probed particular Southern trade issues, such as those related to services and intellectual property.[56] General edited collections focused on Southern WTO members have also emerged in recent years, with the emphasis on explaining the recent history of different trade problems.[57] In addition, as already referenced, civil society analysts have also been sensitive to the position of Southern countries in the WTO and have offered interesting snapshots on aspects of negotiations.[58] Thus my argument aims to speak to, and enrich, the study of Southern countries posed in this wider literature.

At the same time, however, there are two important qualifications to note. First, in regards to the problems raised by agricultural trade, one cannot possibly examine all Southern country concerns that have emerged in the Doha Round. Such an objective would be a multi-volume undertaking. Thus 'the South' in question in this book is inevitably restricted. The argument makes no claim to capture some immutable 'Southern viewpoint', one which is seemingly fit for all, since such a position would do violence to the extraordinary complexity of concerns in this area. Rather, I have tailored the book to focus on some specific clusters of countries with common concerns. The analysis is also restricted in another sense: for how it remains Geneva-focused, with limited background context on the domestic political economy forces at work in different countries. Again, this decision reflects a concern with designing a feasible enquiry within the boundaries available here. Second, although the orientation is biased towards Southern countries, this clearly does not denote an objectified analysis where such actors are located in a vacuum. With an eye on Bourdieu, the discussion is always relational, including exploring in detail various struggles that have taken place along North–South and South–South lines.

THE IMPORTANCE OF AGRICULTURE

As even a casual observer of WTO negotiations will have noticed, agriculture has come to dominate the agenda of the Doha Round, to an extent that was arguably not easily foreseen in the heat of Qatar in November 2001. While the US and the EU congratulated themselves on the advance of their 'post-modern' trade agenda, shifting attention towards further liberalization of industrial products, services, and other 'behind-the-border' issues such as investment, many Southern countries argued strongly that their concerns in agriculture had been inadequately addressed. This was not a new complaint. The implicit North–South 'grand bargain' that defined the Uruguay Round (1986–1994), where agricultural trade was brought under the multilateral disciplines of the AoA, featured a common belief on the part of Southern countries that significant economic opportunities would emerge. But the Uruguay Round hangover proved serious for many Southern countries: the average depth of tariff cuts was substantially greater than that agreed to by high-income countries and, in addition, costly commitments were bundled into the 'single undertaking'.[59] As the projected gains from agriculture have often proved elusive, this bargain has become increasingly unstable. In advance, as well as in the aftermath, of the Doha Ministerial, Southern countries were thus determined that agriculture would not be so easily sidelined in the future.

But why is agricultural trade of paramount importance for many Southern countries? From one policy perspective it may seem puzzling why the sector is so contentious in the WTO system. Trade in agricultural goods accounts for only 4% of world GDP and 9% of global exports. As a contribution to the international economy, agriculture has been steadily declining for decades, not only within Northern countries but within Southern countries as well. For instance, as a share of international merchandise trade, agriculture has fallen from 42 to 11% in Southern countries.[60] But these figures do not reveal the disproportionate reliance of Southern countries on agricultural trade for export revenue, employment, and, by association in many instances, political stability. One can consider sets of economic and political reasons that help explain why the issue has absorbed extraordinary amounts of political capital during the Doha Round.[61]

The substantive economic reasons have become increasingly clear for many analysts: agriculture represents a core sector for most Southern countries, an area in which they often have comparative advantage. The production of agriculture is a critical source of foreign exchange, investment, and economic growth for many Southern countries. For instance, as a percentage of GDP, agriculture averages 10.3% in Southern countries, with an annual growth rate of 2.9%. By contrast, in Northern countries, the sector forms just 2.4% of GDP, growing only slightly by 0.8% per year.[62] In terms of the economically active population in Southern countries, 53% are engaged in agriculture-related work. Dependence upon the export of three or fewer agricultural products for foreign exchange remains a critical problem for many countries. For instance, 43 Southern countries rely upon a single commodity for more than 20% of their total revenues from merchandise exports.[63]

At the same time, Northern country support programmes that restrict access to wealthy markets, generate large surpluses and subsidize exports. Many critics have noted the transferring of government support funds to a concentrated number of large agricultural firms. For instance, according to the Washington, DC-based Environmental Watch Group, among subsidy recipients, the top 10% of US farms collected 73% of all subsidies ($121 billion out of $165 billion) from 1995–2005, an annual average of $34,190 per recipient.[64] In 2004, across the countries of the Organisation for Economic Co-operation and Development (OECD) as a whole, it was estimated that the value of support to producers was $279 billion or €226 billion. As measured by percentage producer subsidy equivalent (PSE), support accounted for 30% of farm receipts.[65] Producers in Southern countries are often excluded from these Northern markets and forced to compete against heavily subsidized competition in international and even local markets.[66]

At the same time, the political relevance of the negotiations on agriculture are now closely associated not only with the completion of the Doha Round, but also with the overall legitimacy of the WTO system itself. It cannot be overestimated how the reform of the AoA is now intimately tied to notions of fairness or 'diffuse reciprocity' in trading relations and, more broadly, international politics. Representatives from Northern governments seldom miss an opportunity to preach the virtues of trade openness and external integration strategies, while remaining resolutely protectionist themselves in key subsectors and categories. The agricultural rules in the WTO system largely perpetuate a system under which the distribution of agricultural trade is shaped not by comparative advantage in terms of competitiveness, but by access to subsidies, an area in which privileged countries have an unrivalled advantage. While some modifications and policy reforms have been introduced by Northern members, failure to fundamentally change these conditions will inevitably reinforce a perception that WTO rules skew the benefits of trade towards the North. The degree to which the increased international awareness of inequities in trading relations actually impacts on the WTO agenda can be debated, but there is no doubt that the backdrop is considerably different compared to the years of the Uruguay Round.

To risk repeating myself, the interests of Southern countries in agricultural trade are in no way uniform. One cannot adequately understand alternative negotiating positions without exploring how Southern countries may have either offensive or defensive interests, or a blend of both. Thus recalling the conceptual framework on symbolic power, Southern countries could have policies anchored around orthodox or heterodox calculations, or a fusion of both. Internationally competitive producers in Argentina or Thailand are clearly different from countries such as India and Kenya that have large numbers of subsistence farmers, while some members such as Brazil have a mix of both offensive and defensive concerns.[67] In the context of Doha economic projections for instance, some authors have argued that the major beneficiaries of agricultural liberalization will likely be those countries in the Cairns group, which features mostly middle-income Southern countries with well-developed export industries, whereas members in sub-Saharan Africa would receive very little.[68] At the same time, one should not forget that some Southern countries and groupings have also become dependent upon preserving the associated benefits of the agricultural regime, notably preferences. Thus, WTO negotiations on agriculture are as much about protectionism and the preservation of the status quo as efforts to advance liberalization and reform the AoA.

CONSTITUTING THE CASE STUDIES

In terms of guiding criteria, the choice of the case studies was structured by three factors. In the first instance, there was an evaluation of the population of potential cases defined as being Southern-led coalitions on agriculture within the Doha Round. The purpose at this stage was to begin the process of 'casing' by examining the interplay and 'fit' between the empirical and the conceptual framework on power. This was not a predetermined method, but involved a considerable degree of research and refinement before settling on the two designated cases.[69] Furthermore, in order to evaluate how symbolic power operates through the WTO system, the choice of cases had to capture degrees of variation. To facilitate cross-comparisons, one case was chosen for its predominant concern with orthodox themes, while the other was mainly characterized by struggles over the definition of heterodoxy. To recall the conceptual discussion, it needs to be underscored that while each of these cases gravitates towards one of these poles, I also highlight considerable tension and interplay between orthodoxy and heterodoxy visions within each case. Re-reading Bourdieu helped to improve my understanding of how he combined theory and practice in his own work. In turn, explaining this intra-case relational complexity was important for enhancing the overall argument. Finally, for purposes of feasibility, each case was selected to provide a sufficient degree of research control. Both cases have a considerable history in the Doha Round, with existing official documentation and policy-related analysis providing a basis for scholarly examination. Where necessary, the analysis featured consideration of national and regional-level policy-making. With these factors in mind, the major arguments of each case can be outlined.

The first case centres on how a group of west- and central-African (WCA) countries—Benin, Burkina Faso, Chad, and Mali—launched a campaign for the reform of international cotton trade by challenging the subsidies of major producers, particularly the US. Since 2003, the cotton initiative in the Doha Round has stood as an ambitious case of Africa's desire to be integrated into the trading system and yet also receive reparations for past injuries. At its core, I argue that the cotton initiative has been a struggle over competitiveness or, more precisely with an eye on symbolic power, competing representations of legitimacy in claims of competitiveness. What makes it distinctive is that strong claims of competitiveness were articulated by a group of less-privileged members against the US, one of the presumed 'teachers' of orthodoxy. The case explores how and why the initiative was born, as well as its subsequent incorporation into the Doha agenda. The genesis of cotton as 'an issue' is critically examined, focusing on how the WCA countries constructed a novel 'competitive victim' frame to define themselves and the problem. This frame was effective in many respects, but it also featured tensions that would later be exploited by the US and other actors who were threatened by the campaign. I argue that what followed was the introduction of a politically driven 'counter-frame', which divided the problem into a 'trade-related' component and a 'development-related' component. It is important to understand why and how this distinction was constructed, institutionalized, and monitored. By scrutinizing the relationship between framing and institutional power, as well as noting incidents of compulsory power, I suggest that the counter-frame won over the original frame, leading to a re-positioning of the demanders and a re-calibration of their expectations.

The second case examines a larger and more diverse coalition of Southern countries, led by Indonesia for much of its history, which has campaigned for the establishment of defensive policy instruments linked to the category of Special and Differential Treatment (SDT). This case can essentially be defined as a struggle over Southern-centric heterodox notions related to food security and rural development in the AoA. This initiative has its origins in a growing dissatisfaction on the part of many Southern members with the classifications and policy tools of the AoA; in particular, how the accord did not provide effective options for enhancing the defence of vulnerable agricultural populations. Following an economic and legal analysis of these problems, the case explores how this group of Southern countries mobilized the symbolic and institutional resources necessary to renew the classification struggle over heretical policy ideas on SDT. This work began with the formulation of a frame called the 'development box' in the late 1990s. Specific attention is devoted to explaining how the often-laborious battle over taxonomies informed the scope for subsequent deliberation and thus the choices and expectations of Southern countries in the negotiations. The final part of the argument continues this examination by analysing the emergence of the now official concepts of Special Products (SPs) and the Special Safeguard Mechanism (SSM). The discussion critically assesses how these heterodox concepts were gradually codified and institutionalized into the Doha agenda through attention to how Southern countries drew upon symbolic power. Throughout the discussion, attention is paid to the enduring battles these agents played with critics who sought to erode their legitimacy.

1.3 Methodology

This book is derived from four main sets of sources. First, existing literature has been consulted and critiqued. Given the central focus on the conceptualization of power and legitimation processes, this has necessitated a broad reading, not only in reference to debates within IR and IPE, but also sociology and political theory. In turn, this analysis provided the context for investigating the thought of Bourdieu. The adaptation of the symbolic power framework is derived from different sources in his *oeuvre*, but of particular importance was *Outline of a Theory of Practice* (1977), a work which attempted to synthesize his thinking at that time.[70] In respect to the international trade literature, a range of scholars and analysts were consulted, with a special focus on the history of Southern-country activism. Studies of agricultural trade policy were also evaluated and, where possible, recent academic literature related to the case studies was integrated into the discussion. Second, the research of international organizations, intergovernmental institutions, and technical NGOs was utilized, most prominently, the Food and Agricultural Organization of the United Nations (FAO), the South Centre, and the International Centre for Trade and Sustainable Development (ICTSD). Third, a range of official documents were accessed and analysed, not only WTO, but also statements and reports issued by coalitions. A small number of these documents were not public records, but given to me privately by country representatives.

In terms of working with these three sets of sources, the research process featured inevitable methodological challenges, which had to be recognized, understood, and frequently reconsidered. One significant concern was the very application of the framework on symbolic power to the WTO setting, something which has never been attempted before. In order to understand the conditions under which symbolic power could aid our understanding of WTO politics, including comparing such theorizing to other rival explanations, a systematic research strategy was adopted. The book has therefore taken seriously the method of process tracing in order to reveal the genesis and struggle over problems in WTO negotiations, including attention to moments that may appear inconsequential at first glance but acquire meaning when considered holistically and in relation to other elements.[71] This included a fine-grained legal and economic analysis of WTO documents in order to appreciate the arguments they contained. But this reading was always overlaid with attention to the potential for political motivations and informational biases contained in each source. For some, this micro-level process tracing may appear rather excessive or dense, but it will be suggested that such a method is necessary in order to better explain the subtleties of power relations that are often missed through conventional conceptual lenses.

The fourth major source was interviews: 37 in total. The decision to adopt interviewing as a strategy was made for three main reasons:

(1) to explore the reasons why actions were taken by actors, not simply the reasons themselves
(2) because some of the areas of analysis concern recent events to which existing literature was of limited help
(3) to verify existing claims in the literature and to establish what I did not know.[72]

Interviews were conducted with Geneva-based and Washington, DC-based ambassadors, attachés, and other political officials. Relevant staff at the WTO Secretariat were also interviewed. Other subjects included civil society analysts (such as from Oxfam International), trade consultants (such as those based at ICTSD), and officials who worked in intergovernmental agencies (such as the South Centre and the International Cotton Advisory Committee). In reference to both case studies, I found that some of these experts were not only monitoring negotiations, but actively contributing to the drafting and formulation of country strategies, indicating their growing importance to the trade policy process of Southern countries. Not all interviewees were incorporated into the writing of the case studies, often because their responses confirmed findings discovered elsewhere. In addition, a small number of subjects requested that their identities remain anonymous.

When reflecting upon the study overall, the use of interviews proved to be important in terms of better exploring a theorization of symbolic power within the WTO system. It was invaluable to hear actors explain particular histories and problems in their own terms and, subsequently, for me to critically question those terms in the time available. In keeping with the conceptual objectives, common themes in all interviews included a focus on the roots and common understandings of trade issues, linguistic terms and argument construction, relations with other actors, and the means for managing criticism. In the two case study chapters, direct quotes are used for particularly telling points; at other times, the opinion of the subject is incorporated into the background of the discussion. In addition, following Bourdieu, since the analysis of symbolic power is concerned with latent forms of power or political activity that is not normally labelled 'power', a careful interviewing technique was adopted. This was in order to tease out not only what was accomplished, but also what options were discarded or indeed not even conceived. In this regard, I sometimes drew upon elements of counterfactual reasoning with subjects. Such methods are, however, never straightforward to conduct, particularly because not all agents possess the same degree of institutional memory or expertise. In short, interviewing is a complex craft, not a science, but most participants proved keen to explain in detail their various experiences.

1.4 Outline plan

The book is organized into five main chapters. Chapter 2 offers a critical introduction and re-examination of the concept of power in relation to the WTO system. It begins by briefly considering some metatheoretical issues related to the notion, including its essentially contested character and purpose in scholarly enquiries. This is followed by an evaluation of the analytical strengths and deficiencies of the two notions of power commonly considered in WTO political analysis: compulsory and institutional. In a bridge to the Bourdieu-inspired framework, the chapter ends with a discussion of the concepts of structural power and productive power, including noting the limited applications of these notions to trade politics. Chapter 3 provides a detailed unpacking of the conceptual approach of symbolic power, including attention to the notion of 'taken-for-granted' doxic relations and the key properties of the linguistic market. Again, examples are drawn from trade politics to illuminate the utility of these notions. The end of the chapter further clarifies and extends Bourdieu's contribution in two ways: through a brief comparison with the literature on argumentation in IR, and through debating the concepts of framing and mimicry as useful ancillary tools for exploring the practical effects of symbolic power.

The fourth chapter focuses on the WCA cotton initiative. It begins by first discussing how cotton was constructed as a problem in the Doha Round through an examination of the political economy of the trade as well as sources of policy debate. The chapter then turns to critically dissect the original WCA proposal, arguing that the dossier was rooted in orthodox justifications, but also features appeals to heterodox reasoning. The remainder of the discussion is devoted to explaining how the cotton issue was politically managed through a complex series of combined symbolic power and institutional power forces. In the final part, the chapter brings the results of these activities into context through debating the most recent phase of cotton negotiations. An examination of the evolution of a set of Southern-centric heretical ideas on agricultural policy over a period of around ten years is the focus of Chapter 5. The discussion begins with an economic and legal analysis explaining why many Southern countries have argued that the AoA does not adequately address their defensive policy needs. This debate, in turn, provides the context for evaluating how a group of countries began to coalesce around the notion of the 'development box', before later constructing the now official categories of SPs and the SSM. Throughout, I pay attention to when and how the struggle over symbolic power mattered in shaping the definition of heterodox issues centred on food security and rural development. The final chapter takes the form of a conclusion where the major findings of the book are summarized.

2

Power analysis and the WTO system

> *. . . a system which replaces the role of power in international trade relations with the rule of law is invariably to the advantage of the smallest and weakest countries.*
>
> Michael Moore, director general of the WTO (1999–2002)[1]

> *Power is best exercised in a situation of uncertainty and unpredictability. That is why the rules and procedures [of the WTO] are so vague.*
>
> Geneva-based Southern country delegate[2]

Both of these statements are telling, offering different ways of understanding power in the WTO system. They represent two voices: a former bureaucrat speaking publicly and a national policy-maker speaking privately. Moore suggests that a new order is being constructed, one where law has substituted power. He predicts it will bring inevitable normative benefits, especially to the small and weak. It is not clear where power has disappeared to, how power is related to law, or who has ushered in this new era. We are simply asked to acknowledge this development as a fact. In contrast, the Southern country delegate argues that power is still at play. He or she sees and feels it. From this perspective there is a connection between power and the rules: not a divorce as Moore puts it, but a fusion. The delegate implies that the rules and procedures are not as certain and predictable as first appears, and that this confusion is due to the exercise of power. Here law is part of an environment that is difficult to navigate for certain actors. Moreover, the unspecified exercisers of power wish this system to remain because it is in their 'best' interests. Moore speaks with confidence in the public sphere; the delegate remains anonymous. The effects of power are of great interest to the delegate; Moore speaks as if power is increasingly irrelevant.

One could suggest, on the basis of these snapshots, that there is some truth to both interpretations. Power clearly 'matters' when political actors give accounts of their policy experiences and preferences; negatively, in Moore's depiction of a system evolving beyond power or positively, in the delegate's expansive definition. The WTO is a regime of complex rules, which have been used, under certain conditions, to benefit Southern countries. But, in contrast to Moore's claims, I would argue that these regulations and procedures were not formed with power 'retreating into history'. For scholarly accounts of the trading system, concepts of power are invoked to better explain how the structures of the WTO are conceived, how participation and actions within them are enabled, and how distributional outcomes are generated. When discussed, one particular—although valuable—reading of power is often privileged: power as the ability of one actor to compel another to do something they would not have done otherwise. For some analysts, this is the 'essence' of power in the WTO system; the fist on the negotiating table to use a popular metaphor. But while such a depiction remains important, it is my argument in this chapter that one needs to go beyond the compulsory power meaning in order to capture other essential features and processes of modern trade politics.

This opening theoretical chapter thus aims to introduce the idea of power and debate how different concepts under its name can be applied to the WTO system. There are three main parts. First, by way of contextualization, the notion is approached in light of two significant themes that run throughout the book:

(1) that power remains an essentially contested concept which invites multiple different readings
(2) that the notion is best studied through a relational, rather than substantialist, lens of analysis.

Attention is also devoted to questioning the analytical purposes of the concept. Second, the chapter draws upon a useful typology designed by Michael Barnett and Raymond Duvall.[3] The discussion focuses first on compulsory power and institutional power as the conventional ways in which the concept has been understood in relation to the WTO system. The third part broadens the analysis to address the other two notions in the Barnett and Duvall framework: structural power and productive power. In general, these latter concepts offer more critical readings on power but, at the same time, such thinking has made relatively little impact on specific WTO debates. Throughout, I point to the strengths and weaknesses, as well as the distinctions and affinities between these different concepts. In addition, the third part also serves as a bridge to the discussion on symbolic power in Chapter 3. The major purpose of the chapter is therefore not to search for some single or dominant notion of power that would command universal assent, but to begin the process of investigating the benefits and limitations of current thinking in this area.

2.1 Entering the conceptual universe of power

Before examining how power operates in the WTO system we need to approach the attributes of the concept itself. From one perspective, it may appear an ill-defined move to choose power as a central category for investigation. Arguably all IR questions orientate directly or implicitly around notions of power. It is a major—perhaps the most important—concept for studying who wins conflicts and who governs. Questions of power and powerlessness, including assessing the degree of stability and change within relations of power, have always been core. What is troubling, however, is not the frequent acknowledgement that power is 'important' and has some role in explanations, but why it remains one of the least well-researched concepts in the IR field. As Roxanne Lynn Doty has remarked, 'it is ironic that a concept as central to international relations as power remains so impoverished in terms of how it is defined and how it is understood to operate in global politics'.[4] Such a situation is quite paradoxical for, as I will argue here, there is nothing obvious or secondary about 'power'. This section seeks to introduce the concept in two ways: first by exploring how it can be understood as an essentially contested notion, and second by examining what purpose the concept serves in political explanations.

2.1.1 *The essentially contested nature of power*

The *Oxford English Dictionary* lists over twenty meanings of 'power', and these cluster around notions of ability or relationship. Power is often seen as both a capacity and the exercise of such capacity. The Latin *potentia* is associated with *posse*, meaning a faculty to exercise might and force, particularly political. Hence, in English, 'potential' and 'power' have their origin in this elision. Such history has continued, for the scope, effects, and meaning of both the capacity and exercise of power still invite examination.

But is power an essentially contested notion, as writers such as Steven Lukes and William E. Connolly claim?[5] The argument in this book is predicated upon treating power as a concept with many faces. However, this orientation is not immediately self-evident and could be questioned. The belief that the notion of power should be tailored to a specific command-and-control meaning is a popular understanding, one found in policy and media debates. In academic terms, the same sense can be traced back to Plato and Aristotle, before being adapted by Machiavelli and Hobbes.[6] But the idea that scholars should strive to find an 'essence' of power became most prominent in the postwar period with the advance of political science and methods of behaviouralism associated with Robert Dahl.[7] Hence, in these accounts, power is not 'conceptually stretched' to illuminate all forms of political action but, rather, is used in explanations at particular points, notably to clarify acts of coercion.[8] Similarly, in the realist tradition in IR, the concept of power has tended to maintain a particular meaning linked to some sense of violence or control.[9] The boundaries of the notion can be further visualized by noting how power is often read in opposition to 'ideas', 'legitimacy', or 'persuasion', concepts that are said to perform different analytical functions and should not be confused with 'power'.

In the last forty years, however, there has been a proliferation of critiques on the concept of power in the social sciences. Today, we increasingly have a situation whereby the 'conception of power as essentially grounded in coercion represents a minority view'.[10] As will be examined in this chapter, different critical literatures have questioned the 'intuitive' sense of power, particularly the focus on the individual and a rigid adherence to materialism. In the process, this has promoted a notion that is more multifaceted, inclusive, and adaptable. To say that power is 'essentially contested' is to call attention to how theorists may agree that the concept is worth having, but disagree about its proper use. In Walter Gallie's classic statement, an essentially contested notion has an internally complex character; is open-ended, vague, and subject to modification; and is often linked to value-based judgements.[11] In particular, the normative assumptions of the author can complicate what definition of power is given a privileged status, although this influence is often unclear to the reader. As Lukes argues, one can distinguish between pluralist, reformist, and radical interpretations of power. Each perspective offers different views on what questions should be asked and what evidence should be selected for understanding what is called power, ranging from Dahl's focus on elite decision-making processes to Foucault's analysis of the 'productive' movements of power without an identifiable centre.[12]

Moreover, such distinctions are often reflective of deeper ontological or epistemological fault lines that go beyond the conceptualization of power *per se*. For instance, one major comparison is between substantialism and relationalism as core logics of thought.[13] As the term suggests, a substantialist perspective on politics is one that locates substances of different kinds—materials, things, beings—as the fundamental units of all analysis. Such substances are often conceived as discrete 'pre-formed' entities. The interaction between substances is studied, but often the entities are treated as internally static in some way. Substantialism has historically provided an underlying ontological basis for theorizing on power, as well as most IR theories. This can be seen in the common metaphors of power as something that is 'accumulated', 'seized', or 'held', as if power could be tangibly touched. Indeed, the very term 'powerful' creates the image of a subject having power embodied within them. In contrast, the relational logic rejects the vision that one can assume certain units as pre-given starting points. Instead, it conceives of social reality in 'dynamic, continuous, and processual terms'.[14] Thus, the concept of power looks different from this vantage point; it is only through a relational analysis that one can accord value to an exercise or effect of 'power'. If social power 'resides' anywhere—to borrow a substantialist metaphor—it is in the relations between subjects and objects. For instance, as Marx often put it, capital and labour are never fixed entities, but processes in constant motion.[15] In this book, a relational logic underpins the analysis of power. As will be explained, this perspective has been strongly promoted by Bourdieu in his theorizing of symbolic power and, more generally, as a methodological way to organize different conceptual tools.[16]

But for all the talk that power remains an essentially contested notion, the risk of conceptual over-extension is real. In social science debates, it sometimes appears as if there is an endless proliferation of 'powers': from hard to soft, economic to political, and material to discursive to name just three major dichotomies. Disentangling the notion is made particularly difficult because of how it sits at the centre of a conceptual universe of connected terms. These expressions include, most notably, 'capacity', 'influence', and 'authority', but also 'domination', 'rule', 'leadership', 'hegemony', 'force', and 'strength'. Thus, authors who use these latter terms may be referring to phenomena that could be explained with the notion of power or, alternatively, a particular understanding of power probably undergirds such accounts (yet this may not be explicit). In light of such difficulties, it is perhaps better to see power as a 'family resemblance' notion in the Wittgenstein sense: the concept has no essence but, rather, it serves as a frame to link a range of associated ideas that share overlapping qualities.[17] This does not mean that power is a 'muddled' concept, only that it is impossible to arrive as a single 'master' definition that could do justice to the variety of uses that fall under its name.[18] In IR, such a point is underscored by Michael Barnett and Raymond Duvall who, in addition to arguing that IR should not be handcuffed to a realist-inspired vision of power, point to the unhelpfulness of treating notions of power as engaged in 'gladiatorial' battles. Rather, with a relational logic in mind, scholars should be striving to understand the connections and comparisons between different notions.[19] This book aspires to contribute to such a research agenda but, initially, we also need to address a more fundamental theoretical problem: what is the point of the concept of power?

2.1.2 *The purposes of 'power'*

Surprisingly, despite everything that has been written and uttered on power, very few scholars have systemically addressed what the notion is actually providing. Peter Morriss' study, *Power: A Philosophical Analysis* (2002 [1987]), is, however, an exception in the literature.[20] Three purposes of 'power' can be noted. First, according to Morriss, the concept is valuable for helping to explain practical struggles between actors. In this sense, in order for agents to make their way around the world, to avoid being hurt and realize opportunities, they need to assess their own abilities. Such examinations clearly do not take place in a vacuum: agents evaluate each other and, moreover, their forms of power will depend on exploiting or evading the power of others. In short, the notion of power is associated with understanding how capabilities can effect outcomes. Second, there is a moral context, an essentially negative connection between power and responsibility. According to Morriss, 'you can deny all responsibility by demonstrating lack of power'.[21] In this sense, we are interested in how what is claimed to be 'power' can affect something; specifically, how an actor suffers blame through disinclination and not inability. Third, there is an evaluative context, referring to the distribution and assessment of power across social systems and units. This is obviously very broad and it is within this category that many debates on power take place. Morriss outlines two possible perspectives: 'the extent to which citizens have the power to satisfy their own ends, or the extent to which one person is subject to the power of another'.[22]

One can debate the merits of the contextual settings offered by Morriss and the extent to which he clarifies power debates; for some authors, the path he offers is not as walkable as it seems.[23] But when applied to the study of IR, the concept of power is commonly considered important for how it helps to illuminate the nature of different polities, which could include questions on the definition of problems deemed 'political' and the organization of resources. More precisely, and in keeping with a richer sociological sense of power promoted in this book, I would argue that the concept is valuable for how it helps to reveal what is potentially hidden or poorly recognized in political life. This objective will be particularly important in discussing the utility of the notion of symbolic power in Chapter 3. The term 'power', when incorporated into a discussion, tends to sharpen the analysis of political relations by prompting classic social scientific questions. Why does the political world take its current forms? Who gains and loses from particular struggles? How could one envisage alternative arrangements? The concept of power is a vehicle to heighten the senses of the reader that fundamental stakes of the social order are being debated. It provides a means to 'capture the different ways in which social relations shape and limit actors' ability to determine their fates'.[24] For all these reasons, the notion of power will remain integral to understanding the history and contemporary form of international affairs. With these remarks in mind, we can now turn to explore how power has conventionally been thought of in relation to the WTO system.

2.2 Power analysis and the WTO: conceptual departures

The notion of power is clearly important for understanding the WTO system, for both practitioners and researchers alike. 'Power' matters when producers and diplomats give accounts of their policy experiences and preferences. Concepts of power are invoked by scholars to better explain how the structures of the WTO are conceived, how actions within them are enabled, and what distributional outcomes are achieved. Here, I begin the process of critically evaluating the existing literature on the role of power in the WTO system. The discussion draws upon the flexible typology developed by Barnett and Duvall.[25] It debates the merits of the two historically dominant conceptual modes within their quartet scheme—compulsory and institutional—and how each notion can be applied to the WTO regime.

2.2.1 *Compulsory power*

The most intuitive understanding of power, from which many concepts have derived their meaning, can be defined as the production of obedience to the preferences of others. As noted, such a view is found in the classic political writings of Machiavelli and Hobbes, among many others.[26] Power has conventionally been conceived in terms of the property notion and this construct has appealed to the realist logic in IR. For the early realists, when one 'added up' the material resources of states, particularly military capabilities, one could judge who were the 'Great Powers' and, therefore, who would compete and have a significant stake in international politics.[27] For E. H. Carr, how major powers were able to coerce other states to adjust was determined by the exercise of various instruments, not only military, but also economic and ideological.[28] The emphasis on competition and managing the balance of power between states has been viewed as an inevitable feature of a self-help world.[29] Within this, as one major author expressed it, the focus on both force and war-winning ability has served as 'not only the *ultima ratio*, but indeed as the first and constant one'.[30]

While the study of power clearly has a long heritage, it was not until the postwar period that theorists began 'more systematic efforts to tie down these [power] concepts than [had] the previous millennia of political thought'.[31] This revolution in power analysis, across many fields in the social sciences and humanities, attempted to move beyond the simple property notion of power to embrace the 'relational power' approach. In this understanding, power is understood in terms of causal relationships between recognizable agents or organizational units. As mentioned, Dahl's work, in part inspired by Weber, was a key conceptual development in this regard. For Dahl, the exercise of power should only be studied through attention to concrete, discernible behaviour, rather than a focus on its potential effects.[32] Dahl was concerned with how power operated through open conflict in decision-making arenas, with a particular concentration on how ruling elites built the necessary bargaining capacities in order to win over opponents.[33] Decades later, this pluralist view of organizational behaviour—that 'A has power over B to the extent that he can get B to do something that B would not otherwise do'[34]—continues to be a template and inspiration for many scholars. As David Baldwin has defined it, power is the capacity of one actor to compel another to do something they would not have done otherwise, not simply in respect to policy behaviour, but also the attitudes, values, and the proclivity to act.[35]

The compulsory view of power is certainly a useful explanatory tool for analysts of trade politics. The social history of international trade is replete with attention to nations, companies, and dynasties that have been defined by their ability to exercise power, in some cases backed by force.[36] In his famous critique of the 'mercantile system' of the seventeenth and eighteenth centuries, Adam Smith often returned to matters of power, particularly the monopoly rents and taxes collected by chartered businesses that he argued inhibited free competition.[37] In Jacob Viner's later interpretation of mercantilism, he proposed that many mercantilist writers believed in a 'long-run harmony' between military power and wealth in the construction of the nation.[38] Such relations between trade and notions of security have been explored by other authors as well. For instance, in *National Power and the Structure of Foreign Trade* (1945), Albert Hirschman debated how trade agreements could shape and reflect international relations of power, leading in some circumstances to the economic domination of one actor over another.[39] Within a similar worldview, Stephen Krasner applied insights derived from neorealism to propose a relationship between international trading structures—deemed to be either 'open' or 'closed'—and the power of leading hegemons. For Krasner, what mattered for the promotion of a 'stable' trade regime was the existence of a hegemon that could discipline others through accumulated power resources, as indicated by its aggregate national income.[40]

While power may not always be visible to researchers today as 'concrete, observable behaviour' in the Dahlian formulation, one can appreciate how privileged trading actors in the international system draw upon a repertoire of techniques in their attempts to directly control the activities of others. Historically, the US and the EU—the 'major' powers in the common vernacular—have been able to adjust the preferences of others through their command of informational resources and the use of threats. Power-as-property, in terms of market access, has been often treated as a first cut towards understanding the presumed strength of trading players. For Kent Jones, the decision-making structure of the GATT/WTO regime has always followed a 'hegemonic trade model' with 'bargaining power' in diplomatic talks equated with a country's share of world trade.[41] At the conclusion of trade rounds, for instance, Richard Steinberg has argued that the US and the EU have used various 'threats to exit' on different issues to compel other actors to conform.[42] On other occasions, disputes between members may be overcome by the most privileged members applying political pressure over the heads of Geneva officials to their superiors in capital, threatening to suspend preferential trade agreements or, externally, aid and debt arrangements with other creditors.[43] Elsewhere, as investigated by Gregory Shaffer, other tactics may be used to forcefully persuade Southern countries to not register complaints at the Dispute Settlement Body (DSB), such as threatening to restrict market access, litigating, forum-shifting, or denying political sympathy in other issue areas.[44] In sum, therefore, on the basis of such examples, one could conclude that the direct, intentional, actor-based, command view of power is very real in the WTO system. With attention to changing material conditions, one can see how different appeals to compulsory power will always play a role in any conceptual understanding of trade politics.

However, while compulsory power may be a valuable tool in certain key respects, it is my argument in this book that a singular focus on the concept cannot adequately capture the complexity of forms of power in WTO talks. In examining the concept more carefully, one can argue that a series of drawbacks and difficulties emerge. At root, these problems can be explained by how trade scholars have been informed—consciously or unwittingly—by the behaviouralist assumptions of the early postwar theorists of power. There are three sets of problems that can be given here.

First, on its own terms, there are concerns regarding how compulsory power is understood in relation to the idea of domination and the agency that actors are presumed to hold. In one respect, the concept contains an understanding that relations of power are relatively pervasive and resilient to change. Actor A constrains the choices of actor B and, subsequently, secures B's compliance. But the recent history of Southern countries in the WTO system shows how this model of power-as-domination does not easily fit with an empirical assessment. For instance, the emergence of the G20 coalition in agriculture, led by Brazil and India, has significantly altered the bargaining dynamics of the Doha Round, undermining the US–EU duopoly that was previously considered by many to be a 'normal' feature of negotiations.[45] According to some reports, Robert Zoellick, United States Trade Representative (USTR), initially believed (or wanted other parties to believe) that the G20 would fracture, either internally or through external pressure.[46] Analysts who use the concept of compulsory power often depict the powerful as alert and adaptable, and such assumptions may be justified when considering a skilled negotiator such as Zoellick. But if taken too far, such thinking can risk caricaturing the power of the powerful as omnipresent or impregnable. It would be wrong, therefore, to suggest that the forces of compulsory power flow in a unidirectional manner from the North to the South, or that all Southern countries have experienced the effects of such compulsory techniques to the same degree. Part of the challenge of understanding power lies in inspecting its presumed durability, not least the commonsensical claims of this sort by both policy-makers and some scholars.

A second, associated issue parallels the initial critique of Dahl's theorizing: the representation of conflict within social relations. Similar to some critical theorists that will be discussed below, the concept of compulsory power is often defined in conflictual terms as an enduring struggle between actors. Part of the instinctive appeal of the notion for trade scholars—one which is exaggerated by journalists when they speak of 'trade wars'—lies in how it creates the impression of recognizable disputes between adversaries. But is 'war' the most appropriate metaphor at all times? To what extent is power exercised through seemingly 'calmer' political processes, some of which may be removed from more intense forms of scrutiny? Thinking counterintuitively, could the very exercise of compulsory power, including an evaluation of its effectiveness, *depend upon* the utilization of other forms of power? For many power theoreticians, these are critical questions that an exclusive focus on compulsory power has difficulty shedding light on. Moreover, the framing of trade in terms of conflict can also lead to a depiction that power is a zero-sum game: if A wins it must, by definition, diminish the power of B. But as Talcott Parsons once argued, while such an outcome may be true in some specific circumstances, particularly monetary relations, it cannot hold for the most complex systems of power.[47] Take, for instance, situations when the power of a privileged player is read by others as being unfair, leading to limits on its actual deployment, or when an actor may deny the existence of their power to evade or deflect questions of responsibility.

Third, such problems can lead one to question if the notion of compulsory power is able to capture other potential indicators of power that may be valuable for explaining political phenomena. While Barnett and Duvall do allow scope for compulsory power to be exercised with 'symbolic' or 'normative' resources—such as transnational activists who shame targeted institutions through campaigning—the dominant conceptualization remains rooted in a materialist philosophy.[48] In this move, what is arguably left out is a sense of the 'manufacturing' or legitimation mechanisms of power, particularly over time and involving multiple actors. As neo-Gramscians would point out, where is the space for consent in the reproduction of power within this concept? Can power be 'negative' or 'naked' in all circumstances? As will be argued in the subsequent chapter on symbolic power, if one broadens the notion of power to examine its links with knowledge and so-called 'authorized languages' of trade politics, then an alternative picture emerges. The maintenance and evolution of the trading system is arguably dependent on many other sources of social power or, more precisely, with an eye towards Bourdieu, the transmutability of state authority into different forms. The shift from the weakly institutionalized GATT regime—no more than a house on Lake Geneva according to some—to the creation of the more complex and legally rigorous WTO system illustrates how the powerful needed new ways to organize and expand their trading relations. It is on this note that we can turn to address the concept of institutional power.

2.2.2 *Institutional power*

Power can be seen in the creation, stabilization, and weakening of international institutions. The architecture and purpose of institutions may reflect power relations, constrain them, or provide the basis for their existence. Institutional power draws attention to the indirect means by which actors control each other. As Barnett and Duvall define it, 'the conceptual focus here is on the formal and informal institutions that mediate between A and B, as A, working through the rules and procedures that define those institutions, guides, steers, and constrains the actions (or non-actions) and conditions of existence of others'.[49]

Institutional power can thus be distinguished from compulsory power on three grounds. First, understanding the significance of institutional relations highlights how A and B operate at a distance from each other, either spatially or temporally. They do not need to physically meet in order to experience the effects of their power relationship. Second, this leads one to focus on not only immediate decision-making, but also *non-decision-making*, a notion that can be attributed to Peter Bachrach and Morton Baratz.[50] Non-decision-making can refer to the dominant values and rules of social games that work, among other ends, to 'effectively prevent certain grievances from developing into full-fledged issues which call for decisions'.[51] Such an idea is important, for it indicates how, depending upon the circumstances, it may be possible for an actor to defend its interests without resorting to an exercise of compulsory power or, alternatively, that non-decision-making could serve as a prelude before the deployment of compulsory power.

Third, the notion of institutional power also sheds light on some basic questions of legitimacy and universality within the management of power relations. For instance, although an institution may contain one or more actors deemed to be powerful, such figures rarely (if ever) claim that they 'own' the institution. Rather, the institution most likely has some degree of independence from the members that constitute it. This does not mean, however, that the so-called 'universal' objectives of the organization are not vulnerable to being distorted by the particular interests of the most privileged agents. Some theorists, in this regard, have concentrated on formal and informal agenda-setting mechanisms, examining how actors use the resources of the institution to establish certain issues.[52] Similarly, one can also mention how the 'relative gains' debate in neoliberal institutionalism in IR theory has sought to address who gains how much from cooperative action, including assessing 'the impact of numbers, of alliance patterns and cooperative clusters, and the extent to which unequal gains can alter power relationships and be plausibly turned into actual strategic advantage'.[53]

When turning to study the dynamics of institutional power in the multilateral trading system, two relevant enquiries can be given here for the purposes of illustration:

(1) How are the architectural rules and practices of the WTO system in part shaped by political agents?
(2) More specifically, to what extent is the WTO Secretariat 'outside' relations of power?

One starting point in addressing these questions is the old politics-versus-law narrative or, more precisely, the relationship between diplomatic flexibility and rule-based certainty.[54] For some, the 'major and unsustainable discrepancy' in the business of rule-making and decision-making in the WTO regime is the coupling of an automatic and binding system of laws under powerful surveillance with the informal, ad hoc practice of bargaining and negotiation.[55] It is this dynamic, frequently unstable, interplay between two forms of legality that arguably represents one of the central sources of tension for less-privileged actors.[56] The importance of informal political practices in establishing agendas and codes of conduct within the WTO system is impossible to overstate, a legacy drawn from the 'club' atmosphere of the GATT. But when informality becomes the institutional *modus operandi*, weaker agents are always vulnerable to manipulation where there is a lack of transparency.[57] Within this explanation, specific concerns lie in several aspects of the negotiating processes, including the use of 'green room'-style forums for select members, the core protocols on the negotiation of rules, the politicizing of types of formula, and issue linkages.[58] To an extent, one could argue that there is an overlap here between the forces of compulsory and institutional power: the historical conventions of informality, in the shadow of hard law, provide the political space for Northern countries to frame particular sets of agendas over others.

Nevertheless, for all these problems, the WTO system also contains institutional principles that have been repeatedly exploited by Southern countries in ways that block and enable particular agendas. The consensus principle is clearly very important here. If no delegation has a fundamental objection to an issue in the presence of the full membership, such as at General Council or ministerial gatherings, it can be said that consensus has been achieved. Most Southern members have advanced the view that the retention of the consensus principle is non-negotiable. Such opinions arise from different fears, but the experience of the Executive Board model at the International Monetary Fund (IMF)—where, until very recently, such countries had no seat at the table—provides a reminder of how the WTO negotiating environment offers more space to shape patterns of institutional power. Even in the rare moments where GATT rules have called for a formal vote—such as on the granting of waivers of GATT obligations to a country (Article XXV)—negotiations and consultations were held prior to the vote in order to achieve the legitimacy that the notion of consensus provides.[59] In addition, the related idea of the 'single undertaking' in respect to the settlement of the Uruguay and Doha rounds—summarized by the diplomatic mantra of 'nothing is agreed until everything is agreed'—also serves to enable Southern players to at least partially control the pace and form of talks.[60] As will be addressed later, one can draw links with both these aspects of institutional power to the concept of symbolic power. What the notion of symbolic power sheds light on, however, is how the authenticity of the deemed 'universal' opinion is a product of political construction and, in particular, one which may still lead to inequitable outcomes beneath such legal platitudes.

Second, the role of the Secretariat itself as the primary 'guardian' or 'teacher' of the rules of the system may initially appear unproblematic and, according to the common conceptualization, divorced from power. However, this view of the 'Secretariat-as-bystander' to the power games played by members is from my perspective an inadequate reading. Those who have investigated the Geneva body have discovered that the presumed disinterestedness and autonomy on the part of the bureaucracy can be questioned.[61] From the Secretariat's position, it is very keen to explain its place in history: it is helping to build a fairer rules-based system that is open to universal membership, unlike the GATT, which tended to marginalize Southern countries.[62] Like the World Bank and the IMF, the Secretariat is quick to claim that it only acts as a facilitator and honest broker for members, as in the production of technical assistance and research advice which, to borrow Michael Barnett and Martha Finnemore's model, is based on rational, legal–economic knowledge.[63] In part, this leads proponents to offer normatively appealing visions of the organization, even suggesting that the Secretariat serves to moderate the abuse of both domestic and international power by protecting market actors and citizens from 'wayward' governments.[64]

To what extent is this representation accurate? Although there is not space here to offer a full critique of these common positions, one major criticism of the Secretariat's management can serve to reveal why some Southern countries have expressed reservations about its projected neutrality: the extent to which the chairs of various committees have developed greater capacity to structure negotiations. This was a particularly sensitive problem in the early years of the WTO's history. For instance, at the Doha Ministerial in 2001, Stuart Harbinson, the chair of the General Council, introduced the practice of drafting the conference text 'under his own responsibility', collating the views of members and judging the terms of consensus. Yet standard diplomatic practice (in many United Nations agencies, for instance) is to debate textual amendments openly, using brackets to note differences of opinion, and to agree consensus collectively. This chair-driven methodology by the Secretariat, producing a 'clean' text without marking where conflicts arose or which views garnered most attention, disrupts this practice. Although the Doha Round has witnessed some improvements in the transparency of texts drafted by chairs, for some members this still remains not only an imperfect process, but an unjust one. The frustrations of one African delegate recounting their experience prior to Doha speak to the problems Southern countries face in managing these dynamics of institutional power:

> We gave texts. We didn't know where they went, but they didn't find their way to the draft declaration. We were expressing our dissatisfaction, and our disgust. Yet the Chair went ahead, taking the draft to Doha. We were shooting, but we didn't know who we were shooting at. We ended up negotiating with the Chair, whereas negotiations should be amongst Members. The onus was left on developing countries to say, 'We don't want this'. But the other side didn't have to do that because the job had already been done for them in the text.[65]

In short, institutional power in this example draws our attention to how certain agents in the Secretariat—often objectively characterized as 'neutral technocrats'—act to make certain decisions over the scope of legitimate debate. Why these moves are made and the extent to which privileged actors exert degrees of control over such processes needs to be qualified. But to underscore, visible decisions are only one side of the coin. Institutional power also considers the governing biases as work in politics since, as Elmer Eric Schattschneider succinctly expressed it, '*organization is the mobilization of bias*. Some issues are organized into politics while others are organized out.'[66] In other words, the grievances of some actors may never rise to become 'official' problems if the dominant decision-makers suppress or thwart such actors in the agenda-setting process. Power, in these terms, may be considered to move in more subtle ways than in the compulsory form.[67] Such analytical concerns, moreover, dovetail with my own focus on the concept of symbolic power, which also seeks to uncover non-explicit or apparently disinterested political shifts on the part of actors. As I will explain in Chapter 3, Bourdieu can enrich the analysis of institutions here, in particular by providing the conceptual tools to help reveal how such mobilizations of bias are legitimately accomplished.

2.3 Critical approaches to power and the WTO system

Together, one can see how the compulsory and institutional concepts of power provide useful approaches for exploring certain processes and outcomes in the WTO system. To use the framing popularized by Lukes, these notions can be considered analogous to the first and second 'faces' of power, respectively.[68] Nonetheless, in my view it is inadequate to stop the analysis of power in trade politics at this point. This is because there are other scholars who have argued that power can be conceived in alternative ways. It is to this so-called 'third' face of power that we turn in this section. The word 'critical' is used as a broad umbrella term for these perspectives. This is not to suggest, in any kind of crude denunciation, that the scholars discussed so far lack 'rigour'. Rather, the term critical is meant to showcase those theorists who draw upon different traditions, including Marxism, neo-Gramscianism, and aspects of continental philosophy. In terms of organization, the discussion continues to follow the Barnett and Duvall conceptual taxonomy, addressing here the notions of structural power and productive power. Both these concepts are distinctive in regards to revealing how power can work through social relations of constitution, either directly or, often, diffusely. While the analysis highlights the advantages of these frameworks when compared to compulsory and institutional notions of power, it also signals some important drawbacks and limitations, which will, in turn, serve as stepping stones to the main examination of symbolic power.

2.3.1 *Structural power*

If institutional power tries to focus on 'differential constraints on action', the idea of structural power aims to examine 'the determination of social capacities and interests'.[69] Concepts of structural power have made an important contribution to the IPE literature, including redefining the environment and boundaries within which action is assessed, the indicators considered important when evaluating capabilities, and the outcomes that should feature in conceptual analysis.[70] The term 'structure' is a complex and difficult notion to grasp in the social sciences, not least because it is used by scholars in so many different ways. Here, it can be regarded in broad terms as webs of relations that 'empower and constrain social action and tend to be reproduced by that action'.[71] In turn, this leads one to concentrate on how regularities of action are established, sustained, and possibly transformed within social spaces. Scholars who have used such concepts have focused on how the position of an actor within the structure informs their competences, subjectivities, and interests. Within this literature, one can identify two alternative structural power approaches.[72]

The first is best associated with the work of Susan Strange, who argued that the command of transnational credit and knowledge were increasingly the most important systemic dimensions of power, beyond a purely state- or military-centric conception. The idea of 'unintentional power', used in her non-Marxist critique of the 1980s thesis of US hegemonic decline, refers to the inherent complexities of the US managing the resources, agents, and effects of the global capitalist order. In this reading, studying power in reverse from its effects, it appears tied to a specific territory, yet its reproduction is founded on the exchange of both explicit and non-intentional (or perhaps unconscious) moves by multiple actors (states, firms, institutions, civil society organizations) within the system. There is, thus, a diverse range of political units contributing towards the functioning of the international economy, many not under the direct control of the hegemon or a single command node. The focus on the knowledge pillar of structural power was particularly important in Strange's assessment. This took two forms:

(1) knowledge as 'technology' in a broad sense, particularly via the trend towards privatizing research and restricting it to certain organizations
(2) as a foundation for societal belief systems, in part derived from the work conducted in universities and professional associations.[73]

In some respects, therefore, one could consider Strange at least nominally attentive to the symbolic power of the academy and the need to reflect on processes of knowledge production.

The second framework on structural power is derived from theorists who emphasize 'impersonal bias' or the role of ideology in international relations.[74] The neo-Gramscian approach within IPE is a link to this conception, identifying power not only in terms of dominance, but also examining how it is expressed through permutations of coercion and consent.[75] In this reading, the structure of capitalism significantly determines both the competences of actors and the interpretative beliefs through which interests are derived. Gramsci was careful to complement Marx, however, stressing the reciprocal relationship between the economic base (capitalism) and the cultural dimensions (superstructure) of the social order. The superstructure, in turn, could be divided into two 'floors' as Gramsci expressed it: 'civil society', which included 'private organisms' such as schools and journals, and 'political society', involving the government, courts, and the police. It was this durable 'material structure of ideology' that aimed to normalize a particular form of class hegemony into which subordinate groups accepted the worldview of the ruling class as the only possible vision.[76] Structural power, defined in these terms, thus represents 'the capacity of a social class to realize its specific objective class interests'.[77]

In the past two decades, neo-Gramscians in IPE have been particularly concerned with explaining 'disciplinary neoliberalism' as 'a concrete form of structural and behavioural power', which has both international and local dimensions, 'and these dimensions of discipline are one dimension of the supremacist transnational historical bloc'.[78] For Stephen Gill, the ideology of neoliberalism cannot remain abstract if it is to succeed. Ideas such as capital account liberalization need to be institutionalized and codified into law or, as he has expressed it, 'constitutionalised'.[79] How this so-called ideological hegemony of neoliberalism operates through international organizations and regimes has been a consistent theme of research in this area.[80] For instance, Ian Taylor has used the Gramscian notions of 'common sense' and 'moral leadership' to explain how the IMF has adopted the 'good governance' agenda in its relations with recipient countries. For Taylor, the policies that stem from the frame of 'good governance', such as 'transparency' initiatives to reduce government corruption, work to 'reconstruct hegemony through a reformulation of the mode of political rule: from the unstable and unpredictable to one that is most attractive to international investors'.[81] Similar themes have also been pursued by Rita Abrahamsen and Graham Harrison who have each explored how the World Bank has managed legitimacy problems with African countries via 'partnership' initiatives involving government and civil society.[82] In sum, in reaction to the more vulgar economism found in forms of Marxism and positive social science, neo-Gramscian theorists have drawn attention to how power operates through an 'historical congruence between material forces, institutions, and ideologies'.[83]

However, when one returns to the literature on international trade in IPE and related fields, it is surprising how concepts of structural power have made comparatively little impact in empirical studies. For sure, neo-Gramscian theorists often read the WTO regime as an institutional manifestation of neoliberalism, part of a larger political project to promote what is defined as 'free trade'.[84] In more historical terms, Rorden Wilkinson has offered a guide to how Gramscian concepts could be applied to international economic law in order to understand how particular configurations of power are generated and stabilized.[85] But it is still very rare to find structural power concepts supported by substantial evidence drawn from, among other potential sources, WTO legal texts, political negotiations, or analysis of relations between relevant class fractions, domestically or internationally. Those few authors on trade politics who have used notions linked to structural power have, nonetheless, developed some interesting accounts. It may be helpful to note these contributions through a critical examination of two prominent themes inspired by neo-Gramscian thought.

First, there is the question of the relationship between power and corporate rewards within the WTO system. As Strange was often at pains to tell audiences, it was firms that traded, not states, with much of international trade being intra-firm. With this in mind, some writers have argued that the ambitions of the US in the Uruguay Round were informed by a recognition among business and political elites that US offensive interests centred on services, investment, and intellectual property rights. In regards to services, Jane Kelsey has drawn upon Gill to argue that the codification of the General Agreement on Trade in Services (GATS) can be understood as being part of a neoliberal 'regime of accumulation'.[86] Kelsey has argued that the benefits of such a system have been channelled towards major corporations, such as American Express and Citigroup, who seek to amend domestic laws and customs 'behind the border' in order to facilitate further profit-generating activities. Similar claims have been made by Susan Sell, who has used the concept of structural power to argue that a dozen leading corporations, including Monsanto and Pfizer, played a crucial role in lobbying for the Agreement on Trade-Related Aspects of Intellectual Property Rights (TRIPS).[87] In broad terms, according to these authors, the capturing of such highly competitive economic sectors through trade law has worked to 'lock in the position of Western countries at the top of the world hierarchy of wealth' and prevent the emergence of other rival models of capitalism.[88]

However, to say that the WTO system benefits Western corporations does not mean that they control the regime, nor that other agents necessarily do their bidding. For instance, lobby organizations such as the Coalition of Service Industries (CSI) and International Financial Services London (IFSL) are sometimes portrayed as handmaidens to trade diplomats. The reality is often more complex and uneven: sometimes these large business networks are inconsistent in their long-term engagement with the WTO process and certainly cannot control how far their interests will be pursued in multi-issue, multi-player negotiations. Furthermore, one should not conflate gains witnessed in agenda-setting stages, although extremely important, with material outcomes. The implementation of TRIPS, in particular, has actually proved to be very difficult with considerable variation and contestation among Southern countries.[89] At other times, however, it appears to be not so much business capture of the WTO, but outright apathy or ignorance of the Geneva body, a situation particularly seen within the Doha Round.[90] According to one study, the lessons from the first ten years of the WTO order illustrate how the structure of opportunities for business is in many ways dependent on nationally defined state–civil society relations and the participation of multiple knowledgeable actors.[91] Thus, while one should never forget that the most powerful corporations remain headquartered in Northern countries, many Southern-based producers have now become active in lobbying government agencies on WTO policy.

Second, not unlike one of the criticisms of compulsory power, there are concerns regarding how the concept of structural power accommodates historical change in political life, particularly at the micro-level. From one perspective, the metaphor of 'structure' is problematic because it implies stability and, in some uses, a rather rigid determinism in social relations.[92] While it may be an appropriate term for mapping consistencies and regularities in politics, the notion of structural power also runs the risk of appearing too abstract and static, without sufficient sensitivity for how social patterns change over time and how various forms of resistance may emerge, in the process reshaping the very structures in question. Still, it is worth acknowledging that the neo-Gramscian approach has attempted to address this weakness by stressing how power is managed and contested through civil society. In this regard, understanding how the WTO system has attracted a plurality of critics within different social movements has been addressed by some authors. For instance, in a short essay penned after the WTO Seattle Ministerial Conference in 1999, a meeting that attracted large-scale protests, Gill argued that the visibility of the demonstrations and the failure of the talks could be explained by the inherent contradictions within the project of neoliberalism. For him, tensions between capital and democracy, as well as enduring social and economic dislocations, created the conditions for the resistance witnessed on the streets.[93] Elsewhere, in a richer examination of the relationship between civil society activism and the WTO order, Bill Paterson has argued that 'hegemonic elites' have been partly effective by adopting the arguments of protesters, most notably through the idea of 'development'. Borrowing from Gramsci, Paterson has suggested that such moves represent a strategy of *trasformismo* which 'has become a significant tool in the armoury of the WTO for resisting reform and manufacturing the "common sense" necessary for maintaining consent and legitimacy'.[94]

In light of these points, what, then, is the core contribution of the notion of structural power? As Barnett and Duvall have more precisely defined it, the concept seeks to examine the 'co-constitutive, internal relations of structural positions' and how these said structures 'define what kind of beings social actors are'.[95] Similar to compulsory power, it points to durable forms of domination tied to the interests of privileged actors, but the neo-Gramscian perspective offers alternative ways of grasping such dominance, ranging from coercion to more consensual forms of enticement and cooption. Students of compulsory power and structural power also tend to share an analytical focus on forces of materialism, although, as noted, writers such as Strange and Gill have also addressed how this informs societal belief systems and identities. A core focal point in the structural power literature remains the struggle between capital and labour, but one clearly does not need to be Marxist to acknowledge how government decisions are often a function of the demands made by domestic pressure groups.[96] In other regards, while the notion of structural power is attentive to processes of institutionalization, it is distinct from the concept of institutional power which, to recall, is chiefly focused on how restrictions on interest-seeking action can take place within more diffuse processes. Nevertheless, one can consider structural power and institutional power to have similar ends when authors seek to use the notions to explain the legitimation of particular ideas and interests within political contests.

For some, therefore, the concept of structural power could be viewed as eclectic and richly textured. For others, on the other hand, it may still appear too abstract or conceptually unwieldy. As will be explained in Chapter 3, Bourdieu's notion of symbolic power shares some affinities with structural power notions, particularly regarding the 'masking' or legitimation of political relations. But the idea of symbolic power also makes other distinct contributions, such as explicitly addressing the relationship between language and power, as well as the non-intentional ways through which the patterns of politics are reproduced. For the moment, however, it is necessary to pause on another theoretical bridge towards Bourdieu, the final notion in Barnett and Duvall's quartet: productive power.

2.3.2 *Productive power*

As we move further away from the presumed 'commonsensical' command view of compulsory power, the definitions of power become more intricate and contested. The traditions and ideas that have informed the concept of productive power further complicate these debates. For Barnett and Duvall, productive power is different because it focuses on objects and subjects that are shaped through ongoing processes of signification; that is, the very social construction of meaning.[97] Analytically, the concept aims to critically address those systems of knowledge and discursive techniques that help to 'define the (im)possible, the (im)probable, the natural, the normal, [and] what counts as a problem' in the political world.[98] In other words, social relations are seen through this lens as being '*simultaneously* the locus of power and the site for the production of meaning'.[99]

The work of Foucault has served as perhaps the key touchstone for scholars who have been inspired by the idea of productive power. While it is difficult to encapsulate a 'single' Foucauldian reading of power, his critique of the dominant Hobbesian or 'juridical' sense of power found in political theory was a reoccurring theme throughout his *oeuvre*. For instance, in one interview he reasoned that such a conception was 'wholly negative', 'narrow', and 'skeletal', arguing that:

> If power were never anything but repressive, if it never did anything but to say no, do you really think one would be brought to obey it? What makes power hold good, what makes it accepted, is simply the fact that it doesn't only weigh on us as a force that says no, but that it traverses and produces things, it induces pleasure, forms knowledge, produces discourse. It needs to be considered as a productive network which runs through the whole social body, much more than as a negative instance whose function is repression.[100]

For Foucault, this interpretation leads to some notable consequences on how to define the movement and constitution of power. First, he argues that power is best conceived through a relational mode of analysis—for which the metaphor of the network is often invoked—rather than thinking of it as something that is 'acquired, seized, or shared', a vision in keeping with substantialist philosophy.[101] As already noted, this is a macro point I agree with, an understanding that Foucault shares with Bourdieu. In this sense, power is said to produce social subjects not via central command units in hierarchical or binary formations, but through impersonal means or relations of forces. Second, this power is characterized by what he terms advanced disciplinary techniques. For Foucault, we no longer live in the Marxian society of antagonistic classes, but a disciplinary society where individuals are regulated and monitored in accordance with a more pervasive regime of power. As he sees it, these methods of discipline were tested in the creation of state institutions, such as the prison, the asylum, and the school, before spreading into other areas of social life. Power is at work in a multiplicity of ways: 'embodied in the state apparatus, in the formulation of law, in various social hegemonies'.[102] Third, and most distinctively, Foucault argues that a mutually constituting relationship exists between power and knowledge, to the extent that knowledge can be considered indissociable from power, thus meriting the term 'power/knowledge'. Such a proposition is provocative because it breaks from the conventional Western philosophical tradition that has viewed power (domination) as antithetical to knowledge (emancipation). But for Foucault the dichotomy between power and knowledge cannot hold because, in his mind, the modern subject is now constituted as an object of knowledge.

Put simply, therefore, one can see how productive power is like structural power in the sense that both concepts are concerned with the social reproduction of agents' capabilities and how these practices, in turn, inform self and mutual understandings of actors. At the same time, similar to both structural power and institutional power, the concept of productive power insists upon a broader definition of conflict, often for the purpose of explaining how some power relations maintain a level of efficiency or consistency.[103] Thus, power is not only seen in more 'observable' large-scale struggles, but also latent and implicit movements at local levels. However, productive power is clearly at odds with compulsory power since, to underscore Foucault's point, the concept is also aimed at revealing how certain forms of behavioural conduct become normalized, rather than how such behaviour is censored or controlled through dictatorial commands.

Despite the theoretical avenues that this concept appears to open, productive power has so far made very little impact on empirical debates associated with international trade politics or the WTO system specifically. This is not to say that analysts have been oblivious to how, for instance, a power/knowledge nexus may operate in international trade and, in turn, how this relationship could shape the agendas, processes, and identities of agents. However, such thinking has tended to be dominated by a particular conceptualization in both the academic literature and the trade policy field: the knowledge-as-property view. In keeping with the general mindset of commodification, the initial orientation here is not necessarily towards what knowledge is, but a second-order epistemological enquiry: how is it acquired? In this respect, knowledge is often treated as an artefact to be retrieved, such as in documents that require specific skills to be appreciated. For instance, one can highlight the common conceptions of 'technical assistance' as an example of how this understanding remains pervasive. Many Southern countries are encouraged to adapt towards the local 'ownership' of trade-related assistance mechanisms, such as through the Integrated Framework for Trade-Related Technical Assistance to Least-Developed Countries (the 'IF') or the Global Trust Fund.[104] To this end, the Secretariat offers a range of increasingly refined 'products', including various policy courses and seminars (in Geneva and capitals), reference centres and databases, as well as training support through academic institutions in member countries.[105]

Thus 'knowledge' is associated here with the ability to acquire 'capacity', a term which has connotations with 'holding power'.[106] But this common reading of an implicit relationship between power and knowledge in trade politics only represents a very partial application of the idea of productive power. For a more explicit and critical treatment of power/knowledge systems in relation to trade, one can highlight Emanuel Adler and Steven Bernstein's re-working of Foucault's notion of *épistémè*. As defined by them, an épistémè represents the 'background intersubjective knowledge—collective understandings and discourse—that adopt the form of human dispositions and practices'.[107] The concept of épistémè does not, therefore, refer to knowledge in the objectified, property sense seen in the example above but, rather, seeks to investigate how forms of institutionally embedded 'expertise' draw upon more profound and durable frameworks of collective appreciation. Adler and Bernstein cite liberalism and, in a more recent development, legalization, as two important épistémès that have strongly shaped the trading system or, to be more exact, the dispositions of agents who inhabit the social space of trade policy. The boundaries of any épistémè should be treated as being relatively porous since, by definition, a successful épistémè 'does not create uniformity of a group or community', but works to organize the differences of agents around 'pervasive understandings of reality'.[108] However, as Adler and Bernstein rightly note, not all actors benefit from the dominant épistémè to the same extent, a situation of particular importance when considering the 'game' of trade legalism, which has established high costs of entry for many Southern countries.[109]

Still, this single-chapter discussion of productive power applied to the trade regime, while noteworthy, inevitably lacks a detailed extrapolation of evidence that would be necessary to fully assess the analytical value of the concept. One can, however, highlight Doerthe Rosenow's more extended treatment of Foucauldian ideas to WTO politics as an indicator of what could be possible. Aiming to critique neo-Marxist perspectives, which she argues often 'gloss over' the 'heterogeneities and divergences in the exercise of power', Rosenow takes the US-initiated *EC Biotech* case on the importing of genetically modified organisms (GMOs) as an object for analysis.[110] She argues that the European Communities (EC) has defended a form of 'neoliberal' social regulation in this area, one which is distinct from the US technological vision of allowing consumers to choose for themselves between GM and non-GM products.[111] Among her points of attention, Rosenow argues that the EC's stringent methods of testing and categorizing GM products has a disciplinary-like quality. The aim of such activity, as she puts it, is to make GMOs more 'governable', 'controllable', and 'manageable'.[112]

Productive power, grasped in these terms, can therefore be understood as a more flexible and nebulous notion than the other concepts of power debated in this chapter. Yet it is not without its major problems, of which two are significant. First, perhaps the most enduring critique of Foucault concerns how his treatment of power appears to offer little prospect of escape and political agency as historically understood. If power moves through the social world in a 'capillary' or networked manner, with no obvious centre, how can less privileged agents protest and direct a campaign of action? More profoundly, if there is no 'outside' to such relations of power, if power produces desire and discourse which constitutes the individual, then what are the prospects for any form of transformation? As Michael Hardt has rather bluntly expressed it, Foucault's studies of power seemed to 'run into a conceptual dead-end', particularly in the first half of his career, despite his claims that resistance strategies could be theoretically pursued at the local level.[113] In my view, the point is not to deny that some power relations can profoundly entrap certain agents and that explanations may be enriched with the use of biological metaphors, but that the actual prospects for disturbing such relations are greater than Foucault often implies. In essence, it is when the idea of productive power appears to divorce strategies from subjects that Foucault 'runs the risk of reducing power to a play of forces unconnected with recognizable human concerns'.[114]

A second problem stems from this tendency of depicting productive power in amorphous terms: the difficulty of empirically grounding the notion. It is particularly unclear, for instance, how one is supposed to connect large-scale épistémès with the concrete practices of disciplinary methods. As Lukes has remarked, 'for all his talk of "micro-physics", "analytics" and "mechanisms", Foucault was a genealogist, concerned with the historical recovery of the formation of norms . . . and as such he had no interest in analysing such mechanisms by examining variation, outcomes and effects: he just asserted that there were such effects'.[115] Thus, as a consequence of being a philosopher and a sceptic of the social sciences, Foucault developed a particular approach to the analysis of power, one which was removed from primary empirical data collection.[116] This has arguably led to methodological problems when authors have tried to apply a Foucauldian sense of discipline—which seems to work most effectively in relation to *closed institutions*—to a whole range of contemporary objects and fields of analysis. Indeed, as Habermas argued in his famous debate with Foucault, the method of genealogy is actually a rather conservative way of engaging in modern political critique.[117] All of these criticisms are, nevertheless, not meant to lead to a crude condemnation of Foucault's complex reflections on power and his entire body of work. Rather, the point is to encourage caution with handling the concept of productive power. It is, I believe, possible that such a conceptual framework could provide inspiration for the analysis of modern trade politics, but this remains a prospect that has yet to be fully realized.

2.4 Conclusion

In sum, I have critically explored how one can apply four conceptual types of power to the WTO regime in order to aid our understanding of how the structures of the trading system are conceived, how the strategies of agents within them are enabled, and how they effect results. The virtues of the compulsory concept often appear self-evident and, as noted, many analysts of the WTO system stop their theorizing of power at this point. To view power in the form of direct, intentional, controlling actions allows one to gain a sense of how some actors adjust relative to others. Yet when scholars in this tradition adopt an essentialist approach to power analysis it can, in turn, delimit the field of enquiry, resulting in a notion of power that is in many respects very restricted. In one important regard, the concept of compulsory power concentrates almost entirely on the locution 'power over', often implying premeditated and durable political relations, and thereby neglecting the more social, dispositional concept of 'power to'.[118] In short, the concept arguably represents an initial (but still necessary) approximation, one which on closer reading cannot adequately explain or uncover how power often moves in less visible ways and depends upon other mechanisms and processes for legitimacy and sustainability.

With this in mind, a richer appreciation of power in the WTO system cannot fail to address how members work through the institutional architecture to shape the core rules and procedures in ways favourable to their interests. The concept of institutional power is most distinctive when it explains the 'second face' of power: the *interested* action of non-decision-making and non-participation, complementing the conventional understanding of bargaining based on explicit preferences.[119] It shares with compulsory power a focus on actor-to-actor (state) coercion and the material basis of power, yet illustrates how this control manifests in different forms and, crucially, operates at a spatial or temporal distance. The concept of institutional power can be considered linked to Bourdieu's own accounts of how legitimation processes operate in relation to symbolic power, although I will argue that Bourdieu offers a much more subtle reading of how interested actions are manifested and organized within a social space. In turn, this would bring us closer to building a more penetrating critique of the behaviouralist perspective, which has shaped the dominant postwar conceptualization of power.

The two critical concepts of power which have been debated—structural and productive—have the advantage of shedding light on the social constitution of power. Both notions are somewhat slippery and remain relatively untested in WTO studies. But each concept is valuable in the attention it affords to how power can seek concealment and incorporation to preserve a certain state, such as through systems of thought, law, or even human bodies. Potential issues, as Lukes strongly argued, can be kept out of politics through a variety of social forces, operating across historical periods, and often occurring without tangible expressions of conflict.[120] In short, as Strange noted, power is as much about the manipulation of symbolic systems, including knowledge and language, as it is about arm-twisting and material threats. The symbolic dimension of power does not simply refer to communication, but the very political meanings ascribed to issues and actors. It is on this note that we turn to examine in more detail how power analysis can be considered from this perspective. By the end of Chapter 3, we will be in a position to compare the value of the concept of symbolic power relative to the notions of structural and productive power.

3

The symbolic face of power

> *Every established order tends to produce...the naturalization of its own arbitrariness.*
>
> Pierre Bourdieu (1977)[1]

Inspired by Bourdieu's theorizing, and considering the limitations of conventional notions of power used to study trade politics, I argue in this chapter that a critical framework on symbolic power is of intellectual importance. At its centre, the notion of symbolic power offers a way to conceptualize how political language, as a pre-eminent symbolic system, both reflects and constitutes power. For Bourdieu, language is taken seriously because of how it is used to legitimize certain material forms and social relations and not others. Linguistic constructions are thus read as being, at the same time, instruments of communication, political domination, and, potentially, resistance. The struggle over political language shapes the fundamental definitions of issues, the organization of agendas, and the mobilization capabilities of agents. Importantly, in the Bourdieusian vision of the political world, there is not a sharp divide between material structures and symbolic structures, but an interdependent relationship. Symbolic power can thus be thought of as a kind of '*worldmaking* power', alerting us to the construction of the 'legitimate vision of the social world and of its divisions'.[2]

This chapter debates the merits of Bourdieu's careful thinking on power, offers illustrations from trade politics to show how such ideas can be empirically applied, and, when needed, explains distinctions and similarities between symbolic power and the other critical notions of power from Chapter 2. Symbolic power should be treated here as a conceptual framework that houses a series of important sub-concepts. With an eye on relational analysis, these sub-concepts work together to form a larger theoretical design. In the subsequent chapters, symbolic power will, in turn, be compared to the concepts of compulsory power and institutional power in order to better explain strategies pursued by Southern countries in recent WTO negotiations. There are three main sections to the chapter.

First, at a deeper level, the analysis of symbolic power begins with attention to those 'background' notions or elements of the political world that pass as 'taken-for-granted' or, as Bourdieu puts it, 'doxic'. Examining the doxic relations that agents have with their social environment helps to shed light on potentially covert features of power, aspects that are arguably missed when using traditional power concepts. These features may prove particularly significant if certain dominant players have shaped the 'common sense' in ways that privilege their particular interests. In the second section, the argument advances to debate the complex relationship between power, language, and processes of political legitimation. Bourdieu's notion of a 'linguistic market' is introduced here, a conceptual device for exploring the competition between political actors for symbolic power and the potential profits that may result. Three major dimensions of the linguistic market are debated: at a macro-level, the role played by classification systems; at a meso-level, the struggle between 'orthodox' and 'heterodox' opinions; and at a micro-level, the social valuation of particular political spaces and speakers. Understanding the relative potency of symbolic power in a given situation, including its potential to shape the definition of problems, identities, and material outcomes, lies in studying the relationships between these elements.

However, although it will be argued that Bourdieu offers a rich theorization of power, his framework is not a radical innovation. This leads to the third section, which explores complementary conceptual resources in IR theory and sociology. In terms of context, Bourdieu is first compared to literature on the relationship between argumentation and power in IR in order to further tease out the distinctiveness of symbolic power. The chapter concludes through briefly discussing two additional notions that offer synergies with Bourdieu's thought: the importance of framing as an agenda-setting device, and the idea of mimicry for studying social adaptation or the subversive appropriation of an opponent's argument. Together, the chapter argues that these added concepts can help refine our understanding for how mechanisms of legitimation work in the service of symbolic power to favour some issues and groups over others. In the larger picture, it will be suggested that symbolic power, as a malleable conceptual framework, aims to dissolve, rather than strictly police, the structure–agency relationship. In one sense, it warns us about how symbolic systems enframe actors, establishing parameters on action. In another sense, however, symbolic power can be interpreted in more instrumental or substantialist terms, potentially to be used by all, like a weapon or a commodity.

3.1 The doxic relationship to the political world

For some readers, the concept of doxa could be considered to be associated with a very old problem in the social sciences: how to theorize the relative stability of political relations. What David Hume referred to as 'implicit submission', others have come to call 'socialization', 'internalization', or 'logical conformity'.[3] Within these critical traditions, many authors have been preoccupied with explaining how certain political arrangements acquire a so-called 'normal' appearance and, in particular, how less-privileged agents may come to adhere to, or identify with, their own subjugation. For instance, as already noted in Chapter 2, in Gramsci's writings on hegemony, he argued that some discourses could reflect and reproduce justifications for the status quo that come to be accepted as the 'common sense'.[4] In a similar vein, Louis Althusser's work on ideology argued that general assumptions about meanings, what he called 'obviousness', are inter-related with the social identities of actors.[5]

Bourdieu was equally sceptical of those presumptions or ideas that appeared 'natural'. In his view, the stability of the political order is not inevitable, but rather remains contingent upon the management of two universes: not only the public arena of discourse and argument, but also a 'background' space of stable beliefs. Doxa or, more precisely, the *doxic relationship agents have with the social world*, is his chosen expression for 'that which is taken for granted'.[6] For Bourdieu, explaining the workings of symbolic power begins with trying to grasp the significance of more latent histories that may pass unacknowledged or be intuitively sensed by agents as 'settled' and thus part of the consensus. Although the empirical debates in this book overwhelmingly concentrate on the 'foreground' of trade negotiations, where conflicts are more visibly represented and documented, the analytical focus here is on how power can be conceived in more covert forms as imagined in the notion of doxa.

3.1.1 *Explaining how the 'common sense' undergirds power*

If a particular perspective exerts such a deep hold upon agents that other alternative schemes become marginalized, then the perspective has the potential to be sensed as not arbitrary (one among many) but, instead, as the 'natural' or, indeed, possibly 'only' vision. In these situations, as Bourdieu puts it, some agents may 'misrecognize' how the particular social order of the day is a product of historical struggle. As he argued with Luc Boltanski, 'Symbolic domination really begins when the misrecognition (*méconnaissance*), implied by recognition (*reconnaissance*), leads those who are dominated to apply the dominant criteria of evaluation to their own practices.'[7] The concept of doxa enters here as a conceptual tool to help shed light on how the common sense is conserved and how, in the process, particular histories and politics may be misrecognized by certain actors.

Like other ideas in Bourdieu's theoretical arsenal, the basic purpose of the concept of doxa is to explain why social relations often remain relatively stable but, at the same time, by no means rigidly impervious to change. In any particular social environment, a doxic relationship can be said to operate when agents hold on to 'cognitive and evaluative presuppositions' that often pass as 'accepted' and hence without criticism.[8] For instance, in different cultures at different historical periods, patriarchy, or the concept of human rights, or racial superiority, or religious belief have often appeared as given, self-evident 'truths'. For Bourdieu, there is thus a limit to the possibilities 'allowed' by the perceptual framework of any actor within the conventional political universe. The constraining effects of the doxa 'work'—without any kind of lead orchestrator, strategic plan, or conspiracy—to define these limits. This does not mean that one is blinded to an analysis of how doxic relations of gender symbolism, for example, are both strictly enforced and yet contested in actual practice.[9] Rather, Bourdieu's main aim is to examine how power can work through the *internalization of previously external structures*, that is, how a successful doxic relationship exists where there is a correspondence or 'fit' between the 'objective structures' of the political world (such as physical institutions or common categories of problems) and the schemes of perception constructed by the agent.[10] The tighter this 'fit', the stronger the effects of the doxa on the actor in question or, in other words, the more likely they will misrecognize how the doxa is operating.

With this in mind, it is useful to mention how Bourdieu uses the related word 'disposition' to give himself further conceptual space to explore this nexus between structure and agency, which defines doxic relations. As he argued, the term 'expresses first the *result of an organizing action*, with a meaning close to that of words such as structure; it also designates *a way of being, a habitual state* (especially of the body) and, in particular, a *predisposition, tendency, propensity, or inclination*'.[11] In Bourdieu's view, agents carry with them sets of 'durable dispositions', which, while being special to their own experiences, are also shaped by external structures. These dispositions tend not to change very easily because they have become historically sedimented and incorporated into each actor, through explicit motivations as well as by a range of tacit means. For instance, one may be able to reveal such qualities when an agent verbally characterizes an action as 'a traditional approach' or explains 'habitual frailties' as 'natural conditions', rather than reflecting upon how such behaviour may be the product of complex patterns of socialization. One should not assume, therefore, that issues of explicit 'constraint' will inevitably be recognized on the part of those who appear (from the perspective of an outsider) to be strongly constrained, since the subject may read their own position or capabilities as 'appropriate' for the time and setting. For Bourdieu, therefore, an adherence to a doxic presupposition is, in short, more fundamental, more effective, and, arguably, pre-reflexive, a 'true foundation of a realistic theory of domination and politics'.[12]

While any particular doxa is most likely embedded in different institutional settings and territories, shaping what is accepted as the *sens pratique*, it is also important to reflect upon its agent- and field-specific qualities. It is here, however, that one needs to raise some qualifications or criticisms regarding how Bourdieu has generally handled the notion. Despite a later acknowledgement that one can find 'variations in the extent of the realm of doxa'—that is, doxic relations can be exposed or broken—the concept still remains part of his general power-as-domination outlook.[13] It can be remarked in passing that his reading of the concept was partly a reaction to Edmund Husserl's conceptualization of doxa within the tradition of phenomenology.[14] However, some scholars in the critical literature have suggested that Bourdieu has tended to 'overpolarize' Husserl's thinking by marking a radical break between opinion as 'undiscussed' (doxa) and opinion as discursively articulated (orthodoxy to heterodoxy).[15] Husserl, instead, preferred to speak of how agents revealed different modes of recognition, from a deeper, 'passive sense' that he called 'urdoxa', before considering other states of awareness such as 'judgement' or 'predictiveness'.[16] In relation to any social space, therefore, one could imagine that an actor may form different sets of appreciation of the world, from a deeper internalization of dominant notions to a more cynical or pragmatic conformity. Not all readers will be convinced, therefore, that there is always complicity between socially diverse actors over certain doxic presuppositions. Moreover, the degree of congruence between any institution and the doxic assumptions in question arguably never reaches a 'perfect' alignment, even within those structures commonly called the 'institutions of power'. Rather, there is often at least a limited struggle between political actors over competing governing principles that may have implications for different doxic features.

That said, what contribution can this concept ultimately perform when compared to the other critical concepts of power discussed in Chapter 2? To return to neo-Gramscian perspectives again, one could argue that the idea of doxic presuppositions appears to be very similar to the notion of hegemony and the ideological means by which powerful actors defend their interests. It may be read as a concept for grasping the 'microstructures' of ideology.[17] There are, however, some important differences. First, while neo-Gramscians place an emphasis on how elites engineer the consent of dominated actors to ensure a predictable common sense, Bourdieu rejects ideology and consciousness as suitable concepts for explaining such processes. For him, ideology is a rather blunt conceptual tool that has been tarnished through different political and scholarly uses (or abuses).[18] In contrast, Bourdieu repeatedly argues that power often works through very obscure processes, especially involving the space occupied by the body, for which the conventional definition of ideology in terms of representation and false consciousness has trouble accounting.[19] Second, on the related question of intentionality, Bourdieu asks researchers to probe, against the Marxist or compulsory-power vision of totalizing control, how behaviour is often regulated without necessarily being the result of 'strategic' purpose. As he once expressed it, 'social mechanisms are not the product of some Machiavellian intention. They are much more intelligent than the most intelligent of the dominant.'[20] Thus, seen in this light, one needs the concept of doxa to avoid treating power as simply the operations of an 'omniscient strategist' whose every move is undertaken with calculation, foresight, and self-interestedness.[21] The powerful themselves are socialized creatures who may misrecognize how certain features of the order have been normalized, a point Bourdieu illustrated in his studies of the making of cultural elites in the French academy.[22]

In comparison with the Foucauldian sense of *épistémè* and productive power, however, the concept of doxa does share some broad similarities. Both Bourdieu and Foucault have, as a starting point, a common education in the history of science, and frame their theorizing of power in terms of techniques of domination and bodily incorporation. The notion of doxic presuppositions, however, does not necessarily need to be referring to large-scale, transhistorical forces that the idea of épistémè attempts to highlight. Rather, a doxic quality, an internal practical sense, could be generated within a narrower institutional or cultural setting. This qualification is, in turn, emblematic of perhaps the major difference between Foucault and Bourdieu; that is, how the latter, by using the tools of social science rather than philosophy is much more sensitive to contemporary forms of legitimation in particular social spaces.[23] Bourdieu's conceptual approach on symbolic power enables, according to Wacquant's reading, an ability 'to link the objective structures bequeathed by history to the historical practices of agents and, therefore, a mechanism to account for the social patterning and objective meaning of strategies'.[24] This distinction will be returned to at the end of this chapter in order to further clarify what contribution symbolic power provides in relation to other critical notions of structural power and productive power.

In essence, as Bourdieu argued in one study of bureaucracy, 'Doxa is a particular point of view, the point of view of the dominant, which presents and imposes itself as a universal point of view—the point of view of those who dominate by dominating the state and who have constituted their point of view as universal by constituting the state.'[25] The task of critically understanding and empirically applying the notion arguably calls for a close attention to history, not only in assessing how one possibility among many became actualized, but also how certain historical presuppositions remain a source of ongoing struggle between agents, even if they take latent forms. But in keeping with the criticism of Bourdieu's use of the concept, it is perhaps better to imagine how political orders could contain doxic elements, particular features or moments when 'the "right" opinion or calculation simply "falls right", in a sense, without knowing how or why... that the agent does what she "has to do" without posing it explicitly as a goal'.[26] Stabilizing these doxic elements, over time and territories, is in part dependent upon how privileged actors preserve ideas of tradition, custom, and deference, and yet, suitably, remain silent about the genesis of such social practices. As Bourdieu encapsulated it, a doxic relationship simply 'goes without saying because it comes without saying'.[27]

3.1.2 *Doxic relations within trade politics*

Whenever the epithet 'common' is uttered or implied—to indicate why a certain agenda, policy, or rule is the prescribed universal starting point—it is possible that an underlying doxic feature is present. Because Bourdieu used this notion across different fields of analysis—including the arts, education, and the economy—it can be viewed as a flexible conceptual tool that could 'come in many empirical guises in modern societies'.[28] With this in mind, when returning to the social space of international trade relations, where can one find doxic elements of significance? One could cite many assumptions and presumptions that pass with little or no criticism. But perhaps an obvious starting point is the very practice of diplomacy itself as the dominant mode of political organization. As explored by Vincent Pouliot in his Bourdieu-inspired account of international security, conditions of inter-state peace could be considered 'a form of doxa'.[29] Once peace has been established and becomes stabilized over time between a group of states, it may come to acquire a certain 'self-evidence' in the minds of relevant diplomats, thus forming part of the 'background knowledge' of exchanges.

There is, of course, a long intellectual tradition that has sought to examine how trade can both reflect and constitute international peace. Immanuel Kant, Richard Cobden, Cordell Hull, and the modern disciples who have defended the democratic peace thesis have all discussed such themes.[30] Even if current trade officials have never dwelt upon the ideas of these thinkers, the practice of negotiating through diplomacy has become deeply entrenched through the institutional establishment of the postwar GATT/WTO system, building on earlier preferential arrangements. As Joseph Weiler has explained in reference to the closeted and 'self-referential' practices of GATT diplomacy, an 'ethos' emerged that contracting parties would work to 'prevent trade disputes from spilling over or, indeed, spilling out into the wider circles of international relations: a trade dispute was an "internal" affair which had, as far as possible, to be resolved ("settled") as quickly and smoothly as possible within the organization'.[31] It was expected that the process for managing disputes would be conducted with discretion, often insulated from not only broader social forces, but other government ministries that were not specifically tasked with a trade remit. In other words, the implicit aim was to prevent possible discord from spreading, in contrast to the interwar period, which served (and continues to serve) as an illuminating negative example.[32] As Robert Howse has expressed it, drawing on Pascal's imagery, a 'sense of pride' existed among this community that they stood above the 'madhouse' of international politics, notably the UN system.[33] Such insiders thus developed, through close engagements, what Bourdieu would call a practical 'sense of the game' regarding how to adapt to the GATT style of diplomatic culture, including all the customs and proclivities that passed as 'natural' or 'appropriate'.[34]

But perhaps what matters most when trying to apply the notion of doxa to trade politics is to examine not diplomacy *per se* as a larger construct, but how the adherence to some predispositions results in distributional consequences. This, indeed, was Bourdieu's chief motivation: to understand how inequities were manifested through agents adhering to seemingly innocuous practices. Take, for instance, how the notion of reciprocity is politically conceived and acted out in trade relations. This idea, one of the oldest in trade and social exchange more generally, was codified into the GATT as a principle to encourage sovereign nations to engage in the mutual submission of their markets to international competition.[35] Governments were said to need certain 'payments' or 'concessions' for engaging in liberalization, particularly for managing the public acceptability of trade deals at home with constituents. The effects of reciprocity, however, are often very ambiguous and difficult to interpret in trade relations, both for negotiators and outside analysts alike. In most trade talks, the meaning of reciprocity takes a diffuse quality, to use Robert Keohane's descriptor, whereby the definition of equivalence (of equity of value) is less precise, more approximate, possibly involving multiple actors, or negotiations that extend over time.[36] Such points are crucial to recall when analysing the struggles over WTO policy and, indeed, will be reflected in the case studies addressed in this book.

But reciprocity is, at the same time, not simply an objective legal fact that is given material reality through codification and the physical exchange of goods. Thinking more sociologically, with an eye to the effects of symbolic power, the normative theme of reciprocity also shapes the very bodily dispositions of the trade diplomat. A trade negotiator is not 'made' when they pronounce from a prepared statement or fold their arms in opposition to another speaker. Rather, the most expert reciprocal dealer is one who senses and judges the intentions (calculated or not) of other parties; explores and discerns the potential pathways to compromise; beckons and entices players together at the right time, in the most appropriate forum, and with the most suitable methods; and anticipates where obstacles could disrupt or derail the process. One could view Pascal Lamy, in his former capacity as EU commissioner for external trade, or Arthur Dunkel, as GATT director general during the Uruguay Round, as figures that have embodied such qualities.[37] What passes in the common vernacular as the 'technique' or 'personality' of the negotiator—expressions that often conflate or obscure a multitude of potential attributes—is, to use Bourdieu, a set of practical dispositions that shape the conduct of the diplomat. Through common patterns of ritualization, such practices are socially tested and refined, yet this sometimes evolves in an almost imperceptible way beyond explicit calculation and consciousness.[38] In these moves, the trade negotiator begins to form what could be considered a doxic relationship with the ideal of reciprocal exchange; that is, it becomes inscribed into their practices in an unquestioning manner, 'guiding' their 'feel' for the game.

However, as Keohane rightly notes, appeals to reciprocity are not necessarily normatively 'good' for all parties concerned and in all contexts. Rather, what is declared as reciprocal, including the desire for reciprocal behaviour, may in some cases be 'fraudulent, hiding domination and exploitation' and that 'even genuinely reciprocal relationships are not power-free'.[39] One is reminded, in this sense, of the related literature on gift exchange, to which Keohane notes in passing through the work of Marcel Mauss.[40] The act of gift giving, as Mauss explored through his studies of traditional societies, often has a double-edged quality. On the one hand, according to the conventional reading, the transferring of a gift from a donor to a recipient results in a bond of solidarity. Often, the giver may appeal to an ethic of 'generosity' or 'sincerity'; that is, they claim or imply that they have transcended their particular (economic) interests to become, in Bourdieu's language, 'disinterested' (an idea that will be returned to below).[41] On the other hand, however, gift exchanges also appear to reveal social inequities or even hierarchies where the donor holds some form of superiority over the recipient. Moreover, 'if this hierarchy already exists, then the gift expresses and legitimizes it'.[42] In one move, therefore, the gift transaction could reinforce relations of power and dependence, yet be intuitively perceived by both participants and observers through the common—and often highly legitimate—lens of 'charity'.

In trade relations involving many Southern countries, the most institutionalized form of gift exchange would probably be the idea of 'technical assistance' (TA). The management of such officialized gifts, such as through the WTO Secretariat, can take different forms, including the provision of training courses on particular topics or internship programmes for select diplomats, to name two services.[43] But prior to even opening a debate on the precise content of such programmes, including concerns regarding objectives, effectiveness, and accountability, one needs to note how the notion of TA often exerts a strong taken-for-granted, doxic effect on many trade policy actors.[44] Discord may exist between policy-makers over the form of TA projects, including some expressions for more serious reforms, but the fundamental principle of conducting such exchanges is rarely doubted. In the broader critical literature on international aid, Tomohisa Hattori has drawn upon Bourdieu to argue how the notion of foreign aid can be conceptualized as a form of symbolic domination.[45] In bestowing a gift, a donor has the potential to transform their status in the relationship 'from the dominant to the *generous*'.[46] When applied to studying trade-related TA, a Bourdieusian vision of symbolic power would thus be attentive to these subtle processes of (mis)recognized power, particularly when inequalities are naturalized through dominated actors adhering to whatever is deemed 'obvious'.

What would Bourdieu's conceptual tools help to reveal in this context? Two points could be raised. First, doxic relationships are defined here through an implicit commitment among a range of actors to a common stake in the trade policy game. But what tends to be marginalized or, indeed, 'abolished' through time is the genesis of such ideas and, crucially, the particular political principles that underpin its ongoing salience. If one does not understand such history there exists a risk of missing a deeper, pre-reflexive logic of symbolic power or, in other words, how an issue such as TA became problematized in only certain terms. For instance, one would need to initially analyse how internationally administered TA was a radical concept born with the UN in the 1940s; how it was given policy direction by President Truman; and how the notion was attached to a belief that world poverty could be solved in the context of decolonization and theories of modernization.[47] Perhaps most significantly for our current period, one would also need to study how TA was conceived within a positivist, compartmentalized model of technocratic rationality and how only certain public agencies and experts became authorized to speak with competence on the subject.[48] Decades later, one can still see the traces of these principles undergirding the TA initiatives led by the WTO Secretariat. In sum, these primary doxic presuppositions pass as 'settled' or, in the most profound sense, 'forgotten'; they are mental constructions that require little, if any, effort to be grasped by trade officials that are part of the diplomatic game.

Second, this doxic relationship—to be precise, the 'fit' between the legally sanctioned category of TA and the cognitive structures of the trade policy agent—is often marked by an apparent sense of permanence. Yet, to clarify again, any particular doxa is never completely insulated from all types of exposure or change. In this regard, one can note a general critique of TA that has resurfaced in different forms over the postwar period: the question of agency, 'dependence', or 'powerlessness' on the side of the recipient. The more recent shift towards naming TA as 'technical cooperation' or 'capacity-building', a development that spilled over into the trade field from debates in international aid politics, can be understood as 'perhaps signalling a more equal, interactive relationship between giver and the receiver'.[49] The appeal to 'partnerships', 'networks', and 'demand-driven' approaches in relation to TA has become common in current policy debates. But these terms also conceal and obfuscate larger historical social forces at work in capitalism, which the trade regime and its institutional manifestations are, in a broad sense, merely reflecting. In this regard, one could argue that what passes as doxic now in social arrangements on TA is, at a deeper level, the shift from the previous 'spirit of capitalism' (with its emphasis on hierarchy, dictation, and authoritarian methods of social organization) to the 'new spirit' that emerged in the 1980s and 1990s.[50] Empirically, what needs to be analysed today, among other enquiries, is whether aspects of the 'older' cultural spirit survive in new forms and the extent to which the agency of some recipients may be constrained through more subtle means.

There are two concluding points that can be made at this stage. First, inspired by Bourdieu's theorizing on symbolic power, I have suggested that one can understand doxic elements as being very stable features of political orders that often present a particular point of view as the universal point of view, sometimes without resorting to any justification. These elements can work to 'smooth' and 'quieten' resistance, to the extent that the very discussion of fundamental critique fades into the background. Since the doxic relation does not stand out as a recognizable 'problem' to be addressed, it may be difficult for some actors (not only the dominated, but the dominant) to recognize the social conditions that have made some presuppositions of the world pass as 'normal'. In turn, this leads to a second conclusion as a bridge to the next part of this chapter; that is, the doxa operates in a relationship with its close ally, orthodoxy, yet denies such a relationship exists. In the 'ideal' theoretical model for Bourdieu, the empirical justifications for orthodoxy begin to align and 'fit' with the internal common sense of agents, both universes in a mutually constitutive relationship. In these moves, the most powerful actors hope to universalize and concretize their systems of classification, the 'authorized' institutional languages, and the policies that derive from them; in sum, to defend 'the integrity of doxa or, short of this, of establishing in its place the necessarily imperfect substitute, orthodoxy'.[51]

3.2 Power and its need for legitimation

This second section continues the examination of Bourdieu's theorizing on symbolic power, but shifts focus to explore how agents engage in the common struggle over the representation of the political world. It is divided into two subsections. First, I explain why an attention to legitimation processes is integral to the broader study of power, including specific reasons advanced by Bourdieu. Second, this discussion provides a basis for further grounding the notion of symbolic power with the WTO empirical context. As a conceptual organizing device, the idea of a 'linguistic market' is introduced and core properties of this market are debated. At relevant points, the argument also integrates insights from constructivist and critical authors in IR and law who have had similar concerns to Bourdieu.

3.2.1 *The importance of legitimation*

Bourdieu consistently argues that social practices—from the faintest of utterances to the hardest of legal rules—almost always require some form of justification and that 'figures' or structures of power are intimately bound up with strategies of legitimation. As he expressed it, 'No power can be satisfied with existing just as power, that is, as brute force, entirely devoid of justification—in a word, arbitrary—and it must thus justify its existence, as well as the form it takes, or at least ensure that the arbitrary nature of its foundation will be misrecognized and thus that it will be recognized as legitimate.'[52] For Bourdieu, what motivates the notion of symbolic power is this concern with analysing the mechanisms of legitimation that are intertwined with power. This aim, however, requires some initial contextualization and clarification in order to unpack its significance and provide a basis for the subsequent discussion in this chapter.

Legitimation is, to be precise, a dimension of the concept of legitimacy, referring to the techniques and methods that agents use to make certain actions appear legitimate. The notion of legitimacy, however, is often opaque, intangible, and inherently contested, being understood and applied in different ways. The academic literature on legitimacy—engaging the social sciences, moral and political philosophy, and law—fully reflects this ambiguity, with scholars adopting a range of epistemological and methodological views.[53] For instance, debates have opposed normative theories with empirical theories of legitimacy, or positioned scholars who adopt procedural accounts of legitimacy against those who hold more substantive conceptions. Many definitions of legitimacy gravitate around a sense of 'belief' or 'oughtness' on the part of the subject. A particular institution or rule, for instance, is seen as legitimate if it is justified in terms of certain common values leading, in turn, to actors obeying or adhering to the institution or rule. Thus, seen through a variety of possible subjective lenses, what makes an object pass as legitimate is, in one major sense, defined by what is absent: coercion or, in other words, the intuitive conventional sense of power-as-domination.[54]

For those theorists who subscribe to the compulsory vision of power there has been, by definition, a tendency to see legitimacy, as defined in terms of consensus, as an oppositional concept. To recall the discussion in Chapter 2, if power is characterized by actions that are commanding and dictatorial, and which constrain the agency of one actor by another, then placing the concept of legitimacy close to power would seem inappropriate. However, in relation to the other major notions of power in IR, I have already raised the issue of legitimacy and legitimation, which appears to be implicated in any adequate understanding of these concepts. For instance, the idea of institutional power aims to grasp how some agents shape the practices and codes of organizational complexes in order to better control other actors. In this way, the actor-to-actor power relation operates indirectly and less obtrusively, thus potentially cultivating less resistance and hence implying that the action has some degree of legitimacy. Similarly, the notion of structural power in the Marxist and Gramscian traditions has highlighted the role of ideology as a 'cloaking' device that aims to secure the legitimation of the dominant order. In this regard, the emphasis is placed on how methods of legitimation are used by actors to maintain particular social relations and how conflict is minimized or 'masked'. One can also note in passing here Jürgen Habermas' contribution to the theorization of legitimation. Borrowing from Marx and Parsons, Habermas likewise argues that legitimacy is a kind of facade or screen, which is necessary for a stable social order, particularly in terms of managing the tensions between capitalism and democracy.[55]

Broadly speaking, Bourdieu falls within this critical tradition. Where he differs on the subject of legitimacy is in his incorporation and extension of Weber's ideas.[56] Why, then, does Bourdieu argue that legitimation is important to study? Three sets of reasons can be suggested. First, put simply, teasing out different mechanisms of legitimation helps to reveal what is hidden in political life, specifically, the complexity of forms of domination. To accomplish this, Bourdieu is keen to expand the concept of interest (following Weber's translation of the economic model into the realm of religion) in order to trace how actions defined as 'self-interested', such as a desire for economic capital, can often mutate and transform into 'disinterested' actions.[57] 'Disinterest' here does not mean an absence of interest but, rather, the projection of an *apparent* sense of impartiality, often through an appeal to whatever is defined as the 'universal'. For Bourdieu, symbolic power is essentially 'denied capital'; it aims to obscure the underlying 'interested' relation, including the original sources of power, through legitimation.[58] Agents need to develop symbolic power, as Bourdieu sees it, because a large number of social practices could not be performed if they were recognized as emanating from the pursuit of pure self-interest. By contrast, he views all notions of legitimacy that are uncritically 'consensus-based', that posit implicitly or explicitly that legitimation works at a distance from 'power', to be fundamentally misleading.[59] Rather, the challenge is to figure out how legitimation is imbricated with power; how it works, through manifold ways, to protect power.

This idea that the 'arbitrary' nature of power needs to be insulated leads us, in turn, to a second reason for studying legitimation: how it helps to explain the regularities in politics. The concept of symbolic power is hence useful in terms of shedding new light on the patterns and continuities in political relations and, in particular, forms of inertia. This is because legitimation strategies are often pursued in ways that attempt to stabilize or 'fix' political relations in certain forms; that is, as Weber put it, to see 'purely factual power relations' transformed 'into a cosmos of acquired rights, and to know that they are thus sanctified'.[60] If a particular power relation or principle is successfully legitimized it could make the job of active policing easier and the intervention of violence less likely. In short, the effects of legitimation may work to enhance the durability or efficiency of the power in question. Third, for Bourdieu, it is only through analysing legitimation techniques that one can better probe and detect the fractures within the walls of symbolic power. Legitimation implies an active process of construction and renewal where symbolic labourers struggle for better positions in their primary social spaces.[61] It is a process that is often unsteady, unpredictable, and, for Bourdieu, increasingly arduous in advanced industrial societies.[62] But the potential for agency is always possible when the fractures are chipped open to reveal vistas, and the vistas lead, in turn, to new visions, including all those perspectives that were closed off or denied under the search for 'consensus'.

3.2.2 *The properties of the linguistic market in trade politics*

Symbolic power thus represents for Bourdieu 'a way of talking about the legitimation of power relations through symbolic forms'.[63] But what exactly are these symbolic forms? Religion and art could be represented as two symbolic systems of prominence, but Bourdieu spends most of his time on perhaps the major symbolic system, one which plays a paradigmatic role in politics: language. His major argument is that language does not simply function as a tool of cognition and communication; that is, as a method for 'coding' and signifying the meanings of objects. Rather, Bourdieu sees symbolic systems as being *simultaneously* 'instruments of domination' that serve political purposes, in particular through enabling the 'legitimation of the established order by the establishment of distinctions (hierarchies) and the legitimation of these distinctions'.[64] In respect to any social environment, when actors meet and engage, they do so within what Bourdieu refers to as a 'linguistic market', which is structured in certain ways.[65] The next sections explore three key properties of this market:

(1) the role of classifications
(2) the organization of arguments into orthodox and heterodox opinions
(3) the social valuation of particular contexts and speakers.

CLASSIFICATION SYSTEMS

In the Bourdieusian social world, it is the 'logic of difference', of 'differential deviation', that matters most.[66] Symbolic systems, from this viewpoint, are essentially classification systems, constructed around principles of inclusion and exclusion, of dividing categories into opposing classes and hence generating meaning through such separation. Binary distinctions—such as between normal or special; distinguished or vulgar; or the master bipolar relationship for Bourdieu, dominant or dominated—are particularly significant, acting as 'primitive classifications' that underpin many mental formulations.[67] A major stake in the contest for symbolic power, often the first, is therefore over which classificatory schemes become legitimized or delegitimized, and who benefits from these processes. Why do classifications matter so much in politics? Two sets of reasons can be given here. First, the struggle over, and 'fixing' of, classifications often takes place at a high level of abstraction in political debates, serving as a kind of conceptual organizing grid. This is significant because the classification may have a determining effect on many issues, policies, and modalities operating at lower levels of abstraction; indeed, this is often a stated goal. The classification may also have a conceptual reach across institutions, territories, or spheres of politics. In other respects, the classification may have a long lifespan, shifting in meaning only gradually through time. Such designs are important to analyse because if an actor wins a classification battle—that is, in other words, if more of its particular interests become attached to a 'universal' category—they will likely have an upper hand in subsequent competitions on that same conceptual terrain.

The significance of classifications has not escaped the attention of IR theorists, particularly those who have adopted constructivist perspectives on international organizations. For instance, Michael Barnett and Martha Finnemore have argued that the ability of international bureaucracies to classify political problems is a major objective for such bodies and that these processes can be considered 'a form of power'.[68] This thinking has, in turn, been utilized by other authors in theorizing classification mechanisms involving the UN Secretariat and the OECD.[69] In trade scholarship, one can identify other writers who have explored the powerful effects of classifications. For example, Jane Kelsey has examined the links between schemes of categorization and political interests in the history of services trade. Building on the earlier work of William Drake and Kalypso Nicolaïdis, Kelsey has examined how 'trade in services'—an alien notion prior to the 1980s—was in part legitimized through the work of institutions such as the OECD, which acted as a restricted forum and knowledge producer for Northern countries to debate how services could be classified in the GATT system. For Kelsey, the point of such enquiries is to trace how 'trade in services' had particular roots in the commercial interests of US, European, and Japanese corporations, but was subsequently legitimized through a 'globalizing' process that was aided by the OECD.[70]

In law, Andrew Lang, who has adopted an explicit constructivist framework, has further enriched such analysis by explaining how this 'regime of knowledge' in services was assembled and monitored by interested actors.[71] As noted in the introduction to the book in respect to the relationship between power and ideas, he draws attention to the potential for law—symbolic power par excellence in Bourdieu's opinion—to 'close' opportunities for contestation over time through the common work of objectification and officialization.[72] For instance, Lang argues that through the legal codification of particular definitions of the General Agreement on Trade in Services (GATS) (such as the four 'modes of supply' in Article I), as well as the ongoing labour of statistical analysis, particular dominant meanings acquire a certain salience and have the potential 'to reflect and embody shared ways of classifying services'.[73] Trade law, in this sense, has not only a 'regulative power', but also an 'imaginative power'.[74] In other related work, Lang has also critically engaged with the 'trade' versus 'non-trade' distinction, otherwise known as the 'trade linkage' debate, as in 'trade and environment' or 'trade and labour'.[75] Through attention to the standard vocabulary and social narratives used by trade lawyers in these discussions, he questions why such a conceptual opposition arose between, on the one hand, a positive and apparently 'self-evident' category of 'trade' and, on the other hand, a more problematic class of 'non-trade'.[76] Lang argues that this distinction has proved to be 'ultimately counter-productive', tending to legitimize and naturalize the *telos* of the liberal trade project via the privileging of those (commercial or political) values attached to 'free trade'.[77] The linkage debate thus gives the appearance of subjecting the trade regime to political contestation but, in practice, such classifications typically work to 'reproduce and reconstitute' a conservative opinion, in the process blunting more profound critiques.[78]

Second, the struggle over the symbolic power of classifications is, at the same time, a struggle over groups. For Bourdieu, the capacity to make groups, to constitute them, to divide them, or to destroy them, is an enduring feature of the workings of symbolic power. This is because classifications can shape the very 'basis of the representation of groups, and therefore, of their mobilization and demobilization'.[79] As Wacquant has argued in his reading of Bourdieu, the 'political work of group-making calls our attention to the panoply of techniques of symbolic aggregation and instruments of claim-making whereby a population is forged into a collective, a "class on paper" turned (or not) into a real collective, endowed with the capacity to move its (putative) members, voice demands, and act as such on the historical stage'.[80] The modern state can be highlighted as a classic object of analysis for analysing the relationship between group-making and classifications. For Bourdieu, the state has evolved to become the 'central bank for symbolic credit' or, in an extension of Weber, the 'holder of the monopoly of legitimate symbolic violence'.[81] By this he means that when the state claims responsibility for adjudicating over a territory, it needs to collect, treat, and redistribute symbolic resources it considers valuable. Among these activities, the logic of which tends towards totalization and objectification, Bourdieu draws attention to the ways in which the state classifies populations for the purpose of managing social problems, most prominently through the education system.[82]

In turning back to the WTO, one can see how political actors form groups to construct as much as to express their reality. Perhaps the most fundamental division is the master tripartite classification between 'developed', 'developing', and 'least developed' members. As in the UN, from where the system is borrowed, this is a self-designated categorization in the WTO. But that has not prevented repeated struggles between countries over the validity of certain members associating themselves to particular groups. The category of 'developing country' has become a notable bone of contention. For instance, China's original accession to the WTO featured negotiations with the US over its 'developing country' designation and the extra legal provisions attached to such categories. This was particularly apparent in agricultural talks, where it was agreed that Chinese domestic support payments would be capped at 8.5% of agricultural production, not the 10% conventionally given to countries that are defined as 'developing'.[83] In recent years, in the context of the Doha Round, the US has tried again to argue that countries such as China, India, and Brazil represent 'advanced developing countries' as a result of their changing economic status and that, due to this distinction, they need to assume 'greater responsibilities'.[84] In general, however, most Southern members have resisted any effort to fundamentally alter the logic of differentiation in this area. One can see how the power of symbolic naming, in this example, is highly significant because it is being used to defend access to potential material benefits. Explaining the design and consequences of classifications is thus, for Bourdieu, an important contribution of the concept of symbolic power. But it is also apparent that we need to address, at a lower level of abstraction, the content of opinions expressed on the linguistic market in question.

ORTHODOX AND HETERODOX OPINIONS

As noted at the end of Section 3.1, in Bourdieu's mind there exists a two-way relationship between the 'background' doxa and the idea of orthodoxy. Some doxic presuppositions that today pass as taken-for-granted were, at a previous period in time, part of public debate on the orthodox point of view. Conversely, some contemporary orthodox judgements contain the traces of doxic elements.[85] To speak of an orthodoxy is to define a particular opinion, which may constitute a broader system of knowledge, as being 'the convention'; a 'straight', 'right', or 'correct' orientation.[86] For Bourdieu, this raises the question of which political languages become recognized as 'authoritative', including all the theories, principles, and modes of expression that acquire a quality of 'good usage'. But the strength of an orthodoxy, perhaps its defining feature, centres on how it defends itself against other *potential orthodoxies*, opinions that are positioned as *heterodox* by virtue of having a marginalized status.[87] In short, the notions of orthodoxy and heterodoxy can be thought of here as conceptual devices for teasing out the range and value of potential positions that can be adopted on the linguistic market.

In this struggle over the symbolic power to define a legitimate opinion, Bourdieu points to three general features. First, following the economic analogy, the idea of a linguistic market implies a space where individuals enter into an exchange of goods, which results in a market price. But like the potential for monopolies in the economic market, the linguistic market also features more dominant producers who structure the scope for deliberation (controlling the price) in ways that may serve their interests. Certain utterances or propositions may thus acquire a greater profit, while others are recognized at a lower value. Second, Bourdieu introduces the related notion of 'linguistic capital' as a way to trace the perceived balance between orthodox and heterodox values. Linguistic capital refers to the 'power over the mechanisms of linguistic price formation, the power to make the laws of price formation operate to one's advantage and to extract the specific surplus value'.[88] For Bourdieu, each linguistic market will experience episodes of 'linguistic inflation' or 'linguistic devaluation'—phrases that highlight the praising or tarnishing of certain ideas—as actors battle to impose their 'correct' definition. Although each interaction can be significant, agents seek, at the same time, to ensure that their stock of linguistic capital can be reproduced over time through structuring key mental frameworks on the world. As noted, this could include classification schemes, premises, or standards.

Third, more specifically, Bourdieu argues that a 'crucial process' to be analysed in this study of symbolic power 'is the work of dissimulation and transfiguration (in a word, euphemization)'.[89] What does this entail? A euphemized discourse is, by definition, concealing something distasteful, something that may provoke if fully revealed. The euphemism represents a substitute for a harsher term that may more accurately reflect reality. Although one could say that all linguistic expressions are, to some degree, euphemized, it is in politics where such formulations are most carefully composed. As George Orwell famously argued, 'political language has to consist largely of euphemism, question-begging and sheer cloudy vagueness'.[90] The primary reason why Bourdieu pays attention to such forms and formalities is because some euphemized utterances can work as a kind of censorship on the structure of the linguistic market. To be clear, this is not censorship defined in terms of explicit repression, directed by an identifiable agency. Rather, it is a softer form of censorship, a 'constrained communication' to be precise, which derives its efficacy from a majority of actors in the game recognizing the same euphemisms.[91] Indeed, over time, some euphemisms may become so normalized that agents may misrecognize what precisely is or was being concealed.

How, then, can one define this relationship between orthodoxy and heterodoxy in the WTO setting? Due to the complexity of literatures in this area, embracing history, economics, and international politics, one cannot possibly conduct an extended analysis of how the contemporary linguistic market on WTO policy has evolved into its present state. Such work would represent a major enquiry beyond the scope of this book.[92] The following points should therefore be read as an initial mapping exercise or conceptual sketch, with further, more detailed applications to come in the fourth and fifth chapters. The more restricted aim here is not to capture some 'immutable essence' or rigid definition of an orthodox or heterodox opinion in the WTO system but rather to highlight the fluid struggle over symbolic power at this level.

Among possible starting points, one can begin with the role of international trade theory, as refined and defended primarily in the academy. As is well known, modern trade theory owes its debt to the canonical work of David Ricardo who, along with James Mill, articulated the principle of comparative advantage: that mutual gains from trade can be realized when nations specialize in the production of a good in which their opportunity cost is lowest.[93] The later neoclassical extensions of Ricardo's thought have provided, in turn, the basis for theorists to justify the orthodox vision of freer commercial exchange.[94] According to writers who fall within this broad tradition, it is claimed, first and foremost, that trade liberalization exists in a positive relationship with economic growth. Increasing trade provides access to worldwide resources and markets, enlarging the consumption capacities of a country and enabling scale economies. Trade helps to reward those countries or, more precisely, sectors and firms, that possess a comparative advantage, whether in terms of labour efficiency or other factor endowments. In turn, it is argued that with more growth, a country is in a better position to reduce poverty, as commonly illustrated by the enlarging middle class in China and India.[95] In the contemporary literature since the 1970s, these arguments have built upon a general critique against import-substitution policies, which are claimed to foster biases against exporting. Economic planning behind import quotas and other instruments is to be severely questioned according to these authors. Among other undesirable outcomes, they argue that such policies can lead to the rationing and misallocation of foreign exchange, the empowering of 'special interests', and the weakening of national institutions.[96]

Nevertheless, such economic ideas do not travel in an uncontested, unidirectional manner from the academy to the WTO negotiating room. Trade practice, as Sidney Weintraub has rightly expressed it, 'draws its legitimacy from trade theory, but by no means does it mimic theory'.[97] Indeed, one of the most common frustrations among trade economists, particularly those who have engagements in public debates, centres on how many WTO agreements function, through a labyrinth of ways, to inhibit freer trade and provide justifications for protection. As Paul Krugman once bluntly put it, 'The compelling economic case for unilateral free trade carries hardly any weight among people who really matter'; that is, the trade diplomats.[98] However, since the 1990s, what is considered 'orthodoxy' in trade policy has shifted. Increasingly, theorists have issued more cautious assessments regarding what precisely international trade can accomplish for different countries, particularly in terms of the linkages between trade, growth, and poverty. For instance, scholars have debated the use of different measurements of 'openness' and encountered problems with evaluating causal relationships. In one prominent analysis, Francisco Rodríguez and Dani Rodrik critiqued the econometrics underpinning some major studies, arguing that the case for the relationship between trade openness and growth was not 'general' and 'unambiguous', but most likely 'contingent' and 'dependent on a host of country and external characteristics'.[99] Such conclusions have dovetailed with a broader concern for examining how the consequences of trade policy changes are connected to factors such as industrial organization, domestic institutions, and the so-called 'sequencing of reforms'.[100] In sum, as a normative baseline, trade liberalization remains a consensus opinion within the community of authorized trade experts, but the consensus is now marked by different shades of grey.

Orthodoxy in the trade policy game, then, is partly founded upon an historical opposition to theories of import substitution. However, although it should be acknowledged that import replacement policies were poorly implemented in a number of Southern countries in the postwar period, this does not automatically equate to a condemnation of the entire vision underpinning such an approach. Rather, as Robert Wade has argued, the task for Southern states should be to rethink how such a strategy could be pursued in the contemporary trading context.[101] As a source of inspiration, this often takes the form of Southern officials in the WTO concentrating their energies on that malleable and often vague idea of 'development'. To speak of 'development'—however conceived—as heterodoxy in the political economy of international trade may strike some readers as unusual. There is not the space here to conduct a larger genealogical analysis, only to note how one needs to acknowledge that ideas associated with development have a deep history in the trading system and cannot be easily encapsulated. In the post-war context of decolonization, one would need to trace how, for instance, the paradigm of modernization theory implied that all 'backward' or 'underdeveloped' areas could advance to the same economic status of the North.[102] In the specific circumstances of multilateral trade policy, 'development', as imagined in terms of exceptions to liberalization, was politically contested in debates surrounding the failed International Trade Organization (ITO), as well as the later GATT 'Haberler Report' into the concerns of Southern countries.[103]

In more recent years, the idea of 'policy space', a notion associated with debates at the United Nations Conference on Trade and Development (UNCTAD), has been seized upon by some scholars, advocates, and government representatives as a way to articulate a vision of trade policy that is slightly removed from, but still 'speaks to', the conventional orthodoxy.[104] Under this heterodox frame, theorists have argued that the Uruguay Round was detrimental for many Southern countries. In areas such as tariff reductions, provisions on patents, and investment rules, many WTO members lost 'development sovereignty' according to Kevin Gallagher.[105] The concept of 'policy space' remains controversial for some, but for proponents it is claimed to offer a vehicle to debate, first, the historical use of trade policy instruments and, second, the inevitable tensions between multilateral obligations and degrees of national political autonomy.[106] The point of such heterodox enquiries is not to condemn multilateral disciplines *per se*, since the complete abandonment of such rules could significantly damage international trade for all. Rather, it provides a spotlight to explore which powerful interests become attached to certain rules and how, in light of such constraints, less-privileged agents can maximize their symbolic power, leading in turn to greater material and political gains.

The labels 'orthodoxy' and 'heterodoxy' thus provide a means to plot the positions of agents within the linguistic market on trade policy. However, this picture is complicated by three important qualifications. First, these terms should not be considered representative of fixed bodies of thought, as in some classical Marxist sense of an actor who unwaveringly defends the so-called 'dominant ideology'. Rather, in contrast to those critical writers who represent the WTO as a monolithic institutional entity dictating 'neoliberalism' to all, it is my argument that the movement and constellation of symbolic power in the trade field is much more complex.[107] Second, I argue that a distinctive feature of this complexity centres on how orthodoxy evolves in a dialectical relationship with heterodoxy. Those agents who are privileged by an orthodox opinion are often found adapting to and, in some cases, integrating heretical criticism into orthodox justifications. This is not a new observation in itself. As Peter Berger and Thomas Luckmann argue with respect to theological doctrines, orthodoxies tend to struggle with, and incorporate, deviant beliefs, so as to better control them.[108] When this labour of incorporation is successfully accomplished, the legitimacy of orthodoxy is often rejuvenated since it has checked the potential advance of the heterodox vision to become a new orthodoxy. In this sense, when applied to the WTO system, one should not crudely pigeonhole all opinions deemed orthodox with Northern countries and all heterodox values as somehow inherently 'Southern'. It follows, in dynamics that will be returned to, that the 'would-be most radical critique' from the heterodox actor 'always has the limits that are assigned to it by the objective conditions' of orthodoxy.[109]

Third, the empirical analysis in this book pays particular attention to how WTO actors struggle over the meaning of keywords within the negotiating environment. This focus can be considered linked to the importance of classifications in the evaluation of symbolic power but allows added conceptual space for critiquing political language. In particular, Bourdieu's eye on the politics of euphemized discourse becomes useful here. Notions such as 'openness', 'reform', 'development', and 'policy space' or, as will be explored later, 'competitiveness', 'poverty reduction', and 'food security' are major terms in the lexicon of trade policy officials. But these expressions often conceal as much as they reveal, containing multiple potential definitions and associations. Crucially, like some classifications, particular political interests are often attached to the common meanings of these keywords, yet these interests are frequently obscured and misrecognized due to appearances of 'neutrality' and 'universality'. Similar to Rorden Wilkinson's analysis of the different catalysing effects of the popular 'crisis discourse' in WTO negotiations, the attention to keywords provides an entry point for discerning larger-scale changes, including shifts in methods of legitimation, the relative importance of trade issues, and the means by which actors mobilize themselves and others.[110]

SPACES AND SPEAKERS

By analysing the discourse of a particular linguistic market, with opinions that tend to oscillate between orthodox and heterodox values, I have suggested how one can uncover some key symbolic properties. But words in themselves carry no intrinsic power. Symbolic power, for Bourdieu, is only generated when there is 'a belief in the legitimacy of the words and of the person who utters them, a belief which words themselves cannot produce'.[111] Any attempt to autonomize language, to abstract it from the competences of the agent within a given social environment, is therefore likely to prove analytically short-sighted. In order to grasp how the inequalities of symbolic power are manifested, one needs to incorporate these additional variables into the overall conceptual design.

At a fundamental level, the recognition of a particular opinion is dependent upon it being heard in the most prized forums of expression. Some actors have an easier passage into those valued spaces—be it a political institution, a media outlet, or a department of the academy—where the crucial work of legitimation takes place. It follows, therefore, that one of the surest forms of control over the reproduction of a given orthodoxy or heterodoxy is to simply deny certain (problematic) players from entering the privileged spaces of expression. Spaces such as courts of justice, for instance, have highly restricted rights of way, including exclusive positions for those actors who have been officially 'anointed' by the institution.[112] This effort to police the membership of the space may produce different effects depending upon the situation. For instance, some agents who are denied entry may rebel and walk away, while others may develop an even greater desire for acceptance and seek the conditions that will ensure their passage. In essence, therefore, the competence to speak in an orthodox or heterodox tongue only has value, and can only begin to acquire a profit, so long as it can be heard within a space that values such competence and can permit the development of expression.[113]

Like other political actors, one can see how trade negotiators struggle among themselves over the social value accorded to particular spaces. Take the example of the so-called 'green room' forums for select delegates in Geneva and at ministerial meetings. Depending upon the precise context, these gatherings, which are commonly called 'informal', tend to feature around 20–30 country representatives. The green room has historically been justified as a means to advance 'consensus-building' among the largest traders at a quicker pace. According to the conventional wisdom, a smaller setting may facilitate the conditions for detailed deliberation that would not be possible in a negotiation involving a large number of players.[114] Yet the green room format has been strongly criticized on the grounds of 'accountability' and 'transparency', particularly at the Singapore Ministerial in 1996 and the Seattle Ministerial in 1999.[115] For instance, in Seattle, USTR Charlene Barshefsky and director general Michael Moore called a green room meeting on the final day in an effort to broker a settlement. It was a move that greatly angered many other delegates, such as Jamaica and Kenya, who were denied entry and feared that a *fait accompli* for the rest of the membership was in the making. The Dominican Republic ambassador, Federico Cuello Camilo, was reported to have accused the participants of the green room of treating the WTO like it was their own 'club' in a manner reminiscent of the GATT: 'They still think 20 countries can decide for the rest of us.'[116]

In contrast to the green room, the WTO General Council, as the top decision-making body, represents a highly legitimate space. Participants and observers rarely question its *raison d'être* because, to use a Bourdieusian interpretation, it symbolically embodies the definition of the universal. All members are present and potentially can be heard (although the agenda formulation begins elsewhere, such as in the lower councils).[117] Decisions are made in the shadow of law which, through its logic of formalization and codification, tends to lay the conditions for social adherence or, at the very least, a stifling of potential dissent. The General Council also bolsters its legitimacy as a prized space through other (apparently) mundane activities deemed 'bureaucratic', such as openly publicizing its meetings and issuing reports that are carefully written to avoid any charge of political bias. Thus the fears and frustrations of the excluded delegates at Seattle can only be understood in comparison to the General Council, which exists to officially 'crystallize' political and economic interests, some of which may, indeed, originate in closeted green rooms. In turn, under the pressure of time constraints, if the universal membership 'blesses' a proposition that was formulated in a green room it makes the subsequent task of critique more difficult for any opposing actor. Now, the particular interests of the green room do not simply exist in an arbitrary form but, instead, will be insulated under the symbolic cover of the 'universal'.

But even if one is accepted into the spaces of negotiation that matter, further problems can confront actors in their efforts to effectively use symbolic power. For Bourdieu, there is also a need to assess the social position of the speaker in the linguistic market because what speaks 'is not the utterance, the language, but the whole social person'.[118] Linguistic capital, in this sense, is not a mere technical capacity, but part of a more complex process of mobilizing and projecting symbolic power in relation to an audience. The so-called 'authoritative' or 'credible' speaker, the one who has the capacity to persuade and intimidate others (which need not be considered mutually exclusive), has typically incorporated the dominant values of the linguistic market.[119] In this sense, to return to the idea of bodily dispositions discussed in Section 3.1 in reference to the notion of doxa, the 'appropriate' speaker often exhibits an assured or relaxed attitude of someone who believes, and wants others to believe, that they should be respected and obeyed (the 'sense of entitlement'). In contrast, the less-privileged speaker, the one who fights to be heard and to be understood, seeks to produce, often at the cost of anxiety and tension, linguistic formulations in keeping with a dominant linguistic market that is not of their making. Such players therefore tend to talk in limited and hesitant ways or, in an effort to overcome such apprehension, to adopt methods of hyper-correction and formality.[120] We thus find, in these instances, a central relationship between the linguistic strategies at the disposal of the agent and their social position in the political game.

We can now summarize the core features of the linguistic market as a way to understand the broader concept of symbolic power. My discussion began by contextualizing how Bourdieu aims to explain the legitimation techniques and mechanisms that are common within the exercise of power. He does not draw any hard division between the concept of power and legitimation but rather seeks to illuminate how such notions need to be braided together. In other words, when applied to practice, they are flipsides of the same coin. For Bourdieu, symbolic power represents a kind of authentic 'credit' that agents draw upon in their social struggles for domination.[121] The precise manner by which this credit is obtained, the fluctuating value it accords over time, and the extent to which such processes are (mis)recognized by agents are core enquiries. Linguistic markets are open environments to a degree, porous in admitting and organizing certain ideas but, at the same time, structured spaces that contain the expression of opinions that only 'make sense' to those who negotiate within the market. For Bourdieu, it is important to study such features because it helps to clarify the particular historical form of political relations within the market, rather than reifying it uncritically as an 'ordinary' state of affairs.

In order to trace the processes by which agents struggle for the accumulation of symbolic power, I have debated three core properties of the linguistic market. First, at a macro-level, it is space which is framed by systems of classification that work to define objects of significance into opposing classes. Classifications are important because of their potential reach and permanence within structures, to the extent that they may be read by agents as 'inevitable' or 'appropriate'; in essence, symbolic resources that must be used. Crucially, classifications can shape, in mutually interdependent ways, the scope for political deliberation and the very constitution of agents, classic problems in any study of power. Second, at a meso-level, agents tend to struggle over the representation of politics by categorizing certain opinions as either orthodox ('straight' or 'correct') or heterodox ('alternative' or 'critical'). In contrast to the deeper doxic sense of *fait accompli*, orthodoxy represents the public face of the dominant opinion. Here, one needs to pay attention to the complex, often arduous, labour of justifications advanced by agents to defend certain interests. Third, at a micro-level, the efficacy of any movement of symbolic power depends upon where it is exercised and by whom. In those highly prized spaces, where material and political stakes are under threat, the struggle for symbolic power is often more intense. In sum, the power of words essentially represents the power to mobilize authority in a field of operation, to establish and insulate 'circuits of legitimation'.[122]

3.3 Beyond Bourdieu: complementary concepts

Bourdieu's theorizing on symbolic power provides a subtle and rich framework for re-examining the objectification of material and political interests, particularly through questioning why and how such interests are protected through legitimation processes. The attention to the relationship between language and power is not, however, a scholarly agenda that Bourdieu monopolizes. For instance, I have already discussed how classification schemes have been examined by constructivist theorists in IR and law. More broadly, there exists a tradition of scholarship that has sought to explain how argumentation can be studied in the social and political world, including the relationship between conceptions of arguing and power. This final part reflects upon debates in this area and how they can be compared to Bourdieu's ideas. It begins by discussing some of the literature on argumentation, before addressing two complementary concepts that will complete the overall design for studying symbolic power in this book: framing and mimicry.

3.3.1 *Argumentation and power*

As a result of constructivist research over the past twenty years, it is now recognized that 'arguing matters' in IR. Among important enquiries, constructivists have sought to explain the appropriation and advocacy of particular norms in world politics, methods of persuasion and reason-giving, and how the logic of argumentation can be compared to other modes of social action (such as the 'logic of consequentialism').[123] Studying the practice of arguing within multilateral negotiations has been a particular theme within this field. Often informed by a Habermasian perspective, 'pure arguing' has been conceived as an ideal type of communication 'in which the power of reasoning prevails' through political agents exchanging empirical and normative assertions.[124] In turn, such scholars have claimed that the effectiveness of an argument can be explained through examining the institutional context, where propositions will be shaped by particular norms, rules, and decision-making procedures; the role of external authorities who pass judgement on validity; as well as the perceived credibility of the speaker in question.[125]

But how precisely does the notion of power relate to this literature? In one important sense, as initially raised in the introduction to this book, constructivist authors have often treated the concept of power as being in opposition to the logic of argumentation. This understanding has been underpinned by a view that power essentially refers to egotistical calculation and domination, the common meaning found in the realist tradition and, more generally, rational choice perspectives. Hence, with this compulsory sense of power reconfirmed, multilateral negotiations are claimed to represent '"hard cases" for arguing, since deliberation as such is not the purpose of such talks, but to accomplish certain goals including the maximization of interests of the negotiating partners'.[126] For these authors, 'power politics', with its associated references to threats and deception, is an analytical problem, a description that fails to adequately capture 'truth-seeking arguing' as a core feature of international relations.[127] In Habermas' theory, communicative action advances the potential for mutual agreement (*verständigung*) through the exchange of arguments. A rational consensus, presented in his earlier work as an 'ideal speech situation', is when reason escapes domination, facilitating not 'distorted communication' through power, but intersubjective understandings in which access to, and empathy for, dialogue is present among parties.[128] Relations of power, according to this sense, are essentially replaced by relations of meaning.[129]

However, this treatment of the relationship between power and argumentation can be criticized. First, from the Bourdieusian perspective I promote here, it is more fruitful to conceptualize how power works *through language*, rather than compartmentalizing the relationship into two autonomous spheres. Even if this Habermas move is read as a counterfactual theoretical exercise, maintaining a strict linguistic analysis neglects how power can seep into all forms of 'speech acts', to use John Austin's idea.[130] Thus the efficacy of a group consensus is derived not (or not only) from illocutionary force or empirical rationality but, rather, through the belief in the authority of the speaker who is situated within a concrete social *milieu*. Relations of meaning are interlaced with relations of material and political power. For Bourdieu, to separate these notions, even in a normative form, is to confuse how domination secures its (mis)recognized legitimacy. Given this understanding of power, it is perhaps not surprising that some constructivists have reported empirical difficulties distinguishing between, on the one hand, arguing and, on the other, the notion of bargaining (which is typically attached to coercive behaviour).[131] Second, the Habermasian framework on argumentation can also be problematic in terms of overlooking how agents acquire the 'entry requirements' to speak and be heard. The idea that all political actors have 'equal access' to a discourse is simply not the case in many fields of world politics.[132] Rather, as Bourdieu often argues, the instruments of expression are always unequally distributed, with seemingly 'common' or 'rational' linguistic devices bearing the traces of particular political interests. In sum, a Bourdieusian framework goes further in unravelling all the power dynamics that inevitably distort communication.[133]

Such criticism is not meant to crudely condemn all IR constructivist work on argumentation. The attention to the broader social conditions of negotiations and how arguing processes can be connected to political change represent valuable theoretical investigations. Nonetheless, perhaps closer to actual political struggles, one can also note other scholars who examine how diplomatic language is deployed by agents, but choose to avoid Habermas as a key inspiration. Frank Schimmelfennig's idea of 'rhetorical action' can be highlighted as an example. For Schimmelfennig, rhetorical action is defined as the 'strategic use of norm-based arguments in pursuit of one's self-interest'.[134] In contrast to communicative action, this notion aims to showcase the instrumental use of arguments, rather than how agents seek to yield to the stylized 'better argument'. Such actors are 'subjectively rational' in the sense that 'they do not possess objective knowledge about the effectiveness of their arguments and do not necessarily use the *most* effective argument (only)'.[135] Schimmelfennig points to how political agents often use multiple types of arguments due to anxiety about the relative effectiveness of claim-making, a point that will be returned to in the subsequent case studies. Importantly, in a bridge to Bourdieu, he also explains why rhetorical action is important: because it helps players acquire and reproduce legitimacy within a community setting. Although Schimmelfennig still categorizes 'power' as being an alternative explanatory notion in his model, the focus on how actors 'manipulate' arguments or become 'rhetorically entrapped' by the legitimacy standards of the community illustrates his desire to link egoistic preferences with collective outcomes.[136] Bourdieu would agree that such potential uses of discourse are possible, but one major difference would centre on how agents also incorporate themselves into a community through less deliberate and conscious processes, as the concept of doxa tries to highlight.

The framework on symbolic power advanced in this chapter is, nonetheless, in need of some extra conceptual support. The properties of the linguistic market already discussed—classification systems; orthodox and heterodox opinions; and the social valuation of spaces and speakers—provide a basis for uncovering the means by which symbolic power is exercised and reproduced. At a lower level of abstraction, however, the discussion would also benefit from two notions that are able to further tease out the links between language and power, as well as patterns of social adaptation. By returning to the empirical focus on the WTO system, we can now introduce these two concepts.

3.3.2 *Framing*

In the WTO regime, as elsewhere in international politics, mental short-cuts are used by actors to distil information, shape understandings on problems, and encourage action. Before coherent arguing begins, there must be at least some provisional resolution of meta-arguments, or 'frames'. Agents have to agree on what they are arguing about or, more precisely, one set of frames (and not another set) has to be recognized as a legitimate starting point.[137] Frame analysis is an analytical tool derived originally from Erving Goffman's formulation and now used widely in the social sciences, including the literature on argumentation in IR.[138] In its broadest sense, according to Michael Barnett, a frame can be understood as a representation tool, 'to fix meanings, organise experience and alert others that their interests and possibly their identities are at stake, and propose solutions to ongoing problems'.[139] As a category of perception, framing may strongly shape subsequent discourse, although not necessarily in a unidirectional or top-down logic. In social movement studies, pioneering work conducted by David Snow and Robert Benford, among others, helped to develop the idea of frames as 'conscious strategic efforts by groups of people to fashion shared understandings of the world and of themselves that legitimate and motivate collective action'.[140] Framing is also clearly an important political resource in wider WTO negotiations, yet its explicit use in scholarly accounts of the trading system has been limited.[141] One only needs to note how the 'masterframe' of the Doha Round—'development'—has been so heavily contested to appreciate how the framing process can be significant.

These contributions offer useful starting points for any researcher keen to study the notion of framing, but I would also argue that one needs to analytically delineate the concept into two phases. According to Snow and Benford, a first stage could be represented as diagnostic framing, referring to problem identification. In social movement analysis, for instance, the 'injustice frame' or 'victim frame' has been often studied.[142] The character of a problem is formed by interpreting the actions of an authority or another player as unjust. In the WTO context, one can see how variations on victim framing are often utilized by Southern countries in their positions, statements, and arguments. A prime example of this would be the emergence of the G20 coalition in 2003 which, according to many trade analysts, was conceived in order to prevent the US and the EU from 'pulling another Blair House'.[143] It must be noted, however, that in some instances identifying the most salient or primary factor underpinning a problem may not be immediately determinable. If multiple systemic forces or agents have contributed to an issue, internal framing contests may emerge at this stage in order to unravel differences of opinion. The task of defining the most empirically credible and consistently appealing diagnostic frame is therefore critical. Once constructed, it has to be defended and sustained. The greater the number of causal stories that can explain why a problem exists, the more space becomes available for opponents to challenge the veracity of the promoted diagnostic frame.[144]

Beyond issue identification, Snow and Benford also draw attention to a second stage of framing: the prognosis of a recognized issue. Even if agents agree on the legitimacy of discussing a certain problem, it does not necessarily lead to accord on what is the best set of solutions. In many situations, one finds that the degree of correspondence between the diagnostic and prognostic frames is not in alignment and, therefore, struggles continue between actors. Importantly, if the linkages between these two stages are not robust enough, openings may emerge for opponents to undermine the overall framing process. Again, this points to how the dynamics of framing often do not proceed along a single path but, rather, are subject to contests, featuring actors that intervene in the linguistic market to reframe or counter-frame. The degree to which such moves are successful is, as Rodger Payne has rightly underscored, in part dependent upon 'material levers' that certain privileged actors can activate.[145] For instance, in his analysis of how 'core labour standards' are debated in reference to the WTO system, Payne argues that the frame has been 'distorted by very strong states or by other claimants making misleading and even troublesome claims'. According to him, US government officials use the frame 'almost exclusively' in reference to poor working conditions in Southern countries, whereas a more comprehensive analysis would also examine urban sweatshops, inequitable pay, and other labour abuses on US soil. Payne suggests that the particular meanings attached to the frame by US representatives can be partly explained by their desire to protect material interests, particularly those of US-based corporations.[146] In sum, in another nod towards Bourdieu's emphasis on symbolic power, such accounts help to tease out how frames are always the product of social and political construction, no matter how self-evident they may appear on the surface.

3.3.3 *Mimicry*

In many political encounters in the WTO system, when actors are closely observing each other, they choose to copy, borrow, or adapt certain ideas for their own ends, rather than inventing anew. This is particularly the case for many Southern countries with resource constraints, but even the most privileged actors are often compelled to adhere to institutional standards or, at the very least, not consistently act in ways that would be deemed 'arbitrary' by others. The method of mimicry can be conceptualized in light of these major concerns.

From the viewpoint of a less-privileged actor, the technique of mimicry could be understood in two main ways. First, it may be used for purposes of social adaptation, whereby a Southern agent appropriates some of the practices of orthodoxy in order to assimilate into the prevailing order. This may not necessarily be for reasons of strategically emulating those actors deemed to be 'successful' but, rather, on a more fundamental level, to simply participate and be acknowledged as a 'player', one who has a stake in the game and a right to be heard. Thus mimicry brings to the fore issues related to political status, recognition, and relations of deference and dependence within power relations. For Alastair Iain Johnston, one of the few IR theorists to discuss the concept, mimicry is often used by actors to manage situations of uncertainty, but this may be 'prior to any detailed ends-means calculation of the benefits of doing so'.[147] Mimicking, in this sense, should be understood as a method of survival for certain agents, providing them with the 'modal procedures, models, norms, languages, and (perhaps) preferences' that will allow them to 'relate' and 'make sense' to orthodoxy.[148] In the WTO context, one could suggest that China's entry into the organization has exhibited elements of this form of mimicry. WTO admission was vital for China's self-proclaimed status as an 'emerging power'. Once inside the institution, it preferred to adopt quiet modes of diplomacy that did not appear to trouble Northern actors unduly. Particularly in its early years, China did not take a leadership role in the conceptualization of trade problems but, rather, preferred to deal with the initial uncertainty of moving through a new organization.[149]

Second, mimicry can also be conceived in a more critical manner. How could an actor both appropriate and critique orthodoxy in the same moment? For Homi Bhabha, the effect of mimicry on the authority of the dominant actor can potentially be 'profound', 'disturbing', and 'menacing'.[150] The threat emerges when the less-privileged agent is able to bridge some of the symbolic distinctions (which may or may not correlate to material distinctions) that are commonly claimed to separate them from the dominant actor. On the surface, it may appear that such actions are in keeping with the work of assimilation and deference to the established order, but this time, however, there is a subversive subtext. I would argue that the force of the critique, including the ability of agents to disguise it as such, is dependent upon how the central relationship between Self and Other is exposed and manipulated. On the one hand, Northern actors often want the validity of orthodoxy to be proven and for others to adjust and conform to them, but on the other hand, the very movement towards homogeneity challenges the inviolability of the Self. For Southern actors, it pays to mimic if one can reveal this unstable '*ironic* compromise' as Bhabha has expressed it, whereby the dominant player desires 'a reformed, recognizable Other, as *a subject of a difference that is almost the same, but not quite*'.[151] In an effort to place the dominant actor in an uncomfortable position, where the distinction between teacher and student is blurred, this form of mimicry can often border on parody. The replication of orthodoxy may appear 'too perfect' to be believed.[152] Again, this partly explains why mimicry can be appealing for actors who hold few other cards at the negotiating table. In the next chapter, I will argue that this method of subversive mimicry was used by a group of west- and central-African cotton-producing countries in their political struggles with the US.

Notwithstanding these critical features, is mimicry as 'menacing' to dominant actors as Bhabha claims? Two points are worth highlighting here. First, one can see that when mimicry becomes a kind of risk management tool—the first approach discussed—it does not seriously jeopardize the legitimation of orthodoxy. On the contrary, it could actually invite 'amusement, tolerance, even encouragement' from the privileged actor (imitation being the sincerest form of flattery).[153] Second, one also has to keep in mind how mimicry can be equally adopted by Northern actors in their efforts to acquire greater legitimacy. Orthodoxy, as I will argue in reference to the case studies, does not advance in the WTO system on its own independent path; rather, it evolves in a relationship with what are deemed heretical ideas. Depending upon the circumstances, it may be in the interests of a Northern actor to 'attach' some of their own legitimacy to a heterodox initiative promoted by a Southern agent. This could be based on an assessment that the risks of ignoring or antagonizing the demander may be greater than acknowledging the heterodox notion. In the Doha Round, at a general level, this can been seen in the efforts of many privileged agents to take the term 'development'—perhaps the most important word in the trade lexicon of many Southern delegates—and affix it to numerous agenda items and proposals, to the point where it has become highly malleable. But it needs to be recalled that this widespread dissemination of 'new development speak' within the WTO system was not an inevitable process. Rather, it was only following the collapse of the Seattle Ministerial in 1999, when Southern animosities were intense, that Northern actors began to repeat the word more frequently and worked towards its codification into the Doha Declaration. Thus part of the Northern reaction to Southern demands for 'more development' has been to mimic and echo such language.

Finally, let me clarify why the notions of framing and mimicry are needed as extensions to a Bourdieu-centred approach to symbolic power. Both concepts can be conceived of here as sociological thinking tools, which are, therefore, amenable to a Bourdieusian vision preoccupied with the intersubjective constitution of ideas and identities. Indeed, Goffman's work, which was used by social movement theorists to define the notion of framing, was a notable inspiration for Bourdieu. The concept of mimicry is also complementary to Bourdieu's analysis of how agents tacitly adapt to social situations, rather than viewing all action through the lens of conscious rule-following. However, Bhabha's notion of mimicry as a form of subversive and ironic social resistance is a slightly different idea that is not found in Bourdieu. In the case studies that follow, framing and mimicry provide conceptual glue at key points in the empirical stories. As will be explained, this is particularly important for unpicking and tracing micro-level practices of legitimation in the WTO negotiating environment. Both notions thus help to sharpen analytical attention on the processes through which subjects actively define and redefine the commercial world. In comparison, the ideas of orthodoxy and heterodoxy discussed in Section 3.2 are, in one sense, initial mapping devices for plotting the position of arguments within a given social space. We need the concepts of framing and mimicry to reveal the active process by which agents draw upon cognitive and cultural resources to win a place in the WTO order and, ultimately, to secure material advantages.

3.4 Conclusion

This chapter has sought to shed new light on how we can conceptualize symbolic power and apply such a framework to the WTO system. I argue that we need to analyse power through this critical lens in order to better understand why and how material structures take their objectified forms, and how agents are either enabled or disabled in their actions. To this end, symbolic power is a kind of '*worldmaking* power' in the sense that it involves the capacity of agents to create and impose the 'legitimate vision of the social world and of its divisions'.[154] Inside this conceptual toolkit, Bourdieu points to doxic relations as a way to reveal the 'taken-for-granted' historical features of the political order. We also find the properties of the linguistic market, a structured, but still fluid, social space where agents struggle over classifications and definitions of the 'conventional wisdom'. As a framework, symbolic power only acquires its full analytical value when conceived within a relational logic of analysis. This refers not only to the links between the internal sub-concepts discussed in this chapter, but also to how Bourdieu's approach can help us understand when and why the notions of compulsory and institutional power acquire added meaning. Importantly, the conceptual framework of symbolic power does not exist to explain some presumed autonomous 'realm of ideas' in the political world but, rather, should be used to study the interdependence between symbolic structures and material structures. In sum, material profits are predicated on the historical and contemporary generation of symbolic profits and vice versa.

In the subsequent empirical chapters, I take forward the three concepts of compulsory, institutional, and symbolic power, but leave behind the notions of structural and productive power. Comparisons between symbolic power and the other two critical concepts have been made at different points in this chapter, but it is worthwhile underlining these differences here. The notion of structural power, specifically its neo-Gramscian variant, shares with symbolic power the attention to diffuse processes of social incorporation. Similar to a Bourdieusian approach, the idea of productive power highlights the relationship between power and knowledge, and how power can be considered a property of the body inscribed in dispositions.

However, the concepts of structural and productive power can be criticized on two key grounds. First, while both notions are useful for illuminating certain patterns in political relations, they are less effective at explaining how precisely such continuities are manifested in practice. For Bourdieu, the social world features elaborate and laboriously constructed schemes of justification. One must explore the mechanisms of social legitimation in detail in order to understand why certain political forms and interests remain enduring. The notion of structural power speaks to the historical relationship between capital and labour, and for some neo-Gramscians this contest features elite-led techniques of 'manufacturing' the consent of the dominated. But while Bourdieu would agree in broad terms to this depiction, he would also argue that there is nothing inevitable about the political order. Rather, the active work of legitimation necessitates continual renewal, conceived topologically rather than hierarchically, and extending from subtle sleights of hand to the most rigorously defended laws. Second, one can also question the scope for agency within the concepts of structural and productive power. The notion of productive power, along with its associated idea of 'disciplinary methods', is particularly troublesome when it appears to marginalize the potential for actor-led strategizing. Similar problems exist in more classical Marxist analysis. While it may also appear that Bourdieu could be accused of underplaying the capacity for historical change and resistance, in reality it is contention and struggle, rather than stasis and reproduction, that lie at the heart of his social vision.[155] Symbolic power thus alerts us to not only the strength of the political world, but also its potential fragility.

In the case study chapters that follow I seek to explain in detail how the conceptual resources of symbolic power can be put to work to enhance our understandings of Southern strategies within the Doha Round specifically, as well as institutional change in the WTO system defined broadly. My major focus is on contests within the linguistic market on trade policy, particularly between orthodox and heterodox opinions, although I do not lose sight of how the regime arose out of a series of historical contests and possibilities. Symbolic power is the major lens through which I analyse these cases, but my explanations are also closely informed by investigating the relationships between symbolic power and the modes of compulsory and institutional power. Each case study stands on its own merit but, at the same time, I also seek to discover patterns and regularities in the dynamics of symbolic power, particularly in terms of assessing when, how, and why it becomes more prominent and valuable for understanding political action. To recall the outline in the original introduction, the empirical issue area is agricultural trade, in respect to both offensive and defensive concerns of some key Southern countries. Turning to the next chapter, I will now begin this examination by exploring how a group of west- and central-African countries have campaigned for the reform of the international cotton regime and the extent to which they have been successful.

4

The competing kings of cotton

> *Without firing a gun, without drawing a sword, should they make war on us, we could bring the whole world to our feet... What would happen if no cotton was furnished for three years? England would topple headlong and carry the whole civilized world with her save the South. No, you dare not to make war on cotton. No power on the earth dares to make war upon it. Cotton is King.*
>
> Senator James H. Hammond of South Carolina replying to Senator William H. Seward of New York, US Senate, 4 March 1858

Since the eighteenth century, the global trade of cotton has been a business deeply informed by politics. Although much has clearly changed since this early history, disputes over the cultivation and sale of this 'humble fiber' continue.[1] One such dispute in the most recent past has centred on a group of west- and central-African (WCA) countries—Benin, Burkina Faso, Mali, and Chad—who since 2003 have been at the forefront of international cotton diplomacy, this time focused on the WTO. When these countries made their first official diplomatic submission, it was ambitious and unexpected. The 'Cotton Four' (C4), as they were quickly named, argued for greater integration into the multilateral trading system and also to receive reparations for past injuries. In conventional parlance, these countries had an offensive agenda focused on liberalization and legal conformity. In turn, it was argued and implied that other leading cotton producers, particularly the US, were not meeting their own responsibilities due to a dependence upon government measures. During the process of negotiations within the ongoing Doha Round (2001–), a connection was made between the declining world price and the use of subsidies. Thus, the cotton initiative has been at its core a struggle over competitiveness or, more precisely as I will argue here, *competing representations of legitimacy in claims of competitiveness*.

This particular international trade problem is a surprising story for three sets of reasons. First, there was nothing inevitable about how four states commonly classified as 'least developed' managed to carve out a significant space on the Doha agenda for their prized interest. If one focused only on economic capabilities such as relative GDP as a guide to achieving policy goals, it would have been difficult to imagine how this group of poor countries could have challenged a trade hegemon like the US. Similarly, from an historical perspective, these African countries have never demonstrated any sophisticated use of WTO institutional or legal mechanisms, tending to act as 'rule takers' rather than 'rule makers' to use the standard dichotomy. Thus, the very genesis of the problem at the WTO level is difficult to immediately explain through conventional compulsory or institutional notions of power. Second, once recognized as a specific 'issue', the question of cotton mobilized groups like few other Southern trade concerns in recent years. The initiative became an exemplary vehicle to debate the regulation of agricultural trade. For some advocates, it also appeared to serve as a touchstone for deeper concerns about economic and political justice within North–South relations. Yet it still remains unclear why and how this single commodity—which represents less than 0.2% of world trade—could consume so much political energy on the part of the C4 and their allies and, significantly, the US, the EU, the WTO Secretariat and other international organizations.

The WCA cotton issue is also puzzling in a third sense: the intense 'heat' surrounding the problem, so prominent from 2003 to 2005, has now dissipated. One reading of this relative decline in interest would attribute it to the inertia of the Doha Round and the lack of a final settlement. While this is certainly correct in the larger context, it would also miss some important, specific factors that explain how the problem was subtly reformulated and, in the process, better controlled by actors who felt threatened by the initiative. This is not to say that the problem does not remain contentious; rather, the focus here is on how the definition of the cotton initiative changed, in the process leading to a recalibration of political expectations on the part of the concerned actors, notably the C4. In respect to all these aspects of the WCA cotton story, existing scholarly accounts have shed little light. Overall, there has been a paucity of dedicated studies. What research has been conducted has tended to underplay the innovation of the original proposal or not adequately capture important junctures and processes in its political management.[2] With Bourdieu in mind, this chapter therefore seeks to offer a better explanation for why and how the C4 initiative evolved from the late 1990s to the present, with a particular focus on its debut and early incorporation into the Doha agenda.

Drawing on the conceptual framework on symbolic power, I advance two major sets of empirical arguments. First, I explain the process by which 'African cotton' was given a privileged, legitimate classification within the WTO linguistic market. The chapter argues that the C4 began their campaign for the reform of the cotton regime by constructing a novel 'competitive victim' frame to define themselves and the problem. This frame was effective in many respects but also featured tensions that would later be unravelled and exploited by other actors. Within this, I discuss why certain arguments were used, such as the orientation towards competitiveness and justice-based demands centred on a compensation mechanism. Second, in order to assess the value of this C4-led diagnosis and prognosis or, in other words, the potency of the symbolic power attached to the WCA countries, one needs to analyse the subsequent management of the cotton problem by Northern actors. I argue that the US was disturbed by the trajectory of the cotton issue and sought ways to control the timing and scope of any outcome within the Doha Round. What followed was the introduction of a counter-frame that appeared to be 'natural', but was in fact politically driven: to divide the problem into a 'trade-related' component and a 'development-related' component. The argument places stress on understanding why and how this distinction was constructed, monitored, and institutionalized. Through attention to the relationship between symbolic power and institutional power, I suggest that the counter-frame won out over the original C4 frame, leading to a re-positioning of the WCA countries. Such a move, in turn, helped to strengthen the symbolic power of the US by insulating it from claims that its representation of orthodoxy in cotton was 'artificial'.

The chapter is divided into four main sections. In the first section, I examine how the problem was constructed. This features a brief analysis of the political economy of cotton trade, as well as a focus on the major sources of policy debate and activity which help to explain why the issue emerged at the WTO. In the second section, I subject the original C4 proposal to a critical analysis, separated into a discussion between 'Africans as orthodox competitors' and 'Africans as heterodox victims'. In the third section, the Northern response to the initiative will be analysed in some detail, divided into three subsections: the role of cotton at Cancún, the origins of the counter-frame, and the institutionalization of the problem from 2004. The final section addresses the most recent period of negotiations and the effects of a major cotton-related dispute-settlement case on the C4. The conclusion draws together some of the major lessons of the cotton story in relation to the importance of understanding the accumulation and exercise of symbolic power.

4.1 Constructing the cotton problem

From 1995 until 2002, no communication made by the Africa Group or any WCA country to any WTO committee explicitly mentioned trade in cotton. While there have always been general debates on the problems of commodity dependence, an isolated focus on cotton was absent from negotiations. From an organizational perspective, it could be suggested that this was logical and intuitive: why should cotton be privileged over other commodities and agricultural policy problems? According to the institutional design of the Agreement on Agreement (AoA), it was technically no more important than any other product. What is thus remarkable in the first instance is how cotton became classified in the WTO as a distinguishable 'issue', separate, but still related to, the main agricultural talks. Cotton was not a specific item during the initiation of the AoA talks in 2000, nor was it on the agenda at the Doha Ministerial the following year. In order to explain the emergence of the problem we have to address both the political economy of the cotton trade and how the C4 originally formulated an agenda for negotiation. This section is thus divided into two subsections in order to help clarify the economic and policy environment from the mid-1990s to early 2003, the eve of the submission of the original dossier to the WTO. The first subsection provides an important discussion of recent trends in cotton trade, with a particular focus on the role of government spending. The second subsection examines different sources of policy activity which, when analysed collectively, help to explain why the case emerged at the international level at this point in history.

4.1.1 *The political economy of cotton*

Cotton is the world's most important fibre in textile production, a fact that has remained unchanged throughout the twentieth century. Although there is increasing growth and competition from synthetic fibres, production has still been rising, from 10.2 million tons in 1960 to 22.9 million tons in 2005–06.[3] In recent years, a decreased cotton area resulted in some subsequent production decline, but by 2008–09 there was a recovery to 23.3 million tons.[4] Most production is highly concentrated in a few countries: nearly half of world output is derived from the US and China, rising to more than two-thirds when India and Pakistan are included, and to more than three-quarters when Brazil and Uzbekistan are added. The EU is a relatively minor producer but still contributes to determining the world price.[5]

The WCA region consists of smaller, but still important producers, accounting for around 11% of world production.[6] Most cotton from the region is exported, with 80% shipped to Asia (China at 46%, South Asia at 17%, and East Asia at 17%).[7] Chinese demand for textiles and other types of manufacturing requiring cotton rose substantially around the turn of the century, with imports from West Africa increasing from 2.2% in 1994 to 18% in 2004.[8] For some countries, such as Benin in 2005, the share of cotton exports to China was 65%. Because access to China has become more important, C4 producers have been competing more closely with US operators for market share, thus underscoring why the US would be singled out for blame at the WTO. As a regional entity, WCA is the world's third largest exporter after the US and Central Asia. When cotton is analysed in relation to the structure of national economies, it is clear that the commodity plays a very significant role as a source of foreign exchange. Cotton provides Benin with 47%, Burkina Faso with 37%, Chad with 33%, and Mali with 22% of total merchandise export revenues.[9] With around 2 million on-farm workers in the cotton industry across the C4 countries, the commodity undoubtedly plays a fundamental role in shaping the quality of livelihoods and national economies.[10] More broadly, according to the OECD, up to 16 million people in the region are estimated to benefit directly or indirectly from the impact of cotton production.[11]

International cotton trade, however, is subject to considerable state-led intervention—subsidization in the US and the EU, border measures in China, and taxation in Africa and Central Asia. According to the International Cotton Advisory Committee (ICAC), the intergovernmental agency with responsibility for cotton statistics, direct state assistance to the cotton sector worldwide was estimated at US$5.8 billion in 2001–02. In 2004–05, the figure declined to US$4.7 billion, but by the 2005–06 season, support levels had rebounded to US$7.7 billion. Recent years have seen some decline, from US $5.6 billion in 2006–07 to US$2.7 billion by 2007–08.[12] Assessing the scale and variety of government measures remains an enduring problem for industry observers. In the 2004–05 season, for instance, the US spent US$2.4 billion, China recorded US$1.1 billion, and the EU expended US$1 billion.[13] In China, the cotton system is administered through a complex system of import quotas and licences, rather than direct payments. Thus, China reports to the WTO that it does not subsidize cotton. However, some analysts have speculated that support levels may be higher than officially claimed, leading to concerns on the transparency of data.[14] In the EU, cotton support was reformulated in 2004 as part of the mid-term review of the Agenda 2000 reforms. The EU now 'couples' only 35% of its payments to current production ('more distorting' measures in the language of the AoA 'Amber Box'), leaving 65% 'decoupled' (or 'non-distorting' payments not linked to production, the 'Green Box' in the AoA).[15] This has resulted in lower production levels in countries such as Spain.

In reference to the US, it is not always clear what types of transfers are included in ICAC numbers, figures often reproduced across many publications. In general, however, a distinction can be drawn between direct US support and total US net outlays. The former refers to three major mechanisms or categories defined by the US Farm Act 2002: direct payments, counter-cyclical payments, and loan deficiency payments.[16] In 2001–02, for instance—a period when local cotton producers in WCA countries were beginning to campaign for action on subsidies—direct support spending by the US government totalled US$2.3 billion. But this figure does not include a range of other programmes that form part of the complete US net outlay to the cotton industry. Other forms of support included emergency payments, export credit guarantees, and subsidies to exporters via the Step 2 programme (the latter facility, prior to the Brazil-initiated *US–Upland Cotton* dispute, was not recognized as illegal by WTO rules). When these transfers are included, it is calculated that 25,000 US cotton growers received a total of US$3.9 billion in government subsidies during the 2001–02 season, a doubling in the value of receipts within ten years.[17] In regards to the farm bill of 2008, the structure of cotton subsidies did not change radically.[18] Direct payments and loan deficiency payments remained the same, while counter-cyclical payments were adjusted down very slightly. The bill did, however, introduce a new loan, broadly defined as a 'marketing provision', that would offer subsidies of four cents for every pound of cotton produced.[19] In short, as Jasper Womach has put it, the data suggest that 'a sizable proportion of [US] cotton would not be profitable' without the aid of government subsidies.[20]

As is increasingly well documented, government measures to the cotton industry in many countries are often highly concentrated and made with domestic political calculations in mind. In the US, agriculture makes only a small contribution to the economy (around 2%) but, as an organized political class, it exerts a disproportionate influence within US politics.[21] In terms of industry organization, the effects of consolidation in ownership have been dramatic: a large majority of US farms—67%—have no access to government support because they do not grow a select group of subsidized commodities in sufficient volumes. In 2009, the top 10% of cotton subsidy recipients were paid 70% of total cotton subsidies, with the top 1% of cotton farms receiving 22% of all payments.[22] In part, one cannot understand why this relationship between government and business has been maintained without noting the formidable, intermediate role played by the National Cotton Council of America (NCC), the main lobby organization which acts on behalf of the entire industry. The NCC is in many respects more than the sum of its parts, campaigning not only for increased consumption of cotton domestically and internationally but also acting as a mediator in disputes between cotton-related industries and closely cooperating with US government agencies when cotton issues are at stake, particularly the Office of the United States Trade Representative (USTR) and the US Department for Agriculture (USDA).[23] These well-established connections and deep resources would prove invaluable as cotton subsidies were put on the agenda at the WTO and subsequently scrutinized by many economists, NGOs, and journalists.

When one turns to the real world price, the data clearly show a decline over postwar decades. During the 1960s, prices averaged US$2.31/kg, but by the 1990s the average had dropped to US$1.34/kg and by May 2002, just US $0.39/kg. After 2002, there was some marginal recovery, with cotton trading in a US$0.55–$0.65 range on average. This pattern has, however, been subject to notable interruptions as a result of spikes in commodity prices, particularly in 2007–08 (when the average increased to US$0.73) and again in 2009–10 (when the average rose to US$0.78).[24] Higher production costs for cotton, financial speculation, as well as more attractive prices for alternative crops (notably biofuels and soybeans) were among the most prominent causes of these price rises. In 2010, a supply squeeze caused by flooding in Pakistan caused the price to break through the US$1.00 barrier. By early 2011, as a result of an unexpected stronger rebound in consumer demand and panic buying by mills, the price rose sharply to above US$3.00/kg. For WCA producers, the increasing expense of fertilizer, which accounts for approximately 20% of the cost of cotton production, has generated particularly negative consequences during this period.[25] In the larger context, these problems have only accentuated what was already an increasingly volatile cotton market, with post-1985 price volatility around twice as high as pre-1973 volatility.[26]

However, despite these lower prices around the turn of the century, US farmers were, in the words of Joseph Glauber, chief economist at USDA, 'insulated via all these subsidies'.[27] During this period, the US posted record levels of cotton production and near-record export volumes. For instance, in the 2003 crop year, the US exported three quarters of its cotton production and took a 41% share of world exports.[28] A number of studies have now examined the relationship between subsidies and cotton prices, although it is important to note that such enquiries were limited in the period prior to the launch of the C4 dossier. The work of Kevin Watkins, then head of research at Oxfam, needs to be credited with mainstreaming the empirical connection between US cotton subsidies and WCA livelihoods. His 2002 report, *Cultivating Poverty*, published on the eve of the official consultation request by Brazil to the US, had a key impact in terms of increasing information awareness. Using ICAC's World Textile Demand Model, Watkins calculated that in 2001 eight countries in West Africa suffered a loss of US$191 million in foreign-exchange revenue.[29] Additional work at this time was done by the economists Louis Goreaux and Daniel Sumner, each closely involved in the C4 and Brazil cotton WTO campaigns respectively.[30] The following years have seen further simulations conducted, especially in the light of Brazil's victory over the US in *US–Upland Cotton*. In a West African-focused study undertaken by Julian Alston, Daniel Sumner, and Henrich Brunke, it was found that the elimination of US subsidies would result in an increase in the price of cotton by between 6 and 14%, adding 2.3–8.8% to the average incomes of cotton-producing households. The authors argued that this money would provide sufficient funds to support food expenditure for one million additional people in the region.[31]

Nevertheless, while these studies are persuasive and remain central to understanding the political economy of cotton, there are additional reasons why cotton prices have remained volatile. Apart from government measures, other factors involved include the increased use of synthetic fibres and general fluctuations in production and exports, especially from China, India, and Pakistan. Fluctuations in exchange rates in the Communauté Financière d'Afrique (CFA) franc zone are also very important. Since cotton is traded on the world market in US dollars, and since the CFA franc is tied to the euro, any appreciation of the US dollar will likely reduce the costs of producing C4 cotton. When the euro is strong, these same costs are higher in US dollar terms.[32] Finally, one also has to note that infrastructure and marketing techniques in C4 countries are not as advanced as in the US or the EU and, subsequently, this may have a bearing on the extent of market access that can be captured by WCA actors. As I will explain in Section 4.3, the difficulty in establishing a direct causal relationship between the world price and government subsidies has always be exploited by the US, as well as other threatened players, in subsequent negotiations with the C4.

4.1.2 *Sources of policy debate and activity*

When analysing how the cotton problem was constructed as a policy issue, there are three sources of activity that need to be addressed: the work of agents at the national and regional level in WCA countries, the Geneva-led process, and, crucially, the intervention of independent analysts working in NGOs and other institutions. The momentum behind legitimizing the cotton issue in the WTO centred on the interplay between these groups of actors.

At the national and regional level, the formation of the initiative is notable for the increased organizational capacity of actors who had a direct stake in the production of cotton. Since the mid-1990s, the region has witnessed the rising power of tens of thousands of small farmers who work through producer organizations (POs).[33] According to some observers, considerable initial responsibility for 'globalizing' the cotton problem lies with the social movements in the region, not Northern-based NGOs.[34] From November 2001, POs led by Union Nationale des Producteurs de Coton du Burkina, followed by others in Mali, Benin, and Cameroon, began to raise awareness of the damaging effects on local livelihoods of the unprecedented slump in world cotton prices. By February 2002, the cotton POs were squarely identifying US and EU subsidies as major impediments to their development and began organizing awareness campaigns targeting government officials.

However, it was not until the conference of West and Central African Ministers of Agriculture (CMA/CWA) in Abidjan in June 2002 that the cotton case began to form and the process of establishing attributional consensus was addressed.[35]

There were three important outcomes of this conference. First, the challenge of technically understanding the complex maze of cotton price supports across key countries was recognized by many actors. The question of linking US subsidies to WCA livelihoods may have seemed straightforward for some farmers and officials in the region, but proving that support measures were illegal in the WTO would necessitate a considerable volume of evidence, as Brazil showed in their dispute settlement case. Second, the conference helped to consolidate organizational plans, of particular note being the establishment of the African Cotton Association. This should not be taken to mean that intra-African tensions were necessarily managed better; on the contrary, strains and divisions (often derived from different colonial relationships and ideological viewpoints) would continue to surface at every stage.[36] Nevertheless, it did demonstrate a greater commitment to a common agenda that united them.

Third, and most importantly, it soon became apparent that any WTO action would have to carefully use scarce political resources. Whether the C4 should negotiate or litigate was an important debate, one which was never entirely settled in the either/or terms it was often posed. Although no fixed decision was made at this point—with some officials advocating a more confrontational approach via the DSB and others counselling diplomacy—the movement began to shift towards the latter option. According to some analysts, this was partly due to enduring fears of political reprisals for being seen to openly challenge the US.[37] However, due to the concurrent work of Brazil through the DSB, the political stakes on cotton continued to rise. By March 2003, a panel was established to investigate the Brazilian complaint that US cotton subsidies were prohibited. It was at this stage that Benin and Chad, as leading members of the C4, decided to act as third parties to the *US–Upland Cotton* case.[38] As examined by Hilton E. Zunckel, this would prove to be something of an 'African awakening' in terms of these countries using the DSB to muster economic and legal knowledge directly relevant to their cause.[39] Both the WCA and Brazilian parties appreciated how their activities complemented each other, particularly in respect to political pressure through international media coverage.[40] Still, for the C4, the diplomatic track through the Doha Round would assume the greatest prominence overall.

Elsewhere at the Geneva level, the period leading up to the Cancún Ministerial featured other C4 concerns, namely that the negotiating agenda did not seem to grasp the extensive prejudicial impact of cotton subsidies. Although specific modalities were far from being established, it was clear from the proposals being circulated in early 2003 by the chairman of the Committee on Agriculture, Stuart Harbinson, that C4 producers would probably not greatly improve their situation in the current round.[41] Various components of the negotiations were not going in the right direction for the WCA countries, who signalled that cotton was their only major interest. For instance, there were worries that the aggregate measure of support (AMS) could remain effectively the same, as well as fears that the Blue Box could potentially be enlarged.[42] One of the few potential benefits of the text was the creation of a category called 'strategic products', although specifying type and range was still to be determined.[43] Nevertheless, the WCA countries saw this as an opportunity to exploit, and proposed in the initiative that cotton, owing to its importance for 'food security, rural development and/or livelihood security', should be recognized as a 'special' commodity.[44]

Finally, one cannot adequately understand the evolution of the initiative and the arguments that would underpin it without considering the key role of NGOs and other consultants who either worked directly with the C4 or sympathized at a distance. The cotton case provides another revealing example of how independent experts have become closely integrated with Southern countries in the WTO system. Although it is often difficult to ascertain the relative significance of these contributions, it is safe to say that the initiative would not have been the same without such input. In the first place, as already referred to, the work of Kevin Watkins needs to be credited with greatly increasing information awareness of the problem. As *Cultivating Poverty* became more widely read and cited (not only in the trade policy field, but the wider media as well), Oxfam's Geneva-based advocacy team began to study how the cotton issue could be articulated in the WTO context. In particular, researchers such as Céline Charveriat and Romain Benicchio started to consult with other lawyers and analysts based at the International Centre for Trade and Sustainable Development (ICTSD).[45] From November 2002, ICTSD became important in terms of building solidarity between African missions in Geneva, as well as connecting ambassadors with other relevant actors, of particular note being a Senegal-based network called Environment and Development Action in the Third World (ENDA or L'organisation Internationale ENDA Tiers-monde).[46]

In addition to these groups, another organization deserves a special note of recognition: a small consultancy in Geneva called the IDEAS Centre, led by a former Swiss ambassador, Nicolas Imboden.[47] Funded by the Swiss State Secretariat for Economic Affairs, along with six other European government agencies, Imboden's work has been acknowledged by many actors close to the initiative as being highly significant.[48] One of the differences between the IDEAS Centre and other civil society organizations was the quality of Imboden's social network: he had the political contacts and acquired expertise to meet regularly with high-level government officials in the region, notably through the Economic Community of West African States (ECOWAS).[49] By April 2003, the contours of a campaign had become more clearly defined, with Imboden, according to some insiders, leading the drafting of the dossier.[50] To what extent the initiative at this time was in reality 'African-branded' rather than 'African-led' is therefore a moot point. But for the purposes of external legitimacy, such issues remained behind-the-scenes. The rest of the trade community waited to hear how these countries would articulate their defining problem and how they best believed it could be resolved.

4.2 The C4-led diagnosis and prognosis

All issues that are recognized as 'trade-related' in the WTO have to be classified within boundaries that are 'politically permissible' or, as I would argue, between orthodox and heterodox values on the linguistic market. In such an environment, where restraints and limits have been imposed largely by others, what would be the most effective starting position for the C4 and their advisers? How could they accumulate the necessary symbolic power to make cotton a recognizable, legitimate issue? My argument here concerns the need to spend time examining why the diagnostic and prognostic frames on this problem took the chosen forms. The outcomes that were later witnessed were, in part, derived from this opening pitch. This section is therefore focused on critically analysing the arguments that underpin the original dossier.[51] This document is germane to my case because it attempts to combine elements of orthodox and heterodox reasoning. On the one hand, it is clear that the C4 attempted to position themselves as *orthodox competitors* who demanded universal liberalization in cotton. In this sense, they did not seek to challenge orthodoxy *per se* but, rather, what they argued concerned misrepresentations of orthodox practices on the part of the US and other privileged actors. On the other hand, the dossier also features a second (if still subordinate) theme: the C4 as *heterodox victims* in the cotton trading system. From this perspective, the WCA countries positioned themselves as the injured party of an injustice, for which compensation was requested. In short, I argue that this opening bargaining move can be classified under a 'competitive victim' frame. My discussion takes each of these aspects in turn.

4.2.1 *The C4 as orthodox competitors*

When trying to understand the cotton initiative, it is important to keep in mind that the C4 possessed one ace card in their relations with other members: in this product they were internationally competitive. According to some studies, after the effects of subsidies are accounted for, WCA cotton is up to three times more competitive than US cotton.[52] In terms of both production costs and fibre quality, cotton from the WCA region is highly regarded by millers and refiners. Compared to the US, the region may have lower yields, but it remains more cost competitive. Cotton farmers are paid less than their foreign counterparts and, in many rural areas, growers rely on unpaid family labour.[53] In terms of quality, African cotton lint is given a premium rating on the Cotlook A Index published by *Cotton Outlook*. Fibre quality is superior because the tropical environment is more favourable and, crucially, the cotton is picked by hand rather than harvested by capital intensive machinery.[54]

References to the C4 advantage in competitiveness are found throughout the original dossier. The signatory countries repeatedly stated that their cotton production was 'competitive . . . among the most competitive',[55] the 'second largest exporter after the United States . . . producing high quality cotton and its production costs are among the lowest in the world'.[56] Yet they argued that the results of these efforts have been 'virtually nullified by the refusal of other cotton-producing countries to accept market forces and competition as defined in the WTO's objectives, by maintaining high levels of support for production and export'.[57] The dossier called for full liberalization and denounced state interference in the market, illustrated by an ICAC study that stated that 'if American domestic subsidies were eliminated, there would be a positive impact on global cotton prices'.[58] Further supporting evidence was provided by Louis Goreux, a former deputy director of the Africa Department at the IMF. In more general terms, the proposal also noted how the C4 countries have made 'the necessary, sometimes painful, adjustments in order to adapt their rural economies to global market requirements'.[59] This reference appeared designed to underscore again that the WCA countries have been orthodox rule abiders not only in the WTO context, but also in relations with the World Bank, IMF, and other external actors. In sum, the core message seemed to be: 'we have been willing reformers'.

This contrast between the so-called 'genuine' competitiveness of the C4 producers and the 'artificial' competitiveness of the US made for a very effective diagnostic frame, one which would repeatedly trouble US negotiators. As Jason Hafemeister, the lead USTR agriculture negotiator contextualized it, 'You have to remember that from the US side, we were the super-aggressors. From 1995 on, all we would ever talk about is liberalization; the need for aggressive, ambitious reforms.'[60] Thus, the efficacy of this C4 frame can only be understood when compared to the historical orthodox opinion that has been championed, above all, by the US. There was little hesitation from WCA representatives and those analysts close to the case that the C4 countries could strongly challenge the US on this specific argument. Indeed, this was precisely the same approach that would later work so successfully for Brazil in *US–Upland Cotton*. As the key leader of the coalition, Samuel Améhou of Benin, argued:

> We are only competitive in one product. This is our major interest. But the biggest economic power in the world is destroying our industries as a result of their subsidies. Furthermore, what we are losing as a result of the decline in cotton prices is not being made up in aid. We want our cotton to be treated as competitive. We do not want to survive on aid.[61]

In his time as ambassador from 2000 to 2008, Améhou became an important speaker in the WTO cotton drama, one noted for his 'dynamism' and ability to 'lobby, convince, and take initiatives'; attributes that would enable the C4 to enhance their symbolic recognition with other actors.[62] In the formulation of the dossier, the type of logic expressed by Améhou was strongly favoured by El Hadji Diouf, a Geneva-based trade lawyer and adviser to the C4. Diouf underscored the importance of building a coherent argument, suggesting at the time that the proposal focus tightly on rights-based claims linked to competitiveness. From this perspective, the initiative was very straightforward: some members are not in accord with WTO rules and others are. In the first order, therefore, Diouf argued that the WCA cotton problem should not be enveloped under any kind of masterframe of 'development' but rather that debate should focus on the content and application of existing rules.[63] This representation of the C4 as orthodox competitors was effective essentially because it was empirically difficult to challenge. Another leading adviser already referred to, Nicolas Imboden of the IDEAS Centre, explained it in these terms:

> How could you be against this argument? They had a case. For the first time, the Africans didn't ask for any money, only that the US and the EU apply those global trade rules to themselves. I think that was a very powerful statement, especially coming from a group of least developed countries. When the Africans said 'we want the rules' you couldn't say anything against that.[64]

Yet it would be unwise to believe that mimicking the dominant orthodoxy was a foolproof strategy for the C4. By design, it remained constrained, deliberately flirting with the values of the most privileged actors. In historical terms, with an eye to the effects of symbolic power, it is significant to note that the government problem of 'international competitiveness' is a relatively recent conceptual innovation. Prior to the late 1970s, the notion of competitiveness was considered only in relation to issues within and between corporations. Today, any state that does not appear to adopt the language of competitiveness is liable to be classed as a pariah by international institutions. The reasons for this broadening of meaning to *inter-national* competitiveness and, later, *global* competitiveness, are complicated and will not be debated here.[65] What matters in the WTO cotton story is understanding why competitiveness carries such an intuitive appeal. I would suggest at least two particular reasons can be advanced, both of which draw attention to how the symbolic power of naming can motivate political action. First, the image of competition is stimulating and exciting, one which can be easily grasped within different political constituencies. From the perspective of policy elites concerned with linkages, competition and struggle define other political issues; therefore, why not trade? Indeed, at the level of individual dispositions, Améhou himself liked to speak of the joy of engaging in 'big fights'.[66] Second, the classification of problems in terms of competitiveness tends to externalize economic threats and problems. In any national setting, it can be 'cloaked as a patriotic issue that nobody can be against, everybody can gain some benefits from it'.[67] This was certainly the case in the formation of the cotton initiative: the C4 countries were able to conceal some of their differences or responsibilities through focusing on one common enemy, the US.[68] This focus provided a bridge for the signatory countries to become united (at least publicly).

4.2.2 *The C4 as heterodox victims*

If the framing of the cotton problem in terms of competitiveness was considered a legitimate touchstone for actors within the WTO, it would be logical to assume that the C4 could conclude their opening argument at this point. What is interesting, however, is why the dossier also incorporated a second (albeit subordinate) theme: the notion of victimhood. Like the competitiveness frame, this theme is also highly political, with opposing actors engaged in a struggle over the legitimacy of each others' claims. Yet the idea of victimhood is in many respects more complicated and contestable than the concept of competitiveness. How it relates to the orthodox theme, moreover, is not entirely clear. Indeed, it could be argued that there is a tension—or even contradiction—at work when notions of victimhood are introduced. How can one explain why this frame was used?

When one turns to the dossier again, an underlying sense of a victim–perpetrator relationship appears in several references. I would argue that such a message is not communicated in an explicit form but is more subtly and less obtrusively transmitted through an association with the dominant category of 'development'. In this move, the C4 continue to 'make political sense' to others in the institution, as well as external viewers. In general terms, the identification is visible from the main title: 'Poverty Reduction' is the primary objective. For sure, all members, the Secretariat, and other external authorities speak at length about the utility of trade, in offensive or defensive terms, as a means to alleviate conditions of poverty.[69] Indeed, as was noted in

Chapter 3, the linking of trade liberalization to poverty reduction has become part of the orthodoxy in academic debates. However, in the WTO, at the time of the debut of this official C4 proposal, such a description was still somewhat unusual. According to Imboden, the orientation towards what he called a 'development-related viewpoint' was justified because the product in question represented such a minor share of world trade.[70] Since it was a small issue relative to the entire agenda of the round, there were genuine concerns that the initiative would have to fight for political attention in the WTO. This sense that the cotton initiative did not 'fit well' and was 'untypical'—or, in other words, it did not easily match conventional practice—was a remark echoed by agriculture analysts and officials within the Secretariat.[71] To link cotton to 'poverty reduction' in a trade round politically defined by 'development' would be one way to minimize any possibility that the dossier could be 'swept under the table', as Imboden expressed it, or that it could be met with placatory remarks of encouragement at best or outright silence at worst.[72]

The prognostic frame selected by the C4 and their advisers would be of crucial importance to how other members responded. Associated with the ultimate removal of government measures, one major remedy stands out in the proposal and I would argue that it is related to a representation of the WCA countries as victims. The initiative specified that least developed countries (LDCs) should be granted 'financial compensation to offset the income they are losing' as a result of the subsidies, but only as a 'transitional measure'.[73] At first glance, this request could appear reasonable and legitimate. If one is faced with an injustice, surely the injured party could argue that the perpetrator must pay reparations? In the WTO context, however, the subject of compensation is very problematic. Procedurally, compensation claims are not available as part of the WTO outside the framework of the DSB, and even that forum has notable flaws.[74] From one perspective, it would seem rather naïve to believe that the US or the EU would be expected to formally recognize that their subsidies caused damages for which payments were due. It would likely set a dangerous precedent for Northern governments, immediately injecting the fear of legal ramifications. More fundamentally, the claim does not fit comfortably with the purer C4 orthodox representation. In Diouf's opinion, the inclusion of compensation was a poor decision, since it risked leading the C4 back to an historical (heterodox) bargaining position, away from the unique strengths of the case (that is, aligning closely with orthodoxy and putting the US under pressure).[75] The dossier reads as if the signatory countries are willing to (temporarily) accommodate further economic regression in the hope of realizing the removal of state-sponsored production measures. But as I will explain in Section 4.3, these extended reduction deadlines were never read by the US or the EU as gifts. Rather, the entire issue of formal compensation was always treated by Northern actors as a non-negotiable item.

Considering this context, why was the proposal for compensation included? There are at least three reasons that could be suggested. First, compensation could have been chosen precisely because it was an inflammatory subject, one that could be easily understood by different constituents and also attract greater media attention. What could be more appealing to unite agricultural officials and cotton farmers in WCA countries than to make a demand for compensation? Second, the idea of compensation has notable historical roots and, according to some analysts, possibly represented an attempt to revive previous policy frameworks that existed in other international forums. For instance, the IMF originally had a Compensatory Financing Facility (CFF) designed to provide relatively easy drawing rights when a country experienced a shortfall in export receipts due to circumstances beyond its control. The CFF proved increasingly popular during the 1970s and early 1980s when Southern countries were attracted by its low levels of conditionality and fast authorization (often within a month). In 1983, however, an important decision was made by the IMF Executive Board, raising the bar on levels of conditionality and leading some critics to claim that the facility had been effectively abolished in all but name.[76] Similarly, under the Lomé Convention (1976) between the EU and African, Caribbean, and Pacific (ACP) countries, the STABEX (Système de Stabilisation des Recettes d'Exportation) was a compensatory finance instrument designed for use in export revenue stabilization. Yet this policy option was eliminated as well, via the Cotonou Agreement in 2000. For Samuel Asfaha of the South Centre in Geneva, there was no question that WCA cotton farmers could have benefited from such tools:

> If those types of mechanisms were in place in 2001–02 when cotton prices collapsed, the African countries would have qualified and would have received assistance. These countries hardly have any instruments to cope with revenue changes triggered by price volatility. So they certainly saw a merit in arguing for some compensation mechanism.[77]

While both these explanations certainly have value, I would suggest that a third reason is also very important. As already mentioned, the request for compensation was at least doubly problematic: not only was there no obvious institutional mechanism for such an idea to be operationalized, but it arguably weakened the overall C4 case. It legitimized the notion of temporarily maintaining the subsidies and it put the WCA spokespersons into the more subservient posture of asking for money (even if such finance could be theoretically justified). Yet when faced with manifold economic and social emergencies, any shorter path towards relief could have been appealing to the C4. The subsidies in dispute could take years to be eradicated (if at all), with multiple advances and retreats needed in negotiations. As Abdoulay Sanoko, counsellor at the Mali mission in Geneva expressed it:

> We are weak countries. We have so many urgencies to deal with. And yet our cotton problem, as far as we could foresee at the time, would not be resolved quickly. So we had to think of some transitional measures in order to keep our heads above the water. Meanwhile, we would continue our negotiation battle with the subsidies.[78]

It is plausible to imagine, therefore, that the dossier contained an implicit 'plan B'. Even if formal compensation was likely to be rejected, the C4 appeared willing to open the door to a more feasible and potentially immediate prospect: future cotton-related 'development assistance' from Northern donors. In short, reflecting upon such realities and fears—both present and anticipated—the door to compromising with the powerful had to remain open.

To summarize so far, I have argued that the C4 countries represented themselves as 'competitive victims' to launch their WTO campaign for the reform of cotton-specific government measures. They consciously deployed profoundly orthodox arguments to claim that their product was highly competitive in comparison with other members. This was the WCA ace card and it was a very unusual move, one rarely seen by countries commonly classified as 'least developed' in the WTO. Yet, at the same time, the C4 drew upon older and more enduring representations of themselves as victims of an injustice, in the process invoking notions of compensation and, by association, 'external assistance' or 'help'. When considered holistically, I have suggested that the 'competitive victim' frame contained certain tensions and could indeed be read as being contradictory. But when one reflects again upon the intractability of material and symbolic conditions faced by the C4, the dossier provided an effective (if still flawed) opening for subsequent bargaining. To return to theory more explicitly, the concept of symbolic power thus adds value to our understanding of the genesis of the WCA cotton issue. In particular, I have tried to draw attention to the *profound labour* that was expended in the political construction of the C4 as a problem. The notion of symbolic power is used here to better explain how the WCA countries appropriated potential arguing positions within the WTO linguistic market. The refining of these arguments would, in turn, encourage an interdependent relationship between framing and group-making; in essence, between the symbolic and the material.

In contrast, if this part of the story was told only through the lens of compulsory power we would have missed many of these key details. In conventional accounts that are premised on a 'hegemonic trade model' there is often an implicit presumption that the US or the EU will act to disable such initiatives from becoming larger 'problems' (for themselves). But what this belief removes from the analysis is the potential for power relations to be considerably more unstable and unpredictable in practice. The concept of compulsory power would be a rather blunt analytical tool in this case. For instance, if one compared the C4 to the US in terms of relative GDP, it would be difficult to foresee how a confrontation would ever be mounted (a presumption of political fear on the part of the WCA countries which often goes underexplored). Thus, to underline my larger argument, there is a need for a different concept of power that can grasp how less-privileged actors, in this example, are able to engage with the techniques of legitimation that are prized in the WTO environment. By design, the concept of compulsory power cannot adequately do this. The notion of institutional power is more helpful in regards to highlighting how, for instance, the C4 engaged with other civil society groups. But this only alerts us to the basic form of such social connections. To understand these political processes we still need to critically investigate the content of struggles on the linguistic market and how precisely symbolic power is acquired through cross-institutional relations.

4.3 The Northern-led management of the C4

In this third section, I discuss how the cotton issue was handled in the period following the original C4 submission. For the sake of clarity I have divided the material into three main subsections. First, I examine how cotton was debated as an agenda item at Cancún, noting the roles played by the US, the EU, the Secretariat, and other actors. While the ministerial was famous for not producing an agreed final text, the major lesson drawn by interested parties was that cotton was a tricky problem that incited strong emotions. Second, I discuss how the issue was resuscitated and re-examined during a very important period immediately following the conference. At this stage, I argue that the centre of gravity in the linguistic market on cotton shifted further towards heterodoxy, to the extent that all members began referring to *two dimensions* of the problem: 'trade-related' aspects and 'development-related' aspects. Beneath these pleasantries, however, I suggest that the diagnostic and prognostic frames on the cotton issue were changing in ways favourable to the US. Third, I examine the most recent period, where the problem has become increasingly bureaucratized and officialized. I focus on the complex relationship between symbolic power and institutional power in order to understand how a particular US-led counter-frame—distinguished by a division between 'trade' and 'development'—became universalized as *the* frame for envisioning and managing the issue.

4.3.1 *Cotton at Cancún*

Much has been written on the Cancún Ministerial as a watershed moment in the WTO's history, with attention focused on why the talks collapsed and the subsequent political and economic fallout.[79] These debates will not be explicitly dealt with here, but it is important to underscore that the emergence of the cotton problem complicated (particularly for Northern actors) an already ambitious working agenda in the Doha Round. This is not to say, in any kind of crude manner, that the C4 directly 'caused' the collapse of the conference as some indignant members insinuated at the time. Cotton was a significant negotiating element at Cancún but it alone did not structurally determine the observed outcome.

As the ministerial approached, the C4 and their supporters became increasingly well organized and quietly confident that their arguments were resonating with others. Political engagement was at the highest levels. On 10 June 2003, for instance, President Blaise Compaoré of Burkina Faso went to Geneva to address the WTO Trade Negotiations Committee, an unusual move rarely seen in a forum dominated by trade ministers and officials. Speaking on behalf of the signatory countries, his presentation recalled the orthodox competitiveness frame introduced in the dossier, arguing that 'our countries are not asking for charity, neither are we requesting preferential treatment or additional aid. We solely demand that, in conformity with WTO basic principles, the free market rule be applied. Our producers are ready to face competition on the world cotton market—under the condition that it is not distorted by subsidies.'[80] In Washington, DC, further political campaigning was conducted by President Amadou Toumani Touré of Mali, who spoke before the Subcommittee on Africa at the US House of Representatives.[81] Both presidents collaborated to write opinion pieces in the US media, including a prominent submission to the *New York Times*, which was bluntly titled, 'Your Farm Subsidies are Strangling Us'.[82] Meanwhile, on a visit to Senegal in early July, President George W. Bush received a memorandum on cotton directly from President Mathieu Kérékou of Benin. Finally, by late summer, the main NGOs concerned orchestrated another series of cotton-focused events in the US, Europe, and West Africa to increase publicity.

Yet while the issue had accumulated greater legitimacy in the eyes of many observers, it did not automatically follow that cotton would assume a privileged position in the draft ministerial text. By 24 August, for instance, two weeks prior to the start of the conference, it was only 'noted' that the C4 had alerted the WTO membership to the issue, with no proposed opinion on why the problem existed or how it should be addressed.[83] This lone sentence was, according to some close observers, a representation of the reticent attitudes on the part of the US and the EU. How the US delegation in particular attempted to manage the cotton problem is an important part of the Cancún story. At the risk of repeating myself, this is because the issue had now grown in size or, more precisely, the symbolic power of the C4 cause was increasingly universalized the more frequently other actors—both internal and external to the WTO—publically attached their expectations to a satisfactory outcome. The question was therefore no longer an exclusive WCA matter, but an institutional concern necessitating incorporation into the universal agenda.

It is noteworthy, therefore, to see how the US and, in particular, ambassador Robert Zoellick, correctly read the political potency of the cotton problem and the need to offer the C4 immediate recognition.[84] This was accomplished by the US granting the WCA countries the first bilateral meeting on the eve of the ministerial, a small signal of deference from the hegemon to the C4. I would argue that one can identify at this point the contours of an alternative US-led counter-framing effort, which was motivated by the need to reconceptualize the cotton problem.[85] The US appeared to have two objectives. First, there was an attempt to broaden the diagnostic frame that had been promoted by the C4: the US supported the elimination of subsidies and lower market barriers in agricultural products—thus swiftly bolstering its status as a legitimate leader of orthodox teaching—but argued that in cotton this was only one element in a complex mix of problems. The reasons prices were falling did not necessarily rest with the support programmes of certain members (of which the EU and China were also cited by the US), but with other factors such as competition from artificial fibres and higher yields due to good weather conditions.[86]

Second, the US moved to distort the C4 prognostic frame in two forms. Procedurally, USTR, backed by the NCC and a bipartisan group of US senators, was strongly against treating cotton differently from other products, preferring instead to classify the matter via linkages with the wider agriculture and textile negotiations.[87] For now, the WCA countries continued to resist this on the grounds that their economic difficulties necessitated quick action that did not seem feasible if the initiative was subsumed under the larger, more complicated agricultural talks. At the same time, and predictably, the proposal for a compensation mechanism was thrown back as a non-negotiable item that the US would never consider, since, as already argued, it was not allowed in WTO jurisprudence. Crucially, however, the US did advance the message of aid-giving through the euphemistically vague word of 'assistance'. As Hafemeister put it, 'We dug as deep as we could go on technical assistance.'[88] In narrow terms, this took the shape of an appeal to the competitiveness dimension of the C4 argument by stressing technology and marketing-based answers, areas in which the US has an unparalleled advantage. More radically, the US also offered a broader argument that the WCA states would be best 'diversifying' their cotton industry from farming to textile manufacturing, a claim that the C4 (and many other members) found to be insulting since it again deflected attention from the problem of the subsidies.[89] Thus, at the very moment when the cotton issue was to be formally integrated into the Doha Round, the US was working to limit the potential damage it could cause their industry.

But the US could not control all actors and elements within the Cancún maelstrom. From one side, there were many other members and coalitions who spoke out in favour of the C4. The Africa group, the ACP group, and the LDC group had all immediately registered their support, despite some reported efforts by the US to fragment sources of allegiance.[90] The question of whether some WTO members seized upon cotton with more instrumental motivations is, however, always worth keeping in mind throughout the history of the C4 case. The deepest interest for some countries, such as Venezuela and Cuba, may not have been with WCA farmers *per se*, but with putting the US under greater political pressure in a key international forum.[91] Interestingly, both the long-established Cairns group and the newly created G20 (led by Brazil and India) had informally offered the C4 the opportunity to collapse the initiative into their coalitions (the WCA countries refused, fearing their careful progress would be knocked off course not strengthened).[92] One could speculate, therefore, that, like any political group, one of the enduring challenges for the C4 and their advisers has always been trying to deduce the potential positive or negative consequences of closer recognized support.

The EU's position was, however, always more delicate and is worthy of special attention. First, while Pascal Lamy, commissioner for external trade, and Franz Fischler, commissioner for agriculture, also expressed sympathy with the concerns of the four countries, they argued that the EU had little or no responsibility for the low cotton prices. In large part, this was true. As Lamy was always quick to note, under the 2003 reform of the Common Agricultural Policy (CAP), the EU had no export subsidies for cotton and already offered quota-free and duty-free access to LDC exports. If there were any concerns about EU support measures, they centred on the timing and effects of the proposed 'decoupled' AoA Green Box payments noted earlier.[93] Second, as is now well recognized, Lamy was concentrating on the Singapore issues, to an excessive degree according to many WTO members and analysts, including some EU member states.[94] Although the EU's agenda was certainly diverse, Lamy was sensitive to any part of the negotiations that could create an obstacle to an agreement on the Singapore issues. According to Imboden's reading, 'Lamy could see that cotton was a problem, but he did not want to hit the US.'[95] The prospect of almost the entire WTO membership aligning with the C4 against the US was not a favourable scenario for the EU. In one important respect, the US would be left consuming valuable time defending itself on a single product, rather than working with the EU to engineer overall consensus. And there was always an issue for Lamy of the unity of his own party. Heidemarie Wieczorek-Zeul, the German federal minister for economic cooperation and development, for example, was a vociferous advocate of the cotton initiative, arguing against Lamy that the EU's remaining subsidies should be cut more aggressively.[96]

Thus, as the ministerial got underway, the US was already preoccupied defending its position on cotton in relation to other members, as well as from an army of NGOs and media organizations waiting outside. Yet the situation became even more complicated. Confusion and 'haphazard improvisation' characterized different parts of the conference, with the appointment of facilitators to chair key negotiations selected within hours of the first meetings.[97] In one remarkable move, encouraged by his own personal convictions and a notable absence of volunteers, the WTO director general (DG), Supachai Panitchpakdi, took it upon himself to chair a separate negotiation group dedicated to cotton. This development appeared to anger some in the US delegation. In the first cotton meeting (11 September), Zoellick heavily criticized Supachai's decision in some of the toughest exchanges witnessed at the ministerial. Zoellick argued that Supachai's role was as the guardian of the WTO system, without preference for any particular sector or country and, therefore, he had no business leading the cotton talks.[98] Following the meeting, according to one representative in the Secretariat, the US applied further pressure on Supachai to back down, threatening that if the C4 demands were elevated any higher his job would be in jeopardy.[99] By the next day, the results of the US intervention were already bearing fruit as Supachai announced that members were converging on a new 'integrated approach covering all measures affecting cotton producers' (that is, the problem would be viewed as being more encompassing than subsidies alone).[100] On the penultimate day (13 September), the US opinion was faithfully reflected in its entirety in the second draft text released by conference chair Luis Ernesto Derbez. The paragraph called for no more than the intention to address the impact of distortions across multiple WTO committees (Agriculture, Non-Agricultural Market Access, and Rules) and for the DG to consult with other international organizations to channel pre-existing resources towards the 'diversification' of the C4 economies.[101]

In this example, we thus see some evidence of compulsory power—a verbal threat—being exercised and the immediate effects of its deployment. This represents one of the more notable incidents in the cotton initiative where the US sought to demand attention and force a particular decision in accordance with its interests. Still, in light of the conceptual motivations of this book, what I would suggest is more interesting is how one can actually better understand this threat in relation to the notion of symbolic power. From this viewpoint, the use of compulsory power is an effort by Zoellick to 'cut through' the processes of legitimation and, specifically, to call a halt to the increasing recognition of symbolic power around the C4 issue. It is particularly necessary here because the symbolic power that is attached to Supachai is of a different quality to that of the common member. As DG, his power is derived from being the embodiment of the universal within the organization; in a figurative sense, he is like the 'king's two bodies': existing as the body natural, but also as the body politic who serves as the temporary custodian of the (seemingly permanent) institution that will survive him.[102] In practical terms, this means that he speaks within a series of linguistic constraints that are consistently aimed at minimizing political offence and encouraging (often vaguely specified) cooperation. The DG, under these conditions, which are policed by members and himself, is not supposed to be an innovator. When Supachai spoke out in favour of the C4, in public view, he loosened these symbolic constraints in a manner that was in advance of what the US could accommodate. This action therefore provoked Zoellick to use a quick technique of compulsory power to check the wayward path of Supachai.

As the conference stumbled towards collapse, the Derbez draft was met with widespread condemnation from the C4 and their sympathizers. As one African official put it: 'That text was outrageous; it was clearly the US position.'[103] Even Glauber of USDA admitted that the language on 'diversification', while valid in the larger picture, 'came out so blatantly US-centric' that it antagonized the C4: 'The Malians were aghast at hearing it. I remember looking at their faces and thinking that this is not going well.'[104] The final hours of the ministerial were highly emotional, with many delegates under intense stress.[105] It is difficult to assess precisely how the cotton problem contributed towards the early closure of the conference. In terms of sequencing, for instance, the conference did not end on cotton, but on the struggles over the Singapore issues and the wider agriculture talks. To say that the C4 purposefully triggered the collapse of the summit would not be accurate, even if they were angered by perceived poor treatment. Still, there are some suggestions that the US felt that the process on cotton was slipping out of its control and, therefore, it sought to deliberately end the ministerial early in order to reorganize itself.[106] But this could equally reflect a US concern with the overall agenda, for which cotton was just one element. Lamy, wounded and desperate to deflect blame to others, also argued subsequently to the Council of Europe that cotton got too hot to handle for the US:

> The United States too keeps a close eye on the tilt of the scales. My feeling is that the fading prospect of any additional access to markets for farm produce or manufactured goods in keeping with their initial hugely ambitious aims upset a precarious balance. What tipped the scales the wrong way was the prospect of separate negotiations on one politically neuralgic commodity, cotton.[107]

There was, however, relief in one sense: the C4 had proved to themselves and others that resolute, well-organized Southern coalitions could at least block

Northern agendas, unlike at Doha in 2001. The larger point of the above discussion is therefore to illuminate this relationship between symbolic power and existing resources of institutional power. The ability to establish recognition was informed by how the C4 navigated the organizational mechanisms in Geneva, as well as at the ministerial itself. The consensus principle and the assistance of NGOs underpins this initial opportunity. But to conceptually divorce the C4 work of group-making from the labour of symbolic power accumulation is unhelpful; rather, these activities are intertwined. In the three months following Cancún, WTO members, the Secretariat, and other international institutions began to revisit the cotton issue. Away from the heat of Cancún, a crucial difference was drawn on how the problem would be classified in the WTO system and—yet again—it bore the strong imprint of the US, only this time it would be recognized as the 'universal' opinion.

4.3.2 *Codifying a 'methodological distinction'*

While the immediate implications of the Cancún collapse were not yet clear, the US could not avoid the cotton issue. At the most fundamental level, I would argue that the initiative was now linked to the overall representation of US legitimacy in the institution. As a consequence of the construction of the issue, the depiction of the US as an orthodox 'competitive' actor in cotton—and, by implication, agriculture in general—was under renewed scrutiny. But, as explained, the reliance upon coercive power techniques, such as in relations with Supachai, was far from ideal as a strategy. Indeed, it had proven costly, leading to a deeply acrimonious exchange in which the US was unwilling or unable to cope with the process. The post-Cancún blame game, often conducted in a direct and brutal manner, featured similar pressure tactics, yet they did nothing to address the main problem for the US, namely, that its classification of the issue was not accepted by others as legitimate.[108] As Lamy expressed it, 'In Cancún, the [Derbez] text fell badly as it failed to capture the middle ground on issues like cotton, where the text strongly took the US line, and delegates stood up to denounce it as an affront to developing countries and as a heresy.' Clodoaldo Hugueney, the Brazilian ambassador, also made it known that the Derbez draft was no basis for negotiations on cotton.[109] From the US perspective, therefore, an appropriate accommodation strategy was required to both manage the demands of the C4 as well as to rebuild its own stock of symbolic power. The 'solution' was already on the cards at Cancún but it required clearer enunciation and, crucially, codification when members returned to Geneva. It centred on establishing a principle of division that appeared to be logical and intuitive, but was in fact profoundly political: a distinction between 'trade' and 'development'.

Procedurally, it seemed from the publicized announcements of the Secretariat that cotton was an urgent matter of concern. It was, for instance, selected as one of four priority issues for a post-Cancún resuscitation of the institution (the others being agriculture, industrial market access, and the Singapore issues).[110] Within the C4 delegations, however, the mood was more anxious, with worries that momentum was flagging. According to Diouf at ICTSD, the C4 appeared to be weakening at this stage, searching for concessions and compromises in order to entice the US.[111] First, the C4 quietly dropped the word 'compensation'—since it had proved so antipathetic to both the US and the EU—and instead argued for a 'transitional cotton sector support fund', one which would remain in place until the subsidies were eliminated. As Améhou of Benin commented, 'There was a recognition, following Cancún, that further calls for compensation could in fact jeopardize the organization. You could imagine scenarios where all sorts of victims [*sic*] of commodity problems came forward to ask for compensation.'[112] Second, a distinction was drawn between export and production subsidies, with the removal of the latter granted a longer period (four years). Again, this appeared to be a signal to the US that the C4 were willing to tolerate—despite their dominated position in the economic order—an extended phasing out period for US direct payments (classified by USDA as 'decoupled').[113] However, the signatory countries continued to be adamant that cotton should be institutionalized in the WTO as a stand-alone issue and not, as the US had insisted, part of the wider agriculture talks.

Under the leadership of Carlos Pérez del Castillo, chair of the General Council, cotton was discussed in a series of informal 'consultations' and 'green room-style' meetings from October to December 2003.[114] In this period, we can see the development of an emerging recognition—reluctantly or realistically depending upon the actor (including the Secretariat)—that the US subsidies were not going to be substantially reformed any time soon. Yet since cotton had been the subject of such scrutiny, there had to be at least a signal or a vision, however ill-defined, that movement on the initiative was progressive not regressive; that a solution was being sought but was not yet at hand. At a meeting on 18 November, which Benin was invited to, there is evidence that a new counter-frame was beginning to resonate. Pérez del Castillo, on the basis of his private discussions, noted two points in reference to cotton. First, and most importantly, he explained that (unspecified) members were calling for a distinction to be made on how to manage the issue: to divide cotton into 'trade-related aspects' *and* 'development-related aspects'. The chair also noted that he had found a 'fairly high degree of convergence' on paragraph 27 (cotton) in the 13 September Derbez text, the same (still unedited) section that most of the WTO membership had rejected at Cancún.[115] Second, procedurally, he said that a majority of members believed that the issue should be integrated into the main agriculture talks, but given some special status. In short, quietly and without any major fuss, a process of structuring the scope for deliberation was underway and it was closely aligning with US opinion.

The next step was to codify what had been discussed informally. This was accomplished through the simple act of repetition in the official (legitimate) public arena of the General Council. At the 15–16 December meeting, Pérez del Castillo explained that the trade *and* development distinction was chosen for 'methodological' purposes. 'Trade-related' would refer to concerns about government measures, including how different domestic support categories in the AoA have been used in respect to cotton. 'Development-related' would mean 'financial and technical assistance', elements that Pérez del Castillo said formed 'an essential part of an overall response'. Crucially, he underscored that 'multilateral [WTO] negotiations require time' and, therefore, 'development support measures that could be implemented in a shorter timeframe could be of great assistance'.[116] International institutions were highlighted for their potential role in future discussions of the 'development-related' side of the issue. To prevent the matter from getting 'bogged down', the chairman noted that the issue should not be considered separate but integrated into the main agriculture negotiations. When it came to member statements, the distinction was reinforced again and again. The US comment was brief, stating that it agreed with the chairman's view.[117] China, which always remained a less vocal actor in the entire history of the cotton dispute, said that 'the solution should focus on financial and technical assistance'.[118] The EU concurred with the new framework.[119] India linked cotton with 'other development-related issues'.[120] Turkey also supported the distinction.[121] When Benin's turn to speak arrived, the process of manufacturing consensus was almost complete. Améhou put up a spirited defence, before acknowledging the new classification with a pragmatic tone that mirrored the US:

> The most important thing now was that work should focus on seeking firm and rapid solutions to the concerns raised, *taking into account their trade and development aspects*, which both fell—exclusively or partially—within the purview of the WTO.[122]

I would suggest that in hindsight the consequences of this reconceptualization have been inadequately interpreted by political actors and trade analysts. In recent academic discussions, for instance, it has somehow escaped the attention of observers.[123] Why was the trade *and* development distinction accepted so easily? To my mind it represented a manipulation of the C4 position on three counts. First, as mentioned, time was on the side of the US and its allies, not the WCA countries. In the face of economic and social emergencies, even the smallest of potential gains could have appeared attractive for the C4. Second, and crucially, the counter-frame legitimized a shifting of the balance between the orthodox and heterodox sides of the cotton equation, or more precisely, *it universalized the very idea of a balance.* The US had thus made a major advance: the problem was being re-centred and the allocation of responsibility was being redistributed. Now 'trade'—complete with all those sensitive debates about US subsidies and competitiveness—was *compartmentalized and considered equal to* that quasi-magical and infinitely adaptable category called 'development'. The problem was no longer exclusively Northern subsidies, but 'African development' (included in which was the implication that the C4 had their own duties). Moreover, how could one disagree with 'trade' *and* 'development' as the categories of choice in a trade round labelled 'the development agenda'? By constructing what seemed to be a twin-track solution, the division created the appearance that, far from neglecting the reform of the subsidies, a more comprehensive result was being sought. From one perspective, therefore, it was the conjunction 'and' that did a lot of the symbolic heavy lifting. If the reframing had been 'trade' *or* 'development', the US position would not have been strengthened to the same degree. Indeed, to construct 'trade' and 'development' as notions that opposed each other would likely invite more open conflict, precisely what the US wanted to avoid. But when 'and' was inserted, it immediately implied coordination and connection, thus enabling the US to legitimately pivot from 'trade' to 'development' without being exclusively tied to either category.

Third, the counter-frame would prove to be particularly effective because it drew upon another source of symbolic power: the legitimacy of the C4's own claims. This was perhaps the subtlest distortion of the C4's position. To understand how this was accomplished, one has to return to the original introduction of heterodox keywords and arguments. The counter-frame established the conditions for broadening the diagnosis and prognosis on the problem, yet this was in part enabled by the C4 attaching their name to phrases such as 'poverty reduction' and, most notably, 'compensation'. Over time, the trade *and* development division would become 'naturalized', to use a term with a Bourdieu inflection, to the extent that its roots were concealed from even those who were close to the action (or the actors who followed in the diplomatic footsteps of their predecessors). As Sanoko at the Mali mission expressed it, 'It *seems natural* to me that it had to be so—to have a trade track and a development track—otherwise I could tell you about it [the origins].'[124] One could even argue, in light of hearing such remarks, that some actors experienced an almost pre-reflexive, doxic sense that attaching the C4 to 'development-related' measures just felt 'right' and 'appropriate'. In short, the codification of the new distinction on the cotton issue happened so swiftly and so effortlessly that one could have easily missed it. Even Imboden, a negotiator groomed in the Uruguay Round and a major author of the C4's strategy, could not quite comprehend what had happened:

> All of a sudden, development became aid, and trade became trade. But I said: wait a minute, this is a negation of the Doha Round! *Trade is supposed to be development, not aid!* But this worked. It was absolutely incredible. I couldn't believe it. The US and EU negotiators loved it. And this new conceptualization that they opened up led all the way to Hong Kong [Sixth WTO Ministerial Conference, December 2005].[125]

4.3.3 *Universalizing the counter-frame*

However, in order to make the trade *and* development distinction a veritable classification, one that would shape the value of arguments expressed on the linguistic market relevant to cotton, the most privileged trading actors could not yet rest. Beginning in 2004, an important process of institutionalizing the cotton problem began to take shape. By drawing upon resources within the WTO and, more importantly, elsewhere in the international system, the issue became increasingly bureaucratized. It took on the appearance of being a multi-dimensional 'global problem', one that was of relevance to many actors, not simply a US–C4 struggle centred on competitiveness. But amidst all the chatter on cotton, particular political interests were being privileged over others. For those who were directly threatened by the C4 initiative, I would argue that the harnessing of institutional power at this stage was motivated by a desire to deflate the expectations of the C4 and enable the issue to move at a pace that was aligned with US interests. This subsection examines the origins and implications of these actions. The major focus is on how symbolic power is related to institutional power; in particular, how other actors were enabled to legitimately participate in the management of the problem.

It is important to keep in mind that the cotton issue was always a thorny problem for the Secretariat, one that necessitated close attention. The trade *and* development distinction opened the possibility for justifying the linkage of cotton to aid and matters of foreign assistance. But since such topics did not fit within the immediate mandate of the WTO, the Secretariat, acting upon the legitimacy granted by members, was compelled to ask for the services of other external organizations. This move was described using the popular and endlessly seductive vulgates of 'engagement' and 'partnership' with the so-called 'development community' (which was often opposed to the 'trade community'). At first glance, some readers may doubt why this common appeal to cross-institutional cooperation—'coherence' in the official mandate of the WTO—is being highlighted for examination. In my reading, it is precisely this connecting of different sources of symbolic power, tied to different institutional contexts, that helps to explain how the C4 definition of the cotton question was complicated and how, in turn, this would enable the issue to be better controlled by players such as the US. In other words, to be more precise, I argue that this collaboration represented a partial transferring of responsibility for the cotton problem from the US to these other actors.

The first institutional manifestation of this strategy was a Secretariat-organized regional workshop in Cotonou, Benin in March 2004. Participation at this event was broad, in keeping with the 'globalizing' of the problem: the four proponent countries were joined by 26 other African countries, 18 intergovernmental organizations, as well as representatives from the US, the EU, Canada, Japan, and China.[126] Out of these actors, the World Bank and the IMF collaborated with the Secretariat to take the lead in structuring the panels and selecting the speakers. In his opening remarks, a now weakened Supachai underscored that the meeting would concentrate 'exclusively' on the 'development assistance aspects', a point justified on the basis that the 'trade component' could only be discussed in the presence of all members in Geneva. Supachai stated that a substantive objective from the workshop would be to link 'existing' financial and technical assistance to cotton.[127] As the presentations got underway, the problem was unravelled from a number of perspectives. The ordering of speakers was not an insignificant detail: it did not begin with C4 representatives explaining their predicament but with officials from international organizations imparting their wisdom.[128] A picture quickly emerged that WCA cotton was a complex, multi-sided issue, one that seemingly defied neat classifications, explanations, and solutions.

The discussion fragmented into a range of questions and concerns, including data on production, consumption, and trade patterns; productivity issues; infrastructure and transportation; marketing techniques; risk management tools; farm credit and grants; and the role of producer associations. In the subsequent discussions, member representatives added their own contributions. The US welcomed the 'comprehensive' approach while also adding other variables into the mix, including the damaging effects of HIV/AIDS, the impact of synthetic fibres, and the potential utility of the Integrated Framework for Trade-Related Technical Assistance.[129] The EU, which always had more room for manoeuvre compared to the US (and sometimes appeared to take delight in such situations), reiterated its earlier arguments for 'an integrated solution', touting its newly created EU–Africa Partnership for Cotton Development.[130] Overall, considerable attention was devoted to process matters, including how different agencies could cooperate and how existing resources could be redirected to the issue. The workshop was summarized by the Secretariat as marking 'a new sense of pragmatic engagement' between actors, one which was 'serious' in 'purpose' and 'realism'.[131]

By July 2004, WTO members put the Doha Round back on the rails with what became known as the July Framework. In another nod to how cotton had not lost its status as an institutional problem, the text placed the subject on page one.[132] It confidently stated that the matter would be addressed 'ambitiously, expeditiously, and specifically'.[133] By providing an extra legal coat of legitimacy, it is clear that this agreement crystallized the trade *and* development distinction. In addition to the repeated underscoring that development 'mattered', the July Framework also established the idea that a new negotiating forum within the Committee on Agriculture should focus on the 'trade-related' aspects of cotton. However, the C4 would have to wait until November 2004—over a year from the collapse of Cancún and 18 months since they published their original dossier—before members would officialize the Sub-Committee on Cotton.[134]

To summarize here, there are two sets of points that need to be made about this key period. First, one can see how the marshalling of symbolic power tended to work in a circular, symbiotic relationship with institutional power, a point I have already alluded to. The trade *and* development division, once recognized as legitimate, *necessitated* the incorporation of external agencies into the management of the problem, most commonly through the appeal for 'comprehensiveness'. Each institution brought their own particular structure of symbolic power (of which a richer investigation would examine sources of legitimacy and relations of interdependence) which, in turn, was 'spent' on reconceptualizing the issue. It follows, therefore, that upon completion of every cotton-related workshop, conference, or symposium, from Washington, DC to Ouagadougou, the international organizations further solidified their symbolic power on this issue.[135] This was particularly useful for the Secretariat, who could illustrate, for the purposes of representation with external audiences (including journalists and civil society groups), how cotton was a 'busy' issue and was not being neglected. Such work was essential for the interests of the US and any other actor (such as the EU) who sensed a threat to the core of orthodox theory. Now the classification was not only spoken by a US personality, but was endlessly reiterated and embellished by an army of 'impersonal bureaucrats', each one an authorized spokesperson who 'pledged allegiance' to whatever was defined as the universal. Thus the symbolic efficacy of the new legitimation process was generally enhanced the more the chief consecrator—the US—did not appear too closely tied to the acts of consecration.[136]

Second, while the distinction appeared to offer the prospect of 'even-handed' treatment, it quickly became apparent that more energy would be expended on viewing the issue through a heterodox lens, at least initially. In this respect, the primary sequencing of discussions—'development-related aspects' before 'trade-related aspects'—was not an arbitrary organization of time and resources but part of a political move to 'mobilize bias' around heterodox opinions.[137] These heretical propositions—from agricultural risk management to the Integrated Framework—were chosen to distance (but in no way silence) debate from the precise relationship between national competitiveness and government measures. What followed would be immediately recognizable to even a casual observer of actors who move among 'the development set': the issue got increasingly ambiguous.[138] A direct causal path between the US Treasury, the world price, and C4 livelihoods now appeared obfuscated, to be considered as only one element in a complex story. In turn, the more the diagnosis and prognosis on WCA cotton became uncertain, the more difficult it became for the C4 to halt the escalating political linkage game (since more ambiguity encouraged a greater call for clarification and, thus, more demand for events and publications from the actors who had helped foster the ambiguity).[139]

Crucially, by their very participation, the WCA countries legitimized this process and to refuse such intellectual and (potential) material gifts would be almost unthinkable. To this end, one might say that there was a doxic aura of acquiescence. We can also see how the symbolic reframing of the cotton problem enabled the US to subtly redefine its identity 'from the dominant to the *generous*'.[140] But this common appeal to the gift only possesses an intuitive, authentic meaning because the C4 countries also immersed themselves into the same political game. As Bourdieu has expressed it:

> In such a social universe, the giver knows that his generous act has every chance of being recognized as such (rather than being seen as a naivety or an absurdity, a 'folly') and of obtaining the recognition (in the form of a countergift or gratitude) from the beneficiary [. . .] because all the other agents operating in that world and shaped by its necessity also expect things to be so.[141]

In the cotton story, not unlike countless other episodes of international aid politics between donors and recipients, the question of the C4's 'gratuity' has never been made clear, at least in official diplomatic language. What one can point to, however, are certain moments when the 'collective expectations' are disturbed, revealing in the process a *sense of limits* on how expansive the boundaries of heterodoxy could be stretched. Such tacit readjustments from the US and major institutions were in part informed by the degree of exasperation expressed by the C4 (as in 'we are faced with a proliferation of conferences on "development aspects", none of which have yet yielded any concrete results'[142]). Thus, in one key sense, the universalization of the new counterframe worked to placate the C4, as well as their wider network of sympathizers, but such efforts could only manage, rather than resolve, the fundamental problems underlying the issue.

4.4 Back to the 'trade dimension' of the cotton problem

In light of the preceding analysis, my concern has been to show how symbolic power can be characterized as a 'denied' form of power in which the explicit declaration of self-interest is downplayed or, in Bourdieu's language, 'misrecognized'.[143] This does not mean that the C4 could find no value in events that highlighted their predicament, nor that such processes were orchestrated with precision by the US. My main point, rather, is to illuminate and politicize the labour of 'symbolic aggregation' and to show how the C4 were being incorporated into larger political agendas.[144] Thus I would argue that the US was now better cushioned from its own legitimacy deficit on the cotton issue but, at the same time, was not completely insulated. In other words, the focus on 'development' aspects of WCA cotton bought (and would continue to buy) time for the US, but the problem of the subsidies still remained on the table. In the most recent phase of the Doha Round, the C4 have repeatedly returned to this question of domestic support. This final section addresses the key elements within this period, divided into two parallel tracks. First, I return to the Brazil dispute settlement case, noting the major outcomes and the extent to which the C4 benefited. Second, I assess the work done within the Committee on Agriculture, including how cotton was handled at the Hong Kong Ministerial in 2005 and subsequent high-profile meetings.

4.4.1 *The Brazilian cotton victory*

At the time of writing, perhaps the only minor and indirect material benefit that the C4 have received from their efforts has come via the Brazilian victory in *US–Upland Cotton*. In September 2004, the panel found in favour of Brazil's complaint.[145] Among the major findings, it declared that the Step 2 programme of subsidies was prohibited; that export credit guarantees were also prohibited; and that such US measures caused significant price suppression on the international cotton market, thereby resulting in 'serious prejudice' to Brazilian farmers.[146] By March 2005, despite a US appeal, the Appellate Body upheld the decision and the DSB adopted the report.[147] Over the following five years, however, the US and Brazil struggled, at times intensely, over the pace and substance of the implementation of these findings. USDA brought the export credit measures into compliance relatively quickly and by August 2006 the Step 2 payments were removed. But Brazil continued to complain that the US marketing loan and counter-cyclical programmes were also responsible for lowering the world price. In September 2006, Brazil requested a separate compliance panel to investigate these claims. By December 2007, the panel ruled that the US marketing loan and counter-cyclical payments did, indeed, cause 'present' serious prejudice to Brazil, a decision that was upheld almost entirely by the Appellate Body and the DSB.[148] With this development, Brazil was free to authorize retaliatory countermeasures, pointing to the suspension of commitments under the Agreement on Trade-Related Aspects of Intellectual Property Rights (TRIPS) as one possible option.[149] Still, it would take until 2010, following a series of Brazilian threats, for the US to eventually yield, yet not in the way Brasília intended. In return for Brazil suspending its threat to impose trade sanctions, the US agreed to award an annual US$147 million 'technical assistance and capacity-building' fund.[150] In essence, the US has decided to subsidize Brazilian cotton farmers, *in addition* to its own, rather than risk reforming further domestic support programmes in the context of broader economic problems.

But how has the Brazilian cotton saga informed the work of the C4? As already mentioned, there has always been an obvious complementarity between Brazil and the WCA countries in regards to facing a common enemy: the US. According to Zunckel, the results of *US–Upland Cotton* were diplomatically beneficial to the C4, helping to 'bolster their existing work on cotton reform within the Doha Round negotiations'.[151] Other researchers have made similar points, arguing that the Brazilian suit enabled the C4 to maintain a higher political profile, lending 'credence' to their arguments.[152] For instance, the WCA countries made reference to the Brazil case in their public talks and statements.[153] In conceptual terms, therefore, the C4 were now tied into a more complex 'circuit of legitimation'—specifically, the independent judgement of the DSB conferred authoritative recognition on the orthodox opinion of the WCA countries.[154] However, notwithstanding these advantages, the material benefits that the C4 have derived from the repeal of such US schemes have probably been very minor, to the extent that the transmission effects may not have registered on WCA farmers. According to a study by Mario Jales, the C4 continue to be penalized as a result of the major subsidies that are still in place.[155] Thus, it is only through a negotiated settlement in the Doha Round that a broader package on cotton will be finalized, including a deeper reduction in domestic support levels.

4.4.2 *Towards a Doha cotton settlement*

In this respect, the Hong Kong Ministerial text, negotiated in December 2005, was important for not only relegitimizing the idea that cotton would be addressed 'ambitiously, expeditiously, and specifically', but also adding an additional qualification relative to the rest of the agricultural talks:

> Members agree that the objective is that, as an outcome for the negotiations, trade distorting domestic subsidies for cotton production be reduced *more ambitiously*

> than under whatever general formula is agreed and that it should be implemented over a shorter period of time than generally applicable. We commit ourselves to give priority in the negotiations to reach such an outcome.[156]

Although such language was still vague and missing quantitative data, from the US perspective it represented a 'big movement'.[157] For the first time, Washington had committed to something exceptional on cotton subsidy reform within the Doha talks. At this point, one could say that the C4 recorded a small note of success. In the subsequent period since Hong Kong, in the context of negotiations that have often slowed, stalled, and sometimes regressed, the WCA countries have continued to demand further detail on what precisely 'more ambitious' could mean for them and when an accord on cotton will be concluded.

It seems that these problems will only be resolved in the closing stages of the broader agriculture negotiations. This is because the US has consistently argued that it needs clarity on the magnitude of the cut in the AMS before addressing what extra reduction will be made in cotton.[158] The C4 have, nonetheless, attempted to advance the process through their proposal for a cotton-based formula, a template that serves as an official basis for discussion (see Appendix A for full details).[159] As of 2012, the value of 'more ambition' remains uncertain. For instance, as Hafemeister has expressed it, the phrase could hypothetically mean merely 'one day sooner and one dollar less'.[160] Under the shadow of the well-organized NCC, the US continues to treat its final cotton numbers on subsidy reductions as a highly prized asset for other countries to earn. This posture has thus led to fears on the part of players and supporters close to the WCA initiative that the US will reveal its cotton hand in the endgame and, under the pressure of time constraints, enforce a consensus close to its terms.

However, this does not mean that the US has completely stonewalled on cotton. For instance, most notably at the July 2008 Ministerial in Geneva, WTO members did appear to be within reach of resolving their differences.[161] At this summit, although cotton was positioned towards the end of agenda items, the US did make a series of private bilateral engagements in the hope of engineering a broader 'cotton package'. Interestingly, as a way to mollify their cotton industry, US policy-makers approached China to ask for further cotton-specific market-access opportunities to Beijing, a long-standing interest of US producers. But China rejected the logic of such a linkage, called the US argument 'absurd', and, instead, reiterated that US subsidies were the principal problem in the cotton affair.[162] In addition, in the event of the overall talks reaching a conclusion, the US was also readying some extra, aid-related policies for the C4.[163] Nevertheless, such advances came to little, as cotton was never seriously debated in a more multilateral discussion. In the immediate aftermath, the cynical interpretation of the July 2008 Ministerial was that the US remained unwilling to adequately address the cotton subsidies and, as a consequence, was happy to see the talks disband over another agricultural issue that involved more parties, shifting blame in the process (see Chapter 5 for details on the special safeguard mechanism).[164] While this may be true in larger terms, it remains difficult to determine if such a strategy of delay and obfuscation was performed with precision or if, simply, in light of the complex agriculture agenda, cotton was predictably classified as being less important since it involved fewer parties. At present, we are thus still searching for the right cotton piece to fit into the Doha jigsaw.

4.5 Conclusion

In conclusion, there are three main points that can be made. First, at the centre of the cotton story is a struggle over competitiveness or, more precisely, *competing representations of legitimacy in claims of competitiveness*. In an effort to dazzle the North (in particular the US) by mimicking its methods of legitimation, the C4 framing strategy used profoundly orthodox arguments within the WTO linguistic market. At the same time, these arguments were also situated in relation to ideas about victimhood and justice claims within North–South relations, a move that alluded to enormously complicated histories. This 'competitive victim' frame had tensions that would later unravel as the US and other actors sensed how a re-positioning of the C4 (and themselves) could be accomplished. Despite the later trajectory of the issue, however, the case remains a very important account of African political will in trade relations—specifically, how a reconsideration of chances and stakes was first internalized, before being externalized as a new definition of 'feasible' diplomatic practice. At the current juncture, in the context of the 'July 2008 Package', the hope of the C4 realizing gains in cotton rests upon the meaning of 'more ambitious' in the current text. With this in mind, as underscored, it is significant that all the major actors involved, including the US, have been on record noting that the Doha Round will not be completed without 'more in cotton' (when compared to the rest of agriculture), a positive if still imprecise sign.

Second, I have argued how the C4 attempt to narrow the inequities of power in the WTO system was managed by a Northern-led mobilization of symbolic and institutional power. The US, the EU, and other international actors dedicated to monitoring the logic of frames used in WTO negotiations were not comfortable during the early stages of the initiative. The essential response of the US, which in turn became the intuitive 'universal' response, was to redefine the C4 from *rights-based proponents* (demanding equal application of the rules), to *charity-based seekers* (hoping for foreign assistance). This repositioning enabled the US to exert a stronger hand over the direction of the issue and to partially deflate the expectations of the C4. Not all these efforts were successful and not all were done with purposeful calculation, but enough was accomplished to slow down the perceived urgency for policy change that characterized the period around Cancún. Crucially, in terms of understanding the cotton drama through the lens of symbolic power, this reframing required a tremendous expenditure of labour in order to make it appear authentic and not arbitrary or, in other words, not unduly shaped by a US personality. Progressively, such legitimation work became less burdensome for the hegemon as the problem was linked into the complex 'chains of delegation' within world politics (the so-called 'globalizing' of the issue), obscuring in the process the original conditions of production and signification.[165]

Third, and related to one of the central arguments in this book, I have suggested that the accumulation and effects of symbolic power have to be understood in the context of a relational struggle between political actors. These dynamics are, on the one hand, often more fluid and unsteady than is commonly appreciated. There are linguistic techniques that can be used by all agents in the game. On the other hand, however, this fluidity can be equally exploited by the privileged in order to further solidify and naturalize their position in the trading order. Symbolic power, for Bourdieu, involves this capacity to impose a 'legitimate vision of the social world and its divisions', one which trumps other visions and divisions.[166] Struggles over cotton thus remind us of a story that has competing narratives, and what I have tried to do here is to uncover the essential story in all its many facets, but always with an eye on symbolic power. To risk repeating myself, this does not in any way preclude an analysis of situations where the processes of legitimation become disrupted, such as when compulsory power is used to meet a challenge that cannot be accomplished with symbolic power alone. Such outcomes are, indeed, often seen in WTO talks. Rather, the concept of symbolic power should be used to better clarify and understand the inherent advantages that privileged groups hold, not only in terms of their ability to control the actions of those who they dominate, but also in the very language and cognitive frameworks through which the subjected comprehend their domination. Many Southern countries in the WTO system may desire to conceive of symbolic power in more prophetic or subversive terms, yet they are constrained at the other end of the linguistic market by what can be considered 'non-orthodox' ideas. It is on this note that we can turn to the second case study, which examines how a larger group of Southern countries have tried to address this problem and the extent to which they have been successful.

5

The heretics in the house

Words wreak havoc when they find a name for what had up to then been lived namelessly.

Jean-Paul Sartre (1971)[1]

This chapter returns to Southern agricultural trade, but shifts attention to defensive political economy perspectives. Unlike the offensive WCA cotton producers who were keen to advance liberalization and reduce government measures, many other Southern WTO members, but by no means all, have been preoccupied with managing the consequences of orthodoxy. In broad terms, these countries can be defined as heterodox by virtue of their historical position in the trading system, in particular the caution that they have expressed towards opening their agricultural markets to external competition. They have often not condemned the orthodox trade vision in blanket terms but rather have struggled within the confines of WTO categories and rules to reduce potential harmful effects of liberalizing trends, especially in respect to resource-poor farmers. In terms of the conceptual ambitions of this book, it follows, according to such logic, that one can only identify the structural position of a heretic (one who 'deviates') via reference to their interdependent but competing relationship with orthodoxy. In other words, the heretic has to 'make sense' to orthodoxy, but orthodox opinions are, in many ways, not of their own making.[2]

The following case study examines a series of negotiations that have spanned a period of approximately ten years, from the late 1990s to 2010. The story is centred on the struggle led by a coalition (later dubbed the G33) to conceptualize and codify a new set of ideas related to special and differentiated treatment (SDT) in agricultural trade policy. Within the negotiations on market access in the AoA, this group has sought limitations on the depth of their tariff reductions, in addition to instruments to protect populations from import surges. Like the previous case on constructing the cotton problem, the major focus in this chapter is devoted to unpacking why and how this G33 agenda was fashioned and defended. In doing so, I again work with Bourdieu's conceptual tools to explore the complicated effects of symbolic power, including the importance of classification systems for structuring arguments, particular orthodox and heterodox opinions on the linguistic market, and the social spaces that are valued by political actors. The G33 cause was, and remains, the product of substantial political labour, an historical process which requires explaining in order to grasp the interplay between material conditions and symbolic power structures.

The chapter advances three major arguments, each one divided into a separate section. First, in an economic and legal analysis, I critically examine why many Southern countries have argued that existing defensive policy instruments in the AoA are inadequate for them to deal with the range of agricultural problems they face. Second, the chapter examines how, from this less privileged position, a group of Southern countries mobilized the symbolic and institutional resources necessary to renew the classification struggle over heretical policy ideas on SDT. The argument traces how this work began with the formulation of a frame called the 'development box', which was designed to highlight Southern food security concerns, before eventually being incorporated into the Doha agenda as the universally recognized notions of Special Products (SPs) and the Special Safeguard Mechanism (SSM). Against the limitations of the concepts of compulsory power and institutional power, this process tracing aims to showcase the experimental and arduous efforts to accumulate new forms of symbolic power around a dedicated group. But against the notion of symbolic power, the argument also reveals those moments when coercion moved to the centre of the stage, such as with US-led efforts to oppose the G33 agenda. The third section continues this examination by debating the most recent history of negotiations on SPs and the SSM. The phase has been characterized by renewed opposition from leading agricultural exporters to the G33 interests. In particular, the argument probes how the full heretical force of the G33's original critique has been steadily downplayed or discarded as the Doha talks have shifted into common bargaining over quantitative modalities. The chapter ends with a summary of the major findings.

5.1 Southern-centric defensive agricultural interests

This section examines the international political economy of agricultural trade from the perspective of Southern countries and how, in particular, the WTO system relates to such problems. Due to the potential wide scope of such an enquiry, the discussion will inevitably be restricted to important issues that provide a context for understanding the evaluation of WTO negotiations taken up in Sections 5.2 and 5.3. In keeping with the conceptual aims of the book, this contextualization is also vital for grasping how new struggles over symbolic power in the Doha Round are partly founded upon the opportunities and constraints found in the Uruguay Round legal agreements. There are two main subsections. First, an economic assessment reviews some of the key vulnerabilities faced by many Southern countries in agricultural trade. Second, a critical assessment of the original AoA text is undertaken with a particular focus on the design of provisions related to SDT.

5.1.1 *Economic vulnerabilities*

In the domain of agriculture, each Southern country has a unique set of economic characteristics and has taken particular political and institutional paths. As noted in the introduction, there is not a single 'Southern experience' in terms of agricultural trade: some are commodity exporters, others are predominately food importers; some are low-income countries with manifold problems, others have acquired greater economic capabilities relative to Northern countries. Nonetheless, what one can say with confidence is that agriculture often assumes a dominant place in the social life of many of these countries, generating considerable spillover and linkage effects with other areas of the national economy.[3] Many Southern states have long argued that agriculture is 'different' from other sectors and demands extra political attention. For instance, 43 countries (most located in sub-Saharan Africa, Latin America, and the Caribbean) depend upon a single commodity (such as coffee, cocoa, sugar, or bananas) for more than 20% of their total revenues from merchandise exports.[4] In terms of the economically active population in Southern countries, 48% are engaged in agriculture-related work, with the average higher in sub-Saharan Africa, including Kenya at 71% and Ghana at 55%.[5] When one considers that food consumption often accounts for a larger share of household expenditure (compared to Northern countries), even small changes in the structure of agricultural employment can result in major socio-economic effects. Thus, as a consequence of having few (if any) alternative employment opportunities, many small-scale subsistence farmers have argued that agriculture will continue to remain their only viable livelihood source for the foreseeable future.

Three important problems of agricultural dependence have informed the political strategies pursued by different Southern WTO members in recent years. First, there has been considerable volatility in world commodity prices. To underscore, the initial focus here is on the condition of commodity prices in the period prior to the organization of the G33 and the start of their major organizing in 2003. As shown in Figure 5.1, until very recently, the evidence has consistently shown that prices have been caught in a structural decline

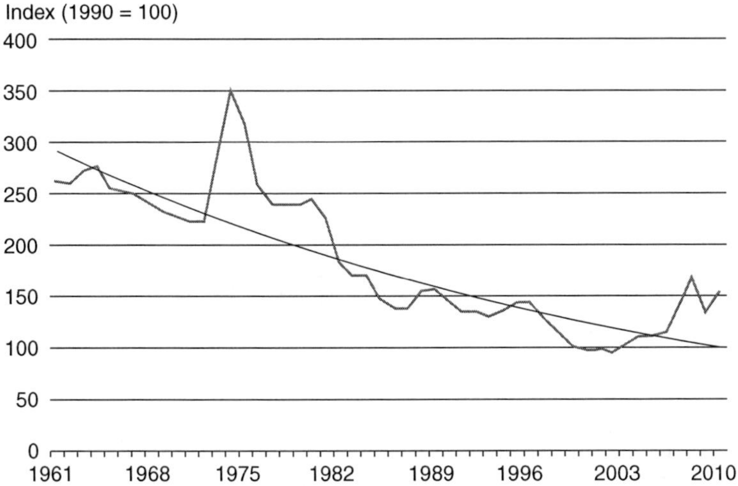

Figure 5.1. FAO Food Price Index in real terms, 1961–2010.

Calculated using international prices for cereals, oilseeds, meats, dairy products, and sugar. The FAO Food Price Index is calculated from 1990 to the present on a regular basis; in this figure it has been extended back to 1961 using proxy price information. Source: FAO, *The State of Food and Agriculture 2010–11*, 68.

over at least the last four decades.[6] Real prices for commodities have declined by almost 50% since the early 1960s, even though nominal prices have risen.[7] Some Southern states that are more prosperous, such as Brazil, have managed to adapt and reduce their exposure, but for many of the poorest, the situation has got worse. For instance, tropical beverages, raw materials, and sugar suffered particularly steep declines on world markets during this period, yet many poor countries who have interests in these products increased their dependence on them for export earnings.[8] The resulting foreign exchange losses relative to the total primary and merchandise exports of many of these countries are substantial. For example, it is estimated that during the period 1995–2000, a group of the poorest countries suffered a cumulative foreign exchange loss of US$37 billion due to weaknesses in commodity prices.[9] Moreover, these countries are likely to experience the greatest price volatility from international markets, a situation that leaves many resource-poor farmers in a more precarious position since they often have fewer opportunities for diversification.[10]

Since 2002, however, there has been a notable rise in the price levels of many commodities, to the extent that the spectre of widespread food crises re-emerged in 2007–08 and again in 2010–11. Figure 5.2 illustrates the trend in the price of major commodity groups over the first decade of this century. There are many potential contributing factors behind the elevated price plateau and extreme variability and, as a consequence, agricultural analysts have

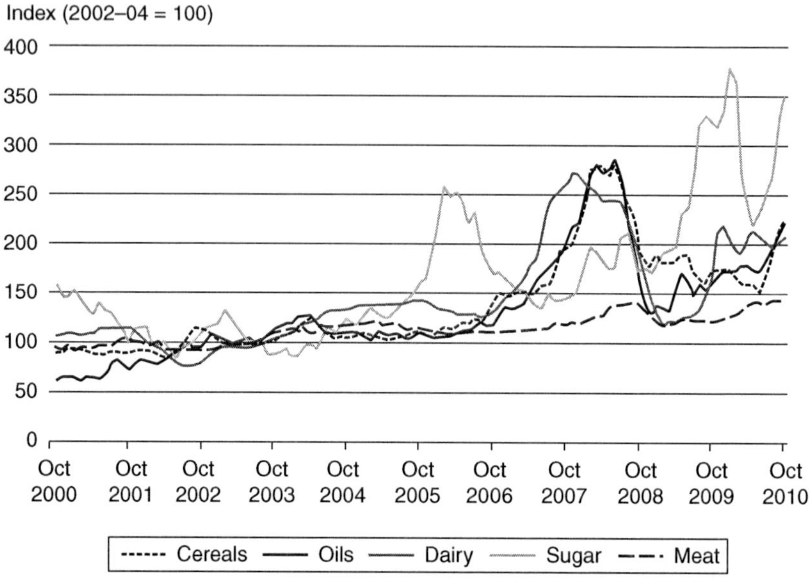

Figure 5.2. Indices of commodity prices included in the FAO Food Price Index, 2000–2010.

Based on FAO and IMF data. Source: FAO, *The State of Food and Agriculture 2010–11*, 77.

found it difficult to unpack a series of complex relationships.[11] On fundamentals, in respect to China and India, rapid economic growth has been accompanied by a rising demand for livestock products, which has in turn increased demand for cereal and oilseed as sources of feed. Another set of explanations focuses on the relationships between energy policies and other commodities. The price of fuel has historically correlated with the price of food, as witnessed in the 1972–74 economic crisis. In the most recent period, the record oil price has also encouraged increased production of biofuels in the US and the EU, which has led to the replacement of traditional food crops. A proportion of price increases can also be attributable to the weakening US dollar in which commodities tend to be denominated. Other factors have spotlighted the role of speculation in the context of the 'financialization' of agriculture.[12] Finally, and perhaps most significantly into the future, the effects of climate change have become increasingly pronounced, including worsening drought conditions and natural catastrophes which have devastated harvests, such as in Russia and Pakistan. On questions of volatility, therefore, there are good reasons to suggest that such trends will become even more serious in the future.

A second and related issue is that the effects of the recent relative rise in prices have in no way been universally beneficial for all Southern countries. In particular, for low-income, food-deficit countries, higher food import bills often represent a threat to livelihood security.[13] Overall, the liberalization of agricultural trade imports has increased faster than exports in the majority of Southern countries.[14] Within this trade, as discussed in the WCA cotton case, there continues to be great concern over how subsidized Northern agricultural programmes generate negative transmission effects to the South.[15] At the same time, when one considers how many of these same countries are compelled to devote a significant proportion of their foreign exchange earnings to service debt repayments, dependence on food imports can become even more critical. Countries where the share of food import expenditure in total export earnings has been increasing include Botswana, Brazil, Honduras, Indonesia, Kenya, Senegal, Uganda, and Zimbabwe.[16] The Food and Agricultural Organization of the United Nations (FAO) has argued that countries where hunger and malnutrition are widespread tend to spend a far higher proportion of their limited export earnings on food imports.[17] Indeed, the average rise in the cost of the annual food import basket for 'least developed' countries in 2007 was approximately 90% more than it was in 2000, thus helping to explain why social unrest has increased in many of these countries.[18] In short, in the context of already low import tariffs, many Southern countries are greatly concerned about the risks of being too dependent on commercial imports. Imports can certainly contribute to food security, but only as a complement to domestic production and based on calculations determined by each country.

Third, and closely related to the experience of liberalization, is the problem of import surges, defined by the FAO as a 30% positive deviation from a three-year moving average of import data.[19] In recent years, import surges have come under greater scrutiny by many political actors and agricultural analysts. To begin, they appear to have become more frequent, particularly since the mid-1990s. In an FAO analysis of 102 Southern countries over the 1982–2003 period, it was found that 13 out of 18 food commodities registered an increase in the frequency of surges.[20] There remains, however, considerable debate over the causes and consequences of such events. In themselves, surges are not inherently 'bad' and do not necessarily cause injury.[21] Indeed, some could be helpful in alleviating domestic shortages following weather-related problems. However, most evidence suggests that surges do tend to disrupt local markets, with common indicators including the transmission of depressed world prices to domestic markets; an increase in the share of the domestic market taken by rising imports; a reduction in sales, production, and profits; and an increase in losses, including rising unemployment.[22]

For instance, in Jamaica, the import of potatoes has increased at an average annual rate of 14% since 1995, rising from 1,600 tons in the 1990–94 period to 11,400 tons in the 2000–03 period. At the same time, domestic production has fallen every year since 1995, dropping from 10,000 tons in the 1990–94 period to 5,500 tons in the 2000–03 period. As a consequence, the share of domestic production in total consumption has declined from 100% in 1985 to 31% in 2003. Similar trends also appear in respect to onion and vegetable oil production in Jamaica.[23] Elsewhere, the collapse of the Honduran rice sector is another widely reported case of how import surges can be particularly devastating for rural communities. FAO and Oxfam analysts calculated that rice production fell 86% in just 11 years (1991–2002), with data indicating key surges of subsidized US (paddy rice equivalent) imports in 1991 and 1997–98. By 2002, rice imports represented 48% of Honduras' domestic production, a remarkable situation given the country was previously almost entirely self-reliant. According to Oxfam, conditions of poverty have been particularly exacerbated as a consequence of the collapse of the rice business, with 70% of the rural population living in extreme poverty.[24]

In the context of the trend towards greater trade liberalization, these three inter-related problems of agricultural dependence represent serious challenges for many Southern countries, often exacerbating structural and institutional constraints on domestic production. With this discussion in mind, to what extent has the international policy environment been designed to address these problems? How have existing WTO rules attempted to pre-empt, manage, or possibly eliminate such vulnerabilities? What types of trade policy instruments and provisions can Southern countries draw upon and where is the scope for improvement?

5.1.2 *Policy environment*

Any analysis of Southern agricultural trade policy-making at the international level cannot ignore the fact that other institutions beyond Geneva have long had a powerful stake in shaping the agenda for domestic reforms. Since the 1980s, as a result of the work of the World Bank and the IMF, many countries have changed their trade policy regimes in profound ways. It is worth recalling that previous structural adjustments programmes had specific objectives related to agriculture. As part of a broader strategy to limit the role of the state, common dictates from these organizations included: efforts to end the involvement of government in the production and distribution of outputs and inputs, such as in the provision of minimum prices and import subsidies; the dismantling or privatization of marketing boards that were involved in activities such as procurement and local credit services for farmers; and the orientation of the economy towards agricultural exports, especially in respect to 'non-traditional' products (such as exotic foods and flowers) that were geared to new consumer markets. Some scholars and activists have subsequently argued that conditions of food security in many Southern countries worsened over these decades, pointing to such policies as a cause.[25] Thus, the WTO agricultural rules provide a legal framework which rests on top of the previous history (and continued involvement) of the World Bank and the IMF in these countries.

The AoA, debated in the previous chapter, is a very complicated text which resists easy explanation. At the outset, the Agreement indicates that all actors have agreed to seek 'a fair and market-oriented agricultural trading system' through 'reductions in agricultural support and protection', while 'correcting and preventing restrictions and distortions in world agricultural markets'.[26] According to some observers, the AoA was primarily designed as a response to an OECD problem: the need to manage mounting production surpluses in a number of food products through rising levels of budgetary support and import protection. The most direct, trade-distorting feature of this issue was the escalating use of export subsidies (subsidy 'wars') to dispose of such surpluses on other countries.[27] In contrast, as Panos Konandreas of the FAO has argued, many other players in the trading regime had precisely the opposite problem: underproduction due to either reduced government agricultural support or the negative effects of Northern interventionist policies. Reflecting upon the Uruguay Round, Konandreas suggests that Southern countries made two potentially harmful commitments in signing the AoA: first, they limited their policy options to increase domestic production; and second, they legitimized past distortions in Northern countries, curtailing their export opportunities.[28] In short, many Southern states agreed to address a problem that they did not have themselves.

But how did the AoA incorporate their concerns, particularly those countries that were not major agricultural exporters? In large part, the process of managing Southern anxieties in the face of anticipated new liberalization was through the refurbishing of an old political category: SDT. Although SDT has a long conceptual history, the meanings that are attached to the notion, as Shelia Page and Peter Kleen have examined, have never been stable.[29] Rather, the definition of SDT adopted by policy-makers and other analysts has always been informed by implicit and explicit assumptions about what is classified as 'normal' or 'non-special treatment', what theories of international trade matter, and what counts as 'development'.[30] Awareness about the differences between countries—epitomized by the use of words such as 'differentiation' or 'graduation'—lies at the centre of many of these debates. Southern countries have often been drawn to (and in equal measure, *directed to*) SDT initiatives for reasons that come under the vulgate of 'flexibility' to liberalization. Specifically, SDT has been commonly founded upon the recognition that exemptions or extra conditions to the trade liberalization model need to be sought, not because the model is fundamentally flawed but because Southern countries need 'help', either narrowly in terms of complying with trade rules or more broadly in regards to their 'development' or 'integration' with the system. Thus, in keeping with the liberal worldview it is attached to, SDT has a melioristic flavour. The notion implies that all countries are taking the same basic economic trajectory, only some are proceeding more slowly than others. Sometimes SDT is compartmentalized into particular elements of WTO negotiations; at other times it is considered as a cross-cutting theme.[31] Above all, it has emerged as an important category, one which is very adaptable and contestable.

Ideas on SDT informed the Uruguay Round AoA negotiations at different points and there are alternative ways to classify the provisions that entered into law in Marrakesh in 1994. The remainder of this section critically discusses four major SDT-related features that were meant to contribute towards enhancing Southern agricultural prospects: flexibility in tariff structures, specific food security provisions, concerns regarding net-food importers, and safeguards available to manage import surges. All of these issues are important because, as I will explain in Sections 5.2 and 5.3, they were incorporated into the G33's larger agenda during the Doha Round.

First, the most immediate policy instrument available for many Southern governments to protect their economies continues to be the use of tariffs. Indeed, following the prohibition of other options, such as quantitative restrictions, it is one of the few border measures left. In general terms, most Southern countries were cautious in their commitments to agricultural liberalization during the Uruguay Round. In many cases, particularly for major foods of interest, they left themselves considerable space to raise applied protection. Although what matters as a policy concern on a short-term basis is the applied rate (the actual border measure), bound rates (the potential border duty) define the legal extent of the flexibility to vary the applied rate in response to particular economic conditions. Negotiations in the Doha Round have focused on establishing the criteria for bound rates and therefore these numbers are of great importance. Figure 5.3 depicts the variance in the mean applied and bound rates, and the range of tariff 'overhang', for select countries that would later join the G33. One can see immediately that there is no archetypal tariff schedule, but rather considerable heterogeneity. Different Southern countries will be affected to different degrees by any given general tariff reduction formula; a one-size-fits-all approach will be insufficient to capture such diversity.[32]

At first glance, it does appear that many of these countries have considerable binding overhang. However, if one applies a hypothetical 40% linear cut on the bound rate—which is likely to be near the maximum average cut for developing countries in a Doha settlement—one can interpret different sets of policy effects.[33] Some countries, such as St Lucia, would face no disruption because of the considerable 'water' still left in their tariff. Another larger cluster of countries, which would include Indonesia, Jamaica, Kenya, and Pakistan, would have to undertake minor efforts to comply with such a cut.

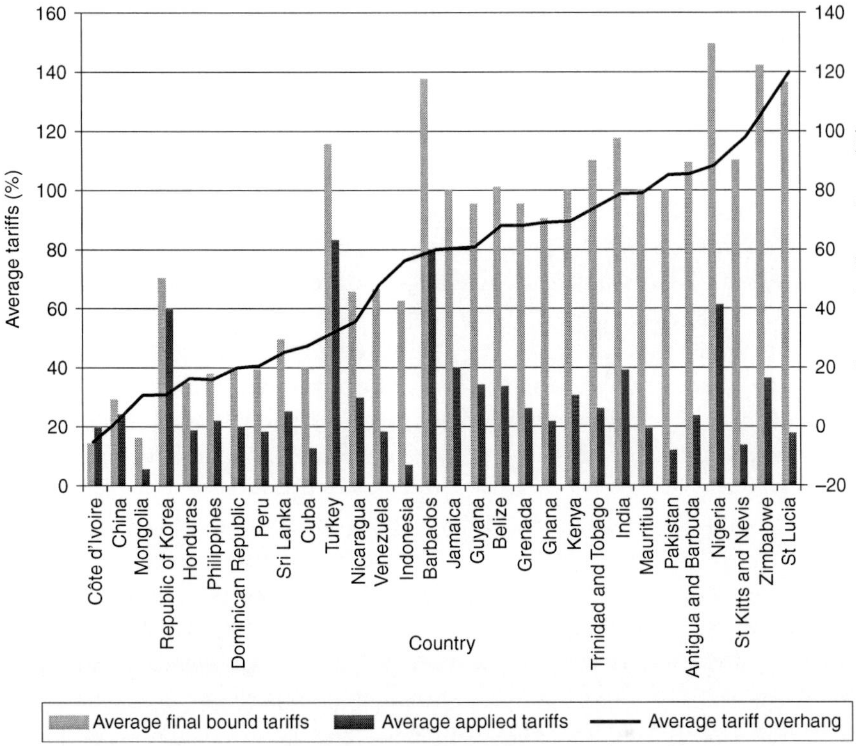

Figure 5.3. Average final bound tariffs, applied tariffs, and tariff overhangs for 16 proxy special agricultural products in selected G33 countries.

The 16 proxy special products of relevance were chicken, rice, milk, dairy products, bovine meat, sugar, corn, pork, potatoes, vegetable oils, sheep meat, goat meat, wheat, tomatoes, onions, and beans. Source: Riza Bernabe, *Treatment of Special Products: Implications of the Chair's May 2008 Draft Modalities Text* (Geneva: International Centre for Trade and Sustainable Development, June 2008).

This would involve these countries having up to six product categories where the tariff overhang is not sufficient to cover a 40% bound rate cut, thus potentially eating into the applied rate. A third grouping would consist of countries that would be forced to make moderate efforts, defined as having between 7 and 20 problematic commodities that would be affected by the same cut. This cluster would include countries such as the Philippines, Peru, and India. Finally, a fourth grouping would feature those countries that would be forced to make substantial changes in order to implement a 40% reduction. This would either be due to the applied tariff being close to the bound tariff or because import restrictions in place affect a number of agricultural products. China, South Korea, and Côte d'Ivoire are particularly affected here.[34] As will be addressed in Section 5.3, exemptions to the general tariff cut formula have proved highly political, between not only Northern and Southern countries, but also among Southern countries.

Second, while food security was incorporated into the AoA text, there have been criticisms that the notion largely privileges Northern concerns. Within the preamble, Article 20, and the SDT-related provisions in Annex 5, food security is classified under what are called 'non-trade concerns'.[35] The basic premise behind this larger category is that agriculture serves many purposes beyond what is commonly recognized as 'trade'—that is, the production and sale of commodities—and that such distinctions need to be integrated into multilateral rules. Since the conceptual debut of 'non-trade' at the end of the Uruguay Round, the naming and classifying of topics under the heading has remained ambiguous. Countries have preferred to offer illustrative (rather than indicative) lists of 'non-trade' items, going beyond food security to include ideas about environmental integrity or cultural preservation.[36] It is crucial to note that the dominant actors who shaped the legal meanings of food security in the Uruguay Round were not Southern members, but principally Japan, the EU, and the Nordic countries. For instance, in one negotiation submission in 1989, Japan argued that food security should be accorded the 'highest priority' and that 'border adjustment measures' were justified to ensure adequate access to 'basic foodstuffs', notably rice.[37] It is true that some Southern countries, such as Jamaica, did make efforts to encourage debate on food security from the perspective of poor farmers, but these interventions were limited and did not have a significant bearing on the provisions that were later codified into law.[38]

When examining the AoA more closely, one can see how the notion of food security under 'non-trade' largely reflects the prerogatives of Northern countries. For instance, under exemptions from reduction commitments within the Green Box (domestic support), food security can be specified as a justification.[39] In the annex to this provision, 'public stockholding for food security purposes' is permitted if a government makes food purchases at prevailing market prices and conducts such activity in a transparent manner.[40] In practice, however, the implementation of this rule has been unclear. If government 'stockholding' provides some form of price support for farmers, which is frequently what such programmes afford, then the measures become classified under the Amber Box and are thus subject to challenge.[41] Perhaps more fundamentally, however, within many Southern countries there are enduring constraints on budget resources, which severely limit the viability of using stockholding. Such situations have led the FAO to conclude that the 'domestic support part of the AoA is oriented towards the types of policies traditionally used by developed countries', and that such policies 'typically have an on-budget financial exposure that developing countries can ill afford'.[42] While it may be the case that some larger Southern countries, such as India, have effectively used stockholding as a price-stabilization tool, such examples remain exceptions.[43]

Yet, when analysed holistically, there are perhaps more profound problems with how food security is conceptualized in the AoA. One only needs to glance at the vast academic and policy literature on the subject to appreciate that it is much more than simply government stockholding. Rather, according to one author, the concept has been progressively stretched in multiple directions and spawned 'a cornucopia of ideas'.[44] Since the 1970s, there have been changes in thinking that have reshaped what 'food security' means: from the global and the national to the household and the individual; from a food-first perspective to a livelihood perspective; and from addressing objective indicators to subjective perceptions.[45] The FAO's 1996 definition often serves as a contemporary starting point for many analysts: 'Food security exists when all people, at all times, have physical and economic access to sufficient, safe and nutritious food to meet their dietary needs and food preferences for an active and healthy life.'[46] Thus, the issue of food security may indeed go beyond the commercial model of farming and the supremacy of the price mechanism. As Aileen Kwa and Walden Bello have argued in their critical reading of the AoA, '*real* food security raises questions such as who has access to the land, who produces, who makes the decisions, who will eat, and whether or not the food produced is culturally appropriate'.[47] And yet these multiple perspectives and meanings, derived from a range of analysts, have found no home at the WTO, or at least not in its early life prior to 2000. In sum, when compared to these wider debates on food security, the WTO has been 'left largely behind'.[48]

Third, another prominent SDT feature that has generated considerable frustration on the part of many Southern countries has been the non-implementation of the Marrakesh decision.[49] This provision was a response to a series of concerns raised during the Uruguay Round that the consequences of deeper agricultural liberalization may not be universally beneficial. In particular, potential problems were highlighted in regards to Southern countries being able to access adequate supplies of basic foodstuffs from external sources on reasonable terms, the erosion of trade preferences as tariffs were reduced, and supply-side constraints inhibiting the flow of exports.[50] The decision outlined four responses to such potential scenarios: food aid, short-term financing of normal levels of commercial imports, favourable terms for agricultural export credits, as well as technical and financial assistance to improve agricultural productivity and infrastructure.[51] However, as many critics have remarked, the decision has never been enforced or taken seriously by Northern governments or institutions, such as the World Bank and the IMF, who were charged with its implementation.[52] When the food crisis intensified from 2007, there was no reference given to the Marrakesh decision in any WTO debates. Thus, in the view of one author, this clause 'must therefore be considered as a piece of political expediency with no chance of making a contribution to improvements in food security'.[53]

Finally, although the problem of import surges was recognized in the Uruguay Round, the utility of the instrument designed to manage such circumstances—the special agricultural safeguard (SSG)—has been strongly criticized by many Southern countries and agricultural analysts. Recourse to the SSG is limited to those members that undertook the process of tariffication (converting non-tariff measures, such as import quotas, into tariffs using a specific formula). During the negotiations, however, countries were given a choice of applying either the tariffication formula or binding tariff ceilings. The majority of Southern members opted for the latter. This has, however, led to the current situation whereby only 22 Southern countries have access to the SSG. Even within this group of eligible actors, the safeguard has been little used in practice, with only two countries (the Philippines and Costa Rica) deploying it from 1995 to 2003.[54] The reasons for this limited use are complex, but in part relate to further procedural restrictions. One significant problem centres on the calculations used to determine the trigger price (the point at which trade restrictions would be activated). In the Uruguay Round, this reference level was set at the average of 1986 to 1988 levels, which is much lower than present real import prices.[55] In contrast, the biggest users of the SSG have historically been the EU-15, Japan, the US, and Poland (representing 87% of all actions taken). For example, the EU-15 has consistently applied the tool to protect fruits and vegetables, while the US has activated the SSG to defend dairy products.[56] As the WTO system has evolved, the inequity in the use of this instrument has been accentuated, fostering resentment on the part of many Southern countries. Such tools, they argue, should not be designed to further cushion already privileged Northern farmers but, rather, absent the institutional resources to achieve domestic support, an effective safeguard instrument should be a right (either exclusively or jointly).

To summarize so far, I have critically discussed some of the major sets of economic and legal problems faced by many Southern countries in the area of agriculture within the WTO system. By way of linking with Section 5.2, it is worth underscoring why this analysis has been important. First, one needs to grasp the complexity of the political challenges confronting many of these members. In order to explain why these actors experience such conditions and, importantly, who shares responsibility for their position in the trading order, one needs to assess the political and economic context, including the history of institutional policy struggles. In blunt terms, as many observers and practitioners have noted, Southern countries were given a 'bum deal' in the Uruguay Round and have been seeking to improve their fortunes ever since.[57] These setbacks put them at a disadvantage in subsequent competitions on the same terrain and, therefore, one needs to understand precisely what baseline they started from in the late 1990s. Secondly, and related to the first reason, I would argue that following this empirical examination it is easier to discern the openings and spaces for heretical critique within the WTO linguistic market. Thus, the discussion helps to frame and inform the arguments in the remainder of the chapter. Already, however, I would suggest that one common theme connects many of the points raised: the critical importance of political classifications. In the WTO, the contests over classifications matter because they strongly shape the structures of debate, the design of policy instruments, and the implementation of technical modalities. In short, the first challenge for Southern countries was to return once more to the classification game.

5.2 Renewing the classification struggle

> What is at stake in the struggles about the meaning of the social world is power over the classificatory schemes and systems which are the basis of the representations of groups and therefore of their mobilization and demobilization.[58]

In the WTO policy game, a fundamental stake is the contest over classifications of trade politics. Through historical reconstruction, one can trace when, and under what conditions, the legitimation of certain classifications prevailed over others. Here in this section, I critically explain how a stronger Southern-centric agricultural heterodoxy was politically crafted from the late 1990s until 2004. Like the cotton case, my argument is that one needs to spend time elucidating the processes by which this new symbolic power arose and how, in particular, it shaped the representations and mobilization capacities of interested actors. Unlike the strategic, calculating behaviour depicted in the compulsory-power vision of politics, the notion of symbolic power alerts us to how agents cautiously and laboriously test new concepts, anticipating opportunities and risks in the process. With a view to the legal cementing of symbolic power to come, these moves were made in the hope of reshaping the WTO linguistic market to better fit their material interests. The discussion is divided into three main subsections. First, I examine the genesis and political purpose of what became known as the 'development box', a framing device used by several countries to organize defensive agricultural concerns. Second, with regard to an important phase during 2003, I explore how the ideas behind this category morphed into the now standardized classification of 'special products' and, in an ancillary move, the 'special safeguard mechanism'. I also debate how the G33 alliance began to coalesce for the first time. Third, the discussion moves to address how a WTO framework agreement in 2004 consolidated the symbolic power gains of the G33.

5.2.1 *Launching a boxing match over 'development'*

Towards the close of the last century, on the basis of discussions within and between a number of Southern countries, civil society groups, and international institutions, a new category for organizing agricultural concerns emerged: the 'development box'. The idea of a distinct 'box' for development was an attractive notion to many of these actors. By its very definition, the category implied that the three existing boxes for organizing exceptions to liberalization disciplines in the AoA (as discussed previously, the Green, Blue, and Amber boxes) either had little or no development in them, or that Southern countries could not easily access them due to resource constraints. The development box presented a possibility that Southern countries could design their own classifications, which could fit into the AoA (communicate to orthodoxy) yet still be recognized as being somewhat subversive. This subsection explains some of the main arguments and tensions which arose when the notion was most prominent and valuable.[59]

By way of context, it is important to recall that during the late 1990s a number of leading policy-makers were increasingly calling for 'more development' in the WTO. For instance, the Brazilian ambassador, Celso Amorim, often argued that the system suffered from a 'development deficit'; while Clare Short, the UK Secretary of State for International Development, was perhaps the first official to attach 'development' to the envisaged 'new round'.[60] Within civil society, some of the most astute critical analysts, residing in groups such as the Catholic Agency for Overseas Development (CAFOD), Oxfam International, and Focus on the Global South, began to sense that the increased chatter on 'development'—however it was conceived—could present new policy openings. Since the FAO-organized World Food Summit in 1996, these groups had already trialled the idea of a 'bread box' category for Southern concerns in the AoA, a concept that tried to heighten awareness of food security problems.[61] By 1999, this notion had transmuted into the development box and was ready to be debated in Geneva with interested country missions. The work of certain individuals, such as Duncan Green at CAFOD, Aileen Kwa at Focus on the Global South, as well as Shishir Priyadarshi and Luisa Bernal at the South Centre, was crucial in terms of formulating ideas as to what purpose the development box could serve.[62] In this sense, similar to the early stages of the C4 case, one can see how it was independent trade analysts (and not immediately government officials) who were trying to make the concept a recognizable 'issue' in the WTO.

For the strongest heretical advocates, the purpose of the development box was to promote trade rules that more openly accommodated, and distinguished between, different social groups, particularly subsistence farmers who had few or no commercial stakes in agriculture at the international level. In slightly weaker arguments, these spokespersons proposed that existing SDT provisions should be strengthened and, where necessary, made permanent legal tools. The keyword of 'flexibility' was used as a means to quickly communicate such demands. For instance, in an October 1999 paper submitted by the Dominican Republic, the first to officially mention the notion of a development box, it was argued that 'food is different from other forms of goods in that it is an absolute daily necessity', and that because 'there is no level playing field between countries' Southern governments should be allowed to '*deviate* from their AoA commitments in order to meet these development and food security needs'.[63] By June 2000, following the collapse of the Seattle Ministerial, a new submission from 11 countries, this time led by Pakistan, put the phrase 'development box' more prominently in the main title. The proposal made a stronger opening pitch than compared to previous efforts: food security was 'inextricably connected to national security and political sovereignty', using GATT Article XXI ('Security Exceptions') as a legal basis for such claims.[64] By drawing upon FAO analysis, the paper stated that key products of interest to Southern countries, particularly food staples, should be 'exempted from liberalisation'.[65]

In the subsequent period leading up to the Doha Ministerial, the development box continued to pick up fans, of particular note being the increased involvement of India. Not to be denied its moment in a new political spotlight, it proposed its own 'food security box', although the contents were almost synonymous with the development box.[66] For S. I. M. Nayyar, a former counsellor at the Pakistan mission who led the initiative at the government level, there was no question that the development box helped to release considerable frustration on the part of the proponent countries: 'The "development box" was about providing meaningful SDT. But like any good negotiator, you start with the maximum opening offer. We said: let's go for everything and then we'll see what happens.'[67] As Nayyar expressed it, the concept was an 'intuitive, catchy phrase', one which had 'value in itself'. Moreover, in light of post-Seattle diplomatic bridge-building between the North and South, it was 'politically difficult for the developed countries to oppose it'.[68] As Duncan Green noted: 'To frame it as a "development box" was absolutely crucial. I even recall Clare Short saying "that's really hard to oppose, you've chosen a great name there". These things may sound simplistic, but are in fact very influential.'[69]

When hearing such insider opinions, one cannot help but be reminded of how performative acts of naming are integral to the accumulation of symbolic power. Such acts are, however, not always easy to engineer, especially for resource-poor actors in the WTO system. I would argue that the category of the development box resonated with a range of constituents because it mimicked existing orthodox classifications. It was 'intuitive' because the words 'development' and 'box' are received ideas for agents in the WTO diplomatic game (each internally 'felt right' or 'fell right').[70] The proposal, therefore, should be read as an effort first, to appropriate orthodox language, and second, to link it with the masterframe of 'development' which, by the Doha Ministerial, had become a highly legitimate and malleable word in the institution. The 'Friends of the Development Box' were essentially motivated by an overriding desire to create a suitable language to explain their political problems, but a language that still *partially deferred to orthodoxy*. The method of mimicry was helpful at this point because the development box aspired to rupture the conventional 'traffic light' classification. But by its very nature, mimicry had its limits: the ambitions of the demanders extended only to complementing the existing Green, Blue, and Amber boxes with a hypothetical 'fourth' or 'missing' box. In short, to borrow from Bourdieu again, one can see how symbolic power was being exercised to reveal problems that were latent and to constitute disparate agents into a group who would, in turn, defend the classification that defined them collectively.[71]

But to make the development box 'an issue' in the WTO system did not mean that it was consecrated and blessed by all actors. In 2001 and 2002 there were a series of struggles over the concept. According to Kwa, there were 'very heated debates' between interested Southern missions in Geneva.[72] For instance, with a keen eye on the general competition over legitimation and the prospect of negotiations to come, she argued the following to a private meeting of national delegates in April 2002:

> What price are we going to pay for [the 'development box']?... The WTO as an institution continues to be in need of gaining legitimacy. Giving developing countries a development box would be a sure way of getting this 'legitimacy', which the rich Members of the institution want so badly... However, depending on what is in the development box, the value of it may be a gross exaggeration... we (as Southern governments and civil society) *have* to do our calculations right. What type of development box should be our bottom-line?[73]

In strategic terms, therefore, Kwa, amongst others, was concerned that the potential utility of the development box might not go far enough to address the complexity of Southern agricultural problems, or that its establishment could become linked to concessions in other areas of negotiations, or that it might absorb valuable symbolic power that could otherwise be directed to disciplining Northern trade-distorting practices.[74] As the evolution of the initiative has shown, these risks were not unique to the early stages, but have continued to resurface throughout the Doha Round.

In turn, such thoughts were associated with the external front: managing anxiety and hostility to the development box from major exporters. In this regard, the strongest detractors were the US and the Cairns group, who saw little commercial benefit for themselves from new border measures, especially in markets such as India.[75] The US in particular seemed keen to organize the development box out of the main negotiating agenda and was not afraid to use compulsory power tools to undermine the political spirits of group members. For instance, Pakistan's position was severely compromised by the aftermath of the 11 September 2001 terrorist attacks and the wholesale reorganization of US–Pakistan relations.[76] By mid-2002, ambassador Munir Akram, an outspoken proponent of the initiative alongside Nayyar, was moved to New York.[77] Central American countries were also targeted. The US signalled to the Dominican Republic that the prospect of extending the Central American Free Trade Agreement to it would be damaged if they continued to be proactive. By September 2002, the ambassador of the Dominican Republic, Federico Cuello Camilo, was pressured out of his post; while El Salvador also reversed its position to fully support the US on tariff reductions (they never returned to the group).[78] At the same time, other actors, including the EU and Switzerland, worked to challenge the legitimacy and veracity of the demanders' claims, suggesting that the category could lead to a detrimental 'two-track' AoA (and thus, by implication, away from the presumed 'one-track' mainstream vision). The notion of allowing Southern countries to potentially raise their tariffs, even on a select range of products deemed significant, was considered anathema to these members.[79]

Yet, within the same moment, in a sign of what was to come, some of these privileged actors also played a more delicate and opportunistic game of expounding upon their own defensive agricultural interests within the context of the development box. For the advocates of the initiative, this was always a possibility that had to be recognized. As noted, the category of 'non-trade' was inserted into the AoA in order to accommodate those members who argued that agriculture served many purposes beyond the production and selling of commodities. This pattern continued into the WTO. For instance, on the eve of the AoA reform negotiations in 2000, the G10 coalition of wealthy net food importers (led by Japan, Switzerland, and Norway) argued for an expansive definition of agriculture to include food security, environmental protection, and the viability of rural areas.[80] The EU's heavy promotion of the concept of 'multifunctionality', characterized as a sub-category within 'non-trade', worked to complement and reinforce these efforts.[81] Although 'multifunctionality' was never explicitly defined, the EU argued that food and 'non-food' outputs were intimately joined together and that this 'jointness' justified increased production-related support. The idea that governments needed to intervene to preserve positive 'non-market' concerns was an argument that was often repeated. But behind such arguments, these actors were acutely concerned about their Amber Box spending reaching the legally allowed limits and thus, were searching for new ways to protect themselves.

For Southern countries, the non-trade label was, in one respect, a useful touchstone to begin any argument on defensive agricultural policies in the WTO, but the category was not sufficient. The primary difficulty of using the non-trade label was that its meanings continued to be shaped by dominant Northern actors. In short, it was 'SDT for the rich'. The development box, therefore, had to be deployed either in conjunction or competition with the concept of the non-trade label. This presented a risk to the Southern advocates of the initiative: namely, that under the vulgate of non-trade some Northern members could *flatten and smooth over* the very inequities and differences that the development box sought to expose. In this respect, as Priyadarshi of the South Centre has remarked, the only 'semblance of relief' that was generated from the Doha Declaration was the 'implicit recognition' that differences did exist on 'non-trade concerns' *between* Northern and Southern countries. This result, however, was still 'purely at a conceptual level' and contained no assurances.[82] Nevertheless, despite these vulnerabilities and contests, the Friends of the Development Box continued to persevere into 2003 as preparations advanced for the Cancún summit. During these months, similar to the evolution of the WCA cotton issue, one saw evidence of Southern countries strengthening their political mobilization. This time, however, the draft negotiating text on agriculture began to change in ways favourable (but by no means entirely satisfactory) to the proponent countries.

5.2.2 *A new category to make a new group*

One can see how the development box frame acted as a rallying point for the socialization of multiple actors. But the salience of any particular frame, within a given social space, rarely stays fixed. A frame may, for instance, fade or indeed 'die' for many reasons. From December 2002, under the leadership of Stuart Harbinson, chair of the Committee of Agriculture, this was precisely the situation that befell the development box. However, as I will argue, this was not necessarily a regressive step from the viewpoint of the food security proponents. In this subsection, I underscore again the important relationship between symbolic power and institutional power through an analysis of events that took place in 2003, focusing on the reframing of the problem and the consolidation of a new group: the G33.

First, 'the fall' of the development box category. Following more than three years of efforts within Geneva to accumulate symbolic power, the proponents of Southern food security registered a small breakthrough within the AoA talks. In a December 2002 'Overview' paper prepared by Harbinson, he proposed that special treatment could be extended to feature 'exemption from reduction commitments for certain agricultural products which are of strategic importance in pursuing food security, product diversification, rural development and employment, and poverty alleviation'.[83] Also mentioned for the first time was the idea of creating 'special safeguard measures' for Southern countries.[84] By February 2003, the phrase 'strategic products' was borrowed from an internal African group submission and inserted into what was optimistically called a 'draft of modalities' text.[85] However, Harbinson also outlined a series of conditions placed in brackets that could be attached to 'strategic products'. Of most importance, the idea of completely escaping envisaged tariff cuts was ruled out; rather, all tariff lines would face at least a 5% cut, regardless of how the crop was associated with food security. At the same time, the choice of tariff line categorization was proposed at the 6-digit Harmonized System (HS) level.[86] This would mean that Southern countries could not, for instance, specify 'rice' as a general product of concern, but would have to indicate what sub-type (such as paddy, husked, or semi-milled) required different treatment. In a revised March version of the same text, prompted mainly by harsh criticism from the rest of the WTO membership, Harbinson kept almost everything he had outlined the same, except for one major change: 'strategic' was removed and replaced with the more common and less politically charged word 'special'.[87]

On the one hand, this change can certainly be read as an important turning point for the advocates of the initiative. As Green of CAFOD expressed it, 'When the idea of strategic products was introduced for the first time I thought, my God, this is real. The issue is *moving from outside to inside* the organization and Harbinson is making it happen.'[88] It represented 'official' recognition that the concerns of the Friends of the Development Box had to be integrated into the discussions on the AoA; that there would be no safe path to Cancún without them. Harbinson, as the 'universal' broker, was 'anointing' the idea of 'strategic products' or 'special products' (SP) (both terms were used interchangeably for the rest of the year). On the other hand, however, these alternative ideas on food security did not easily 'enter' the WTO and the classification schemes of the AoA. The struggle over language reveals that this was not a straightforward process. As one prominent adviser recalled, 'A lot of people, the Americans included, didn't like the word "strategic" and sought to take it out of discussions.'[89] In the opinion of Jason Hafemeister, the lead US agriculture negotiator at the time, the US was trying to be 'pragmatic' but, at the same time, expressed 'huge concerns over the use and misuse of these concepts'. In particular, Hafemeister was sensing how the classification struggle was in flux with unclear consequences: 'We always have these big fights between countries. They try to fit in particular words and get their foot in the door. Then later it comes back to you when they say, "Well you've already agreed to this. We can take this as a given".'[90]

Second, in terms of group mobilization, the weeks leading up to Cancún were very important in terms of building solidarity amongst Southern countries, within both Geneva and national capitals. At this stage, Indonesia and the Philippines assumed a more proactive leadership position, taking on the mantle originally filled by Pakistan. But the formation of a specific group to defend SPs and the SSM was also triggered by perceptions of the US and the EU. As alluded to in the cotton case, many countries feared that the two trade hegemons were colluding in order to 'pull another Blair House' over Southern members.[91] When the US and EU tabled a joint text on agriculture on 13 August 2003, the fears of the demanders were realised: there was no reference to the concept of SPs anywhere.[92] When asked at a subsequent press conference why the category had been excluded, the EU representative, Peter Carl, rather dismissively remarked that the US and the EU were 'working out solutions for ourselves' and that it was the job of Southern countries to respond.[93] As one Geneva-based Asian delegate expressed it, 'That proposal was a tipping point, especially because it was used as a basis for the main agriculture text prepared by [conference chair Luis Ernesto] Derbez. We were determined at that point to better organize ourselves.'[94]

On the eve of the ministerial, Indonesia called a press conference to announce that an Alliance for Special Products and the Special Safeguard Mechanism had been established. In a communiqué signed by 23 countries, the members of the group argued that they spoke for 'the interests of a majority of the world's small vulnerable resource-poor farmers'.[95] Three major demands were issued:

(1) that Southern countries should have the right to self-designate a certain percentage of tariff lines as SPs which would not face any tariff reductions nor be subjected to new Tariff Rate Quota (TRQ) commitments
(2) that an SSM should be established
(3) that crops selected as SPs should also have access to the SSM.[96]

By the end of the third day of the ministerial, the membership of the Alliance had grown by ten, leading many to dub them the G33. Established Southern coalitions also backed the position of the Alliance, including the African Union (AU), the ACP countries, and LDCs. Relations with the offensive G20 were cordial (some countries such as Indonesia, Nigeria, and Pakistan were members of both groups), but the G33 quickly understood that its energies were best focused on managing its own heterogeneity and specific cause. At the same time, this distancing from the G20 was a relief to both the US and the EU, who fought to prevent any form of collaboration between the two coalitions.[97] While Cancún proved significant in terms of reinforcing group cohesion, confronting opposing actors, as well as engaging in political theatre, the coalition was still fighting to earn the symbolic power that mattered most:

legal codification of its members' interests. It is on this note that we can turn to address how the G33—armed with their experiences in the classification struggle over defensive policy ideas—worked to strengthen their suit as the Doha Round entered another difficult and protracted chapter.

5.2.3 *The July 2004 Framework*

As discussed in Chapter 4, the July 2004 Framework was an important junction in the Doha Round. The process of drafting the text was arduous and stressful, particularly for the new G33. In the main negotiating sessions, no detail was too small for scrutiny, but because time was finite—due to the collective pressure to clinch a deal—not all details could be equally well debated. There were the inevitable scuffles. For instance, when the subject of how to designate crops as SPs was raised in a green room meeting on 31 July, the Indonesian ambassador and G33 coordinator, Gusmardi Bustami, clashed with a 'very reluctant' USTR, Robert Zoellick, over the line 'under conditions to be agreed in the negotiations'. Zoellick wanted to keep the reference, presumably to facilitate greater temporal space for the US, but Bustami succeeded in removing the line.[98] However, the G33 also suffered a key loss: the US and other Northern actors did not accept a blanket exemption from tariff reductions. While the language was therefore weaker than desired, the July Framework was significant. Five years after the development box began to surface, the heterodox opinions of the G33 had at last been legally integrated into the regime. When compared to the conservatism of the Uruguay Round, the following two paragraphs were certainly an achievement to savour:

> 41. Developing country Members will have the flexibility to designate an appropriate number of products as Special Products, based on criteria of food security, livelihood security and rural development needs. These products will be eligible for more flexible treatment. The criteria and treatment of these products will be further specified during the negotiation phase and will recognize the fundamental importance of Special Products to developing countries.
> 42. A Special Safeguard Mechanism (SSM) will be established for use by developing country Members.[99]

However, within this same moment, the G33 and their institutional sympathizers also had to grapple with a rival concept that crept on to the agenda prior to the July Framework. It had a name so similar to 'special products' that one could have either misconstrued it as being synonymous with Southern interests or missed it entirely. But the introduction of the category of 'sensitive products' was principally a European creation, initially advanced by Pascal Lamy, commissioner for external trade. Its origins can be found in the EU–US pre-Cancún joint text which, to recall, was criticized by other members.[100]

What was remarkable about this conceptual debut was how decisively it was incorporated into the Doha agenda, particularly when compared to the laborious social and symbolic struggle that the G33 experienced to have their needs recognized. At first glance, it appeared that the idea of sensitive products was the same as SPs: to seek 'flexibility' from the envisaged effects of liberalization. In the July Framework text, the section on sensitive products preceded SPs and was not limited to any particular type of country, thereby leading one to assume that Southern members could also access it. While the outline on sensitive products was vague, it was still more precise than the paragraph on SPs, in terms of selection and treatment from a commercial orthodox perspective.[101] Crucially, the text made an implicit linkage between the two defensive agricultural notions: special products (categorized within SDT) would be an 'integral' consideration in all elements of the negotiations, which included sensitive products (categorized outside SDT).[102]

In the contest over language, it was difficult to judge what the category of sensitive products might entail, in particular, what relationship it had to SPs. But some insiders immediately believed that the G33 faced a potential obstacle: 'When "sensitive products" began to be thrown around, my heart sank. The attitude from the EU was "you've got your special products, but we've got our sensitive products". It just complicated the entire process.'[103] How can this moment in the negotiations be interpreted? If one invokes the framework on symbolic power again, I would argue that this form of mimicry—constructed here as mimicry of the Other by the dominant, not the other way around—was an ingenious political move on two counts.

First, it swiftly enabled Northern members, particularly the EU, but also the G10 and the US to an extent, to accumulate greater symbolic power in order to justify their own protectionist concerns. Now there was a new policy tool, in addition to the legally allowable Green Box spending, which was being legitimized.[104] Like the C4 mimicking of the logic of US-style competitiveness, the EU approached the G33 under the sign of 'flexibility' to liberalization. This move was subtle and difficult to contest because it was precisely the same starting point that the G33 began from. As Bernal expressed it, 'From that point on, it became a tricky chess game for the G33. The EU was trying to use the concept of SPs to legitimize their own sensitive items.'[105] In this example, the beauty of the 'sensitive products' notion was how it could open a space to reinvigorate the older policy framework on multifunctionality. When hearing such comments, one is reminded of Bourdieu's point about how symbolic power can often appear non-contentious, particularly in respect to the use of a common vocabulary which is recognized not as 'power' as such (in the conventional compulsory sense) but, rather, as 'apolitical communication'.[106]

Second, by implying that sensitive products and SPs were united by a conceptual bridge, the US and the EU could indirectly better control the

G33 critique and advance their own desired liberalization agenda in other areas of agriculture. Again, this was a troubling development for the G33 because it risked obfuscating their core message—within the restricted WTO linguistic market—that agriculture served many *non-commercial* purposes in the South, which the category of SPs was designed to defend. Thus, to borrow Homi Bhabha's description, the EU's strategy of mimicry was 'disturbing' to the G33 because it invoked the principle of reciprocity instead of differentiation.[107] The EU was inferring that SPs would be bartered over like any other negotiating item and that the provision was not quite as unique and 'special' as originally claimed. As Bustami recalled, 'In a green room meeting [for the July Framework] I strongly argued against the linkage. Why should we accept that? The concept of special products was born before sensitive products. It is a stand-alone category. It is not a commercial problem. Special products are about social and political problems.'[108]

Nevertheless, at the same time, it would be wrong to overanalyse the significance of the rapid ascent of the concept of sensitive products in relation to the work of the G33. For some observers, there was a strong sense that the very incorporation of SPs and the SSM into the Doha agenda would be met with 'the death of a thousand cuts'; that is, the heretical content would be gradually 'diluted' in order to bring it into closer alignment with orthodox interests.[109] Yet the July Framework was the only template in town and the G33 had already invested a tremendous amount of political energy to reach this point. According to Ricardo Meléndez-Ortiz, executive director at ICTSD, these new concepts, while still ill-defined, were 'probably the most innovative' provisions ever devised in WTO SDT talks.[110] The challenge now was to seize what some of their supporters were calling a 'strategic window of opportunity' to explain how the inter-related needs of food security, livelihood security, and rural development could be operationalized in the AoA.[111]

5.3 Codifying special treatment

This final section examines how the G33's agenda has evolved from the post-July 2004 period until 2008. In an effort to codify new definitions of agricultural special treatment, this phase featured debates at a lower level of conceptual abstraction. Within the space constraints here, however, it is not possible to fully explore the complexity of these negotiations. Rather, with a view to understanding the building and tarnishing of symbolic power attached to the G33 cause, the argument showcases some significant contests and episodes. The discussion does not engage in over-ambitious speculation about potential material effects of the agreements to date, of which the final content remains unresolved. There is, nevertheless, a general 'take-away' message to note: that is, the full heretical force of the G33's critique, complete with attention to concerns about hunger and nourishment, has been partially sidelined or lost as the negotiations shifted into conventional bargaining over quantitative modalities, including market-access demands. It will be suggested that this was an inevitable process of legally translating the G33's heterodox ideas into the existing WTO schemes of classification, a struggle marked by reoccurring clashes with opponents. The discussion consists of three subsections. First, I examine a prominent debate regarding how criteria for the use of SPs could be legitimized, an effort that involved other interested stakeholders beyond the G33. Second, the argument shifts to consider the ways in which the US, along with its allies and sympathizers, sought to undermine the potential scope and effectiveness of SPs. Finally, the section concludes with a focus on the most recent tensions surrounding the SSM.

5.3.1 *Crafting heterodox indicators*

With the July 2004 Framework, SPs had become blessed with institutional legitimacy. The next challenge for the G33 was to begin the process of specifying measures on their potential use. In the subsequent two years, a series of indicators were designed to guide any Southern country towards the selection of their SPs. Here, I argue that this period was marked by renewed experimentation on how to formulate and translate heretical ideas into the 'authorized' language of the AoA, but compared to the earlier classification struggles debated in Section 5.2, this activity featured more refined empirical analysis. In particular, I focus on how this process of accumulating further symbolic power around the G33 cause was, in part, facilitated by drawing upon external institutional power resources.

It is crucial to underscore that the G33 has never developed an 'in house' research capacity. Rather, as examined by Paul Mably, the group has tried to distil relevant knowledge from outside sources into negotiating positions.[112] The major institutions who helped to shape debates have been ICTSD, the South Centre, and the FAO. When studying the July Framework, specialists working for these organizations concentrated on two keywords: 'criteria' and 'treatment'.[113] To this end, independent of any direct call from the G33, ICTSD began to convene a series of meetings in late 2004 in order to clarify the intellectual terrain on SPs, as well as the SSM. For instance, at one event, Bernal of the South Centre argued that SPs could potentially be determined by different sets of factors, such as the relative contribution of any specific product to the national economy.[114] The results of these brainstorming sessions were then brought to a gathering of G33 negotiators. At this stage, a plan was developed to build a longer, two-year ICTSD-organized research programme in order to better facilitate the G33's objectives. This process was not necessarily designed to offer direct advice on negotiation tactics (although this was provided discreetly by the South Centre) but, rather, to develop the analytical frameworks to better understand how SPs and the SSM could be 'scientifically applied' within the AoA.[115] The major purpose of ICTSD's initiatives—including country-level consultations, workshops, and research papers—was to create the conditions for nationally led investigations into SPs which could, in turn, be synthesized into a collective strategy at the multilateral level.[116]

However, there were tensions within the G33 on how to handle these developments. For some negotiators, there was a strong desire to keep talk on 'criteria' at the highest level of abstraction possible. As Bernal expressed it, 'Moving towards the idea of indicators was politically very difficult. The political line was that food security, livelihood security, and rural development were *the* criteria and that you didn't need anything else.'[117] How can one explain this tentative behaviour? Two sets of reasons can be given. First, in many G33 countries, there are serious practical problems regarding data collection, including their availability and form. For instance, agricultural data are often spread across government departments, a problem that has long been appreciated by statisticians from the FAO. Thus, it is not hard to appreciate how G33 representatives could have been perturbed by any requirements for new or reconstituted data, which would have to fit into the conceptual framework on SPs. A second, and related reason was that Indonesia, as coordinator, was always preoccupied with group cohesion in a changing multilateral environment. As noted in Section 5.1 in relation to tariff overhangs, countries such as India and the Philippines considered the issue of SPs more urgent than others. By June 2005, at a high-level G33 ministerial in Jakarta, the group membership had begun to stabilize at around 42, and now included China. In broad terms, the coalition seemed to grasp how its legitimacy was linked to universalist appeals and a diverse membership (internal speaking notes prepared for negotiations emphasized these perceived strengths).[118]

But as the December 2005 Hong Kong Ministerial approached, the G33 faced mounting pressure from other actors, chiefly the US and Australia, that it needed to specify what the 'flexibility' within SPs actually entailed.[119] Interestingly, to recall the notion of compulsory power again, this period saw the G33 denied entry to informal agriculture meetings, a signal that other critical members retained the capacity to marginalize them.[120] In response, the coalition relaxed its negotiating stance and submitted an 'illustrative list' of 16 main indicators that could guide the selection of SPs. In a proposal characterized as 'a major shift from its original position', the group argued that SPs could be defined by considering evidence such as how the product formed part of a basic national food basket, how the product contributed towards the total calorific intake of the population, or what proportion of the agricultural labour force was employed in the production of the product.[121] The research of the South Centre, in addition to ICTSD-commissioned work, became invaluable for the G33 at this point.[122] For instance, Bernal confirmed that she was directly involved in the drafting of group submissions, a contribution that was greatly appreciated by the Indonesian mission in Geneva.[123] Elsewhere, according to Mably, one can identify parallels between the indicators suggested by Anwarul Hoda, a member of the Indian Planning Commission, and the arguments advanced by the G33 at Hong Kong.[124] What finally emerged in the Hong Kong Ministerial text was, in one respect, a conservative outcome for the G33 in the sense that the coalition consolidated their existing gains:

> 7. Developing country Members will have the flexibility to self-designate an appropriate number of tariff lines as Special Products *guided by indicators* based on the criteria of food security, livelihood security and rural development.[125]

But within this key paragraph a sequencing was implied: the criteria would shape the indicators, and the indicators would inform the specific modalities. The use of the word 'guided' (and not, for instance, 'decided' or 'determined') was deliberately weak because the opponents of the G33, as well some coalition members, did not want to commit to an exclusive use of qualitative evidence for the selection of SPs. By May 2006, the debate on indicators began to fade as the chair of the Committee on Agriculture, Crawford Falconer, directed all actors to focus on quantitative figures. Following this point, it is noteworthy that the G33 did not appear to face much resistance from other members regarding their choice of indicators, to the extent that Falconer would use the indicative measures crafted by the group as *the* list for guiding the rest of the negotiations (see Appendix B).

Let me summarize this phase by returning directly to the conceptual ambitions of the book. In Mably's analysis, he explains how ICTSD research, among others, worked to 'legitimize' the G33 and to grant its members 'a higher level of credibility' in WTO talks.[126] With a Bourdieusian interpretation, we can enrich this basic point on two counts. First, in large part, the symbolic power orchestrated by these organizations is derived from their historical command and critique of conventional trade knowledge, particularly in respect to questions of inequality. With a vigilant eye on protecting this stock of symbolic power, these institutional spokespersons are often adept at discerning how the linguistic market is subtly reconfiguring and how, in turn, to take advantage of such fluidity to further 'universal' goals (in this case, Southern perspectives on food security). To fully understand these effects of symbolic power one would need to conduct a detailed historical study of the making of the modern trade policy field. Among other enquiries, this would include attention to the micro-level behaviour of these experts, including their everyday social networking, event management, and how, in particular, they write in a dispassionate tone. Understanding these practices would help to reveal how such players earn the 'admission rights' to speak as credible analysts and, at the same time, to potentially undermine other actors who may privately view their work as politically 'inappropriate' or 'disruptive'.

Second, once these institutions had mobilized themselves to echo and expound upon the G33 cause, coalition members further refined what Erving Goffman would call a 'sense of one's place'.[127] In this respect, the very activity generated by these research bodies enhanced the 'visibility' and distinctiveness of the G33 in relation to other agricultural players, particularly within the Geneva social space. A sense of one's place implies that G33 members were more assured, but by no means supremely confident, of their own position within the overall agricultural negotiations. This is not to infer, in some kind of crude characterization, that intra-coalition relations were now harmonious. Nor does it mean that all G33 countries were dutiful students who read, referenced, and practically applied all the outputs of such institutions. Rather, the cultivation of a sense of place speaks to the enduring desire for recognition, a need which has to be understood historically through previous troubles to earn recognition (such as in the Uruguay Round). In particular, it points to how the G33 was now, at the very least, tolerated by the major powers as a 'player of note' that would, as a consequence, have to be incorporated into the inner circle of talks. To risk repeating myself, these results were the product of considerable symbolic labour since, like any process of political legitimation, one can never say for sure how many events and publications will secure a higher degree of recognition from the audiences that matter.

5.3.2 *Opening up the 'black box'*

Although the Hong Kong Ministerial appeared to offer some optimism that a larger Doha deal was in sight, by the time negotiators returned to Geneva, a downgrading of expectations was already underway. There were still too many unknowns and differences of opinion in the agriculture talks. From 2006 to 2008, deadlines would be repeatedly made and then abandoned, provoking exasperation from many political actors and observers. In terms of the G33 agenda, SPs assumed a more privileged status, although work on trying to unpack the SSM also emerged in this period. The role of the US and tensions between Southern countries can be highlighted here.

Ahead of a July 2006 deadline, the US made a new offer on SPs, one which would prove to be inflammatory from the G33's perspective.[128] The paper stated that SPs should be assigned to 'no more than 5 tariff lines at the detailed duty level'.[129] When one considers that many Southern countries have hundreds of tariff lines to represent agricultural trade, such a proposal, if enacted, would have enabled these members to categorize a minuscule percentage of their crops as SPs.[130] In part, the US argued that this proposal was valid because, in percentage terms, the majority of agricultural trade in many Southern countries tends to be concentrated within a few lines. But this submission needs to be compared to the G33's pre-Hong Kong dossier where they argued, in addition to outlining the indicators, that Southern countries should have the right to self-designate at least 20% of tariff lines as SPs, with at least half of this selection excluded from any tariff reduction.[131] For Susan Schwab, the new USTR, the G33 were depicted as 'obstructionists' who sought 'loopholes' and 'black boxes' in the AoA, negative labels that the US would contrast with their own aim for 'new trade flows'.[132] Inevitably, the US paper was strongly condemned by not only the G33, but nearly the entire WTO membership, as well as provoking scepticism from Falconer.[133] As one delegate expressed it, 'If they [the US] were trying to sabotage the negotiations, they were doing a good job', while Bustami recalled that 'the proposal just wasn't serious at all and we were not prepared to deal with it'.[134]

However, while the US continued to be the most aggressive champion of restrictions on SPs, it is important to note that some Southern members were also opposed to the G33 agenda. As noted, since the time of the development box, a cluster of countries have expressed worries regarding potential negative effects of defensive instruments on South–South trade. The main members who have been proactive on this issue have been Thailand and Malaysia, although Argentina, Uruguay, Costa Rica, and Paraguay have also been critics. For instance, in a paper that was seemingly timed to coincide with the US submission, Thailand argued that SPs should be viewed in light of a desire for 'substantial improvements in market access'. Among other issues, Thailand proposed that when Southern countries account for more than half of all exports of a given agricultural product, that product should not be designated as an SP.[135] As the lead rice exporter in the world, Thailand was concerned that other countries would specify rice as one of their own SPs. Malaysia also signalled that exports of its palm oil could be undermined if other countries, such as India, chose that product as an SP.[136] While these countries voluntarily made such moves, US prodding behind the scenes was certainly important.[137] In this respect, therefore, the idea of institutional power can resurface as a way to explain the efforts of this US-led orchestration.

How the G33 have handled the question of South–South trade has varied depending upon the context. The issue has certainly put pressure on the group. As Bustami remarked, 'In many talks, the US negotiators simply folded their arms and hoped that developing countries would fight it out among themselves'.[138] One tactic has been to downplay the extensiveness of the problem. For instance, overall, trade among Southern countries is growing and one could assume that this trend will continue for the near future. More specifically, one study suggested that only six products are likely to spark potential disputes, leading to the hope that bilateral deals between concerned parties could be found.[139] As the negotiations moved into 2007, the G33 did indeed attempt to do this by quietly speaking to Thailand.[140] But other problems surfaced at the same time. For instance, in a move that drew suspicion from many G33 countries, Pakistan (a coalition member) appeared to offer itself as a 'middle-ground' broker between Indonesia and Thailand with its own proposal on SPs. Among other options, Pakistan suggested that SPs should be subjected to a tiered tariff-cutting formula whereby the reduction rate for SPs would be two thirds of a general formula. However, this contradicted the G33 position that at least 50% of SPs should not be subjected to any tariff reduction; that another 25% would have a 5% reduction; and that the remaining SPs would have no more than a 10% cut.[141]

By early 2008, the G33 appeared to buckle under these stresses or, in other words, submitted to a weakening of their heretical ambitions as the price for 'consensus-building'. The coalition indicated that it would be prepared to accept a minimum of 12% of tariff lines as SPs, a drop of 8% from its previous position.[142] But this was still not sufficient for the US and other major exporters who pressed for further delimiting. In an informal Falconer working paper, designed to collate the opinions of all and offer impressions for future directions, a minimum target for tariff lines as SPs was pitched at a lower level of between 6 and 9%.[143] However, this text came under renewed criticism from the G33. By early July 2008, a new structure was agreed. It proposed at least 10% and a maximum of 18% of products could be declared as SPs. Within this range, the average tariff cut would be between 10 and 14%, with up to 6% of lines having no cut. Throughout all these negotiations, extra special treatment, such as slightly more SP coverage, was reserved for recently acceded WTO members (including China), as well as countries classified as 'small and vulnerable'.

In reference to the distinct, but still linked, question of the SSM concept, negotiations moved more slowly or indeed often not at all. According to Robert Wolfe's reading, the principles and commercial implications of the SSM were never adequately explored by members prior to July 2008. For some actors, this was due to a mistaken notion that the SSM would be somehow easier to negotiate than SPs. As Wolfe summarizes it, there were essentially two core disputes with the SSM: first, how to design an operational trigger, in terms of price or volume, that would be deemed justifiable; and second, whether such a tool would work in reference to lower Doha tariff levels or existing Uruguay Round tariff levels. Underpinning these points were deeper differences over the purpose of the SSM: should it be designed to manage the potential negative consequences of Doha-related liberalization, or should it be an instrument for any kind of market disruption, whether or not due to import surges?[144] Once again, the US opinion has consistently been conservative, arguing that the SSM should have a range of conditions attached to it, including limitations on the number of products that would be eligible as well as treating it as a 'transitional tool' that would be eliminated at the end of the Doha implementation period.[145] As with SPs, countries such as Thailand, Malaysia, and Argentina were also worried about the potential for the SSM to be used indiscriminately. Such views ran contrary to the G33's long-held opinion that the SSM should be 'simple, effective and easy to implement', for use in relation to any import surge and without any termination clause.[146] In short, the conditions were set for an acrimonious showdown at the next major gathering, a 'mini-ministerial' in Geneva.

5.3.3 *The July 2008 package*

This final subsection discusses the most recent period of struggle over the legitimacy of the G33's agenda. The July 2008 meeting was significant for further exposing the political tensions surrounding the SSM. Spanning nine days of tense negotiations, the gathering eventually ended in a stalemate, overshadowed by recriminations and a pervasive sense of mistrust on many sides.[147] The SSM problem was cited by many as a primary cause of the breakdown, one that appeared to be 'technical', but was in fact profoundly political, reflecting alternative orthodox and heterodox visions on the use of defensive trade policy instruments.[148] In the process, it marked a renewed assault on the potential effectiveness of the SSM as originally conceived by G33 members.

The major blockage centred on the G33 idea that the SSM could be used to temporarily raise tariffs above existing Uruguay Round bound rates (the size of the increase being known as the 'remedy'). This proposal, which was endorsed most vociferously by Kamal Nath, the charismatic lead Indian negotiator, was again justified by an appeal to protecting subsistence farmers from subsidized import surges. A significant objective for India was earning an SSM that was free from excessive conditionalities, not only for commercial reasons but also for its self-identified status as a 'leader of the Global South'. In this sense, Nath, like Celso Amorim, the Brazilian foreign minister, consistently drew upon the pre-existing symbolic power attached to the normative appeal of 'helping the poor'.[149] But other G33 members beyond India, such as China, arguably needed the SSM more urgently. To recall the data in Figure 5.3, China has little 'water' between its bound and applied rates, a consequence of its demanding accession to the WTO. For instance, Beijing's maximum allowable tariff on soybeans is only 3%. The G33 proposed that the SSM should be allowed to raise bound tariffs by at least 5%, with disagreements among coalition members over whether a cap on tariff hikes should be set at between 30 and 70%.

In contrast, the US, led by Schwab, along with other major agricultural exporters within the Cairns group, condemned such treatment on the SSM. One US approach to limit access to SSM remedies was to insist upon a high volume-based 'trigger' or threshold before the instrument could be operationalized. A figure of 150% (of the base import volume) was suggested. Other conditions included a proposed limit on the number of lines that could avail the SSM within a 12-month period or a demand for evidence that domestic prices were indeed falling in tandem with the surge (a 'cross-check'). At one point, director general Lamy floated his own compromise, which involved SSM remedies surpassing pre-Doha bindings by up to 15% when import volumes rose by 140% over a three-year average.[150] But by the seventh day, this proposal was declared inadequate by a larger group of around 100 countries, which included the G33, revealing that opposition was widespread.[151] On the penultimate day, Lamy proposed discarding the trigger system altogether and replacing it with a more qualitative assessment of 'demonstrable harm' caused by import surges. This suggestion was backed by India, but the US refused. In the main negotiations, the US became increasingly agitated with the assertiveness of China and India, both of whom were blamed for stymieing the talks.[152] The US was most concerned that an SSM in the hands of China would enable Beijing to undo its accession commitments, such as restricting imports of US soybeans. If such an outcome arose, a Doha deal would be politically unsaleable in Washington.[153] In the end, the talks collapsed with no agreement.

In sum, as Wolfe expressed it, many members failed to adequately read the fault lines on the SSM prior to July 2008. Serious engagements were arguably left too late. One could have speculated that a breakdown might have been avoided if there was '[b]etter research, more preparation, and more negotiations'.[154] However, through 2009 and 2010, the SSM impasse continued to plague the Doha negotiations, with positions that did not radically change, notwithstanding the conducting of further background analytical research.[155] The major agricultural exporters have continued to renew their attacks on the tool, shifting the burden of proof from the original G33 vision of safeguarding vulnerable farmers to the question of avoiding restrictions on 'normal trade'. In conclusion, these demands for conditionalities need to be considered in light of two core sets of concerns. First, to recall the discussion in Section 5.1, the US has been a regular user of the existing Uruguay Round-designed SSG, an instrument that contains far less onerous usage restrictions than the imagined SSM for Southern countries. For instance, there are no limits on the number of times a country can invoke the SSG, while the US in particular has raised its own tariffs beyond bound rates. Second, many G33 members face enduring resource constraints that necessitate an SSM that could be activated quickly in response to an import surge. An SSM weighed down with conditions on use would, in short, effectively disable it from meaningful operation.

5.4 Conclusion

When examined through the lens of symbolic power, what are the major conclusions that can be drawn from this case study? In comparison with the cotton chapter, which largely pivoted around orthodox, offensive debates over competitiveness, this case has been preoccupied with broader struggles over heterodox, defensive concerns in agricultural trade. The major objective has been to investigate how a particular set of Southern heretical interests has evolved through the WTO system over a period of around ten years. This recent negotiating history began with examining how the concept of the development box arose in the late 1990s, before being translated into the notion of 'strategic products' in 2003 and, finally, incorporated into the Doha agenda as the policy instruments of SPs and the SSM in 2004. The evolution of the G33 agenda has been very complex but, on the basis of the preceding analysis, there are four main sets of points which can be made here.

First, despite the less prominent position of many G33 countries in the history of the GATT/WTO system, these members have been partly effective at legitimizing some of their agricultural interests into a reformed AoA. This accomplishment, although still fragile and incomplete, needs to be acknowledged, particularly when compared to how the Uruguay Round meanings of food security were narrowly conceived with Northern countries in mind. Following Bourdieu, I have placed considerable emphasis on understanding how classification contests in the WTO policy game shape, but in no way preset, the scope for deliberation—in terms of agendas and modalities at lower levels of abstraction—and are thus a central stake in the gruelling struggle for symbolic power. Once a classification is concretized into an 'officially' recognized text, the actor whose political interests are attached to the classification tends to acquire a greater stock of symbolic power. In other words, they become more insulated from critique when all members of the institution have at least nominally 'anointed' them. Thus, the codification of the G33's heterodox taxonomy in the July Framework of 2004 was significant for increasing the prospect that stronger SDT policy tools could be created. In short, actors do not start new trade talks with equal volumes of symbolic power, but are constrained by the symbolic power contests of the past which, in turn, become crystallized into 'objectified' legal forms. Without adequately unpacking these patterns, one would miss the everyday, opportunistic, and at times subtle efforts to explore gaps in the WTO linguistic market.

Second, one can see how the struggle over symbolic power is, at the same time, a struggle over groups. In the early days of the development box, only eight Southern countries participated in its conceptualization, but by the Cancún Ministerial in 2003, 33 Members had joined forces and, by 2005, this group had enlarged to 42, with even more countries lending political sympathy. At the July 2008 meeting, around 100 countries registered support for the agenda. Frames such as the development box did not simply point to an imagined 'missing link' in the AoA, but offered a means by which different agents could coalesce into a group with the aim of acquiring institutional recognition and, thus, to win a place in the political order. As Bourdieu would express it, 'The power to impose and to inculcate a vision of divisions, that is, the power to make visible and explicit social divisions that are implicit, is political power par excellence.'[156] Such efforts are, however, not easy to engineer in trade policy, not only due to internal group frictions, but also because I have explained how outside critics have sought to tarnish the symbolic power of the G33 cause. In this regard, one can point to moments in the development box phase or in the post-Hong Kong Ministerial period after 2005, where the notion of compulsory power provides some extra analytical insights, notably in respect to US-led attacks that have downgraded the expectations of G33 countries.

Third, and closely related to the work of group-making, the argument has underscored the existence of a reoccurring and interdependent relationship between symbolic power and institutional power. Institutional supporters of G33 countries made significant contributions at several stages, including helping to maintain the visibility of the declared problems, organizing research and policy analysis, drafting official submissions, and strengthening group identity. Each organization within this loose network of institutional power held, or could generate, sources of symbolic power that could be utilized by G33 members, either directly or tacitly (depending upon their position in the chain of legitimation). Such work enhanced the recognition and uniqueness of the G33 in relation to other agricultural interests. Again, not all these inputs were purposefully exploited by the G33 and such work does not ensure successful negotiation outcomes, but it is safe to say that without the activism of ICTSD, the South Centre, and the FAO, the question of SPs and the SSM would probably not be occupying such a key position in the Doha agenda.

Finally, despite these developments, it is important not to overstress the explanatory value of the conceptual framework on symbolic power. As the Doha negotiations advanced through to July 2008 and beyond, major exporters have steadily eroded the potential operational value of the concepts of SPs and the SSM. It remains to be seen how far this renewed orthodox assault will go. Over time, there has been a dilution of the original potency of the G33 agenda. In the larger picture, this also helps to clarify that one person's view of 'ambition' in the WTO house on Lake Geneva is another person's version of 'timidity'. Mapping the boundaries of the linguistic market is important if one is to uncover what makes some notions acquire the appearance of being 'unconventional' and how, in turn, the definition of 'inappropriate' can be controlled by certain actors. When analysed critically and with an eye on the disparities between WTO members, the G33 agenda has always represented what I would suggest is a rather weak critique, one that largely 'makes sense' to orthodoxy, but does not fundamentally threaten it.

6

Conclusion

Questions of power are necessarily at the centre of the study of politics and no account of the WTO system can afford to avoid at least an acknowledgement of the concept. A closer examination of power can help us to understand why the structures and rules of the trading order take their objectified forms, how the actions of agents are either enabled or disabled, and what distributional outcomes have been achieved. In the preceding chapters of this book, my argument has sought to show how one can be inspired by a sociologically informed understanding of power in order to explain processes of change within the WTO system. Specifically, the argument has concentrated on analysing the strategies adopted by Southern countries in their pursuit of a more equitable trading order. This type of enquiry was deemed necessary because critical concepts of power and legitimacy have tended to be absent not only in the literature on this important institution, but also with regards to the politics of trade in general. From an historical perspective, the book began with the propensity on the part of many WTO scholars either to overemphasize legalization and institutionalized cooperation, or to bind concepts of power too narrowly to a single reading, namely the actor-based, direct, coercive understanding. My argument is that each of these approaches betrays certain limitations which, in turn, have cut short, or worked against, the emergence of more critical appraisals of power.

To address these intellectual shortcomings, I have been motivated by Bourdieu's theorizing on symbolic power, a malleable conceptual framework which captures how language is intertwined with power. In particular, the notion alerts us to the struggles over the legitimation of the social world, including the visions and dispositions held by agents. Since symbolic power often takes latent, subtle, or disguised forms, one needs to spend time unravelling its properties and uses. In scholarly terms, this necessitates analyses that reconfigure the argument of the conventional wisdom and probe the complex methods of justification used by political actors. These methods can appear systematic and mechanistic at certain times, haphazard and opportunistic at other times. However, I have also been careful not to cast Bourdieu as a prophet or a seer, one to be slavishly followed. Rather, I have borrowed and adapted the conceptual tools I considered valuable for an empirical investigation of Southern agricultural trade policy-making. The objective was never to arrive at a single master category or theory of power, but to open IPE and IR scholars, and WTO analysts in particular, to a more rigorous and, at the same time, flexible interrogation of this central concept. Thus, the point has been not only to debate the value of a Bourdieusian framework, but to note when and why the traditional concepts of power retain analytical usefulness. Through the empirical examination of two Southern-centric agricultural coalitions, this book has aimed to critically dissect how symbolic power is manifested in the WTO system. The main results can be organized here into three sets of concluding points:

(1) an encapsulation of major conceptual themes
(2) a review of the main empirical findings
(3) a discussion of broader implications of the study.

6.1 Symbolic power in the universe of power

In writing this book, I have been driven by an interest to go beyond the compulsory definition of power in order to explore new ways of understanding international trade politics broadly, and WTO talks in particular. The Dahlian, coercive, agent-centric vision of power—the capability of actor A to force actor B to yield to their wishes—has historically been read as the most 'fundamental' or 'intuitive' sense of power, in both political theory and practice.[1] This conceptualization has strongly informed academic analysis of the WTO system, not only when scholars appeal directly to 'power' as a term, but also implicitly through numerous other references, including the common dichotomy between 'power' and 'rules'. There is no question that we need this notion of power in order to point to those examples of more aggressive trade diplomacy, the fist on the negotiating table to use one metaphor. Coercion 'works' in trade relations, in the sense that political actions that merit the term repeatedly appear and generate consequences that need explaining. However, I have also argued that the notion of compulsory power is analytically limited in respect to what political action it privileges. Rooted in a conservative and materialist understanding of behaviour, users of the concept tend to depict trade relations as rather resilient or, indeed, even static. My argument is that if one interprets power only in this sense of domination or conflict, there exists a risk of missing other signs of power that could be crucial for explaining the struggle over trade politics.

The notion of institutional power, as conceived in the Barnett and Duvall framework, offers a way to consider how political relations are mediated through organizational complexes of various forms.[2] Power is at work in the making, reproduction, and undermining of international institutions, of which the WTO system represents an excellent illustration. As a concept, institutional power draws attention to the direct and indirect means through which certain players are able to constrain the movements of others, notably via rules, codes, and decision-making practices. In particular, it highlights how certain interests may be nullified over time due to seemingly 'normal' or 'quieter' processes of political incorporation. Depending upon the empirical context, it may help us learn more about which interests become attached to agenda-setting processes and which concerns fail to gain traction.[3] Again, this concept is quite naturally bound up with any evaluation of WTO negotiations and thus is relevant to my argument. Nevertheless, institutional power, as conventionally understood, also has limitations, particularly when compared to the notion of symbolic power. Perhaps most significantly from my perspective, although institutional power does thinly note the question of legitimacy, the concept is less useful for explicating the manifold ways in which language is intertwined with power within organizational settings. It is this richer, sociological sense of legitimation processes that Bourdieu's conceptual tools aim to address.

In response to these criticisms, a framework on symbolic power has been advanced in order to better understand why and how the structures of the WTO system take their objectified forms, and the extent to which political agents are enabled in their actions. It is worth clarifying here what I see as five major contributions of this Bourdieusian conceptual approach to the study of trade politics. First, it offers new objects of analysis that are not present or are underplayed in conventional notions of power. Language is taken seriously as a complex and difficult symbolic system to understand, one which both expresses and constitutes other forms of power. Unlike the compulsory-power vision, which tends to ignore linguistic entry requirements as some byproduct or 'ephemeral' feature of political life, the notion of symbolic power probes the historical making of key classifications and contested definitions of the 'conventional wisdom' (orthodoxy to heterodoxy). Other complementary conceptual tools, including framing and mimicry, were used in the spirit of Bourdieu to tease out how symbolic power is polished and tarnished. In the wider context, the book also highlighted how the social space of trade policy-making features 'taken-for-granted', doxic relations between agents and the political world. Again, compared to common positivistic treatments of power that ignore the space occupied by the body, the notion of doxa addresses the internalization of power and, subsequently, its externalization in the form of durable dispositions of diplomatic practice.

Second, once power is understood to operate through acts of linguistic construction, I then considered how it enhances our understanding of key political processes. Symbolic power is never evenly distributed or, to be more precise, some material practices are surrounded by a greater degree of social (mis)recognition than others. In particular, a Bourdieusian approach is valuable in terms of unpacking the intricate schemes of justification that are common within WTO politics, an issue which is particularly salient for agricultural debates. My argument has explored how the contest for symbolic power should be grasped through different temporal and spatial dimensions. Over the long term, this is reflected in how major taxonomies, categories, scripts, and tropes, such as those crafted in the Uruguay Round, continue to constrain the scope for deliberation in the modern linguistic market. The trade policy game thus has a particular political genesis and trajectory, which requires mapping. Such a point is admittedly captured in some uses of the institutional power notion or in wider constructivist theorizing that has examined the legal evolution of WTO rules and norms. However, Bourdieu's perspective differs in how deeply the politics of law is dissected, uncovering the many euphemistic guises, facades, and subtle sleights of hand used by interested agents. These elements are woven into a larger tapestry of power, providing further clues as to how and why material interests are defended and contested. Crucially, they only make sense to those who are immersed within the space of the game, who understand the location of allies and adversaries or, in other terms, the differences between orthodox and heterodox values.

The book has thus underscored how symbolic power can be conceived as a ceaseless, often arduous, social struggle for recognition; it is a labour of creating and denigrating the meanings of the commercial world. Such work is intensive because symbolic power is like a type of 'credit' which, depending upon the empirical context, tends to rise in profitability following a long period of institutionalization.[4] This helps to explain why the book has needed to focus on quotidian practices in WTO politics. Hence, in one key sense, although symbolic power finds its high point in law—the public codification and formalization of 'particular' interests into the 'universal'—one needs to trace how such moments are often the product of considerable prior deliberation. To concentrate only on major gatherings that are bathed in the glare of media cameras would ignore how the legitimacy of, say, a ministerial declaration, can only be properly understood in the historical context of what it excludes as much as what it seals under the name of 'consensus'. Strategies of symbolic glorification and discrimination are therefore put to work, and continually revised, long before the ministerial. In another respect, I have also argued that the battle over symbolic power cannot be easily foreseen, particularly within multi-issue, multi-actor environments. Thus, to hedge against the possibility of 'misfiring' or the unknown, agents often anxiously (over)elaborate upon their reasoning to ensure the advance of a particular legitimation process. Once again, to risk repeating myself, if one remained fixated on calculating, arm-twisting demonstrations of trade diplomacy, these quieter, everyday agenda-setting practices would become marginalized, impoverishing our explanatory analysis.

Third, and related, it can appear that the competition over symbolic power, centred on the attractive banks of Lake Geneva, acquires a certain autonomy from the material world it supposedly represents. The trade policy game seems to turn upon itself, with players engrossed in the chips and prizes that they have collectively valued. But this depiction is only partially correct. The stakes for controlling symbolic power are high because they shape the configuration and stabilization of particular economic interests. As Bourdieu expresses it, 'codification goes hand in glove with discipline and the normalization of practices'.[5] Yet, as I have argued through the empirical cases, symbolic power should not be crudely depicted as a structuralist notion, but rather, since it can only be grasped relationally, necessitates an examination of heretical protest. A relational approach does not assume fully constituted actors with immutable subjectivities but implies active resistance, even if such resistance is imagined and articulated through the prism of orthodox schemes of perception.[6] Unlike the fixed rationality presumed by mainstream neoclassical economics, many forms of symbolic power are arbitrary, unstable, and ambiguous at the moment of creation, yet may acquire a post-hoc rationalization through the passage of time. The outcome of making certain classifications 'real' is doubly significant because, in addition to shaping economic inequities, such contests also inform the making of classes themselves. Thus, far from denying agency, this analysis helps to reveal more precisely what spaces for political expression actually exist in WTO diplomacy and how, in particular, the making of symbolic power moulds, but in no way predetermines, the legitimation of group identities.

Fourth, at a higher level of abstraction, in a manner reminiscent of Bourdieu's metatheory, this book has aimed to critique, dissolve, and overcome what I view as unhelpful conceptual dichotomies, which plague the analysis of power. Most notably, this includes efforts to transcend the opposition between 'power' versus 'legitimation' or 'interests' versus 'ideas', which are, in turn, reflective of master dichotomies between 'structure' versus 'agency' or 'objectivism' versus 'subjectivism'. These distinctions, which are sometimes strictly policed, are found in conventional IPE theorizing on trade politics, including some thinner versions of constructivist thinking. Instead, I argue here that the historical form of the international trading system, including its distribution of resources and potential for political opportunities, rests upon the interdependence between symbolic structures and material structures. Significantly, and responding to calls made by other theorists, this book has aimed to explore the ways in which the three chosen forms of power—compulsory, institutional, and symbolic—relate to each other, rather than setting up a 'gladiatorial' battle between them for intellectual supremacy.[7]

On this point, let me stress how I have sought to advance such an agenda. In one crucial sense, my argument is not only that a vision of power that is fixated on materialism represents a narrow interpretation but, in addition, how a symbolic-power framework can help us to better grasp under what conditions forms of materialism, including coercive acts, acquire added analytical meaning. For instance, actions of compulsory power are sometimes used to deal quickly with a threat that cannot be accomplished by more time-consuming and strenuous processes of symbolic power. The coercive move may be used to cut short or disfigure a rival process of legitimation, but one would need to examine the content of such symbolic power to understand why compulsory power was being exercised at that point in time. Equally, if following the deployment of compulsory power, a certain actor has a damaged reputation, it may be very necessary for them to rebuild their stock of symbolic power around an issue. Such episodes reveal that coercion is usually rare and expensive because of the fundamental need to appeal to different logics of legitimacy in politics, a systemic trend that has arguably become more widespread. Indeed, because of the importance of protecting symbolic power, the agent who has potential compulsory power may resort to exercising their dictates behind closed doors; that is, away from other audiences who could expose the contradictions and cruelty of such measures.

Finally, it is worth noting again the core affinities and distinctions between symbolic power and the other two critical concepts—structural and productive—that were left behind in Chapter 2. Symbolic power is not a radically new notion when one considers how, in the larger theoretical context, both structural power and productive power are also alert to complex social processes of constitution. The Foucauldian ideas of power/knowledge and performativity, the neo-Gramscian sense of manufacturing the consent of the dominated, and the classical Marxist appeal to ideology as a 'mask' for power, can all be closely compared to Bourdieu's own conceptual ambitions. Yet, beyond the perennial research-design risk of juggling too many conceptual balls, I have also discussed drawbacks with both these structural and productive power notions. One caveat centres on asking whether structural power and productive power are too unwieldy or blunt to capture the labyrinthine methods of justification surrounding WTO negotiations. Another related concern is the extent to which the potential for political critique and agent-led strategizing is still underplayed in such notions. Symbolic power is a slightly different concept in how it allows for the durability and inertia of certain political relations and conditions of (mis)recognition, yet still facilitates scope for examining how agents actively remake the social world through historical instruments of cognitive construction. Importantly, the definition of symbolic power cannot be succinctly fixed and applied to all situations but rather should be treated as an 'open concept' that acquires meaning through the labour of empirical research. In short, in a point Bourdieu often underscored, concepts are no good unless they are put into action in a 'systematic fashion'.[8]

6.2 Empirical findings

The purpose of this book was not to investigate all Southern countries, coalitions, and issues in WTO agricultural talks but, instead, involved selection of two groups to illuminate a range of offensive and defensive concerns. With the conceptual framework in mind, what key conclusions can be drawn from these enquiries? One set of findings concerns the relationship between time, space, and symbolic power. With respect to both cases, I argued how in phases prior to major multilateral gatherings, the boundaries of the WTO linguistic market became more unstable and porous, facilitating discursive openings that were later constrained (or indeed closed off) under the search for 'consensus'. For instance, prior to restarting the AoA negotiations in 2000 or in other periods before ministerial conferences, a broader range of opinions—both orthodox and heterodox—were voiced by political actors. Thus the construction of the 'problem of cotton' required a gradual accumulation of symbolic power in the months prior to the Cancún Ministerial in 2003. The dossier could not have been produced on the eve of the summit because such processes of conceptualization and mobilization require time. Likewise, in the other case study, the notion of the development box was nurtured over a three-year period of intellectual and institutional gestation. Throughout, I have placed particular importance on understanding how classification schemes during these periods are a fundamental prize in the struggle for symbolic power. However, even if opening framing efforts do gain a degree of validity, this does not mean that the legitimation process will move in a quasi-functional, logical fashion towards an agent's desired material outcome.

In part, this is because the argument has also underscored that symbolic power is very important in distinct legal 'writing moments', which call for actors to declare their political commitments. This is most obvious in the drafting of texts at the ministerial level or in the case of the July Framework in 2004. The contest for symbolic power is particularly intense at these points because what is at stake, under timed constraints, is the legal codification of particular political interests which are, in turn, intertwined with commercial interests. In these high-profile events, all members have some sense of the political configurations that they are seeking to at least 'crystallize' into textual form. The most potent concentration of symbolic power is found in the ministerial—an official space of both formalized rituals and underhand practices—where all members are potentially prepared to 'lend' a degree of their own legitimacy in order to construct and justify the 'universal' agenda. When the full membership has participated in this process, each actor who has successfully incorporated their own interests into the text can now claim that they work on behalf of the 'universal'. This provides such members with greater insulation when faced with future critiques of their actions. For instance, to recall the cotton case again, the US used a General Council meeting in December 2003 to begin the process of legally justifying the new distinction between 'trade' and 'development', but it took the July Framework to make it seem authoritative and certifiable, an effort that became naturalized over time. The C4's own complicity in the counter-framing exercise enabled the US, along with its allies, to better control the management of the problem.

In another sense, while political attention tends to gravitate towards core writing moments where time is (made) short, one should not miss how the process of WTO negotiations through time tends to solidify or even further constrain the boundaries of the linguistic market. Such processes are slow, interspersed by official or informal proposals, signals, and engagements. From one perspective, this movement towards fixing meanings should not necessarily be viewed as a problem. For instance, if an actor wins an earlier classification struggle—such as with the G33's codification of Southern understandings of food security—then the establishment of modalities under such categories will probably provide (at least some of) the policy tools desired. On the other hand, however, as has been witnessed in the Doha Round, the formulation of modalities takes time or, perhaps more precisely in many circumstances, the most privileged actors try to manipulate time to their own advantage. In the G33 case, particularly after the Hong Kong Ministerial in 2005, one saw renewed efforts on the part of the US and major exporters to belittle and degrade the symbolic power attached to SPs and the SSM. For the cotton case, in the most recent period, the C4 have been waiting for a larger agricultural settlement to be finalized. Waiting does not erode symbolic power as such, but it can generate anxiety on the part of those who defer and submit to timelines they cannot easily control, timelines that are often hidden or unclear.

In turn, this brings us to another set of findings centred on the analytical relationships between symbolic power and the conventional notions of compulsory power and institutional power. Bourdieu's framework is not some conceptual *deus ex machina* capable of encapsulating and revealing every aspect of power. It has certain limits. Thus, the compulsory power explanation is most valuable in reference to particular moments in WTO talks. For example, in the aftermath of the Doha Ministerial, when talk on the 'development box' gathered pace, the US tried to splinter the group of Southern countries who promoted the issue. Elsewhere, in respect to the cotton story, I explained how the US chose to pressure director general Supachai at the Cancún Ministerial when he sought to appeal personally for a rapid result on the issue. By attempting to force adjustments on to others, such actions can certainly have important consequences. But these moves are not without political limitations, even for a player such as the US. One can see, for instance, how the cotton conundrum could not be resolved with compulsory power alone; rather, such acts of intimidation provided only temporary fixes for the US. Indeed, in some respects it made matters worse since, by offending so many parties, Washington was forced to return to rebuild its own volume of symbolic power on the issue. The US always reserves the option to produce actions that commonly fall under the category of compulsory power—a phone call from the White House, a warning to cut an aid deal, a threat to shift to another trade forum—but these incidents are also exceptional (and thus precious) in comparison with the daily, micro-level labour of constructing symbolic power.

My argument has also underlined at different stages why and how the links between symbolic power and institutional power are significant for explaining processes and outcomes. In the G33 case, for instance, the task of refining the meaning of heretical indicators on SPs required the resources of the South Centre and the International Centre for Trade and Sustainable Development. The research that these institutions provided or facilitated was, in turn, utilized by G33 countries to enhance the wider recognition of their own interests and disarm opponents who disputed their wishes. Similarly, in the cotton story I explained how the incorporation of organizations such as the World Bank into monitoring the problem was crucial for universalizing the lower ambitions of the US (relative to the C4). Through multiple events and publications, these international bodies helped gradually to shift the centre of the linguistic market away from the C4-attached focus on competitiveness, which included attention to US subsidies. In short, both cases show how the concept of symbolic power can often work in a symbiotic relationship with the notion of institutional power. These institutions or, perhaps more precisely, the seemingly apolitical professionals housed within them, can offer tokens for formal political agents to use in their trade struggles. But the profit of these symbolic resources, that is, the degree to which they 'pass' as legitimate in the trade field, 'varies in direct proportion to the real or visible distance (independence) between the praiser and the praised'.[9] The legitimacy of the trade expert is thus dependent upon not only how they 'make sense' to (particular) states and their problems, but also how they can disguise political objectives (which often align with the state) under the screen of 'universalism', 'impartiality', or 'disinterestedness'.

Finally, this book has also helped, in small ways, to better explain some of the economic effects of WTO rules. In one respect, my argument has contributed to understanding the remarkable lasting impact of the Uruguay Round settlement in agriculture, including the difficulty of reforming its complex architecture of rules. Thus the cases outlined have explored how economic privileges are preserved in this area of world trade. At the same time, I have been equally preoccupied with examining the attempts of others to minimize the material inequities associated with such rules. The most tangible, if still indirect, outcome in this regard can be seen in how the C4 associated themselves with the successful Brazil cotton case against the US. Yet, from a normative perspective, the book did not explicitly stray into defending a personal preference on the Doha Round and adopt some sermonizing tone on the strategies of the countries under examination. To be clear, I certainly do not advocate every effort advanced by the C4 and the G33, nor have I aimed to demonize every action taken by the US. It was noted, for instance, that the resolution of the C4 problem depends upon more than the abolition of Northern subsidies, particularly in the light of the growth of synthetic fibres. Likewise, the idea of SPs and, in particular, the SSM, will create uneven distributional effects, and therefore political frictions, across Southern countries. Thus one should not assume that food security, however defined, will inevitably be enhanced in all Southern countries if such instruments become law. Multilateral trade policy is no panacea for food security in the context of agricultural markets that are shaped through not only policy legacies specific to each nation, but also by the financialization of commodities, the price of energy, and the worsening impact of climate change.

6.3 Wider implications

In what ways could this Bourdieusian study of the political economy of WTO practices hold research implications for the broader analysis of international trade, as well as IPE and IR? As a starting point, the intellectual environment today is arguably more receptive to critical conceptual approaches. The development of international political sociology and sociological rethinking in IPE, including trade politics, speaks to the desire for alternative frameworks. These debates should certainly be welcomed. Yet there remains considerable scope for building and enhancing research agendas on world politics through the theory contained in this book. By way of example, and to further provoke discussion, I sketch out here three potential avenues that extend the main themes already addressed.

First, examining symbolic power in relation to the space of 'the international' offers a fresh approach for understanding the ties between knowledge construction and agency. How and why certain material interests win over others in different issue domains is, of course, an enduring problem for

IPE scholarship. But such questions are difficult to answer when the movement and reproduction of power becomes obfuscated, depoliticized, and thus, in Bourdieu's terminology, misrecognized. In one major sense, therefore, a deeper sociological excavation of power is needed to uncover the many techniques and mechanisms of legitimation deployed within the modern capitalist system. From the legal codification of particular agendas, to the making of dominant theoretical frameworks, to the explicit and tacit regulation of economic cooperation, and to the internalization of doxic presuppositions, the struggle for accumulating and transforming capital is unrelenting, experimental, and resists easy summation. The circuits of symbolic power in the world economy are made all the more complex because privileged elites often need to appeal to different audiences (sometimes simultaneously) and therefore play multiple legitimacy games, each one of which may obey alternative logics and rewards. At the same time, one also needs to reckon with how the problems of capitalism continually provoke forms of social critique and, in turn, how the system renews itself through the incorporation of such critiques (yet often selectively and in a distorted manner to disarm rival heterodoxies from becoming a new orthodoxy).

How might one advance IPE research that could respond to these tricky analytical problems? Different projects could be suggested. For one, it remains remarkable how the world of trade politics, including its population of political and academic players, continues to lack any strong sense of critical reflexivity or, in other words, a sociology of itself.[10] What is sorely needed is a political investigation into the making of trade experts. Such a study could plot how, in particular, authoritative figures struggle to acquire legitimacy among themselves and shape the material stakes of the trading game. Research in this mould could also offer new resources for understanding historical change in the trading system, notably the shift from a closeted community of insider intellectuals and bureaucratic officials to a heterogeneous space featuring competing groups of acknowledged players. But a Bourdieusian vision is not limited to trade. The political economy of finance, long transfixed by rationalist accounts, is also ripe for critical interrogation. Here, a few constructivist IPE scholars have shown the way by exploring the role of meaning-making and cognitive schemes in financial relations.[11] But other enquiries could also be explored, including how financial elites organize within 'transnational guilds' that straddle state boundaries, how political classes and financiers become embroiled in hubristic attitudes, the ways in which the 'social purpose' of finance is promoted, and, in a crucial but neglected theme, how incentive methods are used to nurture and socialize new cadres into becoming financial professionals.[12]

Second, within the larger IR community, an interest in Bourdieu has been most obvious in the literature on the international politics of security. In this area, researchers have used his thinking tools to undertake a re-examination of the links between culture, political identity, and diplomacy in the post-Cold War period.[13] The best work has surrounded the so-called 'Paris School' of security studies, which has unpicked webs of relations between European security professionals (police, intelligence agents, military counterterrorist players, and border guards) in order to reveal a richer political process of problematizing (in)security.[14] Inspired by such explorations, there is arguably a need for further research into how physical violence is, in a practical sense, intertwined with symbolic violence within different spheres of political life. For instance, how can we compare and contrast the strategies used by different militaries to legitimize force, including the justification and denigration of symbolic resources at the UN and other universal bodies?[15] How do wider cultural narratives of 'national defence' and forms of honour associated with 'public duty' become sedimented into the minds of different social groups, in the process concealing and justifying the reoccurring horror of militarized violence? Or in the spirit of Loïc Wacquant's work on advanced urban marginality, how do politicians and 'security experts' stigmatize certain problem populations on the basis of geography, instead of connecting the lines of historical responsibility between practices of penalization, bouts of civil unrest, ethno-racial divisions, and the erosion of the social state model?[16]

Third, in order to explain the arguments contained in the previous chapters, I have illuminated the importance of detailed, relational process tracing methods. Too often, even among those who are sympathetic to a Bourdieusian reading in IR, the hard work of empirical analysis is either underplayed or inevitably curtailed due to article-length constraints on space. In some ways, as discussed in Chapter 2, similar problems afflict those researchers who gravitate towards structural power and productive power frameworks of analysis. Book-length expositions are thus vital for exploring the true value of the concepts debated in this study. But beyond process tracing, IPE and IR research would also benefit from examining the potential utility of ethnographic methodological techniques. It is through careful ethnography that the researcher can immerse themselves in social settings, capturing in the process apparently mundane expressions of power that may offer important clues for understanding the complexity of political life. From this viewpoint, research objects should be selected cautiously and probed with a variety of tools. If Bourdieu offers anything for the study of world politics it therefore lies in how his vision of intellectual work re-examines the relationship between theory and practice. Theoretical ideas should not assume a totalizing meaning for all times and locations but, rather, should be considered as flexible resources that are repeatedly refined on the basis of what is discovered in the field.

In sum, in writing this book I have tried to conceive of power in the world trading system not simply in terms of units or locations, but more broadly as the mobilization of relations of forces. Power does, in part, derive from, and reside within, particular physical bodies and centres. But one must understand the transnational political space within which the symbolic labourers occupy their positions, a space which has been socially constructed across time and territories to leave certain possibilities open and others closed. Although it is easier to think in terms of substantial objects within a particular historical snapshot, one must endeavour continually to assemble social facts in order to better understand their collective sets of relations. In the analysis of power, as elsewhere in the social sciences, 'the real is the relational'.[17]

APPENDIX A

Extract taken from WTO, 'Proposed Modalities for Cotton Under the Mandate of the Hong Kong Ministerial Decision', Communication from the Co-Sponsors of the Sectoral Initiative in Favour of Cotton, 1 March 2006 (TN/AG/SCC/GEN/4), 2.

Operationalizing the term 'more ambitious'

More ambitious reduction must be construed, as the co-sponsors of the Sectoral Initiative in Favour of Cotton already outlined in their contribution of 17 February 2006 (TN/AG/GEN/12 and TN/AG/SCC/GEN/3), in relation to the general result of the agriculture negotiations on domestic support.

Correction coefficient *(c)*: the co-sponsors of the Sectoral Initiative in Favour of Cotton propose the following formula for determining the specific rate of reduction of the AMS for cotton:

Rg = General reduction as a percentage; final result for reduction of the AMS
Rc = Reduction for cotton as a percentage; final result for cotton in order to meet the requirement for specificity and more ambition.

$$Rc = Rg + \frac{(100 - Rg)*100}{3*Rg}$$

This formula meets Members' expectations:

- It provides an ambitious result for cotton in the event of a modest result in agriculture;
- it imposes a higher level of ambition in the event of an ambitious result in agriculture;
- it is degressive in relation to the additional effort required for cotton based on the level of ambition of the result for agriculture in general.

For the purpose of illustration, the following table shows hypothetical Rg values and the corresponding Rc values, starting at 60 per cent, which is deemed to be a modest result.

Rg %	>>>	*Rc %*	Difference %
60	>>>	*82.2*	22.2
70	>>>	*84.3*	14.3
80	>>>	*88.3*	8.3
90	>>>	*93.7*	3.7
100	>>>	*100*	0

APPENDIX B

The following extract is taken from the 10 July 2008 revised draft modalities report submitted by the Chair of the Committee on Agriculture, Crawford Falconer, to WTO members. It details proposed qualitative indicators that could be used to guide the selection of special products (SPs) within Southern countries. Source: WTO, 'Revised Draft Modalities for Agriculture', 10 July 2008 (TN/AG/W/4/Rev.3), Annex F, 51–52.

Annex F: Illustrative List of Indicators for the Designation of Special Products

1. The product is a staple food, or is a part of the basic food basket of the developing country Member through, *inter alia*, laws and regulations, including administrative guidelines or national development plan or policy or historical usage, or the product contributes significantly to the nutritional or caloric intake of the population.
2. A significant proportion of the domestic consumption of the product in its natural, unprocessed or processed form, in a particular region or at a national level, is met through domestic production in the developing country Member concerned.
3. Domestic consumption of the product in the developing country Member is significant in relation to total world exports of that product; or a significant proportion of total world exports of the product are accounted for by the largest exporting country.
4. A significant proportion of the total domestic production of the product in a particular region or at the national level is produced on farms or operational land holdings of up to and including 10 hectares, or is produced on farm or operational land holdings which are of a size equal to or less than the average farm size of the developing country Member concerned, or a significant proportion of the farms or operational land holdings producing the product are up to and including 10 hectares in size or of the average farm size or less of the developing country Member concerned.
5. A significant proportion of the total agricultural population or rural labour force, in a particular region or at the national level, is employed in the production of the product.
6. A significant proportion of the producers of the product, in a particular region or at the national level, are low income, resource poor, or subsistence farmers, including disadvantaged or vulnerable communities and women or a significant proportion of the domestic production of the product is produced in disadvantaged

regions and areas including, *inter alia,* drought-prone or hilly or mountainous regions.

7. A significant proportion of the total value of agricultural production or agricultural income of households, in a particular region or at the national level, is derived from the production of the product.
8. A relatively low proportion of the product is processed in the developing country Member as compared to the world average; or the product contributes a relatively high proportion to value addition in the rural areas, in a particular region or at the national level, through its linkages to non-farm rural economic activities, including handicrafts and cottage industries or any other form of rural value addition.
9. A significant proportion of the agricultural customs tariff revenue is derived from the product in a developing country Member.
10. A significant proportion of the total food expenditure, or of the total income, of households in a particular region or at the national level in the developing country Member concerned, is spent on the product.
11. The product in respect of which product specific AMS or blue box support has been notified by any WTO Member and which has been exported by that notifying Member during any year from 1995 to the starting date of the implementation of Doha Round.
12. The productivity per worker or per hectare of the product in the developing country Member, in a particular region or at the national level, is relatively low as compared to the average productivity in the world.

Endnotes

Chapter 1

1. The classification of 'North/South', rather than 'developed/developing/least developed', will be used throughout this book as a generic name for groups of countries. This decision has been made in order to critically examine some of the major terms used by participants and analysts of the trading regime, of which 'development' is a dominant category. In this regard, I follow so-called 'post-development' theorists, including Gilbert Rist and Arturo Escobar, who have chosen to objectify 'development' in order to better explain its complex meanings and uses. See Gilbert Rist, *The History of Development: From Western Origins to Global Faith* (London: Zed Books, 2008), and Arturo Escobar, *Encountering Development: The Making and Unmaking of the Third World* (Princeton: Princeton University Press, 1995). At the same time, it is appreciated that the conceptual distinction between 'North' and 'South' in the international system is not free from definitional problems and can be traced to particular forms of politics. See Jean-Philippe Therien, 'Beyond the North-South Divide: The Two Tales of World Poverty', *Third World Quarterly*, 20 (1999), 4, 723–42.
2. Quotes taken from interviews conducted by Aileen Kwa in *Power Politics in the WTO* (Bangkok: Focus on the Global South, 2003), and Fatoumata Jawara and Aileen Kwa in *Behind the Scenes at the WTO: The Real World of International Trade Negotiations* (London: Zed Books, 2003).
3. Following the Doha Ministerial the US announced a package for Pakistani textiles worth US$476 million over three years, including quota increases of 15% in seven categories. This was widely seen as a reward for Pakistan's support for the US-led invasion of Afghanistan. See *Inside U.S. Trade*, 'White House Grants Pakistan Quota Concessions Worth Half a Billion', 15 February 2002.
4. Quoted in Ronen Palen, 'The Constructivist Underpinnings of the New International Political Economy', in Ronen Palen (ed.), *Global Political Economy: Contemporary Theories* (London: Routledge, 2000), 228.
5. This classification is drawn from Michael Barnett and Raymond Duvall, 'Power in International Politics', *International Organization*, 59 (2005), 1, 39–75.
6. Pierre Bourdieu, *Language and Symbolic Power* (Cambridge: Polity Press, 1991).
7. Pierre Bourdieu, 'What Makes a Social Class? On the Theoretical and Practical Existence of Groups', *Berkeley Journal of Sociology*, 32 (1987), 1–18, quoted at 13, italics in original.

8. In legal scholarship, the distinction can be traced to John Jackson, 'The Crumbling Institutions of the Liberal Trade System', *Journal of World Trade Law*, 12 (1978), 93–106. The same characterization appears in John Jackson, *The World Trading System: Law and Policy of International Economic Relations* (Cambridge, MA: MIT Press, 1997). Also see J. Michael Finger and Sumana Dhar, 'Do Rules Contain Power?', in Alan V. Deardorff and Robert Mitchell Stern (eds.), *Analytical and Negotiation Issues in the Global Trading System* (Ann Arbor: University of Michigan Press, 1994).
9. Robert Keohane and Joseph Nye, 'The Club Model of Multilateral Cooperation and the World Trade Organization: Problems of Democratic Legitimacy', in Roger Porter, Pierre Sauve, Arvind Subramanian, and Americo Beviglia Zampetti (eds.), *Efficiency, Equity, and, Legitimacy: The Multilateral Trading System at the Millennium* (Cambridge, MA: Brookings Institution Press, 2001).
10. For instance, see John McGinnis and Mark Movsesian, 'World Trade Constitution', *Harvard Law Review*, 114 (2000), 2, 511–605; and the work of Ernst-Ulrich Petersmann, including an early articulation in *Constitutional Functions and Constitutional Problems of International Economic Law* (Fribourg: Fribourg University Press, 1991), and 'The WTO Constitution and Human Rights', *Journal of International Economic Law*, 3 (2000), 1, 19–25. For an evaluation of the debates surrounding constitutionalization and the WTO system, see Deborah Cass, *The Constitutionalization of the World Trade Organization: Legitimacy, Democracy and Community in the International Trading System* (Oxford: Oxford University Press, 2005).
11. Judith Goldstein, Miles Kahler, Robert O. Keohane, and Anne-Marie Slaughter, 'Introduction: Legalization and World Politics', *International Organization*, 54 (2000), 3, 385–99, quoted at 389.
12. Andrew Hurrell, 'Power, Institutions, and the Production of Inequality', in Michael Barnett and Raymond Duvall (eds.), *Power in Global Governance* (Cambridge: Cambridge University Press, 2005), 34.
13. Kenneth W. Abbott, Robert O. Keohane, Andrew Moravcsik, Anne-Marie Slaughter, and Duncan Snidal, 'The Concept of Legalization', *International Organization*, 54 (2000), 3, 401–19. Also see Lisa Martin and Beth Simmons, 'Theories and Empirical Studies of International Institutions', *International Organization*, 52 (1998), 4, 729–58.
14. Asif Qureshi, *The World Trade Organisation: Implementing International Trade Norms* (Manchester: Manchester University Press, 1996).
15. Judith Goldstein and Joanne Gowa, 'US National Power and the Post-war Trading Regime', *World Trade Review*, 1 (2002), 2, 153–70.
16. Robert Keohane, 'Governance in a Partially Globalized World', *American Political Science Review*, 95 (2001), 1, 1–13, quoted at 7.
17. E. H. Carr, *The Twenty Years' Crisis 1919–1939: An Introduction to the Study of International Relations* (London: Macmillan, 1946), 177–8.
18. Robert Howse, 'The Legitimacy of the World Trade Organization', in J. Coicaud and V. Heiskanen (eds.), *The Legitimacy of International Organizations* (New York: United Nations University Press, 2001); Matthew Dunne, 'Redefining Power Orientation: A Reassessment of Jackson's Paradigm in Light of Asymmetries of Power, Negotiation, and Compliance in the GATT/WTO Dispute Settlement System', *Law and*

Policy in International Business, 34 (2002), 277–342; Joost Pauwelyn, 'The Transformation of World Trade', *Michigan Law Review*, 104 (2005), 1–66; Robert Howse, 'From Politics to Technocracy—And Back Again: The Fate of the Multilateral Trading Regime', *American Journal of International Law*, 96 (2002), 1, 94–117; and Joseph A. Conti, *Between Law and Diplomacy: The Social Contexts of Disputing at the World Trade Organization* (Stanford: Stanford University Press, 2010).

19. Andrew T. F. Lang, 'Reconstructing Embedded Liberalism: John Gerard Ruggie and Constructivist Approaches to the Study of the International Trade Regime', *Journal of International Economic Law*, 9 (2006), 1, 81–116; and Robert Wolfe, 'See You in Geneva? Legal (Mis)Representations of the Trading System', *European Journal of International Relations*, 11 (2005), 3, 339–65. Also see Martha Finnemore and Stephen Toope, 'Alternatives to "Legalization": Richer Views of Law and Politics', *International Organization*, 55 (2001), 3, 743–58. For a particularly good synthesis and critical analysis of blind spots and biases at work in the disciplines of public international law, international economic law, and comparative law, see David Kennedy, 'The Disciplines of International Law and Policy', *Leiden Journal of International Law*, 12 (1999), 1, 9–134.
20. Joseph Weiler, 'The Rule of Lawyers and the Ethos of Diplomats: Reflection on the Internal and External Legitimacy of Dispute Settlement', in Roger B. Porter, Pierre Sauvé, Arvind Subramanian, and Americo Beviglia Zampetti (eds.), *Efficiency, Equity, and Legitimacy: The Multilateral Trading System at the Millennium* (Washington, DC: Brookings Institution Press, 2001). Also see Emanuel Adler and Steven Bernstein, 'Knowledge in Power: The Epistemic Construction of Global Governance', in Michael Barnett and Raymond Duvall (eds.), *Power in Global Governance* (Cambridge: Cambridge University Press, 2005).
21. There is a long legacy of this thinking explored in more detail in Chapter 2. For example, in terms of a general history, see Ronald Findlay and Kevin H. O'Rourke, *Power and Plenty: Trade, War, and the World Economy in the Second Millennium* (Princeton: Princeton University Press, 2007). More specifically, see Albert Hirschman, *National Power and the Structure of Foreign Trade* (Berkeley: University of California Press, 1945); Jacob Viner, 'Power Versus Plenty as Objectives of Foreign Policy in the Seventeenth and Eighteenth Centuries', *World Politics*, 1 (1948), 1, 1–29; Stephen Krasner, 'State Power and the Structure of International Trade', *World Politics*, 28 (1976), 317–47; and John Barton, Judith Goldstein, Timothy Josling, and Richard Steinberg, *The Evolution of the Trade Regime: Politics, Law, and Economics of the GATT/WTO* (Princeton: Princeton University Press, 2006).
22. For a general introduction, see Rorden Wilkinson, 'The Political Economy of International Economic Law: A Neo-Gramscian Perspective', in Asif Qureshi (ed.), *Perspectives in International Economic Law* (London: Kluwer Law International, 2002). Also see Stephen Gill, 'Toward a Postmodern Prince? The Battle in Seattle as a Moment in the New Politics of Globalisation', *Millennium: Journal of International Studies*, 29 (2000), 1, 131–41. On the role of a dozen leading corporations in the drafting and implementation of the Agreement on Trade-Related Aspects of Intellectual Property Rights (TRIPS), see Susan Sell, *Private Power, Public Law: The Globalization of Intellectual Property Rights* (Cambridge: Cambridge University Press,

2003). Also see Gregory Shaffer, *Defending Interests: Public-Private Partnerships in WTO Litigation* (Washington, DC: Brookings Institution Press, 2003).

23. Robert Dahl, 'The Concept of Power', *Behavioural Science*, 2 (1957), 201–15, quoted at 202.
24. David Baldwin, *Paradoxes of Power* (Oxford: Blackwell, 1989), 7.
25. Richard Steinberg, 'In the Shadow of Law or Power? Consensus-Based Bargaining and Outcomes in the GATT/WTO', *International Organization*, 56 (2002), 2, 339–74.
26. Gregory Shaffer, 'The Challenges of WTO Law: Strategies for Developing Country Adaptation', *World Trade Review*, 5 (2006), 2, 177–98, note 66.
27. Peter Bachrach and Morton Baratz, *Power and Poverty: Theory and Practice* (Oxford: Oxford University Press, 1970), 44.
28. Elmer Eric Schattschneider, *The Semi-Sovereign People: A Realist's View of Democracy in America* (New York: Holt, Rinehart and Winston, 1960), 71, italics in original.
29. For an introduction, see Rawi Abdelal, Mark Blyth, and Craig Parsons (eds.), *Constructing the International Economy* (Ithaca: Cornell University Press, 2010). The attention to constructivism has been more advanced in the political economy of finance, rather than trade. For instance, for highly commendable studies, see Jacqueline Best, *The Limits of Transparency: Ambiguity and the History of International Finance* (Ithaca: Cornell University Press, 2005); Jeffrey M. Chwieroth, *Capital Ideas: The IMF and the Rise of Financial Liberalization* (Princeton: Princeton University Press, 2010); and Timothy J. Sinclair, *The New Masters of Capital: American Bond Rating Agencies and the Politics of Creditworthiness* (Ithaca: Cornell University Press, 2005).
30. John Gerard Ruggie, 'International Regimes, Transactions, and Change: Embedded Liberalism in the Postwar Economic Order', *International Organization*, 36 (1982), 2, 379–415, quoted at 382.
31. Judith Goldstein, 'The Impact of Ideas on Trade Policy: The Origins of U.S. Agricultural and Manufacturing Policies', *International Organization*, 43 (1989), 1, 31–71, quoted at 71. Likewise, in respect to the rise of 'trade in services' as a conceptual and political innovation with US roots, see William Drake and Kalypso Nicolaïdis, 'Ideas, Interests, and Institutionalization: "Trade in Services" and the Uruguay Round', *International Organization*, 46 (1992), 1, 37–100.
32. Andrew Lang, *World Trade Law after Neoliberalism: Re-imagining the Global Economic Order* (Oxford: Oxford University Press, 2011).
33. Lang, 'Reconstructing Embedded Liberalism: John Gerard Ruggie and Constructivist Approaches to the Study of the International Trade Regime'.
34. Andrew T. F. Lang, 'Reflecting on Linkage: Cognitive and Institutional Change in the International Trading System', *Modern Law Review*, 70 (2007), 4, 523–50. For an introduction to the debate which serves as the basis for Lang's critique, see David Leebron, 'Linkage', *American Journal of International Law*, 96 (2002), 1, 5–27, part of an issue symposium on 'The Boundaries of the WTO'.
35. Lang, 'Reflecting on Linkage: Cognitive and Institutional Change in the International Trading System', 538.
36. Lang, 'Reconstructing Embedded Liberalism: John Gerard Ruggie and Constructivist Approaches to the Study of the International Trade Regime', 115.

37. Joseph A. Conti, *Between Law and Diplomacy: The Social Contexts of Disputing at the World Trade Organization* (Stanford: Stanford University Press, 2010), 2.
38. Ibid., 12.
39. Cornelia Woll, *Firm Interests: How Governments Shape Business Lobbying on Global Trade* (Ithaca, Cornell University Press, 2008).
40. Mark Blyth, *Great Transformations: Economic Ideas and Institutional Change in the Twentieth Century* (Cambridge: Cambridge University Press, 2002), 270.
41. Mark Laffey and Jutta Weldes, 'Beyond Belief: Ideas and Symbolic Technologies in the Study of International Relations', *European Journal of International Relations*, 3 (1997), 2, 193–237, quoted at 207.
42. Vincent Pouliot, 'The Logic of Practicality: A Theory of Practice of Security Communities', *International Organization*, 62 (2008), 2, 257–88. Also see Emanuel Adler and Vincent Pouliot (eds.), *International Practices* (Cambridge: Cambridge University Press, 2011).
43. In this vein, Didier Bigo's work has been the most impressive for its theoretical sophistication and empirical labour. For a summary, see Didier Bigo, 'Pierre Bourdieu and International Relations: Power of Practices, Practices of Power', *International Political Sociology*, 5 (2011), 3, 225–58, as well as *Terror, Insecurity and Liberty: Illiberal Practices of Liberal Regimes after 9/11* (Abingdon: Routledge, 2008). Overlapping with IR, and informed by Bourdieu's conceptual tools, Yves Dezalay and Bryant G. Garth have written absorbing studies of how economists and lawyers construct transnational fields of expertise. See in particular, Yves Dezalay and Bryant G. Garth, *The Internationalization of Palace Wars: Lawyers, Economists, and the Contest to Transform Latin American States* (Chicago: University of Chicago Press, 2002); and *Dealing in Virtue: International Commercial Arbitration and the Construction of a Transnational Legal Order* (Chicago: University of Chicago Press, 1996). Elsewhere in IR, see the work of Iver B. Neumann, including 'Returning Practice to the Linguistic Turn: The Case of Diplomacy', *Millennium: Journal of International Studies*, 31 (2002), 3, 627–51; and 'To Be a Diplomat', *International Studies Perspectives*, 6 (2005), 1, 72–93. Also see Frank Gadinger and Christian Büger, 'Reassembling and Dissecting: International Relations Practice from a Science Studies Perspective', *International Studies Perspectives*, 8 (2007), 1, 90–110; Emanuel Adler, 'The Spread of Security Communities: Communities of Practice, Self-Restraint, and NATO's Post-Cold War Transformation', *European Journal of International Relations*, 14 (2008), 2, 195–230; and Peter Jackson, 'Pierre Bourdieu, the "Cultural Turn" and the Practice of International History', *Review of International Studies*, 34 (2008), 1, 155–81.
44. For instance, see Rebecca Adler-Nissen (ed.), *Bourdieu in International Relations: Rethinking Key Concepts in IR* (Abingdon: Routledge, 2012); and the excellent 'Bourdieu and the International', a special issue of *International Political Sociology*, 5 (2011), 3. However, single-authored book-length investigations that are strongly imbued with Bourdieusian terminology are still rare. The exceptions are Michael Williams, *Culture and Security: Symbolic Power and the Politics of International Security* (London: Routledge, 2007); Frédéric Mérand, *European Defence Policy: Beyond the Nation State* (Oxford: Oxford University Press, 2008); and Vincent Pouliot, *International*

Security in Practice: The Politics of NATO–Russia Diplomacy (Cambridge: Cambridge University Press, 2010).

45. The only notable references so far to Bourdieu in IPE-related work have been in Tomohisa Hattori, 'Reconceptualizing Foreign Aid', *Review of International Political Economy*, 8 (2001), 4, 633–60; Anna Leander, 'Do We Really Need Reflexivity in IPE? Bourdieu's Two Reasons for Answering Affirmatively', *Review of International Political Economy*, 9 (2002), 4, 601–9; and Liliana Pop, 'Time and Crisis: Framing Success and Failure in Romania's Post-communist Transformations', *Review of International Studies*, 33 (2007), 3, 395–413.
46. The notion of a 'field of power' is Bourdieu's attempt to conceptually free himself from categories such 'the ruling class' or 'the elite' which he argues are derived from a substantialist mode of thinking. In particular, see Pierre Bourdieu, *The State Nobility: Elite Schools in the Field of Power* (Cambridge: Polity Press, 1996). For further introductions, see Loïc Wacquant, 'Reading Bourdieu's "Capital"', *International Journal of Contemporary Sociology*, 33 (1996), 2, 151–69; and David Swartz, *Culture and Power: A Sociology of Pierre Bourdieu* (Chicago: University of Chicago Press, 1998).
47. Bourdieu, *Language and Symbolic Power*. In addition, for other relevant Bourdieu texts that will be used to explain the conceptual framework on symbolic power see, in particular, *Outline of a Theory of Practice* (Cambridge: Cambridge University Press, 1977); 'The Economics of Lingusitic Exchanges', *Social Sciences Information*, 16 (1977), 6, 645–68; 'Symbolic Power', *Critique of Anthropology*, 4 (1979), 77–85; 'The Force of Law: Toward a Sociology of the Juridical Field', *Hastings Law Journal*, 38 (1987), 805–53; 'Social Space and Symbolic Power', *Sociological Theory*, 7 (1989), 1, 14–25; and *Pascalian Meditations* (Cambridge: Polity Press, 1997).
48. Bourdieu, *Outline of a Theory of Practice*, 85.
49. Max Weber, 'The Meaning of Discipline', in H. Gerth and C. Wright Mills (eds.), *From Max Weber: Essays in Sociology* (London: Routledge, 1991).
50. Barnett and Duvall, 'Power in International Politics', 67.
51. Bourdieu, 'What Makes a Social Class? On the Theoretical and Practical Existence of Groups'.
52. The term 'modality' does not have a precise definition in the WTO, but usually refers to the specification of formulas or approaches for final legal commitments.
53. Bhagirath Lal Das, *The Current Negotiations in the WTO: Options, Opportunities, and Risks for Developing Countries* (Third World Network: Penang, and Zed Books: London, 2005); Donna Lee and Rorden Wilkinson (eds.), *The WTO After Hong Kong: Progress in, and Prospects for, the Doha Development Agenda* (Abingdon: Routledge, 2007); and Kent Jones, *The Doha Blues: Institutional Crisis and Reform in the WTO* (Oxford: Oxford University Press, 2010).
54. Among the few notable books written on Southern countries in the GATT system, see Diana Tussie, *The Less Developed Countries and the World Trading System: A Challenge to the GATT* (London: Francis Pinter, 1985); and Robert E. Hudec, *Developing Countries in the GATT Legal System* (London: Trade Policy Research Centre, 1987).
55. For instance, for samples of Odell's work, see John S. Odell, 'Negotiating from Weakness in International Trade Relations', *Journal of World Trade*, 44 (2010), 3,

545–66; and 'Breaking Deadlocks in International Institutional Negotiations: The WTO, Seattle, and Doha', *International Studies Quarterly*, 53 (2009), 2, 273–99. For Narlikar, see Amrita Narlikar and Diana Tussie, 'The G20 at the Cancun Ministerial: Developing Countries and Their Evolving Coalitions in the WTO', *World Economy*, 27 (2004), 7, 947–66; and *International Trade and Developing Countries: Coalitions in the GATT and WTO* (London: Routledge, 2003).

56. For instance, see Olivier Cattaneo, Michael Engman, Robert M. Stern, and Sebastian Saez, *International Trade in Services: New Trends and Opportunities for Developing Countries* (Washington, DC: World Bank, 2010); and Carolyn Deere, *The Implementation Game: The TRIPS Agreement and the Global Politics of Intellectual Property Reform in Developing Countries* (Oxford: Oxford University Press, 2009).
57. Garry Sampson and W. Bradnee Chambers (eds.), *Developing Countries and the WTO: Policy Approaches* (Tokyo: United Nations University Press, 2008); G. A. Bermann and P. C. Mavroidis (eds.), *WTO Law and Developing Countries* (Cambridge: Cambridge University Press, 2007); Larry Crump and S. Javed Maswood (eds.), *Developing Countries and Global Trade Negotiations* (London: Routledge, 2007); and John S. Odell (ed.), *Negotiating Trade: Developing Countries in the WTO and NAFTA* (Cambridge: Cambridge University Press, 2006).
58. Jawara and Kwa, *Behind the Scenes at the WTO: The Real World of International Trade Negotiations*.
59. J. M. Finger and L. A. Winters, 'Reciprocity in the WTO', in Bernard Hoekman, Philip English, and Aaditya Mattoo (eds.), *Development, Trade and the WTO: A Handbook* (Washington, DC: World Bank, 2002); and J. M. Finger and P. Schuler, 'Implementation of Uruguay Round Commitments: The Development Challenge', in Bernard Hoekman and Will Martin (eds.), *Developing Countries and the WTO: A Pro-Active Agenda* (Oxford: Blackwell, 2001). For example, according to some economists, Southern countries transfer at least US$40 billion in rents every year to the US as part of the Agreement on Trade-Related Aspects of Intellectual Property Rights (TRIPS) and this figure does not account for total welfare losses which may be six times the transfer costs. See Keith Maskus, *Intellectual Property Rights in the Global Economy* (Washington, DC: Institute for International Economics, 2000).
60. United Nations Statistics Division (UNSD), COMTRADE Database.
61. For a more detailed contextualization, see Kym Anderson and Will Martin (eds.), *Agricultural Trade Reform and the Doha Development Agenda* (Washington, DC: World Bank, 2006).
62. Food and Agriculture Organization of the United Nations (FAO), *The State of Food and Agriculture 2006: Food Aid for Food Security?* (Rome: FAO, 2006), Part III Statistical Annex, Table A7: Economic Indicators. Data are for 2004 with annual percentage growth calculated over the period 1992–2004.
63. Food and Agriculture Organization of the United Nations (FAO), *The State of Agricultural Commodity Markets 2004* (Rome: FAO, 2004).
64. See Environmental Watch Group, 'Farm Subsidy Database', <http://www.ewg.org/farm>.
65. Organisation for Economic Co-operation and Development (OECD), *Agricultural Policies in OECD Countries: Monitoring and Evaluation 2005* (Paris: OECD, 2005).

Producer subsidy equivalent (PSE) statistics measure aggregate government assistance to farmers. The PSE is calculated by totalling the value of price supports, direct payments, and other transfers to producers of agricultural commodities. Percentage PSE is a measure of the rate of assistance to producers by calculating the PSE as a percentage of total production valued at internal prices.

66. Merlinda Ingco and John Nash (eds.), *Agriculture and the WTO: Creating a Trading System for Development* (Washington, DC: World Bank, 2004); and Michael Cardwell, Margaret Rosso Grossman, and Christopher Rodgers (eds.), *Agriculture and International Trade: Law, Policy and the WTO* (Cambridge, MA: CABI Publishing, 2003). Notable exceptions include the EU's provisions for former colonies in Africa, the Caribbean, and the Pacific (ACP) and more recently for so-called Least Developed Countries (LDCs) under the Everything But Arms (EBA) agreement. Elsewhere, the US has sponsored the Africa Growth and Opportunity Act (AGOA) and the Caribbean Basin Initiative (CBI).
67. Sandra Polaski, 'Agricultural Negotiations at the WTO: First, Do No Harm', Policy Outlook (Washington, DC: Carnegie Endowment for International Peace, June 2005).
68. See the results of simulations conducted by Sandra Polaski in *Winners and Losers: Impact of the Doha Round on Developing Countries* (Washington, DC: Carnegie Endowment for International Peace, March 2006). Also see Timothy A. Wise and Kevin P. Gallagher, 'The Doha Round's Development Impacts: Shrinking Gains and Real Costs', RIS Policy Brief 19, November 2005. Southern Members of the Cairns group include Argentina, Brazil, and South Africa. Established in 1986, the Cairns group is a diverse coalition of 19 agricultural exporting countries. Prominent members include Argentina, Australia, Brazil, Canada, South Africa, Thailand, and Uruguay. The group has historically campaigned for the elimination of all trade-distorting domestic subsidies and export subsidies.
69. See Audie Klotz, 'Case Selection', in Audie Klotz and Deepa Prakash (eds.), *Qualitative Methods in International Relations: A Pluralist Guide* (Basingstoke: Palgrave Macmillan, 2008); John S. Odell, 'Case Study Methods in International Political Economy', in Detlef F. Sprinz and Yael Wolinsky-Nahmias (eds.), *Models, Numbers and Cases: Methods for Studying International Relations* (Ann Arbor: University of Michigan Press, 2004); and Charles Ragin and Howard Becker, *What Is a Case? Exploring the Foundations of Social Inquiry* (Cambridge: Cambridge University Press, 1992).
70. Bourdieu, *Outline of a Theory of Practice*.
71. See Jeffrey Checkel, 'Process Tracing', in Klotz and Prakash (eds.), *Qualitative Methods in International Relations: A Pluralist Guide*; and Alexander L. George and Andrew Bennett, *Case Studies and Theory Development in the Social Sciences* (Cambridge, MA: MIT Press, 2005).
72. On interviewing techniques and strategy, Elliot Mishler's *Research Interviewing: Context and Narrative* (Cambridge, MA: Harvard University Press, 1991) was particularly valuable. I also turned to some of Bourdieu's work on interview methodologies for additional guidance. See Pierre Bourdieu, 'Understanding', in Pierre Bourdieu et al. (eds.), *The Weight of the World: Social Suffering in Contemporary Society* (Stanford: Stanford University Press, 1999).

Chapter 2

1. Michael Moore, *Ten Years of the WTO: A Success Story of Global Governance* (Bonn: Friedrich-Ebert-Stiftung, 2005), 19.
2. Quoted in Aileen Kwa, *Power Politics in the WTO* (Bangkok: Focus on the Global South, 2003), 38.
3. Michael Barnett and Raymond Duvall, 'Power in International Politics', *International Organization*, 59 (2005), 1, 39–75.
4. Roxanne Lynn Doty, *Imperial Encounters: The Politics of Representation in North–South Relations* (Minneapolis: University of Minnesota Press 1996), 165. Similar arguments have been advanced in Janice Bially Mattern, 'The Concept of Power and the (Un)discipline of International Relations', in Christian Reus-Smit and Duncan Snidal (eds.) *The Oxford Handbook of International Relations* (Oxford: Oxford University Press, 2008); Felix Berenskoetter and Michael J. Williams (eds.), *Power in World Politics* (London: Routledge, 2007); Barnett and Duvall, 'Power in International Politics'; Stefano Guzzini, 'The Use and Misuse of Power Analysis in International Theory', in Ronen Palen (ed.), *Global Political Economy: Contemporary Theories* (London: Routledge, 2000); and Cynthia Enloe, 'Margins, Silences, and Bottom Rungs: How to Overcome the Underestimation of Power in the Study of International Relations', in Steve Smith, Ken Booth, and Marysia Zalewski (eds.), *International Theory: Positivism and Beyond* (Cambridge: Cambridge University Press, 1996).
5. Steven Lukes, *Power: A Radical View* (Basingstoke: Palgrave Macmillan, 2005); and William Connolly, *The Terms of Political Discourse* (Oxford: Martin Robertson, 1974).
6. While the study of power has a long history, many theorists, including Aristotle, presumed that terms such as 'power', 'influence', or 'rule' were intrinsically understood by audiences and did not require any technical specification. See Robert Dahl, 'Power', in David Sills (ed.), *International Encyclopaedia of the Social Sciences* (New York: Free Press, 1968), 406. Also see Niccolò Machiavelli, *The Prince* (Oxford: Oxford University Press, [1532] 2008); and Thomas Hobbes, *Leviathan* (London: Penguin, [1651] 1985).
7. Robert Dahl, 'The Concept of Power', *Behavioural Science*, 2 (1957), 201–15.
8. Giovanni Sartori, 'Concept Misformation in Comparative Politics', *American Political Science Review*, 64 (1970), 4, 1033–53.
9. In the classical variant, see Hans Morgenthau, *Politics Among Nations: The Struggle for Power and Peace* (New York: Alfred Knopf, 1948). In the neorealist interpretation, see Kenneth Waltz, *Theory of International Politics* (London: McGraw-Hill, 1979).
10. Mark Haugaard and Stewart R. Clegg, 'Introduction: Why Power is the Central Concept of the Social Sciences', in Stewart R. Clegg and Mark Haugaard (eds.), *The SAGE Handbook of Power* (London: Sage, 2009), 3.
11. Walter Gallie, 'Essentially Contested Concepts', *Proceedings of the Aristotelian Society*, 56 (1956), 167–98.
12. Lukes, *Power: A Radical View.*
13. The following points are inspired by Mustafa Emirbayer, 'Manifesto for a Relational Sociology', *The American Journal of Sociology*, 103 (1997), 2, 281–317.

14. Ibid., 281.
15. Karl Marx, *Capital: Volume 1: A Critique of Political Economy* (London: Penguin Books, [1867] 1990).
16. This does not preclude that certain expressions to characterize 'power' in this book will appear to have a substantialist colour. Part of the intuitive appeal of the substantialist vision of power arguably concerns how it reflects and constitutes a sensory perception and codification of the world. This is what makes it easier to grasp cognitively. However, even in cases where I depict power as being 'accumulated' or 'deployed', such metaphors are still linked, in larger terms, to a process analysis whereby the 'power' in question is always viewed as being in a state of flux with potential for transformation.
17. Ludwig Wittgenstein, *Philosophical Investigations* (Oxford: Basil Blackwell, [1953] 1972).
18. Haugaard and Clegg, 'Introduction: Why Power is the Central Concept of the Social Sciences', 4.
19. Barnett and Duvall, 'Power in International Politics', 67.
20. Peter Morriss, *Power: A Philosophical Analysis* (Manchester: Manchester University Press, [1987] 2002).
21. Ibid., 39.
22. Ibid., 40.
23. Stefano Guzzini, '"Power" in International Relations: Concept Formation Between Conceptual Analysis and Conceptual History', paper presented at International Studies Association Annual Convention, New Orleans, 24–27 March 2002.
24. Barnett and Duvall, 'Power in International Politics', 67.
25. Ibid.
26. Machiavelli, *The Prince*; and Hobbes, *Leviathan*. For a survey of Machiavelli's and Hobbes' readings on power, see Stewart Clegg, *Frameworks of Power* (London: Sage, 1989).
27. Hans Morgenthau, *Politics Among Nations: The Struggle for Power and Peace* (New York: Knopf, 1949); Martin Wight, *Power Politics* (London: Royal Institute for International Affairs, 1946); and Harold Sprout and Margaret Sprout, *Foundations of National Power* (Princeton: Princeton University Press, 1945).
28. E. H. Carr, *The Twenty Years' Crisis 1919–1939: An Introduction to the Study of International Relations* (Basingstoke: Palgrave Macmillan, [1939] 2001).
29. Richard Little, *The Balance of Power in International Relations: Metaphors, Myths and Models* (Cambridge: Cambridge University Press, 2007).
30. Waltz, *Theory of International Politics*, 113.
31. Robert Dahl, *Modern Political Analysis* (London: Prentice Hall, [1963] 1991), 27–8. Perhaps the earliest examination in the literature was Herbert A. Simon, 'Notes on the Observation and Measurement of Political Power', *Journal of Politics*, 15 (1953), 500–16.
32. Robert Dahl, *Who Governs? Democracy and Power in the American City* (New Haven: Yale University Press, 1961).
33. Ibid., 4.
34. Dahl, 'The Concept of Power', 202.

35. David Baldwin, *Paradoxes of Power* (Oxford: Blackwell, 1989), 7.
36. Ronald Findlay and Kevin H. O'Rourke, *Power and Plenty: Trade, War, and the World Economy in the Second Millennium* (Princeton: Princeton University Press, 2007).
37. Adam Smith, *An Inquiry into the Nature and Causes of the Wealth of Nations* (Oxford: Oxford University Press, [1776] 1993). In particular, see Book IV for Smith's criticism of mercantilist authors. For a review, see John Elliott, 'Adam Smith's Conceptualization of Power, Markets, and Politics', *Review of Social Economy*, 58 (2000), 4, 429–54.
38. Jacob Viner, 'Power Versus Plenty as Objectives of Foreign Policy in the Seventeenth and Eighteenth Centuries', *World Politics*, 1 (1948), 1, 1–29, quoted at 10. For the classic account of the period of mercantilism, see Eli Heckscher, *Mercantilism* (London: Allen & Unwin, 1934).
39. Albert Hirschman, *National Power and the Structure of Foreign Trade* (Berkeley: University of California Press, 1945).
40. Stephen Krasner, 'State Power and the Structure of International Trade', *World Politics*, 28 (1976), 3, 317–47.
41. Kent Jones, *The Doha Blues: Institutional Crisis and Reform in the WTO* (Oxford: Oxford University Press, 2010), 88. This is also a common argument in textbooks. For instance, see Bernard M. Hoekman and Michel M. Kostecki, *The Political Economy of the World Trade System: The WTO and Beyond* (Oxford: Oxford University Press, 2009), 68–70. In discussing WTO decision-making processes, Hoekman and Kostecki argue that a positive relationship exists between 'influence' in negotiations and indicators such as the GDP of a member. Also see John Barton, Judith Goldstein, Timothy Josling, and Richard Steinberg, *The Evolution of the Trade Regime: Politics, Law, and Economics of the GATT/WTO* (Princeton: Princeton University Press, 2006), 10–14.
42. Richard Steinberg, 'In the Shadow of Law or Power? Consensus-Based Bargaining and Outcomes in the GATT/WTO', *International Organization*, 56 (2002), 2, 339–74.
43. Fatoumata Jawara and Aileen Kwa, *Behind the Scenes at the WTO: The Real World of International Trade Negotiations/Lessons of Cancún* (London: Zed Books, 2004).
44. Gregory Shaffer, 'The Challenges of WTO Law: Strategies for Developing Country Adaptation', *World Trade Review*, 5 (2006), 2, 177–98.
45. For example, see Andrew Hurrell and Amrita Narlikar, 'The New Politics of Confrontation: Developing Countries at Cancún and Beyond', *Global Society*, 20 (2006), 4, 415–33; and Amrita Narlikar and Diana Tussie, 'The G20 at the Cancún Ministerial: Developing Countries and their Evolving Coalitions in the WTO', *World Economy*, 27 (2004), 7, 947–66.
46. At the early stages of the WTO Ministerial Conference in 2003 in Cancún, Zoellick 'was convinced that it [the G20] was an artificial alliance that wouldn't last very long, given the conflicting interests of its leading members—especially Brazil and India—and he didn't want to elevate its status by granting it a special meeting'. Paul Blustein, *Misadventures of the Most Favored Nations: Clashing Egos, Inflated Ambitions, and the Great Shambles of the World Trade System* (New York: Public Affairs, 2009), 147.
47. Talcott Parsons, 'On the Concept of Political Power', *Proceedings of the American Philosophical Society*, 107 (1963), 3, 232–62.

48. Barnett and Duvall, 'Power in International Politics', 50.
49. Ibid., 51.
50. Peter Bachrach and Morton Baratz, 'Two Faces of Power', *American Political Science Review*, 56 (1962), 947–52.
51. Peter Bachrach and Morton Baratz, 'Decisions and Nondecisions: An Analytical Framework', *American Political Science Review*, 57 (1963), 3, 632–42, quoted at 641.
52. For instance, see Mark Pollack, *Engines of European Integration: Delegation, Agency, and Agenda Setting in the EU* (Oxford: Oxford University Press, 2003); and William Zartman and Jeffrey Rubin (eds.), *Power and Negotiation* (Ann Arbor: University of Michigan Press, 2000).
53. Andrew Hurrell, 'Power, Institutions, and the Production of Inequality', in Michael Barnett and Raymond Duvall (eds.), *Power in Global Governance* (Cambridge: Cambridge University Press, 2005), 34. For an early introduction, see Robert Axelrod and Robert Keohane, 'Achieving Cooperation Under Anarchy: Strategies and Institutions', *World Politics* 38 (1985), 1, 226–54.
54. In legal scholarship on trade, the distinction between 'law' and 'power' can be traced to John Jackson, 'The Crumbling Institutions of the Liberal Trade System', *Journal of World Trade Law*, 12 (1978), 93–106. The same characterization appears in John Jackson, *The World Trading System: Law and Policy of International Economic Relations* (Cambridge, MA: MIT Press, 1997). Also see J. Michael Finger and Sumana Dhar, 'Do Rules Contain Power?', in Alan V. Deardorff and Robert Mitchell Stern (eds.), *Analytical and Negotiation Issues in the Global Trading System* (Ann Arbor: University of Michigam Press, 1994).
55. Amrita Narlikar, *The World Trade Organization: A Very Short Introduction* (Oxford: Oxford University Press, 2005), 42.
56. Joost Pauwelyn, 'The Transformation of World Trade', *Michigan Law Review*, 104 (2005), 1–66. See also Robert Howse, 'From Politics to Technocracy—And Back Again: The Fate of the Multilateral Trading Regime', *American Journal of International Law*, 96 (2002), 1, 94–117.
57. Narlikar, *The World Trade Organization: A Very Short Introduction*.
58. Ibid. For an overview, see Jawara and Kwa, *Behind the Scenes at the WTO: The Real World of International Trade Negotiations/Lessons of Cancún*. On internal representation in the green room process, see Kent Jones, 'Green Room Politics and the WTO's Crisis of Representation', *Progress in Development Studies*, 9 (2009), 4, 349–57.
59. Jackson, *The World Trading System: Law and Policy of International Economic Relations*; and Amrita Narlikar, 'WTO Decision-Making Processes and Developing Countries', TRADE Working Paper, 11 (South Centre: Geneva, November 2001). Calls for the creation of an executive committee for the WTO system are periodically raised by some trade officials and scholars, but little movement has been formally made in this direction. For instance, see the report by the Consultative Board to the Director-General Supachai Panitchpakdi, *The Future of the WTO: Addressing Institutional Challenges in the New Millennium* (WTO: Geneva, 2004); and for a critical analysis, Robert Wolfe, 'Decision-Making and Transparency in the "Medieval" WTO: Does the Sutherland Report have the Right Prescription?', *Journal of International Economic Law*, 8 (2005), 3, 631–45.

60. For an evaluation of the social purpose of the Single Undertaking, see Robert Wolfe, 'The WTO Single Undertaking as Negotiating Technique and Constitutive Metaphor', *Journal of International Economic Law*, 12 (2009), 4, 835–58.
61. Gregory Shaffer, 'The Role of the WTO Director-General and Secretariat', *World Trade Review*, 4 (2005), 3, 429–38.
62. For a re-evaluation of the role of Southern countries in the GATT system, including the argument that many members were more active in negotiations than is conventionally appreciated, see Rorden Wilkinson and James Scott, 'Developing Country Participation in the GATT: A Reassessment', *World Trade Review*, 7 (2008), 3, 473–510.
63. Michael Barnett and Martha Finnemore, *Rules for the World: International Organizations in Global Politics* (Ithaca: Cornell University Press, 2004).
64. The concentration of rule-making power at the WTO has been justified from both utilitarian and constitutional perspectives. For instance, see John McGinnis and Mark Movsesian, 'World Trade Constitution', *Harvard Law Review*, 114 (2000), 2, 511–605; and the work of Ernst-Ulrich Petersmann, including an early articulation in *Constitutional Functions and Constitutional Problems of International Economic Law* (Fribourg: Fribourg University Press, 1991), and 'The WTO Constitution and Human Rights', *Journal of International Economic Law*, 3 (2000), 1, 19–25.
65. Aileen Kwa, *Power Politics in the WTO* (Bangkok: Focus on the Global South, 2003), 23.
66. Elmer Eric Schattschneider, *The Semi-Sovereign People: A Realist's View of Democracy in America* (New York: Holt, Rinehart and Winston, 1960), 71, italics in original.
67. Peter Bachrach and Morton Baratz, *Power and Poverty: Theory and Practice* (Oxford: Oxford University Press, 1970).
68. Lukes, *Power: A Radical View*.
69. Barnett and Duvall, 'Power in International Politics', 53.
70. Guzzini, 'The Use and Misuse of Power Analysis in International Theory', 60.
71. William H. Sewell, 'A Theory of Structure: Duality, Agency, and Transformation', *The American Journal of Sociology*, 98 (1992), 1, 1–29, quoted at 27.
72. Stefano Guzzini, 'Structural Power: The Limits of Neorealist Power Analysis', *International Organization*, 47 (1993), 3, 443–78. In the context of IR theory, one should not confuse defensive and offensive variants of structural realism with this discussion. Kenneth Waltz's structural theory of international relations necessitates an 'elements of national power approach', leading to a 'lump notion' of power in order to rank states. Many scholars have criticized this as a confusing assumption, failing to accurately specify scope, weight, and costs. This needs to be understood as a different meaning of 'structure' compared to the scholars discussed here. See Stefano Guzzini, *Realism in International Relations and International Political Economy* (London: Routledge, 1998).
73. Susan Strange, *States and Markets: An Introduction to International Political Economy* (London: Pinter, 1988), and for a critical examination, see Lynn K. Mytelka, 'Knowledge and Structural Power in the International Political Economy', in Thomas Lawton, James Rosenau, and Amy C. Verdun (eds.), *Strange Power: Shaping the Parameters of International Relations and International Political Economy* (Aldershot: Ashgate Publishing Company, 2000).

74. Guzzini, 'Structural Power: The Limits of Neorealist Power Analysis'. The notion of 'impersonal bias' is derived from Bachrach and Baratz, *Power and Poverty: Theory and Practice*.
75. Robert W. Cox with Timothy Sinclair, *Approaches to World Order* (Cambridge: Cambridge University Press, 1996); and Stephen Gill (ed.), *Gramsci, Historical Materialism and International Relations* (Cambridge: Cambridge University Press, 1993).
76. Adam David Morton, *Unravelling Gramsci: Hegemony and Passive Revolution in the Global Economy* (London: Pluto Press, 2007), 92. Also see Thomas R. Bates, 'Gramsci and the Theory of Hegemony', *Journal of the History of Ideas*, 36 (1975), 2, 351–66.
77. Nicos Poulantzas, *Political Power and Social Classes* (London: Verso, [1968] 1987), 104.
78. Stephen Gill, 'Globalisation, Market Civilisation, and Disciplinary Neoliberalism', *Millennium: Journal of International Studies*, 24 (1995), 3, 399–423, quoted at 411–12. It is worth noting that there exists a methodological and ontological sub-debate regarding how the ideas of Gramsci, developed in the particular context of inter-war Italy, can be applied to problems in contemporary international relations. Such issues go beyond the points here, but for details see Randall D. Germain and Michael Kenny, 'Engaging Gramsci: International Relations Theory and the New Gramscians', *Review of International Studies*, 24 (1998), 3–21; and Craig N. Murphy, 'Understanding IR: Understanding Gramsci', *Review of International Studies*, 24 (1998), 417–25.
79. Stephen Gill, 'New Constitutionalism, Democratisation and Global Political Economy', *Pacifica Review*, 10 (1998), 1, 23–38.
80. Fred Gale, 'Cave "Cave! Hic Dragones": A Neo-Gramscian Deconstruction and Reconstruction of International Regime Theory', *Review of International Political Economy*, 5 (1998), 2, 252–83; and Robert W. Cox, *Production, Power, and World Order: Social Forces in the Making of World History* (New York: Columbia University Press, 1987). Cox has occasionally made use of the term 'structural power', but more commonly has referred to political and social power in the context of production.
81. Ian Taylor, 'Hegemony, Neoliberal "Good Governance" and the International Monetary Fund: A Gramscian Perspective', in Morten Bøås and Desmond McNeill (eds.), *Global Institutions and Development: Framing the World?* (London: Routledge, 2004).
82. Rita Abrahamsen, *Disciplining Democracy: Development Discourse and Good Governance in Africa* (London: Zed Books, 2000); Graham Harrison, *The World Bank and Africa: The Construction of Governance States* (London: Routledge, 2004).
83. Stephen Gill and David Law, 'Global Hegemony and the Structural Power of Capital', *International Studies Quarterly*, 33 (1989), 4, 475–99, quoted at 476.
84. For instance, in an article by Mark Rupert, he draws upon one opposing source of evidence in order to critique the purpose of the WTO system, Lori Wallach and Michelle Sforza, *Whose Trade Organization?: Corporate Globalization and the Erosion of Democracy* (Washington, DC: Public Citizen, 1999). The WTO is summarized as: 'In general, the neoliberal agenda of integrating and depoliticising the global

economy fosters a "race to the bottom" which enhances capitalist power through intensified market competition and the dull compulsion of the economic. Such an implicit class bias is evident in the WTO's governance of the global trading system'. Mark Rupert, 'Globalising Common Sense: A Marxian-Gramscian (Re-)vision of the Politics of Governance/Resistance', *Review of International Studies*, 29 (2003), S1, 181–98, quoted at 192.

85. Rorden Wilkinson, 'The Political Economy of International Economic Law: A Neo-Gramscian Perspective', in Asif H. Qureshi (ed.), *Perspectives in International Economic Law* (London: Kluwer Law International, 2002).
86. Jane Kelsey, *Serving Whose Interests? The Political Economy of Trade in Services Agreements* (Abingdon: Routledge-Cavendish, 2008), 5.
87. Susan Sell, *Private Power, Public Law: The Globalization of Intellectual Property Rights* (Cambridge: Cambridge University Press, 2003).
88. Robert Hunter Wade, 'What Strategies are Viable for Developing Countries Today? The World Trade Organization and the Shrinking of "Development Space"', *Review of International Political Economy*, 10 (2003), 4, 621–44, quoted at 621.
89. Carolyn Deere, *The Implementation Game: The TRIPS Agreement and the Global Politics of Intellectual Property Reform in Developing Countries* (Oxford: Oxford University Press, 2009).
90. Peter Gallagher, *Global Trade Advocate: A Handbook for Managers and Association Executives* (Melbourne: Inquit Communications Pty Ltd, 2005).
91. Peter Gallagher, Patrick Low, and Andrew Stoler (eds.), *Managing the Challenges of WTO Participation: 45 Case Studies* (Cambridge: Cambridge University Press, 2005).
92. Sewell, 'A Theory of Structure: Duality, Agency, and Transformation'.
93. Stephen Gill, 'Toward a Postmodern Prince? The Battle in Seattle as a Moment in the New Politics of Globalisation', *Millennium: Journal of International Studies*, 29 (2000), 1, 131–40.
94. Bill Paterson, '*Trasformismo* at the World Trade Organization', in Mark McNally and John Schwarzmantel (eds.), *Gramsci and Global Politics: Hegemony and Resistance* (London: Routledge, 2009), 43.
95. Barnett and Duvall, 'Power in International Politics', 52–3.
96. For instance, see Judith Goldstein, 'Ideas, Institutions, and American Trade Policy', *International Organization*, 42 (1988), 1, 179–217.
97. Barnett and Duvall, 'Power in International Politics'.
98. Clarissa Hayward, *De-Facing Power* (Cambridge: Cambridge University Press, 2000), 35.
99. Charlotte Epstein, *The Power of Words in International Relations: Birth of an Anti-Whaling Discourse* (Cambridge, MA: MIT Press, 2008), 4, italics in original.
100. Michel Foucault, *Power/Knowledge: Selected Interviews and Other Writings 1972–1977*, edited by Colin Gordon (London: The Harvester Press, 1980), 119.
101. Michel Foucault, *The History of Sexuality: The Will to Knowledge Volume I* (London: Penguin, 1978), 94.
102. Ibid., 93.
103. Barnett and Duvall, 'Power in International Politics'.

104. The Integrated Framework for Trade-Related Technical Assistance to Least-Developed Countries was established at the WTO Ministerial in Singapore in 1996. It is a multi-agency initiative, featuring the WTO and other international organizations. The Global Trust Fund, commenced at the Doha Ministerial in 2001, represented a 'new strategy' according to the Secretariat, incorporating a 'demand-driven' approach to technical assistance. The knowledge-as-property understanding of technical assistance is seen in Susan Prowse, 'The Role of International and National Agencies in Trade-related Capacity Building', *World Economy*, 25 (2002), 9, 1235–61. Prowse argues that 'the efficacy of "aid for trade" is probably indisputable', acting to 'reinforce' market access opportunities. With this assumption seemingly confirmed, the emphasis is placed on how 'delivery' mechanisms of technical assistance can be improved. Quoted at 1248, 1235.
105. For an overview, see WTO, 'Biennial Technical Assistance and Training Plan 2010–2011; Revision', 21 October 2009 (WT/COMTD/W/170/Rev.1).
106. *Oxford English Dictionary Online.*
107. Emanuel Adler and Steven Bernstein, 'Knowledge in Power: The Epistemic Construction of Global Governance', in Michael Barnett and Raymond Duvall (eds.), *Power in Global Governance* (Cambridge: Cambridge University Press, 2005), 295. Foucault originally referred to the concept of *épistémè* in even more encompassing, historical terms: 'This episteme may be suspected of being something like a world-view, a slice of history common to all branches of knowledge, which imposes on each one the same norms and postulates, a general sense of reason, a certain structure of thought that the men of a particular period cannot escape—a great body of legislation written once and for all by some anonymous hand.' Michel Foucault, *The Archaeology of Knowledge* (London: Tavistock Publications, 1972), 191.
108. Adler and Bernstein, 'Knowledge in Power: The Epistemic Construction of Global Governance', 296.
109. Ibid., 314.
110. Doerthe Rosenow, 'Decentring Global Power: The Merits of a Foucauldian Approach to International Relations', *Global Society*, 23 (2009), 4, 497–517. See WTO, 'European Communities—Measures Affecting the Approval and Marketing of Biotech Products', Dispute DS291, <wto.org/english/tratop_e/dispu_e/cases_e/ds291_e.htm>.
111. Rosenow, 'Decentring Global Power: The Merits of a Foucauldian Approach to International Relations', 503.
112. Ibid., 516.
113. Michael Hardt, 'Militant Life', *New Left Review*, 64, July/August 2010, 151–60, quoted at 152.
114. Ciaran Cronin, 'Bourdieu and Foucault on Power and Modernity', *Philosophy & Social Criticism*, 22 (1996), 6, 55–85, quoted at 60.
115. Lukes, *Power: A Radical View*, 98.
116. For a broader investigation into how philosophy is ascribed a prestigious status in the French academy, traditionally above the social sciences, and for Foucault's position in this field, see Pierre Bourdieu, *Homo Academicus* (Stanford: Stanford

University Press, 1988). Also see, in addition, Staf Callewaert, 'Bourdieu, Critic of Foucault: The Case of Empirical Social Science against Double-Game-Philosophy', *Theory, Culture & Society*, 23 (2006), 6, 73–98.
117. For an overview, see Michael Kelly (ed.), *Critique and Power: Recasting the Foucault/ Habermas Debate* (Cambridge, MA: MIT Press, 1994).
118. Connolly, *The Terms of Political Discourse*, 93.
119. Bachrach and Baratz, *Power and Poverty: Theory and Practice.*
120. Lukes, *Power: A Radical View.*

Chapter 3

1. Pierre Bourdieu, *Outline of a Theory of Practice* (Cambridge: Cambridge University Press, 1977), 162.
2. Pierre Bourdieu, 'What Makes a Social Class? On the Theoretical and Practical Existence of Groups', *Berkeley Journal of Sociology*, 32 (1987), 1–18, quoted at 13, italics in original.
3. David Hume, 'Of the First Principles of Government' [1741], in *Selected Essays* (Oxford: Oxford University Press, 2008), 24.
4. Carl Boggs, *Gramsci's Marxism* (London: Pluto Press, 1976), 39.
5. Louis Althusser, *Lenin and Philosophy, and Other Essays* (New York: New Left Books, 1971), 128.
6. Bourdieu, *Outline of a Theory of Practice*, 166.
7. Pierre Bourdieu and Luc Boltanski, 'Le fétichisme de la langue', *Actes de la recherche en sciences sociales*, 4 (1975), 2–32. Quoted in John B. Thompson, *Studies in the Theory of Ideology* (Cambridge: Polity Press, 1984), 46.
8. Pierre Bourdieu, *Pascalian Meditations* (Cambridge: Polity Press, 1997), 100.
9. Pierre Bourdieu, *Masculine Domination* (Cambridge: Polity Press, 2001).
10. Pierre Bourdieu and Loïc Wacquant, *An Invitation to Reflexive Sociology* (Chicago: University of Chicago Press, 1992), 168.
11. Bourdieu, *Outline of a Theory of Practice*, 214, note 1, italics in original.
12. Bourdieu and Wacquant, *An Invitation to Reflexive Sociology*, 168.
13. Bourdieu, *Pascalian Meditations*, 173.
14. Edmund Husserl, *Experience and Judgement: Investigations in a Genealogy of Logic* (London: Routledge, 1973 [1939]).
15. John Myles, 'From Doxa to Experience: Issues in Bourdieu's Adoption of Husserlian Phenomenology', *Theory, Culture & Society*, 21 (2004), 2, 91–107, quoted at 91. Also see John Myles, 'Making Don't Knows Make Sense: Bourdieu, Phenomenology, and Opinion Polls', *The Sociological Review*, 56 (2008), 1, 102–16; as well as Jeremy Lane, *Pierre Bourdieu: A Critical Introduction* (London: Pluto, 2000).
16. Husserl, *Experience and Judgement: Investigations in a Genealogy of Logic.*
17. Terry Eagleton, *Ideology: An Introduction* (London: Verso, 1991), 158.
18. Pierre Bourdieu and Terry Eagleton, 'Doxa and Common Life: An Interview', *New Left Review*, 191 (1992), 111–21.

19. Bourdieu, *Pascalian Meditations*. See also Michael Burawoy, 'Durable Domination: Gramsci Meets Bourdieu', paper presented at the Havens Center, University of Wisconsin, April 2008 <http://burawoy.berkeley.edu/Bourdieu/Lecture%202.pdf>.
20. Pierre Bourdieu, *Sociology in Question* (London: Sage, 1993), 71.
21. Loïc Wacquant, *Punishing the Poor: The Neoliberal Government of Social Insecurity* (Durham, NC: Duke University Press, 2009), xx.
22. Pierre Bourdieu, *Homo Academicus* (Stanford: Stanford University Press, 1988).
23. To be precise, Bourdieu does not abandon philosophy, but uses social science methods to contribute to answering philosophical questions.
24. Bourdieu and Wacquant, *An Invitation to Reflexive Sociology*, 25, note 46.
25. Pierre Bourdieu, 'Rethinking the State: Genesis and Structure of the Bureaucratic Field', *Sociological Theory*, 12 (1994), 1, 1–18, quoted at 15.
26. Bourdieu and Wacquant, *An Invitation to Reflexive Sociology*, 128.
27. Bourdieu, *Outline of a Theory of Practice*, 167.
28. Cécile Deer, 'Doxa', in Michael Grenfell (ed.), *Pierre Bourdieu: Key Concepts* (Stocksfield: Acumen, 2008), 122.
29. Vincent Pouliot, *International Security in Practice: The Politics of NATO–Russia Diplomacy* (Cambridge: Cambridge University Press, 2010), 45. Elsewhere, in another Bourdieusian approach to diplomacy which examines the socialization of European elites, see Rebecca Adler-Nissen, 'The Diplomacy of Opting Out: A Bourdieudian Approach to National Integration Strategies', *Journal of Common Market Studies*, 46 (2008), 3, 663–84.
30. See, for instance, Immanuel Kant, 'Perpetual Peace: A Philosophical Sketch' [1795] in H. S. Reiss (ed.), *Kant: Political Writings* (Cambridge: Cambridge University Press, 2003); Richard Cobden, *The Political Writings of Richard Cobden*, L. Mallet (ed.) (London: William Ridgway, Vol. I, 1867; Vol. II, 1878); Cordell Hull, *The Memoirs of Cordell Hull* (New York: Macmillan Company, 1948); and Michael Edward Brown, Sean M. Lynn-Jones, and Steven E. Miller (eds.), *Debating the Democratic Peace* (Cambridge, MA: MIT Press, 1996).
31. Joseph Weiler, 'The Rule of Lawyers and the Ethos of Diplomats: Reflection on the Internal and External Legitimacy of Dispute Settlement', in Roger B. Porter, Pierre Sauvé, Arvind Subramanian, and Americo Beviglia Zampetti (eds.), *Efficiency, Equity, and Legitimacy: The Multilateral Trading System at the Millennium* (Washington, DC: Brookings Institution Press, 2001), 336–7.
32. Robert Keohane and Joseph Nye, 'The Club Model of Multilateral Cooperation and the World Trade Organization: Problems of Democratic Legitimacy', in Roger Porter, Pierre Sauve, Arvind Subramanian, and Americo Beviglia Zampetti (eds.), *Efficiency, Equity, and, Legitimacy: The Multilateral Trading System at the Millennium* (Cambridge, MA: Brookings Institution Press, 2001).
33. Robert Howse, 'From Politics to Technocracy—And Back Again: The Fate of the Multilateral Trading Regime', *American Journal of International Law*, 96 (2002), 1, 94–117, quoted at 98.
34. Bourdieu, *Pascalian Meditations*, 11.

35. Article XXVIII bis of the General Agreement on Tariffs and Trade (1947) states that negotiations 'on a reciprocal and mutually advantageous basis... are of great importance to the expansion of international trade', p. 1. Strictly speaking, this does not mean that negotiations must produce what is sometimes referred to as a 'balance of concessions'. Rather, as interpreted by Kenneth Dam, 'From the formal legal principle that a country need make concessions only when other contracting parties offer reciprocal concessions considered to be "mutually advantageous" has been derived the informal principle that exchanges of concessions must entail reciprocity.' Kenneth Dam, *The GATT: Law and International Economic Organization* (Chicago: University of Chicago Press, 1970), 59. For further interpretation on the political potency of the notion of reciprocity in the GATT, see John Jackson, *The World Trading System: Law and Policy of International Economic Relations* (Cambridge, MA: MIT Press, 1997), 147–50.
36. Robert Keohane, 'Reciprocity in International Relations', *International Organization*, 40 (1986), 1, 1–27.
37. For instance, on details regarding Lamy's preparatory work ahead of the Doha Ministerial in 2001, including his close working relationship with US Trade Representative Robert Zoellick, see Paul Blustein, *Misadventures of the Most Favored Nations: Clashing Egos, Inflated Ambitions, and the Great Shambles of the World Trade System* (New York: Public Affairs, 2009). On the eulogizing of Dunkel's diplomacy by a range of trade officials and prominent academics see Jagdish N. Bhagwati and Mathias Hirsch (eds.), *The Uruguay Round and Beyond: Essays in Honor of Arthur Dunkel* (Ann Arbor: University of Michigan Press, 1998).
38. Christer Jönsson and Martin Hall, *Essence of Diplomacy* (Basingstoke: Palgrave Macmillan, 2005).
39. Keohane, 'Reciprocity in International Relations', 8.
40. Marcel Mauss, *The Gift: The Form and Reason for Exchange in Archaic Societies* (Abingdon: Routledge, 2002 [1924]).
41. Bourdieu, *Outline of a Theory of Practice*, 192.
42. Maurice Godelier, *The Enigma of the Gift* (Chicago: University of Chicago Press, 1999), 12.
43. For an overview, see WTO, 'Biennial Technical Assistance and Training Plan 2010–2011; Revision', 21 October 2009 (WT/COMTD/W/170/Rev.1). Also see the 'Doha Development Agenda Trade Capacity Building Database', an initiative coordinated by the WTO Secretariat and the OECD, which groups together sources of data and projects, <http://tcbdb.wto.org/>.
44. For politically informed critiques, see Carolyn Deere, *International Trade Technical Assistance and Capacity Building* (United Nations Human Development Report Office, Occasional Paper, 2005); and Gregory Shaffer, 'Can WTO Technical Assistance and Capacity-Building Serve Developing Countries?' in Ernst-Ulrich Petersmann (ed.), *Reforming the World Trading System: Legitimacy, Efficiency, and Democratic Governance* (Oxford: Oxford University Press, 2005).
45. Tomohisa Hattori, 'Reconceptualizing Foreign Aid', *Review of International Political Economy*, 8 (2001), 4, 633–60. See also elsewhere, R. L. Stirrat and Heiko Henkel, 'The Development Gift: The Problem of Reciprocity in the NGO World', *The Annals*

of the American Academy of Political and Social Science, 554 (1997), 1, 66–80; and Rosalind Eyben, 'The Power of the Gift and the New Aid Modalities', *IDS Bulletin*, 37 (2006), 6, 88–98.
46. Hattori, 'Reconceptualizing Foreign Aid', 640.
47. Peter Morgan, 'Technical Assistance: Correcting the Precedents', *Development Policy Journal* (UNDP), December 2002, 1–22. On the early history, including the official debut of TA at the UN General Assembly in 1946, see David Owen, 'The United Nations Program of Technical Assistance', *Annals of the American Academy of Political and Social Science*, 270 (1950), 109–17. For further historical context, see Craig Murphy, *The United Nations Development Programme: A Better Way?* (Cambridge: Cambridge University Press, 2006).
48. Morgan, 'Technical Assistance: Correcting the Precedents'.
49. Gordon Wilson, 'Knowledge, Innovation and Re-inventing Technical Assistance for Development', *Progress in Development Studies*, 7 (2007), 3, 183–99.
50. Luc Boltanski and Eve Chiapello, *The New Spirit of Capitalism* (London: Verso, 2007).
51. Bourdieu, *Outline of a Theory of Practice*, 169.
52. Pierre Bourdieu, *The State Nobility: Elite Schools in the Field of Power* (Cambridge: Polity Press, 1996), 265.
53. For the best introductory exposition, see David Beetham, *The Legitimation of Power* (Basingstoke: Macmillan, 1991).
54. For good accounts of the study of legitimacy in IR and law that have explored these debates, see Thomas M. Franck, *The Power of Legitimacy Among Nations* (Oxford: Oxford University Press, 1990); Ian Clark, *Legitimacy in International Society* (Oxford: Oxford University Press, 2005); and Ian Hurd, *After Anarchy: Legitimacy and Power in the United Nations Security Council* (Princeton: Princeton University Press, 2007).
55. Jürgen Habermas, *Legitimation Crisis* (Cambridge: Polity Press, 1988).
56. In particular, on Weber's theorizing of religion, see Max Weber, *Economy and Society, Volume 1* (Berkeley, CA: University of California Press, 1978 [1922]), Ch. VI. For an explanation of how Bourdieu draws upon Weber in debating religion, see Pierre Bourdieu, 'Legitimation and Structured Interests in Weber's Sociology of Religion', in Scott Lash and Sam Whimster (eds.), *Max Weber, Rationality and Modernity* (Abingdon: Routledge, 2006). Also see Pierre Bourdieu, 'Genesis and Structure of the Religious Field', *Comparative Social Research*, 13 (1991), 1–44.
57. Bourdieu, *Outline of a Theory of Practice*, 192.
58. Pierre Bourdieu, *The Logic of Practice* (Stanford: Stanford University Press, 1990), 118.
59. The same point is also made by Beetham, *The Legitimation of Power*, 103–4.
60. Max Weber, 'The Meaning of Discipline', in H. Gerth and C. Wright Mills (eds.), *From Max Weber: Essays in Sociology* (London: Routledge, 1991), 262.
61. Bourdieu, *Outline of a Theory of Practice*.
62. Bourdieu, *The State Nobility: Elite Schools in the Field of Power*.
63. David Swartz, *Culture and Power: The Sociology of Pierre Bourdieu* (Chicago: University of Chicago Press, 1997), 92.

64. Pierre Bourdieu, 'Symbolic Power', *Critique of Anthropology*, 4 (1979), 77–85, quoted at 79–80.
65. Pierre Bourdieu, 'The Economics of Lingusitic Exchanges', *Social Sciences Information*, 16 (1977), 6, 645–68.
66. Pierre Bourdieu, 'The Social Space and the Genesis of Groups', *Theory and Society*, 14 (1985), 6, 723–44, quoted at 730.
67. Émile Durkheim and Marcel Mauss, *Primitive Classification* (Abingdon: Routledge, 2010 [1903]).
68. Michael Barnett and Martha Finnemore, *Rules for the World: International Organizations in Global Politics* (Ithaca: Cornell University Press, 2004), 31.
69. See Touko Piiparinen, 'The Rise and Fall of Bureaucratic Rationalization: Exploring the Possibilities and Limitations of the UN Secretariat in Conflict Prevention', *European Journal of International Relations*, 14 (2008), 4, 697–724; and Rianne Mahona and Stephen McBridea, 'Standardizing and Disseminating Knowledge: The Role of the OECD in Global Governance', *European Political Science Review*, 1 (2009), 1, 83–101.
70. Jane Kelsey, *Serving Whose Interests? The Political Economy of Trade in Services Agreements* (Abingdon: Routledge-Cavendish, 2008); and William Drake and Kalypso Nicolaïdis, 'Ideas, Interests, and Institutionalization: "Trade in Services" and the Uruguay Round', *International Organization*, 46 (1992), 1, 37–100. Among other interested groups examined, both Kelsey, and Drake and Nicolaïdis highlight the role played by American Express.
71. Andrew T. F. Lang, 'Legal Regimes and Regimes of Knowledge: Governing Global Services Trade', LSE Law, Society and Economy Working Paper Series, WPS 15-2009, July 2009. In the GATS, 'trade in services' is defined as the 'supply of a service', for which four methods or 'modes' are given: cross-border supply (mode 1), consumption aboard (mode 2), commercial presence (mode 3), and the presence of natural persons (mode 4). More generally, also see Andrew T. F. Lang, 'Reconstructing Embedded Liberalism: John Gerard Ruggie and Constructivist Approaches to the Study of the International Trade Regime', *Journal of International Economic Law*, 9 (2006), 1, 81–116.
72. Pierre Bourdieu, 'The Force of Law: Toward a Sociology of the Juridical Field', *Hastings Law Journal*, 38 (1987): 805–53.
73. Lang, 'Legal Regimes and Regimes of Knowledge: Governing Global Services Trade', 34.
74. Ibid., 7.
75. Andrew T. F. Lang, 'Reflecting on Linkage: Cognitive and Institutional Change in the International Trading System', *Modern Law Review*, 70 (2007), 4, 523–50. For an introduction to the debate which serves as the basis for Lang's critique, see David Leebron, 'Linkage', *American Journal of International Law*, 96 (2002), 1, 5–27, part of an issue symposium on 'The Boundaries of the WTO'.
76. Lang, 'Reflecting on Linkage: Cognitive and Institutional Change in the International Trading System', 538.
77. Ibid., 549.
78. Ibid., 538.

79. Pierre Bourdieu, *Distinction: A Social Critique of the Judgement of Taste* (London: Routledge, 1984), 479.
80. Loïc Wacquant, 'On Symbolic Power and Group-Making: Pierre Bourdieu's Reframing of Class', Preface to Pierre Bourdieu, *Et klassespørsmål* (Oslo: Forlaget Manifest, 2007).
81. Bourdieu, *The State Nobility: Elite Schools in the Field of Power*, 376; and Bourdieu, 'The Social Space and the Genesis of Groups', 732, respectively.
82. Bourdieu, 'Rethinking the State: Genesis and Structure of the Bureaucratic Field'.
83. Jeffrey L. Gertler, 'What China's WTO Accession is All About', in Deepak Bhattasali, Shantong Li, and Will Martin (eds.), *China and the WTO: Accession, Policy Reform, and Poverty Reduction Strategies* (Washington, DC: World Bank, 2004). For the original legal reference, see Uruguay Round Agreement on Agriculture, Part IV: Article 6, p. 4 (b).
84. As an example of this common discourse, see the quotes by US Ambassador Michael Punke at a press conference held to discuss the Doha Round. In an effort to explain the delays in reaching a final settlement, Punke shifted the spotlight away from the US to argue that China, India, and Brazil are 'advanced developing economies' and should be 'ready to accept the responsibility and the leadership that goes along with their new position in the global economy'. Quoted in Kanaga Raja, 'India, China, Brazil Leadership Key to Doha Success or Failure, says US', Third World Network Info Service, 27 May 2010.
85. With this relationship in mind, it is perhaps not surprising that the etymology of 'orthodoxy' is literally '*orthós*' plus 'doxa'. Eric Partridge, *Origins: A Short Etymological Dictionary of Modern English* (London: Routledge, 1977).
86. Bourdieu, *Outline of a Theory of Practice*, 169.
87. Jacques Berlinerblau, 'Toward a Sociology of Heresy, Orthodoxy, and *Doxa*', *History of Religions*, 40 (2001), 4, 327–51.
88. Bourdieu, *Sociology in Question*, 80.
89. Bourdieu, 'Symbolic Power', 83.
90. George Orwell, 'Politics and the English Language', in *Shooting an Elephant and Other Essays* (London: Penguin, 2009 [1950]), 370.
91. Pierre Bourdieu and Loïc Wacquant, 'Neoliberal Newspeak: Notes on the New Planetary Vulgate', *Radical Philosophy*, 105 (2001), 2–5.
92. For instance, on the historical struggle over the meaning of 'free trade', with roots that pre-date Adam Smith to the influence of authors in the mercantilist tradition, the French physiocrats, and the moral philosophy of David Hume and Francis Hutcheson, see Douglas Irwin, *Against the Tide: An Intellectual History of Free Trade* (Princeton: Princeton University Press, 1996). Also see, in addition, Lars Magnusson, *The Tradition of Free Trade* (Abingdon: Routledge, 2004); Jacob Viner, *Essays on the Intellectual History of Economics*, ed. Douglas Irwin (Princeton: Princeton University Press, 1991), particularly 'The Intellectual History of Laissez Faire'; Charles P. Kindleberger, 'The Rise of Free Trade in Western Europe, 1820–1875', *The Journal of Economic History*, 35 (1975), 1, 20–55; and Karl Polanyi, *The Great Transformation: The Political and Economic Origins of Our Time* (Boston: Beacon Press, 2001 [1944]).

93. David Ricardo, *On the Principles of Political Economy and Taxation* (Mineola, NY: Dover Publications, 2004 [1817]); and James Mill, *Elements of Political Economy* (London: Baldwin, Cradock, & Joy, 1821).
94. Among the most significant contributions, see the Heckscher-Ohlin model, originally designed in 1933 by Eli Heckscher and Bertil Ohlin. The model proposes that nations will tend to have comparative advantage in the production of goods that extensively use factors of production that are relatively cheap and abundant locally. For a critical discussion of more recent refinements and applications, see Robert E. Baldwin, *The Development and Testing of Heckscher–Ohlin Trade Models: A Review* (Cambridge, MA: MIT Press, 2008).
95. For a literature review of recent work, see L. Alan Winters, 'Trade Liberalisation and Economic Performance: An Overview', *The Economic Journal*, 114 (2004), 493, F4–F21. For strong claims of links between trade liberalization and growth, see David Dollar and Aart Kraay, 'Trade, Growth, and Poverty', *The Economic Journal*, 114 (2004), 493, F22–F49; and Jeffrey D. Sachs and Andrew M. Warner, 'Economic Reform and the Process of Global Integration', *Brookings Papers on Economic Activity* (1995), 1, 1–118.
96. For instance, see the pioneering studies by Ian Malcolm, David Little, Tibor Scitovsky, and Maurice FitzGerald, *Industry and Trade in Some Developing Countries: A Comparative Study* (Oxford: Oxford University Press for the OECD Development Center, 1970); Béla Balassa and Associates, *Development Strategies in Semi-industrial Economies* (Baltimore: Johns Hopkins University Press for the World Bank, 1982); and Deepak Lal, *The Poverty of 'Development Economics'* (London: Institute of Economic Affairs, 1983).
97. Sidney Weintraub, 'Theory and Practice in the Conduct of Trade Policy', in William Alexander Kerr and James D. Gaisford (eds.), *Handbook on International Trade Policy* (Cheltenham: Edward Elgar Publishing, 2007), 11.
98. Paul Krugman, 'What Should Trade Negotiators Negotiate About?', *Journal of Economic Literature*, 35 (1997), 1, 113–20, quoted at 113.
99. Francisco Rodríguez and Dani Rodrik, 'Trade Policy and Economic Growth: A Skeptic's Guide to the Cross-National Evidence', *NBER Macroeconomics Annual*, 15 (2000), 261–325, quoted at 266.
100. On debating the role of trade relative to other economic reforms, see the OECD's work, including Patrick Love and Ralph G. Lattimore, *International Trade: Free, Fair, and Open?* (Paris: OECD, 2009). More generally, see the argument that the 'Washington Consensus' has now been 'augmented' through attention to issues of institutions and 'governance' in Dani Rodrik, 'Goodbye Washington Consensus, Hello Washington Confusion? A Review of the World Bank's Economic Growth in the 1990s: Learning from a Decade of Reform', *Journal of Economic Literature*, 44 (2006), 4, 973–87.
101. Robert Hunter Wade, 'What Strategies are Viable for Developing Countries Today? The World Trade Organization and the Shrinking of "Development Space"', *Review of International Political Economy*, 10 (2003), 4, 621–44. More historically, see Robert Hunter Wade, *Governing the Market: Economic Theory and the Role of Government in East Asian Industrialization* (Princeton: Princeton

University Press, 2002); and Ha-Joon Chang, *Kicking Away the Ladder: Development Strategy in Historical Perspective* (London: Anthem Press, 2003).

102. See Gilbert Rist, *The History of Development: From Western Origins to Global Faith* (London: Zed Books, 2008), and Arturo Escobar, *Encountering Development: The Making and Unmaking of the Third World* (Princeton: Princeton University Press, 1995).
103. On how the 'science of development' became codified into the GATT, see in particular Donatella Alessandrini, *Developing Countries and the Multilateral Trade Regime: The Failure and Promise of the WTO's Development Mission* (Oxford: Hart Publishing, 2010). Also see Rorden Wilkinson, *The WTO: Crisis and the Governance of Global Trade* (Abingdon: Routledge, 2006).
104. Jörg Mayer, 'Policy Space: What, for What, and Where?', *Development Policy Review*, 27 (2009), 4, 373–95; Kevin Gallagher, 'Understanding Developing Country Resistance to the Doha Round', *Review of International Political Economy*, 15 (2008), 1, 62–85; Kevin Gallagher (ed.), *Putting Development First: The Importance of Policy Space in the WTO and IFIs* (London: Zed Books, 2005). In respect to official UNCTAD references to 'policy space', see United Nations Conference on Trade and Development, *Trade and Development Report* (Geneva: UNCTAD, 2002); and United Nations Conference on Trade and Development, *Trade and Development Report* (Geneva: UNCTAD, 2006).
105. Gallagher, 'Understanding Developing Country Resistance to the Doha Round', 63.
106. On criticism of the notion, see Patrick A. Messerlin, 'Enlarging the Vision for Trade Policy Space: Special and Differentiated and Infant Industry Issues', *World Economy*, 29 (2006), 10, 1395–407. The US has previously argued that the term 'policy space' in relation to trade is of 'dubious value' and should not be used as a new principle in economic debates. See Martin Khor, 'Heated Fight on Policy Space Dominates UNCTAD Review', Third World Network Info Service on WTO and Trade Issues, 13 May 2006.
107. For instance, as discussed in Chapter 2, see Mark Rupert, 'Globalising Common Sense: A Marxian–Gramscian (Re-)vision of the Politics of Governance/Resistance', *Review of International Studies*, 29 (2003), S1, 181–98.
108. Peter L. Berger and Thomas Luckmann, *The Social Construction of Reality: A Treatise in the Sociology of Knowledge* (New York: Anchor, 1967).
109. Bourdieu, *Outline of a Theory of Practice*, 169.
110. Rorden Wilkinson, 'Language, Power and Multilateral Trade Negotiations', *Review of International Political Economy*, 16 (2009), 4, 597–619.
111. Bourdieu, 'Symbolic Power', 83.
112. Bourdieu, 'The Force of Law: Toward a Sociology of the Juridical Field'.
113. Bourdieu, *Sociology in Question*.
114. Kent Jones, 'Green Room Politics and the WTO's Crisis of Representation', *Progress in Development Studies*, 9 (2009), 4, 349–57; and Robert Wolfe, 'Informal Political Engagement in the WTO: Are Mini-Ministerials a Good Idea?', in Dan Ciuriak and John M. Curtis (eds.), *Trade Policy Research 2004* (Ottawa: Department of Foreign Affairs and International Trade, 2004). Negotiating environments that have had similar features to the green room format can be found in the early history of the

GATT. For instance, the Principal Supplier rule was premised on key countries negotiating among 'principal suppliers' in smaller bilateral exchanges, before extending the results to the rest of the membership via the most favoured nation rule. The precise term 'green room' came into usage during Arthur Dunkel's leadership as Director General of the GATT (1980–1993) apparently to note the colour of his office.

115. Richard Blackhurst, 'Reforming WTO Decision Making: Lessons from Singapore and Seattle', in Klaus-Günter Deutsch and Bernhard Speyer (eds.), *The World Trade Organization Millennium Round: Freer Trade in the Twenty-first Century* (London: Routledge, 2001); and Richard Blackhurst and David Hartridge, 'Improving the Capacity of WTO Institutions to Fulfil their Mandate', *Journal of International Economic Law*, 7 (2004), 3, 705–16. This criticism has been amplified by many civil society groups, such as Third World Network and Focus on the Global South.
116. Quoted in John S. Odell, 'Breaking Deadlocks in International Institutional Negotiations: The WTO, Seattle, and Doha', *International Studies Quarterly*, 53 (2009), 2, 273–99, quoted at 286.
117. In the WTO institutional architecture, the General Council is positioned above three lower councils: the Council for Trade in Goods, the Council for Trade in Services, and the Council for Trade-Related Aspects of Intellectual Property Rights.
118. Bourdieu, 'The Economics of Lingusitic Exchanges', 653.
119. Ibid.
120. Bourdieu, *Distinction: A Social Critique of the Judgement of Taste.*
121. Bourdieu, *Outline of a Theory of Practice*, 197.
122. Bourdieu, *The State Nobility: Elite Schools in the Field of Power*, 382.
123. For instance, see Friedrich V. Kratochwil, *Rules, Norms, and Decisions: On the Conditions of Practical and Legal Reasoning in International Relations and Domestic Affairs* (Cambridge: Cambridge University Press, 1989); Jürgen Haacke, 'Theory and Praxis in International Relations: Habermas, Self-Reflection, Rational Argumentation', *Millennium: Journal of International Studies*, 25 (1996), 2, 255–89; Thomas Risse, '"Let's Argue!": Communicative Action in World Politics', *International Organization*, 54 (2000), 1, 1–39; Neta Crawford, *Argument and Change in World Politics: Ethics, Decolonization, and Humanitarian Intervention* (Cambridge: Cambridge University Press, 2002); Cornelia Ulbert, Thomas Risse, and Harald Müller, *Arguing and Bargaining in Multilateral Negotiations* (Berlin: Center for Transnational Relations, Foreign and Security Policy, May 2004); Harald Müller, 'Arguing, Bargaining and all that: Communicative Action, Rationalist Theory and the Logic of Appropriateness in International Relations', *European Journal of International Relations*, 10 (2004), 3, 395–435; Markus Kornprobst, 'Argumentation and Compromise: Ireland's Selection of the Territorial Status Quo Norm', *International Organization*, 61 (2007), 1, 69–98; Christian Grobe, 'The Power of Words: Argumentative Persuasion in International Negotiations', *European Journal of International Relations*, 16 (2010), 1, 5–29; and Corneliu Bjola and Markus Kornprobst (eds.), *Arguing Global Governance: Agency, Lifeworld and Shared Reasoning* (Abingdon: Routledge, 2011). On the logic of consequentialism, see James G. March and Johan P. Olsen, *Rediscovering Institutions: The Organizational Basis of Politics* (New York: Free Press, 1989).

124. Cornelia Ulbert and Thomas Risse, 'Deliberately Changing the Discourse: What Does Make Arguing Effective?', *Acta Politica*, 40 (2005), 351–67, quoted at 352.
125. Ulbert, Risse, and Müller, *Arguing and Bargaining in Multilateral Negotiations*.
126. Ulbert and Risse, 'Deliberately Changing the Discourse: What Does Make Arguing Effective?', 352.
127. Risse, '"Let's Argue!": Communicative Action in World Politics', 2.
128. Jürgen Habermas, *The Theory of Communicative Action: Reason and the Rationalization of Society, Volume 1* (Cambridge: Polity Press, 2004 [1981]), and earlier in Jürgen Habermas, 'On Systematically Distorted Communication', *Inquiry*, 13 (1970), 205–18.
129. Franck Poupeau, 'Reasons for Domination, Bourdieu versus Habermas', in Bridget Fowler (ed.), *Reading Bourdieu on Society and Culture* (Oxford: Blackwell, 2000).
130. John L. Austin, *How to do Things with Words* (Oxford: Oxford University Press, 1962).
131. Nicole Deitelhoff and Harald Müller, 'Theoretical Paradise—Empirically Lost? Arguing with Habermas', *Review of International Studies*, 31 (2005), 1, 167–79.
132. Risse, '"Let's Argue!": Communicative Action in World Politics'.
133. Nick Crossley, 'On Systematically Distorted Communication: Bourdieu and the Socio-analysis of Publics', *The Sociological Review*, 52 (2004), 88–112.
134. Frank Schimmelfennig, 'The Community Trap: Liberal Norms, Rhetorical Action, and the Eastern Enlargement of the European Union', *International Organization*, 55 (2001), 1, 47–80, quoted at 62.
135. Frank Schimmelfennig, *The EU, NATO and the Integration of Europe: Rules and Rhetoric* (Cambridge: Cambridge University Press, 2003), 199.
136. Ibid., 196, 222.
137. Crawford, *Argument and Change in World Politics: Ethics, Decolonization, and Humanitarian Intervention*.
138. Erving Goffman, *Frame Analysis: An Essay on the Organization of Experience* (New York: Harper & Row, 1974). For IR constructivists who have utilized the notion of framing see, for instance, Kornprobst, 'Argumentation and Compromise: Ireland's Selection of the Territorial Status Quo Norm' and Schimmelfennig, *The EU, NATO and the Integration of Europe: Rules and Rhetoric*.
139. Michael Barnett, 'Culture, Strategy and Foreign Policy Change: Israel's Road to Oslo', *European Journal of International Affairs*, 5 (1999), 1, 5–36, quoted at 25.
140. Doug McAdam, John McCarthy, and Mayer Zald, 'Introduction: Opportunities, Mobilizing Structures, and Framing Processes—Towards a Synthetic, Comparative Perspective on Social Movements', in Doug McAdam, John McCarthy, and Mayer Zald (eds.), *Comparative Perspectives on Social Movements: Political Opportunities, Mobilizing Structures, and Cultural Framings* (Cambridge: Cambridge University Press, 1996), 6. Also see David Snow, E. Burke Rochford, Steven Worden, and Robert Benford, 'Frame Alignment Processes, Micromobilization and Movement Participation', *American Sociological Review*, 51 (1986), 464–81.
141. Odell, 'Breaking Deadlocks in International Institutional Negotiations: The WTO, Seattle, and Doha'; John Odell and Susan Sell, 'Reframing the Issue: The WTO Coalition on Intellectual Property and Health, 2001', in John Odell (ed.),

Negotiating Trade: Developing Countries in the WTO and NAFTA (Cambridge: Cambridge University Press, 2006); and Rodger Payne, 'Persuasion, Frames and Norm Construction', *European Journal of International Relations*, 7 (2001), 1, 37–61.

142. For instance, see Bert Klandermans, Marga de Weerd, and Jose-Manuel Costa, 'Injustice and Adversarial Frames in a Supranational Political Context: Farmers' Protest in the Netherlands and Spain', in Donatella della Porta, Hanspeter Kriesi, and Dieter Rucht (eds.), *Social Movements in a Globalizing World* (Basingstoke: Macmillan, 1999).
143. Quoting a Southern country interview subject in Amrita Narlikar and Diana Tussie, 'The G20 at the Cancun Ministerial: Developing Countries and their Evolving Coalitions in the WTO', *World Economy*, 27 (2004), 7, 947–66, quoted at 949–50. The so-called Blair House Accord of November 1992 marked a key point in the Uruguay Round when the US and the EU settled their outstanding differences on agriculture. The agreement centred on establishing a ceiling on oilseed production in Europe, facilitating the creation of the Blue Box category in the Agreement on Agriculture, and thus allowing the EU to pursue its reform of the Common Agricultural Policy without making cuts in actual spending. Within the WTO, the phrase 'Blair House' has subsequently carried negative overtones for many members, synonymous with underhand practices.
144. Snow and Benford, 'Ideology, Frame Resonance, and Participant Mobilization'.
145. Payne, 'Persuasion, Frames and Norm Construction', 41.
146. Ibid., 52–3.
147. Alastair Iain Johnston, *Social States: China in International Institutions, 1980–2000* (Princeton: Princeton University Press, 2008), 20.
148. Alastair Iain Johnston, 'Conclusions and Extensions: Toward Mid-Range Theorizing and Beyond Europe', *International Organization*, 59 (2005), 4, 1013–44, quoted at 1021.
149. See Robert Lawrence, 'China and the Multilateral Trading System', in Barry Eichengreen, Yung Chul Park, and Charles Wyplosz (eds.), *China, Asia, and the New World Economy* (Cambridge: University Press, 2008); and Henry Gao and Donald Lewis (eds.), *China's Participation in the WTO* (London: Cameron May, 2005).
150. Homi Bhabha, 'Of Mimicry and Man: The Ambivalence of Colonial Discourse', *October*, 28 (1984), 125–33, quoted at 126, 132.
151. Ibid., 126, italics in original.
152. Baruch Knei-Paz, *The Social and Political Thought of Leon Trotsky* (Oxford: Oxford University Press, 1978), 91.
153. L. H. M. Ling, 'Cultural Chauvinism and the Liberal International Order: "West vs Rest" in Asia's Financial Crisis', in G. Chowdhry and S. Nair (eds.), *Power, Postcolonialism and International Relations: Reading Race, Gender and Class* (London: Routledge, 2002), 117.
154. Bourdieu, 'What Makes a Social Class? On the Theoretical and Practical Existence of Groups', 13, italics in original.
155. Loïc Wacquant, 'Pierre Bourdieu', in R. Stones (ed.), *Key Sociological Thinkers* (Basingstoke: Palgrave Macmillan, 1998).

Endnotes

Chapter 4

1. See Stephen Yafa, *Big Cotton: How A Humble Fiber Created Fortunes, Wrecked Civilizations, and Put America on the Map* (London: Penguin, 2005); and Sven Beckert, *The Empire of Cotton: A Global History* (New York: Alfred A. Knopf, forthcoming).
2. See Elinor Lynn Heinisch, 'West Africa Versus the United States on Cotton Subsidies: How, Why and What Next?', *Journal of Modern African Studies*, 44 (2006), 2, 251–74; Donna Lee, 'The Cotton Club: The Africa Group in the Doha Development Agenda', in Donna Lee and Rorden Wilkinson (eds.), *The WTO After Hong Kong: Progress In, and Prospects For, the Doha Development Agenda* (London: Routledge, 2007); Donna Lee and Nicola J. Smith, 'The Political Economy of Small African States in the WTO', *The Round Table*, 97 (2008), 395, 259–71; and Magda Shahin, 'The Cotton Initiative', in Gary Sampson and W. Bradnee Chambers (eds.), *Developing Countries and the WTO: Policy Approaches* (Tokyo: United Nations University Press, 2008).
3. International Cotton Advisory Committee, *The Outlook for Cotton Supply in 2005/06* (Washington DC: ICAC, 2005).
4. International Cotton Advisory Committee, *Cotton This Month*, 2 August 2010.
5. International Cotton Advisory Committee, *The Outlook for Cotton Supply in 2005/06*.
6. John Baffes and Gérald Estur, 'Market Context', in David Tschirley, Colin Poulton, and Patrick Labaste (eds.), *Organization and Performance of Cotton Sectors in Africa: Learning from Reform Experience* (Washington, DC: World Bank, 2009).
7. COMTRADE Database, United Nations Statistics Division. Data sourced from 2007.
8. ECOWAS-SWAC/OECD, *Atlas on Regional Integration in West Africa* (2006), <http://www.atlas-westafrica.org>.
9. FAOSTAT database, Food and Agriculture Organization of the United Nations. Data sourced from 2007.
10. Julian Alston, Daniel Sumner, and Henrich Brunke, *Impacts of Reductions in US Cotton Subsidies on West African Cotton Producers* (Boston, MA: Oxfam America, 2007).
11. OECD/Sahel and West Africa Club, *Cotton in West Africa: The Development Dimension* (Paris: OECD, 2006).
12. International Cotton Advisory Committee (ICAC), *Production and Trade Policies Affecting the Cotton Industry* (Washington, DC: ICAC, November 2008).
13. International Cotton Advisory Committee (ICAC), *Production and Trade Policies Affecting the Cotton Industry* (Washington, DC: ICAC, September 2006).
14. John Baffes, 'Cotton and Developing Countries: A Case Study in Policy Incoherence', Trade Note 10 (Washington, DC: World Bank, 10 September 2003). Also see Daniel A. Sumner, 'Reducing Cotton Subsidies: The DDA Cotton Initiative', in Kym Anderson and Will Martin (eds.), *Agricultural Trade Reform and the Doha Development Agenda* (Washington, DC: World Bank, 2006).
15. Giannis Karagiannis, 'The EU Cotton Policy Regime and the Implications of the Proposed Changes for Producer Welfare', Food and Agriculture Organization of the United Nations Commodity and Trade Policy Research Working Paper 9 (Rome: FAO, April 2004).

16. Under the Farm Security and Rural Investment Act of 2002 ('Farm Act 2002'), direct payments were categorized as being based on the value of production and yields during a previous production period. In this respect, the US has claimed that such support does not have any distorting effect on the world price since it is 'decoupled' and, therefore, provides no incentive to farmers to increase production. The US has argued that direct payments can be legitimately placed in the Green Box in the AoA (subsidies which result in minimal or no distortion of trade). However, this argument has been debated. For instance, direct payments are only authorized when farmers use their land for agricultural purposes, yet this must not be for cultivating fruits, vegetables, or other crops. Such a situation tends to encourage farmers to grow crops that are eligible for support, including cotton. Counter-cyclical payments refer to subsidies that are transferred when the price of cotton drops through a specified threshold (since 2002 this has been $0.72 per pound). The US Department of Agriculture (USDA) has described such payments as forming a 'safety net', but since the transfer is linked to the price falling to a set level, they are classified as being part of the Amber Box in the AoA (support measures linked to trade distortion and subject to removal). Loan deficiency payments are triggered when world prices fall below $0.52 per pound. The further prices fall below that level, the more they increase. These subsidies also fall into the Amber Box in the WTO. See Jasper Womach, 'Cotton Production and Support in the United States', CRS Report for Congress (Washington, DC: Congressional Research Service, 24 June 2004).
17. Oxfam International, *Cultivating Poverty: The Impact of US Cotton Subsidies on Africa*, Oxfam Briefing Paper 30 (Oxford: Oxfam International, September 2002).
18. The bill was officially titled The Food, Conservation, and Energy Act of 2008.
19. Jim Monke, 'Farm Commodity Programs in the 2008 Farm Bill', CRS Report for Congress (Washington, DC: Congressional Research Service, 23 July 2008). The reduction in counter-cyclical payments for cotton from the 2002 bill to 2008 bill was 0.0115%.
20. Womach, 'Cotton Production and Support in the United States', 14.
21. The historical, political, and economic reasons for the privileged voice that US agriculture receives in Washington, DC are complicated and go beyond the confines of this particular chapter. For general debates see Judith Goldstein, 'The Impact of Ideas on Trade Policy: The Origins of US Agricultural and Manufacturing Policies', *International Organization*, 43 (1989), 1, 31–71; Kishore Gawande, 'The Structure of Lobbying and Protection in US Agriculture', in Bernard Hoekman and Simon Evenett (eds.), *Economic Development and Multilateral Trade Cooperation* (Basingstoke: Palgrave Macmillan, 2006); and Kishore Gawande and Bernard Hoekman, 'Lobbying and Agricultural Trade Policy in the United States', *International Organization*, 60 (2006), 3, 527–61. For a particular focus on cotton, see Omer Gokcekus and Richard Fishler, 'The Cotton Influence Index: An Examination of US Cotton Subsidies', *American Journal of Agricultural Economics*, 91 (2009), 2, 299–309.
22. Environmental Working Group (EWG), Farm Subsidy Database, 'Cotton Subsidies in the United States', <http://farm.ewg.org>. The three largest cotton trading

companies in the world have major US affiliates: Allenberg Cotton Co (a member of the Paris-based Louis Dreyfus Group), Cargill Cotton, and Dunavant Enterprises Inc (also owned by Allenberg Cotton Co). According to the EWG, Allenberg Cotton Co received US$186 million in Step 2 payments from 1995–2004. See Ken Cook and Chris Campbell, 'EWG Analysis of Step 2 Data for 2004; US Taxpayers Spent $264 Million in 2004 On Cotton Export Subsidies Ruled Illegal By WTO', 9 June 2005, <http://www.ewg.org/node/21053>.

23. Gawain Kripke, 'King Cotton: Abdicate or Subjugate? The Political Economy of US Cotton and Prospects for a Pro-development Policy Reform', in Eric Hazard (ed.), *International Trade Negotiations and Poverty Reduction: The White Paper on Cotton* (Dakar: Enda Prospectives Dialogues Politiques, 2005). Also see Donna Lee, 'The Cotton Club: The Africa Group in the Doha Development Agenda', in Donna Lee and Rorden Wilkinson (eds.), *The WTO After Hong Kong: Progress In, and Prospects For, the Doha Development Agenda* (London: Routledge, 2007).
24. Prices are based on the Cotlook A Index, a reliable barometer of world cotton values used by the ICAC, governments, commodity exchanges, and industry groups. See Cotton Outlook, <http://www.cotlook.com>.
25. Terry Townsend, 'World Cotton Situation', paper presented at WTO Director General's framework mechanism on cotton, 11th round of consultations, 24 April 2009, Geneva.
26. John Baffes, 'Cotton: Market Setting, Trade Policies, and Issues', World Bank Research Working Paper, WPS 3218 (Washington, DC: World Bank, 2004).
27. Joseph Glauber, Chief Economist, US Department of Agriculture, interview with the author, Washington, DC, 13 July 2010.
28. Nicholas Minot and Lisa Daniels, 'Impact of Global Cotton Markets on Rural Poverty in Benin', *Agricultural Economics*, 33 (2005), 3, 453–66.
29. Oxfam International, *Cultivating Poverty: The Impact of US Cotton Subsidies on Africa*.
30. Louis Goreux, 'Prejudice Caused by Industrialized Countries to Cotton Sectors in Western and Central Africa', mimeo, July 2002; and Daniel Sumner, 'A Quantitative Simulation Analysis of the Impacts of US Cotton Subsidies on Cotton Prices and Quantities', mimeo, Department of Agricultural and Resource Economics, University of California: Davis, 2003.
31. Alston, Sumner, and Brunke, *Impacts of Reductions in US Cotton Subsidies on West African Cotton Producers*.
32. Louis Goreux, 'Prejudice Caused by Industrialized Countries Subsidies to Cotton Sectors in Western and Central Africa', mimeo, June 2003.
33. Joost Nelen, 'Farmers' Organisations in West Africa: Emerging Stakeholders in Cotton Sector Reforms', in Giel Ton, Jos Bijman, and Joost Oorthuizen (ed.), *Producer Organisations and Market Chains: Facilitating Trajectories of Change in Developing Countries* (Wageningen: Wageningen Academic Publishers, 2007). For instance, see the Senegal-centred Le Réseau des Organisations Paysannes et de Producteurs de l'Afrique de l'Ouest (ROPPA), a network of West African farm organizations which campaigns at both regional and international levels. According to Sally Baden, Economic Justice Policy Adviser for Oxfam International's West Africa Regional

Programme, ROPPA should be considered the major forum for cotton producers across Francophone countries. Sally Baden, interview with the author, Oxford, 10 October 2006.

34. El Hadji A. Diouf, Programme Coordinator, Africa Trade Programme, International Centre for Trade and Sustainable Development, interview with the author, Geneva, 28 September 2006.
35. Denis Pesche and Kato Nubukpo, 'The African Cotton Set in Cancún: A Look Back at the Beginning of Negotiations', in Eric Hazard (ed.), *International Trade Negotiations and Poverty Reduction: The White Paper on Cotton* (Dakar: Enda Prospectives Dialogues Politiques, 2005), 49.
36. The partial involvement or absence of other African countries that could potentially stand to benefit from inclusion in the initiative will not be debated here. The reasons are complicated and country-specific, stemming not only from the relative contribution of cotton to the economy, but also intra-African and North–South relations. For instance, some analysts have speculated that Senegal's marginal involvement could be due to fears of not wanting to damage long-standing relations with the US.
37. Pesche and Nubukpo, 'The African Cotton Set in Cancún: A Look Back at the Beginning of Negotiations'. Also see El Hadji Diouf and Eric Hazard, 'Sectorial Initiative on Cotton: A Balancing Act of Alliances in Africa and at the WTO', in Hazard (ed.), *International Trade Negotiations and Poverty Reduction: The White Paper on Cotton*.
38. Third party signatories have the right to submit testimony before panels during the first round of litigation, but are not allowed to participate in the main panel hearings or appeal panel reports. On Brazilian approaches to the C4, Pedro de Camargo Neto, a major strategist on the cotton case and former Secretary of Production and Trade with the Ministry of Agriculture, has remarked that he tried to persuade the WCA countries to join as co-complainants but they refused. See Ray A. Goldberg, Robert Z. Lawrence, and Katie Milligan, 'Brazil's WTO Cotton Case: Negotiation Through Litigation', in Charan Devereaux, Robert Z. Lawrence, and Michael D. Watkins (eds.), *Case Studies in US Trade Negotiations: Resolving Disputes Volume 2* (Washington, DC: Peterson Institute for International Economics, 2006).
39. Hilton E. Zunckel, 'The African Awakening in *United States–Upland Cotton*', *Journal of World Trade*, 39 (2005), 6, 1071–93. Also see Romain Benicchio, 'The WTO Ruling on the Brazil–US Cotton Dispute: Implications for African Countries and Agriculture Negotiations', in Hazard (ed.), *International Trade Negotiations and Poverty Reduction: The White Paper on Cotton*. For an historical overview of the participation of African countries in the DSB, see Victor Mosoti, 'Africa in the First Decade of WTO Dispute Settlement', *Journal of International Economic Law*, 9 (2006), 2, 427–53.
40. Among hundreds of articles which would later appear in the world media, see in particular Roger Thurow and Scott Kilman, 'Hanging by a Thread: In US, Cotton Farmers Thrive; in Africa, They Fight to Survive', *Wall Street Journal*, 26 June 2002.

41. WTO, 'Negotiations on Agriculture; First Draft of Modalities for the Further Commitments; Revision', 18 March 2003 (TN/AG/W/1/Rev.1). The term 'modality' does not have a precise definition in the WTO, but usually refers to the specification of formulas or approaches for final legal commitments.
42. Reduction commitments in the AoA are expressed in terms of an aggregate measure of support (AMS) that combines estimated support levels from all non-exempt policies for all commodities into one overall spending amount. The Blue Box exemption category contains subsidies that are considered to be possibly trade-distorting and not immune to challenge, but still permitted under the AoA. In the Uruguay Round negotiations it was implied that Blue Box policies were temporary and transitional, although by the Doha Round, the US and the EU began making attempts to broaden the category.
43. The concept of the 'strategic product' was associated with an original group of approximately 20 Southern countries led by Indonesia. The term was designed to express how certain commodities were intimately connected to ideas about political sovereignty. Under pressure from some Northern countries, however, later draft texts by Harbinson changed the term to the more neutral 'special', thus leading the group to reclassify itself as the 'Alliance on Special Products and the Special Safeguard Mechanism', and by Cancún, the G33. See Chapter 5.
44. The reference is drawn from WTO, 'Negotiations on Agriculture; First Draft of Modalities for the Further Commitments; Revision', p. 11.
45. Romain Benicchio, Advocacy Officer, Oxfam International, interview with the author, Geneva, 26 September 2006.
46. El Hadji A. Diouf, Programme Coordinator, Africa Trade Programme, International Centre for Trade and Sustainable Development, Geneva, interview with the author, Geneva, 29 September 2006.
47. For details, see IDEAS Centre, <http://www.ideascentre.ch>.
48. Other agencies providing financial support included the Danish Ministry of Foreign Affairs, the Dutch Ministry of Foreign Affairs, the French Ministry of Foreign Affairs, the German Ministry of Economic Cooperation and Development, the Swedish Ministry of Foreign Affairs, and the UK Department for International Development. For details, see IDEAS Centre, <www.ideascentre.ch>. In interviews conducted for this book, Imboden's contribution was recognized by WCA policy-makers, including Ambassador Samuel Améhou at the Benin mission in Geneva; Jason Hafemeister, former Deputy Assistant US Trade Representative for Agriculture and lead negotiator on agriculture during the Doha Round (until 2007); two officials at the WTO Secretariat who declined to be named; and another trade analyst who also wished to remain anonymous.
49. Nicolas Imboden, Executive Director, IDEAS Centre, interview with the author, Geneva, 27 September 2006.
50. Ibid. On the specific point of Imboden's role in drafting the cotton dossier, two other interview subjects, including an official in the WTO Secretariat and another civil society representative, stated that his contribution was significant. Both these individuals preferred anonymity on this issue. Imboden's contribution is also discussed in Adam Sneyd, *Governing Cotton: Globalization and Poverty in Africa*

(Basingstoke: Palgrave Macmillan, 2011); and Paul Blustein, *Misadventures of the Most Favored Nations: Clashing Egos, Inflated Ambitions, and the Great Shambles of the World Trade System* (New York: Public Affairs, 2009).

51. WTO, 'Poverty Reduction: Sectoral Initative in Favour of Cotton', Joint Proposal by Benin, Burkina Faso, Chad and Mali, 16 May 2003 (TN/AG/GEN/4).
52. Goreux, 'Prejudice Caused by Industrialized Countries to Cotton Sectors in Western and Central Africa', June 2003.
53. Gérald Estur, 'Is West African Cotton Competitive with the US on the World Cotton Market?', paper presented at Beltwide Cotton Conference, New Orleans, 7 January 2005. On the use of child labour in the cotton industry in West Africa, as well as other regions, see Environmental Justice Foundation, *The Children Behind Our Cotton* (London: Environmental Justice Foundation, 2007).
54. However, the value of hand-picked cotton is not always superior to machine-picked cotton due to the risk of contamination by foreign matter. See Baffes and Estur, 'Market Context'.
55. WTO, 'Poverty Reduction', p. 2.
56. Ibid., p. 10.
57. Ibid., p. 15.
58. Ibid., p. 24. The ICAC study is not referenced.
59. Ibid., p. 15.
60. Jason Hafemeister, former Deputy Assistant US Trade Representative for Agriculture and lead agricultural negotiator during the Doha Round (until 2007), interview with the author, Washington, DC, 12 July 2010.
61. Samuel Améhou, Ambassador, Permanent Mission of the Republic of Benin to the United Nations Office and other International Organizations in Geneva, interview with the author, Geneva, 26 September 2006.
62. Emily Jones, Carolyn Deere-Birkbeck, and Ngaire Woods, *Manoeuvring at the Margins: Constraints Faced by Small States in International Trade Negotiations* (London: Commonwealth Secretariat, 2010), 19. In this study, there were 20 interviews conducted for a case study on Benin by Isaline Bergamaschi. All these interview subjects praised the contribution of Améhou as 'second to none'. His command of English and previous experience stationed at the UN in New York were other valuable qualities. Personal communication with Isaline Bergamaschi, 9 September 2010.
63. El Hadji A. Diouf, Programme Coordinator, Africa Trade Programme, International Centre for Trade and Sustainable Development (ICTSD), interview with the author, Geneva, 29 September 2006. Also see El Hadji Diouf, 'The Survival of African Cotton Between Negotiation and Dispute at the WTO', *Trade Negotiations Insights*, 2, 3, June 2003.
64. Imboden, Executive Director, IDEAS Centre, interview with the author.
65. For an attempt to trace the conceptual genealogy, see Tore Fougner, 'The State, International Competitiveness and Neoliberal Globalisation: Is There a Future Beyond "the Competition State"?', *Review of International Studies*, 32 (2006), 1, 165–85.
66. Jones, Deere-Birkbeck, and Woods, *Manoeuvring at the Margins: Constraints Faced by Small States in International Trade Negotiations*, 19.

67. Karlyn H. Keene, Paul G. Kirk Jr, Norman Ornstein, Edward J. Rollins, and John H. Makin, 'The Meaning of Competitiveness', in Claude E. Barfield and John H. Makin (eds.), *Trade Policy and US Competitiveness* (Washington, DC: American Enterprise Institute, 1987), 131.
68. Pesche and Nubukpo, 'The African Cotton Set in Cancún: A Look Back at the Beginning of Negotiations'.
69. As stated in the Doha Ministerial Declaration, 'International trade can play a major role in the promotion of economic development and the alleviation of poverty... We recognize the particular vulnerability of the least-developed countries and the special structural difficulties they face in the global economy.' WTO, 'Ministerial Declaration', Ministerial Conference, Fourth Session, Doha, 20 November 2001 (WT/MIN(01)/DEC/1), p. 2, 3. From 1999, one can also note how the expression 'poverty reduction' was firmly institutionalized by the World Bank and the IMF through their Poverty Reduction Strategy Papers, a new mechanism for debt relief with recipient countries. Also see Alan Winters, Neil McCulloch, and Andrew McKay, 'Trade Liberalization and Poverty: The Evidence So Far', *Journal of Economic Literature*, 42 (2004), 1, 72–115. For a brief critical examination of the popularity of the phrase 'poverty reduction' in the field of development studies, see John Toye, 'Poverty Reduction', *Development in Practice*, 17 (2007), 4–5, 505–10.
70. Imboden, Executive Director, IDEAS Centre, interview with the author.
71. Interviews with two WTO Secretariat representatives.
72. Imboden, Executive Director, IDEAS Centre, interview with the author.
73. WTO, 'Poverty Reduction', p. 7.
74. Marco Bronckers and Naboth van den Broek, 'Financial Compensation in the WTO: Improving the Remedies of WTO Dispute Settlement', *Journal of International Economic Law*, 8 (2005), 1, 101–26.
75. Diouf, Programme Coordinator, Africa Trade Programme, International Centre for Trade and Sustainable Development (ICTSD), interview with the author.
76. Sidney Dell, 'The Fifth Credit Tranche', *World Development*, 13 (1985), 2, 245–9. Also see Graham Bird, 'Restructuring the IMF's Lending Facilities', *World Economy*, 26 (2003), 2, 229–45. In 1988 the facility was renamed the Compensatory and Contingency Financing Facility.
77. Samuel Asfaha, Programme Officer on Commodities and Economic Diversification, Trade for Development Programme, South Centre, interview with the author, Geneva, 28 March 2007.
78. Abdoulay Sanoko, Counsellor, Permanent Mission of the Republic of Mali to the United Nations Office and other International Organizations in Geneva, interview with the author, Geneva, 27 March 2007.
79. For example, see Andrew Hurrell and Amrita Narlikar, 'The New Politics of Confrontation: Developing Countries at Cancún and Beyond', *Global Society*, 20 (2006), 4, 415–33; Amrita Narlikar and Diana Tussie, 'The G20 at the Cancún Ministerial: Developing Countries and their Evolving Coalitions in the WTO', *World Economy*, 27 (2004), 7, 947–66; Amrita Narlikar and Rorden Wilkinson, 'Collapse at the WTO: A Cancún Post Mortem', *Third World Quarterly*, 25 (2004), 3, 417–30; and Rorden Wilkinson, 'Crisis in Cancún', *Global Governance*, 10 (2004), 2, 149–55.

80. WTO, 'Minutes of Meeting', Trade Negotiations Committee, 10–11 June 2003 (TN/C/M/10), 64–5.
81. US House of Representatives, Hearing before the Subcommittee on Africa, Committee on International Relations, One Hundred Eighth Congress, First Session, 24 June 2003, Serial No: 108–30.
82. Amadou Toumani Touré and Blaise Compaoré, 'Your Farm Subsidies are Strangling Us', *New York Times*, 11 July 2003.
83. WTO, 'Preparations for the Fifth Session of the Ministerial Conference, Draft Cancún Ministerial Text; Revision', 24 August 2003 (JOB(03)/150/Rev.1). The text was drafted under the supervision of the Chair of the General Council, Carlos Pérez del Castillo, and the Director General, Supachai Panitchpakdi.
84. Glauber, Chief Economist, US Department of Agriculture, interview with the author.
85. This analysis is also informed by interviews with Henry Schmick, Agricultural Attaché, and Christine Strossman, Agricultural Attaché, both at the Office of Agricultural Affairs, US Mission to the WTO, interviews with the author, Geneva, 28 March 2007. Also see United States Trade Representative, 'Remarks on the African Cotton Initiative', Ambassador Josette Sheeran Shiner, 10 September 2003.
86. As already noted, the increased production of synthetic fibres relative to cotton certainly does play a role in determining the world price and the distributional impact on C4 farmers.
87. It is interesting, for instance, that one senator, Republican Thad Cochran of Mississippi and Chair of the Senate Agriculture Committee, was at Cancún to lend support to the US delegation. Also see National Cotton Council of America, 'USTR Proposal on Trade Distortion Discussions Much Needed', Press release, 11 September 2003; and National Cotton Council of America, 'NCC Lauds Cochran's Declaration on WTO Ag Trade Negotiations', Press release, 9 September 2003.
88. Hafemeister, former Deputy Assistant US Trade Representative for Agriculture and lead agricultural negotiator during the Doha Round (until 2007), interview with the author.
89. *Bridges Daily Update on the Fifth Ministerial Conference*, 2, 11 September 2003 (Geneva: International Centre for Trade and Sustainable Development). Also see Fatoumata Jawara and Aileen Kwa, *Behind the Scenes at the WTO: The Real World of International Trade Negotiations/Lessons of Cancún* (London: Zed Books, 2004); and Blustein, *Misadventures of the Most Favored Nations: Clashing Egos, Inflated Ambitions, and the Great Shambles of the World Trade System*.
90. Before the start of the Ministerial, according to one African official who spoke to Fatoumata Jawara and Aileen Kwa, 'We were told not to talk so loudly on the cotton issue. Let the four of them [Benin, Burkina Faso, Chad, and Mali] fight it. It was portrayed to be a war against the US. There was some pressure to quieten some countries. I don't think it worked. It was like you were trying to fight against the US, which you know is not acceptable in this setting. It is like you are committing a sin or a crime.' Quoted in Jawara and Kwa, *Behind the Scenes at the WTO: The Real World of International Trade Negotiations/Lessons of Cancún*.
91. Glauber, Chief Economist, US Department of Agriculture, interview with the author.

92. Pedro da Motta Veiga, 'Brazil and the G-20 Group of Developing Countries', in Peter Gallagher, Patrick Low, and Andrew L. Stoler (eds.), *Managing the Challenges of WTO Participation: 45 Case Studies* (Cambridge: Cambridge University Press, 2005); and Imboden, Executive Director, IDEAS Centre, interview with the author. Established in 1986, the Cairns group is a diverse coalition of 19 agricultural exporting countries. Prominent members include Argentina, Australia, Brazil, Canada, South Africa, Thailand, and Uruguay. The group has historically campaigned for the elimination of all trade-distorting domestic subsidies and export subsidies and, thus, shares an affinity with the C4 cause.
93. Pascal Lamy, 'Speech by Commissioner Lamy on the "Cotton Initiative" at the 5th WTO Ministerial Conference (Cancun)', 10 September 2003; and Pascal Lamy, 'Result of the WTO Ministerial Conference in Cancún', Remarks to Plenary Session on the Ministerial Conference of the WTO in Cancún, Council of Europe, Strasbourg, 24 September 2003.
94. The Singapore issues referred to four working groups established at the First WTO Ministerial Conference in Singapore in 1996. The groups focused on investment protection, competition policy, transparency in government procurement, and trade facilitation. The UK Department for Trade and Industry (DTI), in a Cancún post-mortem, accused Lamy of 'tactical misjudgement' in offering concessions in the Singapore issues too late. See Larry Elliott, 'DTI Leak Blames Lamy for Cancun Failure', *The Guardian*, 22 October 2003.
95. Imboden, Executive Director, IDEAS Centre, interview with the author.
96. This point is courtesy of a European civil society representative who was present at Cancún and wishes to remain anonymous. For Wieczorek-Zeul's noted support of the C4, see Wolfgang Uchatius, 'Der Norden sät den Hunger', *Die Zeit*, 14 August 2003.
97. Narlikar and Wilkinson, 'Collapse at the WTO: A Cancún Post Mortem', 450.
98. Blustein, *Misadventures of the Most Favored Nations: Clashing Egos, Inflated Ambitions, and the Great Shambles of the World Trade System.*
99. Interview with WTO Secretariat representative.
100. Report of the Cotton Initiative, Heads of Delegations Meeting, 12 September 2003, <http://www.wto.org/english/thewto_e/minist_e/min03_e/min03_12sept_e.htm>.
101. WTO, 'Preparations for the Fifth Session of the Ministerial Conference; Draft Cancún Ministerial Text; Second Revision', 13 September 2003 (JOB(03)/150/Rev.2), p. 27.
102. Ernst H. Kantorowicz, *The King's Two Bodies: A Study in Mediaeval Political Theology* (Princeton: Princeton University Press, 1957).
103. Interview with Geneva-based African representative.
104. Glauber, Chief Economist, US Department of Agriculture, interview with the author.
105. Martin Khor, 'Analysis of the Collapse of the Cancun Ministerial', Third World Network Info Service on WTO Issues, 16 September 2003.
106. Blustein, *Misadventures of the Most Favored Nations: Clashing Egos, Inflated Ambitions, and the Great Shambles of the World Trade System.*

107. Pascal Lamy, 'Result of the WTO Ministerial Conference in Cancún', Remarks to Plenary Session on the Ministerial Conference of the WTO in Cancún, Council of Europe, Strasbourg, 24 September 2003.
108. As an example of a prominent US rebuttal, see Robert Zoellick, 'America Will Not Wait for the Won't-Do Countries', *Financial Times*, 22 September 2003. Also see Jawara and Kwa, *Behind the Scenes at the WTO: The Real World of International Trade Negotiations/Lessons of Cancún*.
109. Quoted in Martin Khor, 'Lamy Still Insists that Singapore Issues are Part of Doha Single Undertaking; Report of Panel Discussion at the UN on WTO and Cancun', Third World Network Info Service on WTO Issues, 7 November 2003.
110. WTO, 'Statements by the Chairman of the General Council and the Director-General; Informal Heads of Delegation Meeting', Press release, 14 October 2003.
111. Diouf, Programme Coordinator, Africa Trade Programme, International Centre for Trade and Sustainable Development, interview with the author.
112. Améhou, Ambassador, Permanent Mission of the Republic of Benin, interview with the author.
113. WTO, 'Poverty Reduction: Sectoral Initiative on Cotton; Wording of Paragraph 27 of the Revised Draft Cancún Ministerial Text', Communication from Benin, 7 October 2003 (WT/GC/W/516).
114. To recall the discussion in Chapters 2 and 3, the 'green room' is a phrase taken from the informal name of the WTO Director General's conference room at the Secretariat. It is used to refer to meetings of 20–30 members, usually at the level of heads of delegations.
115. Quoted in *Bridges Weekly Trade News Digest*, 'WTO: Green Room Highlights Limited Progress in Trade Talks', 7, 39, 19 November 2003.
116. WTO, News Item, 'General Council: Follow-up to the Cancún Ministerial Conference; Key Issues Clearer, Possible Solutions Becoming Visible—General Council Chair', 15 December 2003, <http://www.wto.org/english/news_e/news03_e/stat_gc_chair_15dec03_e.htm>.
117. WTO, General Council, 'Minutes of Meeting', 15–16 December 2003 (WT/GC/M/84), p. 23.
118. Ibid., p. 50.
119. Ibid., p. 56.
120. Ibid., p. 81.
121. Ibid., p. 91.
122. Ibid., p. 133, italics added for emphasis.
123. See, for instance, Heinisch, 'West Africa Versus the United States on Cotton Subsidies: How, Why and What Next?'; Lee, 'The Cotton Club: The Africa Group in the Doha Development Agenda', in Lee and Wilkinson (eds.), *The WTO After Hong Kong: Progress In, and Prospects For, the Doha Development Agenda*; Lee and Smith, 'The Political Economy of Small African States in the WTO'; and Shahin, 'The Cotton Initiative', in Sampson and Chambers (eds.), *Developing Countries and the WTO: Policy Approaches*.

124. Sanoko, Counsellor, Permanent Mission of the Republic of Mali to the United Nations Office and other International Organizations in Geneva, interview with the author, italics added for emphasis.
125. Imboden, Executive Director, IDEAS Centre, interview with the author, italics added for emphasis.
126. Participating international institutions included the African Development Bank, the African Union, the ACP Secretariat, the Economic Community of West African States, the Intergovernmental Francophone Agency, the International Cotton Advisory Committee, the International Monetary Fund, the International Trade Centre, the New Partnership for Africa's Development, the Organisation for Economic Co-operation and Development, the United Nations Conference on Trade and Development, the United Nations Development Programme, the United Nations Economic Commission for Africa, the United Nations Food and Agriculture Organization, the United Nations Industrial Development Organization, the West African Development Bank, the West African Economic and Monetary Union, and the World Bank.
127. WTO, 'WTO African Regional Workshop on Cotton; Cotonou, Republic of Benin; 23–24 March 2004', Note by the Secretariat, Annex 1, Opening Remarks by Dr Supachai Panitchpakdi, 17 November 2004 (WT/L/587).
128. Representatives on the first session included John Baffes of the World Bank, Cyrille Brainçon of the IMF, and Karim Hussein of the OECD/Sahel and West Africa Club.
129. WTO, 'WTO African Regional Workshop on Cotton', p. 19; and Annex 7, Statement by the US Delegation, Assistant Administrator Simmons.
130. WTO, 'WTO African Regional Workshop on Cotton', p. 14, 52; and Annex 4, Statement by the European Communities Delegation.
131. WTO, 'WTO African Regional Workshop on Cotton', p. 72.
132. WTO, 'Doha Work Programme; Decision Adopted by the General Council on 1 August 2004', 2 August 2004 (WT/L/579), p. 1(b).
133. Ibid., Annex A, Framework for Establishing Modalities in Agriculture, p. 4.
134. WTO, 'Establishment of the Sub-Committee on Cotton; Decision Adopted by the Committee on Agriculture, Special Session on 19 November 2004', 26 November 2004 (TN/AG/13). For further details, see WTO, Agriculture, The Cotton Sub-Committee, <www.wto.org/english/tratop_e/agric_e/cotton_subcommittee_e.htm>.
135. Other prominent events that showcased the C4's plight during the subsequent period included an OECD-organized 'Briefing on the Development Dimensions of African Cotton' in January 2005; and the 'IMF/Benin Joint High-Level Regional Conference on Cotton', held in Cotonou, Benin, in May 2005. In addition, more direct leadership from USDA, USTR, and the US Agency for International Development included sponsoring the 'Ministerial Conference on Harnessing Science and Technology to Increase Agricultural Productivity in Africa: West African Perspectives', held in Ouagadougou, Burkina Faso in June 2004; and pushing the NCC to assist in meeting West African ministers on a 'US Cotton Tour' in July 2004. In November 2005, the US extended and reorganized these efforts through the launch of the 'West African Cotton Improvement Program' which

concentrated on trying to enhance farmer productivity and efficiency in the ginning industry.

136. Pierre Bourdieu, *The State Nobility: Elite Schools in the Field of Power* (Cambridge: Polity Press, 1996), 383.
137. The phrase 'mobilization of bias', to recall the conceptual discussion on institutional power in Chapter 2, is derived from Elmer Eric Schattschneider, *The Semi-Sovereign People: A Realist's View of Democracy in America* (New York: Holt, Rinehart and Winston, 1960), 71.
138. Ross Coggins, 'The Development Set', *Journal of Communication*, 28 (1978), 1, 80.
139. To reiterate, as noted in Section 3.1, this does not mean that a material interpretation of the WCA cotton problem should retreat into simplistic explanations. Rather, the point here is to illuminate how the most politically potent feature of the problem—domestic support subsidies on the part of players such as the US—was diminished through complicating definitions of historical responsibility.
140. Tomohisa Hattori, 'Reconceptualizing Foreign Aid', *Review of International Political Economy*, 8 (2001), 4, 633–60, quoted at 640, italics in original.
141. Pierre Bourdieu, *Pascalian Meditations* (Cambridge: Polity Press, 1997), 193.
142. WTO, 'Ouagadougou Declaration on the Cotton Situation Since the Adoption of the July 2004 Package', Communication from Burkina Faso, 7 April 2005 (TN/AG/SCC/GEN/1), p. 3.
143. Pierre Bourdieu, *The Logic of Practice* (Stanford: Stanford University Press, 1990), 118.
144. Loïc Wacquant, 'On Symbolic Power and Group-Making: Pierre Bourdieu's Reframing of Class', Preface to Pierre Bourdieu, *Et klassespørsmål* (Oslo: Forlaget Manifest, 2007).
145. WTO, 'United States—Subsidies on Upland Cotton; Report of the Panel', 8 September 2004 (WT/DS267/R).
146. For a detailed analysis, see Karen Halverson Cross, 'King Cotton, Developing Countries and the "Peace Clause": The WTO's *US Cotton Subsidies* Decision', *Journal of International Economic Law*, 9 (2006), 1, 149–95; as well as Richard H. Steinberg, 'United States: Subsidies on Upland Cotton, WTO Doc. WT/DS267/AB/R', *American Journal of International Law*, 99 (2005), 4, 852–61. The Panel also addressed the so-called 'Peace Clause' within the AoA which, until its expiry in 2004, protected members from potential litigation against subsidy schemes.
147. WTO, 'United States—Subsidies on Upland Cotton; Report of the Appellate Body', 3 March 2005 (WT/DS267/AB/R).
148. WTO, 'United States—Subsidies on Upland Cotton; Recourse to Article 21.5 of the DSU by Brazil; Report of the Panel', 18 December 2007 (WT/DS267/RW).
149. Karen Halverson Cross, 'United States: Subsidies on Upland Cotton, Recourse to Article 21.5 of the DSU by Brazil', *American Journal of International Law*, 103 (2009), 1, 110–16.
150. USTR Press Release, 'US, Brazil Agree Upon Path Toward Negotiated Solution of Cotton Dispute', 4 June 2010. Also see *Bridges Weekly Trade News Digest*, 'Brazil, US Strike "Framework" Deal in Cotton Dispute', 14, 23, 23 June 2010.

151. Zunckel, 'The African Awakening in *United States–Upland Cotton*', 1079–80.
152. Mosoti, 'Africa in the First Decade of WTO Dispute Settlement', 447. Also see Jumoke Oduwole, 'Nothing Ventured, Nothing Gained? A Case Study of Africa's Participation in WTO Dispute Settlement', *International Journal of Private Law*, 2 (2009), 4, 358–70.
153. For example, see Arsene Omichessan, 'Navigating the Dispute Settlement Understanding (DSU): How Benin Took on the Challenges in Cotton', International Centre for Trade and Sustainable Development Africa Dialogue on WTO Dispute Settlement and Sustainable Development, Mombasa, Kenya, 2–3 November 2006.
154. Bourdieu, *The State Nobility: Elite Schools in the Field of Power*, 382.
155. Mario Jales, 'How Would A Trade Deal On Cotton Affect Exporting And Importing Countries?', Issue paper 26 (Geneva: International Centre for Trade and Sustainable Development, May 2010).
156. WTO, 'Doha Work Programme; Ministerial Declaration; Adopted on 18 December 2005', 22 December 2005 (WT/MIN(05)/DEC), p. 11, italics added for emphasis.
157. Glauber, Chief Economist, US Department of Agriculture, interview with the author.
158. Under the AoA, the Total Aggregate Measure of Support (AMS) collapses all product-specific support and non-product-specific support into one single figure.
159. WTO, 'Proposed Modalities for Cotton Under the Mandate of the Hong Kong Ministerial Decision', Communication from the Co-Sponsors of the Sectoral Initiative in Favour of Cotton, 1 March 2006 (TN/AG/SCC/GEN/4).
160. Hafemeister, former Deputy Assistant US Trade Representative for Agriculture and lead agricultural negotiator during the Doha Round (until 2007), interview with the author.
161. WTO, 'Revised Draft Modalities for Agriculture', 10 July 2008 (TN/AG/W/4/Rev.3).
162. Agence France-Presse, 'Cotton Tangles up Collapsed WTO Talks', 30 July 2008.
163. Glauber, Chief Economist, US Department of Agriculture, interview with the author.
164. Martin Khor, 'Reflections Begin on the WTO Failure and the Future Work', *South–North Development Monitor (SUNS) Report #6530*, 4 August 2008.
165. Pierre Bourdieu, 'From the King's House to the Reason of State: A Model of the Genesis of the Bureaucratic Field', *Constellations*, 11 (2004), 1, 16–36.
166. Pierre Bourdieu, 'What Makes a Social Class? On the Theoretical and Practical Existence of Groups', *Berkeley Journal of Sociology*, 32 (1987), 1–18, quoted at 13.

Chapter 5

1. Jean-Paul Sartre, *L'idiot de la famille* (Paris: Gallimard, 1971), 1, 783, quoted in Pierre Bourdieu, *Outline of a Theory of Practice* (Cambridge: Cambridge University Press, 1977), 170.
2. Jacques Berlinerblau, 'Toward a Sociology of Heresy, Orthodoxy, and *Doxa*', *History of Religions*, 40 (2001), 4, 327–51.

3. For instance, see Christopher L. Delgado, Jane Hopkins, and Valerie A. Kelly, *Agricultural Growth Linkages in Sub-Saharan Africa,* IFPRI Research Report 107 (Washington, DC: International Food Policy Research Institute, 1998).
4. Food and Agricultural Organization of the United Nations (FAO), *The State of Agricultural Commodity Markets 2004* (Rome: FAO, 2004), 20.
5. Food and Agriculture Organization of the United Nations (FAO), *The State of Food and Agriculture 2010–11: Women in Agriculture; Closing the Gender Gap for Development* (Rome: FAO, 2011), Part III Statistical Annex, Table A4.
6. Such arguments have been advanced since the late 1940s when Raul Prebisch and Hans Singer contradicted the neoclassical expectation of declining terms of trade for manufactures relative to agricultural produce. For more recent analysis, see Roman Grynberg and Samantha Newton (eds.), *Commodity Prices and Development* (Oxford: Oxford University Press, 2007); José Antonio Ocampo and María Angela Parra, 'The Terms Of Trade For Commodities In The Twentieth Century', *CEPAL Review*, 79 (2003), 7–35; and Paul Cashin and C. John McDermott, 'The Long-Run Behavior of Commodity Prices: Small Trends and Big Variability', IMF Staff Papers, 49, 2 (Washington, DC: International Monetary Fund, 2002).
7. FAO, *The State of Agricultural Commodity Markets 2004.*
8. Ibid.
9. Roman Grynberg and Samantha Newton, 'Introduction', in Grynberg and Newton (eds.), *Commodity Prices and Development,* 3. The figures group together states classified as least developed countries (LDCs), small vulnerable states (SVs), and heavily indebted poor countries (HIPCs).
10. FAO, *The State of Agricultural Commodity Markets 2004.*
11. For good overviews, see Shenggen Fan and Derek Headey, *Reflections on the Global Food Crisis: How Did It Happen? How Has It Hurt? And How Can We Prevent the Next One?* (Washington, DC: International Food Policy Research Institute, 2010); Baris Karapinar and Christian Häberli (eds.), *Food Crises and the WTO* (Cambridge: Cambridge University Press, 2010); Organisation for Economic Co-operation and Development (OECD) and Food and Agricultural Organization of the United Nations (FAO), *OECD–FAO Agricultural Outlook 2010–2019* (OECD–FAO, 2010); and Food and Agricultural Organization of the United Nations (FAO), *The State of Agricultural Commodity Markets 2009: High Food Prices and the Food Crisis—Experiences and Lessons Learned* (Rome: FAO, 2009).
12. Jennifer Clapp and Eric Helleiner, 'Troubled Futures? The Global Food Crisis and the Politics of Agricultural Derivatives Regulation', *Review of International Political Economy*, 19 (2012), 181–207; and Jennifer Clapp, 'Food Price Volatility and Vulnerability in the Global South: Considering the Global Economic Context', *Third World Quarterly*, 30 (2009), 6: 1183–96.
13. The FAO has created a dedicated country category called Low-Income Food-Deficit Countries, comprising 82 countries (as of November 2006). For details on the criteria for classification and listings, see FAO Country Profiles and Mapping Information System, <http://www.fao.org/countryprofiles/default/en>. It must be noted that there is not a precise correlation between lower commodity prices and lower food import bills in Southern countries. In the 1990s, for instance, the cereal

import bills for so-called least developed countries increased from US$4.9 billion in 1993–94 to US$8.4 billion in 1997–98.

14. Luisa Bernal, 'Guidelines for Approaching the Designation of Special Products and SSM Products in Developing Countries', paper presented at International Centre for Trade and Sustainable Development (ICTSD) Informal Consultation, 'Special Products and Special Safeguard Mechanism After the July Framework: How Do We Move Forward?', Geneva, 30 September 2004.
15. Kevin Watkins and Akhtar Mahmood, 'WTO Negotiations on Agriculture: What Can Be Achieved?', in Thomas Lines (ed.), *Agricultural Commodities, Trade and Sustainable Development* (Geneva: International Centre for Trade and Sustainable Development/London: International Institute for Environment and Development, 2005).
16. Food and Agricultural Organization of the United Nations (FAO), *WTO Agreement on Agriculture: The Implementation Experience—Developing Country Case Studies* (Rome: FAO, 2003).
17. Ibid.
18. Food and Agricultural Organization of the United Nations (FAO), *Food Outlook: Global Market Analysis* (Rome: FAO, June 2007).
19. There is no universal definition of an 'import surge'. Common references are drawn from WTO disciplines in the Agreement on Safeguards and the Special Safeguard provision of the Agreement on Agriculture. See Maurizio de Nigris, 'Defining and Quantifying the Extent of Import Surges: Data and Methodologies', Food and Agricultural Organization of the United Nations (FAO) Import Surge Project, Working Paper 2 (Rome: FAO, May 2005).
20. Among individual commodities, those most affected were pig and poultry meats, palm oil, sugar, and eggs, all ranging from 20–23% in frequency. Only in the case of wheat, rice, maize, palm oil, and rape oil did the frequency of surges decline. Food and Agricultural Organization of the United Nations (FAO), Briefs on Import Surges, 2, 'Import Surges: What is Their Frequency and Which are the Countries and Commodities Most Affected?' (Rome: FAO, October 2006).
21. Maurizio de Nigris, 'Defining and Quantifying the Extent of Import Surges: Data and Methodologies', FAO Import Surge Project Working Paper No. 2 (Rome: FAO, May 2005).
22. Food and Agricultural Organization of the United Nations (FAO), 'Import Surges: Analysis, Preliminary Findings and Lessons Learned', Committee on Commodity Problems, Sixty-sixth Session, Rome, 23–25 April 2007 (Rome: FAO).
23. Mario Jales, *Tariff Reductions, Special Products, and Special Safeguards: An Analysis of the Agricultural Tariff Structures of G-33 Countries* (Geneva: International Centre for Trade and Sustainable Development, June 2005). Jales drew on information from the FAOSTAT database. Also see Food and Agricultural Organization of the United Nations (FAO), Briefs on Import Surges—Countries, 6, 'Jamaica: Poultry, Dairy Products and Onions' (Rome: FAO, November 2006).
24. Oxfam International, *A Raw Deal for Rice Under DR-CAFTA: How the Free Trade Agreement Threatens the Livelihoods of Central American Farmers* (Oxford: Oxfam International, November 2004).

25. See particularly, Structural Adjustment Participatory Review International Network (SAPRIN), *Structural Adjustment: The SAPRI Report: The Policy Roots of Economic Crisis, Poverty and Inequality* (London: Zed Books, 2004). Reluctantly, the World Bank has begun to show more recognition that its actions produced adverse effects, arguing that domestic investment in agriculture should now be at the heart of national economic strategies in many countries. See World Bank, *World Development Report 2008: Agriculture for Development* (Washington, DC: World Bank, 2007).
26. Uruguay Round Agreement on Agriculture, Preamble.
27. John Croome, *Reshaping the World Trading System: A History of the Uruguay Round* (London: Kluwer Law International, 1998).
28. Food and Agricultural Organization of the United Nations (FAO) Secretariat, 'Some Issues Relating to Food Security in the Context of the WTO Negotiations on Agriculture', paper presented at FAO Geneva Roundtable, 'Food Security in the Context of WTO Negotiations on Agriculture', United Nations, Geneva, 20 July 2001. Also see Bhagirath Lal Das, *The WTO Agreements: Deficiencies, Imbalances and Required Changes* (London: Zed Books, 1998).
29. Shelia Page and Peter Kleen, *Special and Differential Treatment of Developing Countries in the World Trade Organization* (Stockholm: EGDI, Ministry for Foreign Affairs, Sweden, 2004). Also see Shelia Page, 'The Evolution of Special and Differential Treatment in the Multilateral Trading System', paper presented at International Centre for Trade and Sustainable Development (ICTSD) Workshop, Geneva, 6 December 2004. The origins of SDT can be found in the GATT 1947 in the context of manufactured products, however it was not until the 'Haberler Report' of 1958 (officially titled *Trends in International Trade*) when issues such as Northern agricultural protectionism and volatile commodity prices became more visible in the eyes of the GATT contracting parties.
30. Page and Kleen, *Special and Differential Treatment of Developing Countries in the World Trade Organization.*
31. Bernard Hoekman, 'Operationalizing the Concept of Policy Space in the WTO: Beyond Special and Differential Treatment', *Journal of International Economic Law*, 8 (2005), 2, 405–24.
32. Anwarul Hoda, *Special Products: Options for Negotiating Modalities* (Geneva: International Centre for Trade and Sustainable Development, July 2005).
33. WTO, 'Revised Draft Modalities for Agriculture', 6 December 2008 (TN/AG/W/4/Rev. 4), p. 64. In this text, the figure is a maximum cut of 36% for developing countries and a minimum cut of 54% for developed countries.
34. This grouping of different countries is derived from Jales, *Tariff Reductions, Special Products, and Special Safeguards: An Analysis of the Agricultural Tariff Structures of G-33 Countries.*
35. AoA, Preamble; Article 20: Continuation of the Reform Process; and Annex 5: Special Treatment with Respect to Paragraph 2 of Article 4.
36. Fiona Smith, 'Non-Trade Concerns and Agriculture in the Post-Doha Environment: Thinking Outside the Green Box', *Environmental Law Review*, 9 (2007), 2, 89–115.
37. General Agreement on Tariffs and Trade (GATT), 'Negotiating Group on Agriculture: Submission by Japan', 6 December 1989 (MTN.GNG/NG5/W/131), 2, 3. For further

analysis, see Terence P. Stewart (ed.), *The GATT Uruguay Round: A Negotiating History (1986–1992); Volume 1: Commentary* (Deventer: Kluwer Law and Taxation Publishers, 1999).

38. General Agreement on Tariffs and Trade (GATT), 'Food Security: Statement by Jamaica at the Eighth Meeting of the Negotiating Group on Agriculture', 30 June 1988 (MTN.GNG/NG5/W/65).
39. The Green Box, which was referred to in the previous cotton chapter, organizes domestic support payments (including items such as research or disaster funds) that must not distort trade, or at most cause 'minimal' distortion. AoA, Annex 2, Domestic Support: The Basis for Exemption from the Reduction Commitments, p. 3.
40. AoA, Annex 2, Domestic Support: The Basis for Exemption from the Reduction Commitments, p. 3.
41. FAO, *WTO Agreement on Agriculture: The Implementation Experience—Developing Country Case Studies*.
42. Ibid. For reference, see <http://www.fao.org/DOCREP/005/Y4632E/y4632e0l.htm>.
43. In 2000, India allocated 70% of its Green Box spending (US$2.02 billion) under this category. See United Nations Conference on Trade and Development (UNCTAD), *Green Box Subsidies: A Theoretical and Empirical Assessment* (Geneva: UNCTAD, May 2007).
44. Simon Maxwell, 'Food Security: A Post-modern Perspective', *Food Policy*, 21 (1996), 2, 155–70, quoted at 155.
45. Ibid. Also see D. John Shaw, *World Food Security: A History since 1945* (Basingstoke: Palgrave Macmillan, 2007).
46. Food and Agricultural Organization of the United Nations (FAO), 'Rome Declaration on World Food Security and World Food Summit Plan of Action', 13–17 November, 1996, p. 1.
47. Aileen Kwa and Walden Bello, *Guide to the Agreement on Agriculture: Technicalities and Trade Tricks Explained* (Bangkok: Focus on the Global South, December 1998), 2.
48. Christopher Stevens, 'The Need for Special Products and Special Safeguard Mechanisms for Agriculture in the WTO: A Situational Analysis', paper presented at International Centre for Trade and Sustainable Development (ICTSD) Informal Consultation, 'Special Products and Special Safeguard Mechanism after the July Framework: How Do We Move Forward?', Geneva, 30 September 2004, 4.
49. The official reference is AoA, Article 16: Least-Developed and Net Food-Importing Developing Countries; Uruguay Round Agreements, 'Decision on Measures Concerning the Possible Negative Effects of the Reform Programme on Least-Developed and Net Food-Importing Developing Countries'.
50. Food and Agricultural Organization of the United Nations (FAO), Commodities and Trade Division, 'Towards Improving the Operational Effectiveness of the Marrakesh Decision on Measures Concerning the Possible Negative Effects of the Reform Programme on Least-Developed and Net Food-Importing Developing Countries', paper presented at FAO Roundtable on Selected Agricultural Trade Policy Issues, Geneva, 21 March 2001.

51. Uruguay Round Agreements, 'Decision on Measures Concerning the Possible Negative Effects of the Reform Programme on Least-Developed and Net Food-Importing Developing Countries', pp. 3–4.
52. The WTO Secretariat is only charged with providing a monitoring and review function. For criticism see, ActionAid, 'The Marrakesh Ministerial Decision on Measures Concerning the Possible Negative Effects of the Reform Programme on Least-Developed and Net Food-Importing Developing Countries: Proposals for Improving its Content and Implementation', Discussion Paper (London: ActionAid, September 2000).
53. Christian Häberli, 'Food Security and WTO Rules', in Karapinar and Häberli (eds.), *Food Crises and the WTO*, 308.
54. Alberto Valdés and William Foster, *The New SSM: A Price Floor Mechanism for Developing Countries* (Geneva: International Centre for Trade and Sustainable Development, July 2005). Original data derived from member notifications to the WTO Committee on Agriculture. See in particular, WTO, 'Special Agricultural Safeguard; Background Paper by the Secretariat; Revision', 19 February 2002 (G/AG/NG/S/9/Rev.1).
55. Valdés and Foster, *The New SSM: A Price Floor Mechanism for Developing Countries.*
56. Ibid.
57. Quoted in Sylvia Ostry, 'Cancun: Can Can't? Can Do?', paper presented at 'Building the Americas' Conference, Centre for International Studies and Globalization, Montreal, 5–7 November 2003.
58. Pierre Bourdieu, *Distinction: A Social Critique of the Judgement of Taste* (London: Routledge, 1984), 479.
59. The highlights of this period have also been touched upon in Robert Wolfe, 'The Special Safeguard Fiasco in the WTO: The Perils of Inadequate Analysis and Negotiation', *World Trade Review*, 8 (2009), 4, 517–44.
60. See Celso L. N. Amorim, 'The WTO from the Perspective of a Developing Country', *Fordham International Law Journal*, 24 (2000), 95–106. Prior to the Seattle Ministerial Meeting, Clare Short advocated the launch of a 'development round' of trade negotiations. In March 1999, in a speech to the Trade and Development Board of the United Nations Conference on Trade and Development (UNCTAD), she argued that 'it is in all our interests that a new round is designed to bring clear benefits to developing countries'. Following this intervention, the phrase 'development round' began to be echoed by Michael Moore, WTO Director General, as well as other Geneva-based delegates. See United Nations Non-governmental Liaison Service (NGLS), 'Build-Up to the Third WTO Ministerial Conference', NGLS Roundup, 39, July 1999, <http://www.un-ngls.org/orf/documents/text/roundup/39wto.txt>.
61. Aileen Kwa, Trade Policy Analyst, Focus on the Global South, interview with the author, Geneva, 6 May 2007. In part, this name was inspired by the work of the long-standing, US-based 'Bread for the World' Christian citizens movement.
62. The South Centre is an intergovernmental organization, not a conventional civil society group.
63. WTO, 'Preparations for the 1999 Ministerial Conference; Agriculture; Proposal under Paragraphs 9(a)(i) and 9(a)(ii) of the Geneva Ministerial Declaration',

Communication from Cuba, Dominican Republic, Egypt, El Salvador, Honduras, Sri Lanka, Uganda, and Zimbabwe, 15 October 1999 (WT/GC/W/374), p. 26, italics added for emphasis. Organizationally, it requires noting that many of the countries who advocated the 'development box' were part of the Like Minded Group (LMG), a coalition that originally formed in 1996 to block the advancement of the Singapore issues, before later addressing the so-called 'implementation issues' of concern to many Southern countries. For an analysis of the larger WTO agenda of the LMG, see Amrita Narlikar and John S. Odell, 'The Strict Distributive Strategy for a Bargaining Coalition: The Like Minded Group in the World Trade Organization, 1998–2001', in John S. Odell (ed.), *Negotiating Trade: Developing Countries in the WTO and NAFTA* (Cambridge: Cambridge University Press, 2006).

64. WTO, 'Agreement on Agriculture: Special and Differential Treatment and a Development Box', Proposal to the June 2000 Special Session of the Committee on Agriculture by Cuba, Dominican Republic, Honduras, Pakistan, Haiti, Nicaragua, Kenya, Uganda, Zimbabwe, Ski Lanka, and El Salvador, 23 June 2000 (G/AG/NG/W/13), 1. For the legal reference, see General Agreement on Tariffs and Trade, Article XXI: Security Exceptions. Article XXI enables members to reserve the right to act in their 'essential security interests', such as in times of war or other emergencies, or in reference to the exchange of arms and ammunition.
65. WTO, 'Agreement on Agriculture: Special and Differential Treatment and a Development Box'.
66. WTO, 'Negotiations on WTO Agreement on Agriculture; Proposals by India in the Areas of: (i) Food Security, (ii) Market Access, (iii) Domestic Support, and (iv) Export Competition', 15 January 2001 (G/AG/NG/W/102).
67. S. I. M. Nayyar, former Counsellor, Permanent Mission of the Islamic Republic of Pakistan to the United Nations Office and Specialized Institutions in Geneva, interview with the author, Geneva, 5 May 2007.
68. Ibid.
69. Duncan Green, former Head of Research, Catholic Agency for Overseas Development, interview with the author, Oxford, 24 November 2007, italics added for emphasis.
70. Pierre Bourdieu and Loïc Wacquant, *An Invitation to Reflexive Sociology* (Chicago: University of Chicago Press, 1992), 128.
71. Pierre Bourdieu, 'Social Space and Symbolic Power', *Sociological Theory*, 7 (1989), 1, 14–25.
72. Kwa, Trade Policy Analyst, Focus on the Global South, interview with the author.
73. Aileen Kwa, 'Development Box: Can It Adequately Address the Agricultural Crisis in Developing Countries?', paper presented at Like Minded Group meeting, Geneva, 10 April 2002, italics in original.
74. Sophia Murphy and Steve Suppan, *Introduction to the Development Box: Finding Space for Development Concerns in the WTO's Agriculture Negotiations* (Winnipeg: International Institute for Sustainable Development, 2003).
75. Established in 1986, the Cairns Group is a diverse coalition of 19 agricultural exporting countries. Prominent members include Argentina, Australia, Brazil, Canada, South Africa, Thailand, and Uruguay.

76. During the Doha Ministerial, Pakistan President Musharraf was visiting US President Bush in Washington, DC. In February 2002, the US announced a package for Pakistani textiles worth US$476 million over three years. This was interpreted by many as a reward for Pakistan's support for the US-led invasion of Afghanistan. See, Anonymous, 'White House Grants Pakistan Quota Concessions Worth Half a Billion', *Inside U.S. Trade*, 15 February 2002.
77. Kwa, Trade Policy Analyst, Focus on the Global South, interview with the author. It is unclear to what extent this was due to US pressure.
78. Aileen Kwa, *Power Politics in the WTO* (Bangkok: Focus on the Global South, 2003).
79. Bridges Weekly Trade News Digest, 'Agriculture: WTO Members Split on "Development Box" and S&D', 6, 5, 12 February 2002. A series of informal special session meetings under the Committee on Agriculture were held from 4–6 February 2002 to discuss the 'development box', among other issues.
80. The G10 includes Bulgaria, Iceland, Israel, Japan, Liechtenstein, Mauritius, Norway, South Korea, Switzerland, and Chinese Taipei. See WTO, 'Negotiating Proposal by Japan on WTO Agricultural Negotiations', 21 December 2000 (G/AG/NG/W/91).
81. European Commission, 'Safeguarding the Multifunctional Role of EU Agriculture: Which Instruments?', Info Paper, October 1999. Also see WTO, 'EC Comprehensive Negotiating Proposal', 14 December 2000 (G/AG/NG/W/90).
82. Shishir Priyadarshi, 'Agriculture Text Poor on Core Development Concerns', *South Bulletin*, 24/25, 30 November 2001, 13–15, quoted at 15. In the final text, there was no mention of a 'development box' as an agenda item for the future, only that food security and rural development would be 'taken account of' within SDT-related work. WTO, 'Ministerial Declaration', Ministerial Conference Fourth Session, Doha, 9–14 November 2001 (WT/MIN(01)/DEC/1), p. 13.
83. WTO, 'Negotiations on Agriculture; Overview', 18 December 2002 (TN/AG/6), p. 15.
84. Ibid., pp. 22–3.
85. WTO, 'Negotiations on Agriculture; First Draft of Modalities for Further Commitments', 17 February 2003 (TN/AG/W/1), p. 10.
86. The Harmonized Commodity Description and Coding System of tariff nomenclature is an internationally recognized system of names and numbers for classifying commodities. It is maintained by the World Customs Organization.
87. WTO, 'Negotiations on Agriculture; First Draft of Modalities for Further Commitments; Revision', 18 March 2003 (TN/AG/W/1/Rev. 1), p. 11.
88. Green, former Head of Research, Catholic Agency for Overseas Development, interview with the author, italics added for emphasis.
89. Luisa Bernal, former Coordinator of the Trade for Development Programme, South Centre, interview with the author, Geneva, 7 May 2008.
90. Jason Hafemeister, former Deputy Assistant US Trade Representative for Agriculture and lead agricultural negotiator during the Doha Round (until 2007), interview with the author, Washington, DC, 12 July 2010.
91. Andrew Hurrell and Amrita Narlikar, 'The New Politics of Confrontation: Developing Countries at Cancún and Beyond', *Global Society*, 20 (2006), 4, 415–33, quoted at 420, based on interviews with Geneva-based delegates. The so-called Blair House Accord of November 1992 marked a key point in the Uruguay Round, when

outstanding differences on agriculture were settled between the US and the EU. Many Southern countries argued that the deal was offered to them as a *fait accompli* without adequate space for negotiation and dialogue. The phrase 'Blair House' has subsequently carried negative overtones within the WTO for many members, associated with underhand practices.

92. WTO, 'Joint Text of the European Communities and the United States; Agriculture', 13 August 2003 (JOB(03)/157).
93. Quoted in Martin Khor, 'US-EC Agriculture Paper Not Acceptable as Basis for Negotiations, Say Developing Countries', *Third World Network Info Reports*, 14 August 2003.
94. Geneva-based Asian delegate, interview with the author, Geneva, 5 May 2007.
95. WTO, 'Ministers' Communiqué; Alliance for Strategic Products and Special Safeguard Mechanism', 9 September 2003 (WT/MIN(03)/14), 1. Members included Barbados, Botswana, Cuba, Dominican Republic, Honduras, Indonesia, Jamaica, Kenya, Mauritius, Mongolia, Nicaragua, Nigeria, Pakistan, Panama, Peru, Philippines, Tanzania, Trinidad and Tobago, Turkey, Uganda, Venezuela, Zambia, and Zimbabwe.
96. Ibid., 3. The category of Tariff Rate Quotas (TRQs) was institutionalized in the Uruguay Round to ensure that minimal opportunities for trade ('market access') would be preserved as a result of the so-called 'tariffication exercise' (the conversion of 'non-tariff barriers' to their tariff equivalents). Whether or not access actually exists is open to interpretation in respect to each member. However, most Southern countries did not incorporate TRQs into their schedules and have opposed calls for TRQ expansion on the grounds that it would expose them to greater liberalization.
97. Bridges Daily Update on the Fifth Ministerial Conference, 4 (Geneva: International Centre for Trade and Sustainable Development), 13 September 2003.
98. Ambassador Gusmardi Bustami, Deputy Permanent Representative, Permanent Mission of the Republic of Indonesia to the United Nations and other International Organizations in Geneva, interview with the author, Geneva, 8 May 2008.
99. WTO, 'Doha Work Programme; Decision Adopted by the General Council on 1 August 2004', Annex A: Framework for Establishing Modalities in Agriculture, 2 August 2004 (WT/L/579), p. 41–2.
100. WTO, 'Joint Text of the European Communities and the United States; Agriculture'. The proposal refers to the need to take account of 'import sensitive tariff lines', p. 2.1.
101. WTO, 'Doha Work Programme; Decision Adopted by the General Council on 1 August 2004', Annex A: Framework for Establishing Modalities in Agriculture, pp. 31–4.
102. Ibid., p. 39.
103. Geneva-based Asian delegate, interview with the author, 5 May 2007.
104. The July Framework also authorized a 'review' and 'clarification' of Green Box use, a move prompted by criticisms from some members that US and EU spending payments in the category were in some respects trade distorting. WTO, 'Doha

Work Programme; Decision Adopted by the General Council on 1 August 2004', Annex A: Framework for Establishing Modalities in Agriculture, p. 16.

105. Bernal, former Coordinator of the Trade for Development Programme, South Centre, interview with the author.
106. Pierre Bourdieu, 'Symbolic Power', in Denis Gleeson (ed.), *Identity and Structure: Issues in the Sociology of Education* (Driffield: Nafferton Books, 1977).
107. Homi Bhabha, 'Of Mimicry and Man: The Ambivalence of Colonial Discourse', *October*, 28 (1984), 125–33, quoted at 129, 126.
108. Bustami, Deputy Permanent Representative, Permanent Mission of the Republic of Indonesia, interview with the author.
109. Green, former Head of Research, Catholic Agency for Overseas Development, interview with the author.
110. Ricardo Meléndez-Ortiz, 'Foreword', in International Centre for Trade and Sustainable Development, *Special Products and the Special Safeguard Mechanism: Strategic Options for Developing Countries* (Geneva: ICTSD, December 2005), viii.
111. Christophe Bellmann, Programmes Director, International Centre for Trade and Sustainable Development, interview with the author, Geneva, 7 May 2008.
112. Paul Mably, 'Centralized Production: The Group of G33', in Diana Tussie (ed.), *The Politics of Trade: The Role of Research in Trade Policy and Negotiations* (Ottawa: International Development Research Centre, 2009).
113. WTO, 'Doha Work Programme; Decision Adopted by the General Council on 1 August 2004', p. 41.
114. Bernal, 'Guidelines for Approaching the Designation of Special Products and SSM Products in Developing Countries'.
115. Bellmann, Programmes Director, International Centre for Trade and Sustainable Development (ICTSD), interview with the author.
116. Ibid. See the ICTSD website for a list of major publications under this theme: ICTSD, Agriculture Programme, Publications on Special Products and the Special Safeguard Mechanism, <http://ictsd.org/programmes/agriculture/special-products-and-special-safeguard-mechanism/>.
117. Bernal, former Coordinator of the Trade for Development Programme, South Centre, interview with the author.
118. G33, 'Arguments Regarding Special Products (SPs) and Special Safeguard Mechanism', 17 March 2004, internal document. For further evidence of G33 caution see, WTO, 'G33 Proposal on Special Products; Communication from G33', 3 June 2005 (JOB(05)/91).
119. Bellmann, Programmes Director, International Centre for Trade and Sustainable Development, interview with the author.
120. Martin Khor, 'G33 Criticises Agriculture Process and US Proposal', *Third World Network Info Reports*, 18 October 2005.
121. WTO, 'Proposal on the Modalities for the Designation and Treatment of Any Agricultural Product as a Special Product (SP) by Any Developing Country Member; Circulated at the Request of Indonesia', 22 November 2005 (JOB(05)/304), p. 5. Including sub-categories, there were 23.

122. Luisa Bernal, *Methodology for the Identification of Special Products (SP) and Products Eligibility Under Special Safeguard Mechanism for Developing Countries* (Geneva: International Centre for Trade and Sustainable Development, October 2005).
123. Bernal, former Coordinator of the Trade for Development Programme, South Centre, interview with the author; and Judha Nugraha, Third Secretary, Permanent Mission of the Republic of Indonesia to the United Nations and other International Organizations in Geneva, interview with the author, Geneva, 8 May 2008.
124. Mably, 'Centralized Production: The Group of G33'. See Hoda, *Special Products: Options for Negotiating Modalities*.
125. WTO, 'Doha Work Programme; Ministerial Declaration; Adopted on 18 December 2005', 22 December 2005 (WT/MIN(05)/DEC), p. 7, italics added for emphasis.
126. Mably, 'Centralized Production: The Group of G33', 267.
127. Erving Goffman, 'Symbols of Class Status', *The British Journal of Sociology*, 2 (1951), 4, 294–304, quoted at 297. Goffman was notably an inspiration for Bourdieu.
128. This deadline was set by Pascal Lamy who became the new Director General in September 2005.
129. WTO, 'United States Communication on Special Products', 3 May 2006 (JOB(06)/137), p. 2.
130. At the six-digit HS level, for instance, most countries have 8 tariff lines for milk and cream products alone, and approximately 20 if the range is extended to account for all dairy products. See note 86 for definition of HS.
131. WTO, 'Proposal on the Modalities for the Designation and Treatment of Any Agricultural Product as a Special Product (SP) by Any Developing Country Member', pp. 3–5.
132. Ambassador Susan C. Schwab, United States Trade Representative, 'Remarks on the Doha Development Agenda', National Press Club, Washington, DC, 7 July 2006, see <http://2001-2009.state.gov/e/eeb/rls/rm/2006/68896.htm>.
133. Martin Khor, 'Agriculture Talks at Boiling Point Over Special Products', *Third World Network Info Reports*, 9 May 2006.
134. Geneva-based Asian delegate, interview with the author; and Bustami, Deputy Permanent Representative, Permanent Mission of the Republic of Indonesia, interview with the author.
135. WTO, 'Thailand Paper on Special Products', 2 May 2006 (JOB (06)/135), p. 1, 6.
136. Bellmann, Programmes Director, International Centre for Trade and Sustainable Development, interview with the author. For the proposal, see Malaysia, 'Discussion Paper on Special Products; Contribution by Malaysia', 23 March 2006, unpublished private paper.
137. Glauber, Chief Economist, US Department of Agriculture, interview with the author; Hafemeister, former Deputy Assistant US Trade Representative for Agriculture and lead agricultural negotiator during the Doha Round (until 2007), interview with the author; and Bernal, former Coordinator of the Trade for Development Programme, South Centre, interview with the author.

138. Bustami, Deputy Permanent Representative, Permanent Mission of the Republic of Indonesia, interview with the author.
139. Christopher Stevens, Jane Kennan, and Mareike Meyn, *South–South Trade in Special Products* (Geneva: International Centre for Trade and Sustainable Development, June 2007).
140. Bustami, Deputy Permanent Representative, Permanent Mission of the Republic of Indonesia, interview with the author.
141. Martin Khor, 'Pakistan's SP Paper Causes Stir as WTO Agriculture Talks Resume', *Third World Network Info Reports*, 26 April 2007.
142. Martin Khor, 'Agriculture: Recent Developments in SPs', *Third World Network Info Reports*, 28 January 2008.
143. The Falconer text, titled 'Working Document No. 15; Special Products' can be found at WTO, Agriculture: Negotiations, Chairperson's Working Documents November 2007–January 2008, <http://www.wto.org/english/tratop_e/agric_e/chair_workdoc_nov07_e.htm>.
144. Wolfe, 'The Special Safeguard Fiasco in the WTO: The Perils of Inadequate Analysis and Negotiation'.
145. WTO, 'United States Communication on Special Agricultural Safeguard (SSG) and the Special Safeguard Mechanism (SSM) Article 5 of the Agreement on Agriculture', 24 April 2006 (JOB(06)/120), p. 2, 3, 19.
146. WTO, 'G33 Proposal on Special Safeguard Measures', 3 June 2005 (JOB (05)/92), p. 3.
147. On heightened levels of suspicion among key countries at this time, see Robert Wolfe, 'Sprinting During a Marathon: Why the WTO Ministerial Failed in July 2008', Groupe d'Économie Mondiale, Sciences Po, Working Paper, April 2009.
148. Some observers argued that the collapse of the meeting over the SSM was only a proxy reason, one which was orchestrated by the US to deflect attention from debating cotton subsidies, the next item on the agenda. See Chapter 4.
149. See Kanaga Raja, 'Kamal Nath Sets Conditions for Success of WTO Talks', *South–North Development Monitor*, 23 July 2008; and Kanaga Raja, 'Kamal Nath Explains How the Geneva Talks Failed', *South–North Development Monitor*, 31 July 2008. To clarify, Brazil was always less keen on the SSM for reasons similar to those expressed by other leading agricultural exporters.
150. Bridges Daily Update, 'G-7 Talks on Special Safeguard Mechanism Inconclusive as Blame Game Heats Up', 29 July 2008.
151. Kanaga Raja, '100 Developing Countries in Show of Strength on SP, SSM', *South–North Development Monitor*, 28 July 2008. The joint statement involved the G33 partnering with the Africa Group, the African, Caribbean and Pacific Group, the Least Developed Countries Group, and the Small and Vulnerable Economies Group.
152. Kanaga Raja, 'Schwab Still Blaming India and China at Press Briefing', *South–North Development Monitor*, 31 July 2008.
153. Wolfe, 'The Special Safeguard Fiasco in the WTO: The Perils of Inadequate Analysis and Negotiation'. The same point was underscored by Glauber, Chief Economist, US Department of Agriculture, interview with the author.

154. Wolfe, 'The Special Safeguard Fiasco in the WTO: The Perils of Inadequate Analysis and Negotiation', 538.
155. For instance, see WTO, 'Negotiating Group on Agriculture; Report by the Chairman, H. E. Mr David Walker, to the Trade Negotiations Committee for the Purpose of the TNC Stocktaking Exercise', 22 March 2010 (TN/AG/25).
156. Bourdieu, 'Social Space and Symbolic Power', 23.

Chapter 6

1. Robert Dahl, 'The Concept of Power', *Behavioural Science*, 2 (1957), 201–15.
2. Michael Barnett and Raymond Duvall, 'Power in International Politics', *International Organization*, 59 (2005), 1, 39–75.
3. Peter Bachrach and Morton Baratz, 'Two Faces of Power', *American Political Science Review*, 56 (1962), 947–52; and Peter Bachrach and Morton Baratz, 'Decisions and Nondecisions: An Analytical Framework', *American Political Science Review*, 57 (1963), 3, 632–42.
4. Pierre Bourdieu, 'Social Space and Symbolic Power', *Sociological Theory*, 7 (1989), 1, 14–25, quoted at 23.
5. Pierre Bourdieu, *In Other Words: Essays Towards a Reflexive Sociology* (Stanford: Stanford University Press, 1980), 80.
6. Didier Bigo, 'Pierre Bourdieu and International Relations: Power of Practices, Practices of Power', *International Political Sociology*, 5 (2011), 3, 225–58.
7. Barnett and Duvall, 'Power in International Politics', 67. Similarly, on the need to examine the relationship between different concepts of power, see Stefano Guzzini, 'Power', in Rebecca Adler-Nissen (ed.), *Bourdieu in International Relations: Rethinking Key Concepts in IR* (Abingdon: Routledge, 2012).
8. Pierre Bourdieu and Loïc Wacquant, *An Invitation to Reflexive Sociology* (Chicago: University of Chicago Press, 1992), 96–7.
9. Pierre Bourdieu, *The State Nobility: Elite Schools in the Field of Power* (Cambridge: Polity Press, 1996), 384.
10. Matthew Eagleton-Pierce, 'Advancing a Reflexive International Relations', *Millennium: Journal of International Studies*, 39 (2011), 3, 805–24.
11. For instance, see Jeffrey M. Chwieroth, *Capital Ideas: The IMF and the Rise of Financial Liberalization* (Princeton: Princeton University Press, 2010); Jacqueline Best, *The Limits of Transparency: Ambiguity and the History of International Finance* (Ithaca: Cornell University Press, 2005); and Timothy J. Sinclair, *The New Masters of Capital: American Bond Rating Agencies and the Politics of Creditworthiness* (Ithaca: Cornell University Press, 2005).
12. The notion of 'transnational guilds' is borrowed from Didier Bigo's work on the professionalisation of fields of expertise in international politics. For a summary, see 'Pierre Bourdieu and International Relations: Power of Practices, Practices of Power', *International Political Sociology*, 5 (2011), 3, 225–58, as well as *Terror, Insecurity and Liberty: Illiberal Practices of Liberal Regimes after 9/11* (Abingdon: Routledge, 2008). For a specific illustration to European banking, see Frédéric Lebaron, 'Central Bankers in the Contemporary Global Field of Power: A "Social Space"

Approach', in Mike Savage and Karel Williams (eds.), *Remembering Elites* (Oxford: Wiley-Blackwell, 2008). The importance of studying how firms secure the commitment of workers is inspired by the magnificent Luc Boltanski and Eve Chiapello opus, *The New Spirit of Capitalism* (London: Verso, 2007).

13. See Michael Williams, *Culture and Security: Symbolic Power and the Politics of International Security* (London: Routledge, 2007); Frédéric Mérand, *European Defence Policy: Beyond the Nation State* (Oxford: Oxford University Press, 2008); and Vincent Pouliot, *International Security in Practice: The Politics of NATO–Russia Diplomacy* (Cambridge: Cambridge University Press, 2010).
14. For instance, see Didier Bigo (ed.), *The Field of the EU Internal Security Agencies* (Paris: Centre d'Études sur les Conflits/L'Harmattan: 2007).
15. See Ian Hurd's use of Bourdieu in *After Anarchy: Legitimacy and Power in the United Nations Security Council* (Princeton: Princeton University Press, 2007).
16. See Loïc Wacquant, *Urban Outcasts: A Comparative Sociology of Advanced Marginality* (Cambridge: Polity Press, 2008); and Loïc Wacquant, *Punishing the Poor: The Neoliberal Government of Social Insecurity* (Durham, NC: Duke University Press, 2009).
17. Pierre Bourdieu and Loïc Wacquant, *An Invitation to Reflexive Sociology* (Chicago: University of Chicago Press, 1992), 97.

Bibliography

Abbott, Kenneth W., Keohane, Robert O., Moravcsik, Andrew, Slaughter, Anne-Marie, and Snidal, Duncan, 'The Concept of Legalization', *International Organization*, 54 (2000), 3, 401–19.

Abdelal, Rawi, Blyth, Mark, and Parsons, Craig (eds.), *Constructing the International Economy* (Ithaca: Cornell University Press, 2010).

Abrahamsen, Rita, *Disciplining Democracy: Development Discourse and Good Governance in Africa* (London: Zed Books, 2000).

ActionAid, 'The Marrakesh Ministerial Decision on Measures Concerning the Possible Negative Effects of the Reform Programme on Least-Developed and Net Food-Importing Developing Countries: Proposals for Improving its Content and Implementation', Discussion Paper (London: ActionAid, September 2000).

Adler, Emanuel, 'The Spread of Security Communities: Communities of Practice, Self-Restraint, and NATO's Post-Cold War Transformation', *European Journal of International Relations*, 14 (2008), 2, 195–230.

Adler, Emanuel, and Bernstein, Steven, 'Knowledge in Power: The Epistemic Construction of Global Governance', in Michael Barnett and Raymond Duvall (eds.), *Power in Global Governance* (Cambridge: Cambridge University Press, 2005).

Adler, Emanuel, and Pouliot, Vincent (eds.), *International Practices* (Cambridge: Cambridge University Press, 2011).

Adler-Nissen, Rebecca, 'The Diplomacy of Opting Out: A Bourdieudian Approach to National Integration Strategies', *Journal of Common Market Studies*, 46 (2008), 3, 663–84.

—— (ed.), *Bourdieu in International Relations: Rethinking Key Concepts in IR* (Abingdon: Routledge, 2012).

Agence France-Presse, 'Cotton Tangles up Collapsed WTO Talks', 30 July 2008.

Alessandrini, Donatella, *Developing Countries and the Multilateral Trade Regime: The Failure and Promise of the WTO's Development Mission* (Oxford: Hart Publishing, 2010).

Alston, Julian, Sumner, Daniel, and Brunke, Henrich, *Impacts of Reductions in US Cotton Subsidies on West African Cotton Producers* (Boston, MA: Oxfam America, 2007).

Althusser, Louis, *Lenin and Philosophy, and Other Essays* (London: New Left Books, 1971).

Amorim, Celso L. N., 'The WTO from the Perspective of a Developing Country', *Fordham International Law Journal*, 24 (2000), 95–106.

Anderson, Kym, and Martin, Will (eds.), *Agricultural Trade Reform and the Doha Development Agenda* (Washington, DC: World Bank, 2006).

Anonymous, 'White House Grants Pakistan Quota Concessions Worth Half a Billion', *Inside U.S. Trade*, 15 February 2002.

Austin, John L., *How to do Things with Words* (Oxford: Oxford University Press, 1962).

Axelrod, Robert, and Keohane, Robert, 'Achieving Cooperation Under Anarchy: Strategies and Institutions', *World Politics*, 38 (1985), 1, 226–54.

Bachrach, Peter, and Baratz, Morton, 'Two Faces of Power', *American Political Science Review*, 56 (1962), 947–52.

—— 'Decisions and Nondecisions: An Analytical Framework', *American Political Science Review*, 57 (1963), 3, 632–42.

—— *Power and Poverty: Theory and Practice* (Oxford: Oxford University Press, 1970).

Baffes, John, 'Cotton and Developing Countries: A Case Study in Policy Incoherence', Trade Note 10 (Washington, DC: World Bank, 10 September 2003).

—— 'Cotton: Market Setting, Trade Policies, and Issues', World Bank Research Working Paper, WPS 3218 (Washington, DC: World Bank, 2004).

Baffes, John, and Estur, Gérald, 'Market Context', in David Tschirley, Colin Poulton, and Patrick Labaste (eds.), *Organization and Performance of Cotton Sectors in Africa: Learning from Reform Experience* (Washington, DC: World Bank, 2009).

Balassa, Béla, and Associates, *Development Strategies in Semi-industrial Economies* (Baltimore: Johns Hopkins University Press for the World Bank, 1982).

Baldwin, David, *Paradoxes of Power* (Oxford: Blackwell, 1989).

Baldwin, Robert E., *The Development and Testing of Heckscher–Ohlin Trade Models: A Review* (Cambridge, MA: MIT Press, 2008).

Barnett, Michael, 'Culture, Strategy and Foreign Policy Change: Israel's Road to Oslo', *European Journal of International Affairs*, 5 (1999), 1, 5–36.

Barnett, Michael, and Duvall, Raymond, 'Power in International Politics', *International Organization*, 59 (2005), 1, 39–75.

Barnett, Michael, and Finnemore, Martha, *Rules for the World: International Organizations in Global Politics* (Ithaca: Cornell University Press, 2004).

Barton, John, Goldstein, Judith, Josling, Timothy, and Steinberg, Richard, *The Evolution of the Trade Regime: Politics, Law, and Economics of the GATT/WTO* (Princeton: Princeton University Press, 2006).

Bates, Thomas R., 'Gramsci and the Theory of Hegemony', *Journal of the History of Ideas*, 36 (1975), 2, 351–66.

Beckert, Sven, *The Empire of Cotton: A Global History* (New York: Alfred A. Knopf, forthcoming).

Beetham, David, *The Legitimation of Power* (Basingstoke: Palgrave Macmillan, 1991).

Benicchio, Romain, 'The WTO Ruling on the Brazil–US Cotton Dispute: Implications for African Countries and Agriculture Negotiations', in Eric Hazard (ed.), *International Trade Negotiations and Poverty Reduction: The White Paper on Cotton* (Dakar: Enda Prospectives Dialogues Politiques, 2005).

Berenskoetter, Felix, and Williams, Michael J. (eds.), *Power in World Politics* (London: Routledge, 2007).

Berger, Peter L., and Luckmann, Thomas, *The Social Construction of Reality: A Treatise in the Sociology of Knowledge* (New York: Anchor, 1967).

Berlinerblau, Jacques, 'Toward a Sociology of Heresy, Orthodoxy, and Doxa', *History of Religions*, 40 (2001), 4, 327–51.

Bermann, G. A., and Mavroidis, P. C. (eds.), *WTO Law and Developing Countries* (Cambridge: Cambridge University Press, 2007).

Bernabe, Riza, *Treatment of Special Products: Implications of the Chair's May 2008 Draft Modalities* Text (Geneva: International Centre for trade and Sustainable Development, June 2008).

Bernal, Luisa, 'Guidelines for Approaching the Designation of Special Products and SSM Products in Developing Countries', paper presented at International Centre for Trade and Sustainable Development (ICTSD) Informal Consultation, 'Special Products and Special Safeguard Mechanism After the July Framework: How Do We Move Forward?', Geneva, 30 September 2004.

—— *Methodology for the Identification of Special Products (SP) and Products Eligibility Under Special Safeguard Mechanism for Developing Countries* (Geneva: International Centre for Trade and Sustainable Development, October 2005).

Best, Jacqueline, *The Limits of Transparency: Ambiguity and the History of International Finance* (Ithaca: Cornell University Press, 2005).

Bhabha, Homi, 'Of Mimicry and Man: The Ambivalence of Colonial Discourse', *October*, 28 (1984), 125–33.

Bhagwati, Jagdish N., and Hirsch, Mathias (eds.), *The Uruguay Round and Beyond: Essays in Honor of Arthur Dunkel* (Ann Arbor: University of Michigan Press, 1998).

Bigo, Didier (ed.), *The Field of the EU Internal Security Agencies* (Paris: Centre d'Études sur les Conflits/L'Harmattan, 2007).

—— *Terror, Insecurity and Liberty: Illiberal Practices of Liberal Regimes after 9/11* (Abingdon: Routledge, 2008).

—— 'Pierre Bourdieu and International Relations: Power of Practices, Practices of Power', *International Political Sociology*, 5 (2011), 3, 225–58.

Bird, Graham, 'Restructuring the IMF's Lending Facilities', *World Economy*, 26 (2003), 2, 229–45.

Bjola, Corneliu, and Kornprobst, Markus (eds.), *Arguing Global Governance: Agency, Lifeworld and Shared Reasoning* (Abingdon: Routledge, 2011).

Blackhurst, Richard, 'Reforming WTO Decision Making: Lessons from Singapore and Seattle', in Klaus-Günter Deutsch and Bernhard Speyer (eds.), *The World Trade Organization Millennium Round: Freer Trade in the Twenty-first Century* (London: Routledge, 2001).

Blackhurst, Richard, and Hartridge, David, 'Improving the Capacity of WTO Institutions to Fulfil their Mandate', *Journal of International Economic Law*, 7 (2004), 3, 705–16.

Blustein, Paul, *Misadventures of the Most Favored Nations: Clashing Egos, Inflated Ambitions, and the Great Shambles of the World Trade System* (New York: Public Affairs, 2009).

Blyth, Mark, *Great Transformations: Economic Ideas and Institutional Change in the Twentieth Century* (Cambridge: Cambridge University Press, 2002).

Boggs, Carl, *Gramsci's Marxism* (London: Pluto Press, 1976).

Boltanski, Luc, and Chiapello, Eve, *The New Spirit of Capitalism* (London: Verso, 2007).

Bourdieu, Pierre, *Outline of a Theory of Practice* (Cambridge: Cambridge University Press, 1977).

—— 'Symbolic Power', in Denis Gleeson (ed.), *Identity and Structure: Issues in the Sociology of Education* (Driffield: Nafferton Books, 1977).

—— 'The Economics of Lingusitic Exchanges', *Social Sciences Information*, 16 (1977), 6, 645–68.

—— 'Symbolic Power', *Critique of Anthropology*, 4 (1979), 77–85.

—— *In Other Words: Essays Towards a Reflexive Sociology* (Stanford: Stanford University Press, 1980).

—— *Distinction: A Social Critique of the Judgement of Taste* (London: Routledge, 1984).

—— 'The Social Space and the Genesis of Groups', *Theory and Society*, 14 (1985), 6, 723–44.

—— 'The Force of Law: Toward a Sociology of the Juridical Field', *Hastings Law Journal*, 38 (1987), 805–53.

—— 'What Makes a Social Class? On the Theoretical and Practical Existence of Groups', *Berkeley Journal of Sociology*, 32 (1987), 1–18.

—— *Homo Academicus* (Stanford: Stanford University Press, 1988).

—— 'Social Space and Symbolic Power', *Sociological Theory*, 7 (1989), 1, 14–25.

—— 'Genesis and Structure of the Religious Field', *Comparative Social Research*, 13 (1991), 1–44.

—— *Language and Symbolic Power* (Cambridge: Polity Press, 1991).

—— *The Logic of Practice* (Cambridge: Polity Press, 1992).

—— *Sociology in Question* (London: Sage, 1993).

—— 'Rethinking the State: Genesis and Structure of the Bureaucratic Field', *Sociological Theory*, 12 (1994), 1, 1–18.

—— *The State Nobility: Elite Schools in the Field of Power* (Cambridge: Polity Press, 1996).

—— *Pascalian Meditations* (Cambridge: Polity Press, 1997).

—— 'The Forms of Capital', in A. H. Halsey, Hugh Lauder, Phillip Brown, and Amy Stuart Wells (eds.), *Education: Culture, Economy, and Society* (Oxford: Oxford University Press, 1997).

—— *Masculine Domination* (Cambridge: Polity Press, 2001).

—— 'From the King's House to the Reason of State: A Model of the Genesis of the Bureaucratic Field', *Constellations*, 11 (2004), 1, 16–36.

—— 'Legitimation and Structured Interests in Weber's Sociology of Religion', in Scott Lash and Sam Whimster (eds.), *Max Weber, Rationality and Modernity* (Abingdon: Routledge, 2006).

Bourdieu, Pierre, and Boltanski, Luc, 'Le Fétichisme de la Langue', *Actes de la recherche en sciences sociales*, 4 (1975), 2–32.

Bourdieu, Pierre, and Eagleton, Terry, 'Doxa and Common Life: An Interview', *New Left Review*, 191 (1992), 111–21.

Bourdieu, Pierre, and Wacquant, Loïc, *An Invitation to Reflexive Sociology* (Chicago: University of Chicago Press, 1992).

—— 'Neoliberal Newspeak: Notes on the New Planetary Vulgate', *Radical Philosophy*, 105 (2001), 2–5.

Bourdieu, Pierre, et al. (eds.), *The Weight of the World: Social Suffering in Contemporary Society* (Stanford: Stanford University Press, 1999).

Bridges Daily Update, 'G-7 Talks on Special Safeguard Mechanism Inconclusive as Blame Game Heats Up', 29 July 2008.

Bridges Daily Update, Fifth Ministerial Conference, 2, 11 September 2003 (Geneva: International Centre for Trade and Sustainable Development).

—— 4, 13 September 2003 (Geneva: International Centre for Trade and Sustainable Development).

Bridges Weekly Trade News Digest, 'Agriculture: WTO Members Split on "Development Box" and S&D', 6, 5, 12 February 2002.

—— 'WTO: Green Room Highlights Limited Progress in Trade Talks', 7, 39, 19 November 2003.

—— 'Brazil, US Strike "Framework" Deal in Cotton Dispute', 14, 23, 23 June 2010.

Bronckers, Marco, and van den Broek, Naboth, 'Financial Compensation in the WTO: Improving the Remedies of WTO Dispute Settlement', *Journal of International Economic Law*, 8 (2005), 1, 101–26.

Brown, Michael Edward, Lynn-Jones, Sean M., and Miller, Steven E. (eds.), *Debating the Democratic Peace* (Cambridge MA: MIT Press, 1996).

Burawoy, Michael, 'Durable Domination: Gramsci Meets Bourdieu', paper presented at the Havens Center, University of Wisconsin, April 2008, <http://burawoy.berkeley.edu/Bourdieu/Lecture%202.pdf>.

Bustami, Gusmardi (Deputy Permanent Representative, Permanent Mission of the Republic of Indonesia to the United Nations and other International Organizations in Geneva), Letter to Paul Wolfowitz, President, World Bank, Washington, DC, 2 October 2006.

Callewaert, Staf, 'Bourdieu, Critic of Foucault: The Case of Empirical Social Science against Double-Game-Philosophy', *Theory, Culture & Society*, 23 (2006), 6, 73–98.

Cardwell, Michael, Grossman, Margaret Rosso, and Rodgers, Christopher (eds.), *Agriculture and International Trade: Law, Policy and the WTO* (Cambridge, MA: CABI Publishing, 2003).

Carr, E. H. *The Twenty Years' Crisis 1919–1939: An Introduction to the Study of International Relations* (London: Macmillan, 1946 [1939]).

Cashin, Paul, and McDermott, C. John, 'The Long-Run Behavior of Commodity Prices: Small Trends and Big Variability', IMF Staff Papers, 49, 2 (Washington, DC: International Monetary Fund, 2002).

Cass, Deborah, *The Constitutionalization of the World Trade Organization: Legitimacy, Democracy and Community in the International Trading System* (Oxford: Oxford University Press, 2005).

Cattaneo, Olivier, Engman, Michael, Stern, Robert M., and Saez, Sebastian, *International Trade in Services: New Trends and Opportunities for Developing Countries* (Washington, DC: World Bank, 2010).

Chang, Ha-Joon, *Kicking Away the Ladder: Development Strategy in Historical Perspective* (London: Anthem Press, 2002).

Checkel, Jeffrey, 'Process Tracing', in Audie Klotz and Deepa Prakash (eds.), *Qualitative Methods in International Relations: A Pluralist Guide* (Basingstoke: Palgrave Macmillan, 2008).

Chwieroth, J. M., *Capital Ideas: The IMF and the Rise of Financial Liberalization* (Princeton: Princeton University Press, 2010).

Clapp, Jennifer, 'Food Price Volatility and Vulnerability in the Global South: Considering the Global Economic Context', *Third World Quarterly*, 30 (2009), 6: 1183–96.

Clapp, Jennifer, and Helleiner, Eric, 'Troubled Futures? The Global Food Crisis and the Politics of Agricultural Derivatives Regulation', *Review of International Political Economy*, 19 (2012), 181–207.

Clark, Ian, *Legitimacy in International Society* (Oxford: Oxford University Press, 2005).

Clegg, Stewart, *Frameworks of Power* (London: Sage, 1989).

Cobden, Richard, *The Political Writings of Richard Cobden*, L. Mallet (ed.) (London: William Ridgway, Vol I, 1867; Vol II, 1878).

Coggins, Ross, 'The Development Set', *Journal of Communication*, 28 (1978), 1, 80.

Connolly, William, *The Terms of Political Discourse* (Oxford: Martin Robertson, 1974).

Conti, Joseph A., *Between Law and Diplomacy: The Social Contexts of Disputing at the World Trade Organization* (Stanford: Stanford University Press, 2010).

Cook, Ken, and Campbell, Chris, 'EWG Analysis of Step 2 Data for 2004; U.S. Taxpayers Spent $264 Million in 2004 On Cotton Export Subsidies Ruled Illegal By WTO', 9 June 2005, <http://www.ewg.org/node/21053>.

Cox, Robert W., *Production, Power, and World Order: Social Forces in the Making of World History* (New York: Columbia University Press, 1987).

Cox, Robert W., with Sinclair, Timothy, *Approaches to World Order* (Cambridge: Cambridge University Press, 1996).

Crawford, Neta, *Argument and Change in World Politics: Ethics, Decolonization, and Humanitarian Intervention* (Cambridge: Cambridge University Press, 2002).

Cronin, Ciaran, 'Bourdieu and Foucault on Power and Modernity', *Philosophy & Social Criticism*, 22 (1996), 6, 55–85.

Croome, John, *Reshaping the World Trading System: A History of the Uruguay Round* (London: Kluwer Law International, 1998).

Cross, Karen Halverson, 'King Cotton, Developing Countries and the "Peace Clause": The WTO's *US Cotton Subsidies* Decision', *Journal of International Economic Law*, 9 (2006), 1, 149–95.

—— 'United States: Subsidies on Upland Cotton, Recourse to Article 21.5 of the DSU by Brazil', *American Journal of International Law*, 103 (2009), 1, 110–16.

Crossley, Nick, 'On Systematically Distorted Communication: Bourdieu and the Socio-analysis of Publics', *The Sociological Review*, 52 (2004), 88–112.

Crump, Larry, and Maswood, S. Javed (eds.), *Developing Countries and Global Trade Negotiations* (London: Routledge, 2007).

Dahl, Robert, 'The Concept of Power', *Behavioural Science*, 2 (1957), 201–15.

—— *Who Governs? Democracy and Power in the American City* (New Haven: Yale University Press, 1961).

—— 'Power', in David Sills (ed.), *International Encyclopaedia of the Social Sciences* (New York: Free Press, 1968).

—— *Modern Political Analysis* (London: Prentice Hall, 1991 [1963]).

Dam, Kenneth, *The GATT: Law and International Economic Organization* (Chicago: University of Chicago Press, 1970).

Das, Bhagirath Lal, *The WTO Agreements: Deficiencies, Imbalances and Required Changes* (Penang: Third World Network, 1998).

—— *The Current Negotiations in the WTO: Options, Opportunities, and Risks for Developing Countries* (Penang: Third World Network and London: Zed Books, 2005).

Deer, Cécile, 'Doxa', in Michael Grenfell (ed.), *Pierre Bourdieu: Key Concepts* (Stocksfield: Acumen, 2008).

Deere, Carolyn, *International Trade Technical Assistance and Capacity Building* (United Nations Human Development Report Office, Occasional Paper, 2005).

—— *The Implementation Game: The TRIPS Agreement and the Global Politics of Intellectual Property Reform in Developing Countries* (Oxford: Oxford University Press, 2009).

Deitelhoff, Nicole, and Müller, Harald, 'Theoretical Paradise—Empirically Lost? Arguing with Habermas', *Review of International Studies*, 31 (2005), 1, 167–79.

Delgado, Christopher L., Hopkins, Jane, and Kelly, Valerie A., *Agricultural Growth Linkages in Sub-Saharan Africa*, IFPRI Research Report 107 (Washington, DC: International Food Policy Research Institute, 1998).

Dell, Sidney, 'The Fifth Credit Tranche', *World Development*, 13 (1985), 2, 245–9.

Dezalay, Yves, and Garth, Bryant G., *Dealing in Virtue: International Commercial Arbitration and the Construction of a Transnational Legal Order* (Chicago: University of Chicago Press, 1996).

—— *The Internationalization of Palace Wars: Lawyers, Economists, and the Contest to Transform Latin American States* (Chicago: University of Chicago Press, 2002).

Diouf, El Hadji, 'The Survival of African Cotton Between Negotiation and Dispute at the WTO', *Trade Negotiations Insights*, 2, 3, June 2003.

Diouf, El Hadji, and Hazard, Eric, 'Sectorial Initiative on Cotton: A Balancing Act of Alliances in Africa and at the WTO', in Eric Hazard (ed.), *International Trade Negotiations and Poverty Reduction: The White Paper on Cotton* (Dakar: Enda Prospectives Dialogues Politiques, 2005).

Dollar, David, and Kraay, Aart, 'Trade, Growth, and Poverty', *The Economic Journal*, 114 (2004), 493, F22–F49.

Doty, Roxanne Lynn, *Imperial Encounters: The Politics of Representation in North–South Relations* (Minneapolis: University of Minnesota Press 1996).

Drake, William, and Nicolaïdis, Kalypso, 'Ideas, Interests, and Institutionalization: "Trade in Services" and the Uruguay Round', *International Organization*, 46 (1992), 1, 37–100.

Dunne, Matthew, 'Redefining Power Orientation: A Reassessment of Jackson's Paradigm in Light of Asymmetries of Power, Negotiation, and Compliance in the GATT/WTO Dispute Settlement System', *Law and Policy in International Business*, 34 (2002), 277–342.

Durkheim, Émile, and Mauss, Marcel, *Primitive Classification* (Abingdon: Routledge, 2010 [1903]).

Eagleton, Terry, *Ideology: An Introduction* (London: Verso, 1991).

Eagleton-Pierce, Matthew, 'Advancing a Reflexive International Relations', *Millennium: Journal of International Studies*, 39 (2011), 3, 805–24.

Elliott, John, 'Adam Smith's Conceptualization of Power, Markets, and Politics', *Review of Social Economy*, 58 (2000), 4, 429–54.

Elliott, Larry, 'DTI Leak Blames Lamy for Cancun Failure', *The Guardian*, 22 October 2003.

Emirbayer, Mustafa, 'Manifesto for a Relational Sociology', *The American Journal of Sociology*, 103 (1997), 2, 281–317.

Enloe, Cynthia, 'Margins, Silences, and Bottom Rungs: How to Overcome the Underestimation of Power in the Study of International Relations', in Steve Smith, Ken Booth, and Marysia Zalewski (eds.), *International Theory: Positivism and Beyond* (Cambridge: Cambridge University Press, 1996).

Environmental Justice Foundation, *The Children Behind Our Cotton* (London: Environmental Justice Foundation, 2007).

Epstein, Charlotte, *The Power of Words in International Relations: Birth of an Anti-Whaling Discourse* (Cambridge, MA: MIT Press, 2008).

Escobar, Arturo, *Encountering Development: The Making and Unmaking of the Third World* (Princeton: Princeton University Press, 1995).

Estur, Gérald, 'Is West African Cotton Competitive with the U.S. on the World Cotton Market?', paper presented at Beltwide Cotton Conference, New Orleans, 7 January 2005.

European Commission, 'Safeguarding the Multifunctional Role of EU Agriculture: Which Instruments?', Info Paper, October 1999.

Eyben, Rosalind, 'The Power of the Gift and the New Aid Modalities', *IDS Bulletin*, 37 (2006), 6, 88–98.

Fan, Shenggen, and Headey, Derek, *Reflections on the Global Food Crisis: How Did It Happen? How Has It Hurt? And How Can We Prevent the Next One?* (Washington, DC: International Food Policy Research Institute, 2010).

Findlay, Ronald, and O'Rourke, Kevin H., *Power and Plenty: Trade, War, and the World Economy in the Second Millennium* (Princeton: Princeton University Press, 2007).

Finger, J. M., and Dhar, Sumana, 'Do Rules Contain Power?', in Alan V. Deardorff and Robert Mitchell Stern (eds.), *Analytical and Negotiation Issues in the Global Trading System* (Ann Arbor: Michigan University Press, 1994).

Finger, J. M., and Schuler, P., 'Implementation of Uruguay Round Commitments: The Development Challenge', in Bernard Hoekman and Will Martin (eds.), *Developing Countries and the WTO: A Pro-Active Agenda* (Oxford: Blackwell, 2001).

Finger, J. M., and Winters, L. A., 'Reciprocity in the WTO', in Bernard Hoekman, Philip English, and Aaditya Matto (eds.), *Development, Trade and the WTO: A Handbook* (Washington, DC: World Bank, 2002).

Finnemore, Martha, and Toope, Stephen, 'Alternatives to "Legalization": Richer Views of Law and Politics', *International Organization*, 55 (2001), 3, 743–58.

Food and Agricultural Organization of the United Nations (FAO), 'Rome Declaration on World Food Security and World Food Summit Plan of Action', 13–17 November 1996.

—— Commodities and Trade Division, 'Towards Improving the Operational Effectiveness of the Marrakesh Decision on Measures Concerning the Possible Negative Effects of the Reform Programme on Least-Developed and Net Food-Importing Developing Countries', paper presented at FAO Roundtable on Selected Agricultural Trade Policy Issues, Geneva, 21 March 2001.

Food and Agricultural Organization of the United Nations (FAO), 'Some Issues Relating to Food Security in the Context of the WTO Negotiations on Agriculture', paper presented at FAO Geneva Roundtable, 'Food Security in the Context of WTO Negotiations on Agriculture', United Nations, Geneva, 20 July 2001.

—— *WTO Agreement on Agriculture: The Implementation Experience—Developing Country Case Studies* (Rome: FAO, 2003).

—— *The State of Agricultural Commodity Markets 2004* (Rome: FAO, 2004).

—— *The State of Food and Agriculture 2006: Food Aid for Food Security?* (Rome: FAO, 2006).

—— Briefs on Import Surges, 2, 'Import Surges: What is Their Frequency and Which are the Countries and Commodities Most Affected?' (Rome: FAO, October 2006).

—— Briefs on Import Surges—Countries, 6, 'Jamaica: Poultry, Dairy Products and Onions' (Rome: FAO, November 2006).

—— 'Import Surges: Analysis, Preliminary Findings and Lessons Learned', Committee on Commodity Problems, Sixty-sixth Session, Rome, 23–25 April 2007 (Rome: FAO).

—— *Food Outlook: Global Market Analysis* (Rome: FAO, June 2007).

—— *The State of Agricultural Commodity Markets 2009: High Food Prices and the Food Crisis—Experiences and Lessons Learned* (Rome: FAO, 2009).

—— *The State of Food and Agriculture 2010–11: Women in Agriculture; Closing the Gender Gap for Development* (Rome: FAO, 2011).

Foucault, Michel, *The Archaeology of Knowledge* (London: Tavistock Publications, 1972).

—— *The History of Sexuality: The Will to Knowledge Volume I* (London: Penguin, 1978).

—— *Power/Knowledge: Selected Interviews and Other Writings 1972–1977*, ed. Colin Gordon (London: Harvester Press, 1980).

Fougner, Tore, 'The State, International Competitiveness and Neoliberal Globalisation: Is There a Future Beyond "the Competition State"?', *Review of International Studies*, 32 (2006), 1, 165–85.

Franck, Thomas M., *The Power of Legitimacy Among Nations* (Oxford: Oxford University Press, 1990).

Friends of the Development Box, Press Statement, Doha, 10 November 2001.

G33, 'Arguments Regarding Special Products (SPs) and Special Safeguard Mechanism', 17 March 2004, internal document.

Gadinger, Frank, and Büger, Christian, 'Reassembling and Dissecting: International Relations Practice from a Science Studies Perspective', *International Studies Perspectives*, 8 (2007), 1, 90–110.

Gale, Fred, 'Cave "Cave! Hic Dragones": A Neo-Gramscian Deconstruction and Reconstruction of International Regime Theory', *Review of International Political Economy*, 5 (1998), 2, 252–83.

Gallagher, Kevin (ed.), *Putting Development First: The Importance of Policy Space in the WTO and IFIs* (London: Zed Books, 2005).

—— 'Understanding Developing Country Resistance to the Doha Round', *Review of International Political Economy*, 15 (2008), 1, 62–85.

Gallagher, Peter, *Global Trade Advocate: A Handbook for Managers and Association Executives* (Melbourne: Inquit Communications Pty Ltd, 2005).

Gallagher, Peter, Low, Patrick, and Stoler, Andrew (eds.), *Managing the Challenges of WTO Participation: 45 Case Studies* (Cambridge: Cambridge University Press, 2005).

Gallie, Walter, 'Essentially Contested Concepts', *Proceedings of the Aristotelian Society*, 56 (1956), 167–98.

Gao, Henry, and Lewis, Donald (eds.), *China's Participation in the WTO* (London: Cameron May, 2005).

Gawande, Kishore, 'The Structure of Lobbying and Protection in U.S. Agriculture', in Bernard Hoekman and Simon Evenett (eds.), *Economic Development and Multilateral Trade Cooperation* (Basingstoke: Palgrave Macmillan, 2006).

Gawande, Kishore, and Hoekman, Bernard, 'Lobbying and Agricultural Trade Policy in the United States', *International Organization*, 60 (2006), 3, 527–61.

General Agreement on Tariffs and Trade (GATT), 'Food Security: Statement by Jamaica at the Eighth Meeting of the Negotiating Group on Agriculture', 30 June 1988 (MTN. GNG/NG5/W/65).

—— 'Negotiating Group on Agriculture: Submission by Japan', 6 December 1989 (MTN.GNG/NG5/W/131).

George, Alexander L., and Bennett, Andrew, *Case Studies and Theory Development in the Social Sciences* (Cambridge, MA: MIT Press, 2005).

Germain, Randall D., and Kenny, Michael. 'Engaging Gramsci: International Relations Theory and the New Gramscians', *Review of International Studies*, 24 (1998), 3–21.

Gertler, Jeffrey L., 'What China's WTO Accession is All About', in Deepak Bhattasali, Shantong Li, and Will Martin (eds.), *China and the WTO: Accession, Policy Reform, and Poverty Reduction Strategies* (Washington, DC: World Bank, 2004).

Gill, Stephen (ed.), *Gramsci, Historical Materialism and International Relations* (Cambridge: Cambridge University Press, 1993).

—— 'Globalisation, Market Civilisation, and Disciplinary Neoliberalism', *Millennium: Journal of International Studies*, 24 (1995), 3, 399–423.

—— 'New Constitutionalism, Democratisation and Global Political Economy', *Pacifica Review*, 10 (1998), 1, 23–38.

—— 'Toward a Postmodern Prince? The Battle in Seattle as a Moment in the New Politics of Globalisation', *Millennium: Journal of International Studies*, 29 (2000), 1, 131–41.

Gill, Stephen, and Law, David, 'Global Hegemony and the Structural Power of Capital', *International Studies Quarterly*, 33 (1989), 4, 475–99.

Godelier, Maurice, *The Enigma of the Gift* (Chicago: University of Chicago Press, 1999).

Goffman, Erving, 'Symbols of Class Status', *The British Journal of Sociology*, 2 (1951), 4, 294–304.

—— *Frame Analysis: An Essay on the Organization of Experience* (New York: Harper & Row, 1974).

Gokcekus, Omer, and Fishler, Richard, 'The Cotton Influence Index: An Examination of U.S. Cotton Subsidies', *American Journal of Agricultural Economics*, 91 (2009), 2, 299–309.

Goldberg, Ray A., Lawrence, Robert Z., and Milligan, Katie, 'Brazil's WTO Cotton Case: Negotiation Through Litigation', in Charan Devereaux, Robert Z. Lawrence, and Michael D. Watkins (eds.), *Case Studies in US Trade Negotiations: Resolving Disputes Volume 2* (Washington, DC: Peterson Institute for International Economics, 2006).

Goldstein, Judith, 'Ideas, Institutions, and American Trade Policy', *International Organization*, 42 (1988), 1, 179–217.

—— 'The Impact of Ideas on Trade Policy: The Origins of U.S. Agricultural and Manufacturing Policies', *International Organization*, 43 (1989), 1, 31–71.

Goldstein, Judith, and Gowa, Joanne, 'US National Power and the Post-war Trading Regime', *World Trade Review*, 1 (2002), 2, 153–70.

Goldstein, Judith, Kahler, Miles, Keohane, Robert O., and Slaughter, Anne-Marie, 'Introduction: Legalization and World Politics', *International Organization*, 54 (2000), 3, 385–99.

Goreux, Louis, 'Prejudice Caused by Industrialized Countries to Cotton Sectors in Western and Central Africa', mimeo, July 2002.

—— 'Prejudice Caused by Industrialized Countries Subsidies to Cotton Sectors in Western and Central Africa', mimeo, June 2003.

Grobe, Christian, 'The Power of Words: Argumentative Persuasion in International Negotiations', *European Journal of International Relations*, 16 (2010), 1, 5–29.

Grynberg, Roman, and Newton, Samantha, 'Introduction', in Roman Grynberg and Samantha Newton (eds.), *Commodity Prices and Development* (Oxford: Oxford University Press, 2007).

Guzzini, Stefano, 'Structural Power: The Limits of Neorealist Power Analysis', *International Organization*, 47 (1993), 3, 443–78.

—— *Realism in International Relations and International Political Economy* (London: Routledge, 1998).

—— 'Use and Misuse of Power Analysis in International Theory', in Ronen Palen (ed.), *Global Political Economy: Contemporary Theories* (London: Routledge, 2000).

——'"Power" in International Relations: Concept Formation Between Conceptual Analysis and Conceptual History', paper presented at International Studies Association Annual Convention, New Orleans, 24–27 March 2002.

—— 'Power', in Rebecca Adler-Nissen (ed.), *Bourdieu in International Relations: Rethinking Key Concepts in IR* (Abingdon: Routledge, 2012).

Haacke, Jürgen, 'Theory and Praxis in International Relations: Habermas, Self-Reflection, Rational Argumentation', *Millennium: Journal of International Studies*, 25 (1996), 2, 255–89.

Häberli, Christian, 'Food Security and WTO Rules', in Baris Karapinar and Christian Häberli (eds.), *Food Crises and the WTO* (Cambridge: Cambridge University Press, 2010).

Habermas, Jürgen, 'On Systematically Distorted Communication', *Inquiry*, 13 (1970), 205–18.

—— *Legitimation Crisis* (Cambridge: Polity Press, 1988).

—— *The Theory of Communicative Action: Reason and the Rationalization of Society, Volume 1* (Cambridge: Polity Press, 2004 [1981]).

Hardt, Michael, 'Militant Life', *New Left Review*, 64, July/August 2010, 151–60.

Harrison, Graham, *The World Bank and Africa: The Construction of Governance States* (London: Routledge, 2004).

Hattori, Tomohisa, 'Reconceptualizing Foreign Aid', *Review of International Political Economy*, 8 (2001), 4, 633–60.

Haugaard, Mark, and Clegg, Stewart R., 'Introduction: Why Power is the Central Concept of the Social Sciences', in Stewart R. Clegg and Mark Haugaard (eds.), *The SAGE Handbook of Power* (London: Sage, 2009).

Hayward, Clarissa, *De-Facing Power* (Cambridge: Cambridge University Press, 2000).
Heckscher, Eli, *Mercantilism* (London: Allen & Unwin, 1934).
Heinisch, Elinor Lynn, 'West Africa Versus the United States on Cotton Subsidies: How, Why and What Next?', *Journal of Modern African Studies*, 44 (2006), 2, 251–74.
Hirschman, Albert, *National Power and the Structure of Foreign Trade* (Berkeley: University of California Press, 1945).
Hoekman, Bernard, 'Operationalizing the Concept of Policy Space in the WTO: Beyond Special and Differential Treatment', *Journal of International Economic Law*, 8 (2005), 2, 405–24.
Hoekman, Bernard M., and Kostecki, Michel M., *The Political Economy of the World Trade System: The WTO and Beyond* (Oxford: Oxford University Press, 2009).
Hobbes, Thomas, *Leviathan* (London: Penguin, 1985 [1651]).
Hoda, Anwarul, *Special Products: Options for Negotiating Modalities* (Geneva: International Centre for Trade and Sustainable Development, July 2005).
Howse, Robert, 'The Legitimacy of the World Trade Organization', in J. Coicaud and V. Heiskanen (eds.), *The Legitimacy of International Organizations* (New York: United Nations University Press, 2001).
—— 'From Politics to Technocracy—And Back Again: The Fate of the Multilateral Trading Regime', *American Journal of International Law*, 96 (2002), 1, 94–117.
Hudec, Robert E., *Developing Countries in the GATT Legal System* (London: Trade Policy Research Centre, 1987).
Hull, Cordell, *The Memoirs of Cordell Hull* (New York: Macmillan Company, 1948).
Hume, David, 'Of the First Principles of Government' [1741], in *Selected Essays* (Oxford: Oxford University Press, 2008).
Hurd, Ian, *After Anarchy: Legitimacy and Power in the United Nations Security Council* (Princeton: Princeton University Press, 2007).
Hurrell, Andrew, 'Power, Institutions, and the Production of Inequality', in Michael Barnett and Raymond Duvall (eds.), *Power in Global Governance* (Cambridge: Cambridge University Press, 2005).
Hurrell, Andrew, and Narlikar, Amrita, 'The New Politics of Confrontation: Developing Countries at Cancún and Beyond', *Global Society*, 20 (2006), 4, 415–33.
Husserl, Edmund, *Experience and Judgement: Investigations in a Genealogy of Logic* (London: Routledge, 1973 [1939]).
Ingco, Merlinda, and Nash, John (eds.), *Agriculture and the WTO: Creating a Trading System for Development* (Washington, DC: World Bank, 2004).
International Cotton Advisory Committee (ICAC), *The Outlook for Cotton Supply in 2005/06* (Washington, DC: ICAC, 2005).
—— *Production and Trade Policies Affecting the Cotton Industry* (Washington, DC: ICAC, September 2006).
—— *Production and Trade Policies Affecting the Cotton Industry* (Washington, DC: ICAC, November 2008).
—— *Cotton This Month*, (Washington, DC: ICAC, 2 August 2010).
Irwin, Douglas, *Against the Tide: An Intellectual History of Free Trade* (Princeton: Princeton University Press, 1996).

Jackson, John, 'The Crumbling Institutions of the Liberal Trade System', *Journal of World Trade Law*, 12 (1978), 93–106.

—— *The World Trading System: Law and Policy of International Economic Relations* (Cambridge, MA: MIT Press, 1997).

Jackson, Peter, 'Pierre Bourdieu, the "Cultural Turn" and the Practice of International History', *Review of International Studies*, 34 (2008), 1, 155–81.

Jales, Mario, *Tariff Reductions, Special Products, and Special Safeguards: An Analysis of the Agricultural Tariff Structures of G-33 Countries* (Geneva: International Centre for Trade and Sustainable Development, June 2005).

—— 'How Would A Trade Deal On Cotton Affect Exporting And Importing Countries?', Issue paper 26 (Geneva: International Centre for Trade and Sustainable Development, May 2010).

Jawara, Fatoumata, and Kwa, Aileen, *Behind the Scenes at the WTO: The Real World of International Trade Negotiations* (London: Zed Books, 2003).

—— *Behind the Scenes at the WTO: The Real World of International Trade Negotiations/ Lessons of Cancún* (London: Zed Books, 2004).

Johnston, Alastair Iain, 'Conclusions and Extensions: Toward Mid-Range Theorizing and Beyond Europe', *International Organization*, 59 (2005), 4, 1013–44.

—— *Social States: China in International Institutions, 1980–2000* (Princeton: Princeton University Press, 2008).

Jones, Emily, Deere-Birkbeck, Carolyn, and Woods, Ngaire, *Manoeuvring at the Margins: Constraints Faced by Small States in International Trade Negotiations* (London: Commonwealth Secretariat, 2010).

Jones, Kent, 'Green Room Politics and the WTO's Crisis of Representation', *Progress in Development Studies*, 9 (2009), 4, 349–57.

—— *The Doha Blues: Institutional Crisis and Reform in the WTO* (Oxford: Oxford University Press, 2010).

Jönsson, Christer, and Hall, Martin, *Essence of Diplomacy* (Basingstoke: Palgrave Macmillan, 2005).

Kant, Immanuel, 'Perpetual Peace: A Philosophical Sketch' [1795], in H. S. Reiss (ed.), *Kant: Political Writings* (Cambridge: Cambridge University Press, 2003).

Kantorowicz, Ernst H., *The King's Two Bodies: A Study in Mediaeval Political Theology* (Princeton: Princeton University Press, 1957).

Karagiannis, Giannis, 'The EU Cotton Policy Regime and the Implications of the Proposed Changes for Producer Welfare', Food and Agriculture Organization of the United Nations Commodity and Trade Policy Research Working Paper 9 (Rome: FAO, April 2004).

Karapinar, Baris, and Häberli, Christian (eds.), *Food Crises and the WTO* (Cambridge: Cambridge University Press, 2010).

Keene, Karlyn H., Kirk Jr., Paul G., Ornstein, Norman, Rollins, Edward J., and Makin, John H., 'The Meaning of Competitiveness', in Claude E. Barfield and John H. Makin (eds.), *Trade Policy and U.S. Competitiveness* (Washington, DC: American Enterprise Institute, 1987).

Kelly, Michael (ed.), *Critique and Power: Recasting the Foucault/Habermas Debate* (Cambridge, MA: MIT Press, 1994).

Kelsey, Jane, *Serving Whose Interests? The Political Economy of Trade in Services Agreements* (Abingdon: Routledge-Cavendish, 2008).

Kennedy, David, 'The Disciplines of International Law and Policy', *Leiden Journal of International Law*, 12 (1999), 1, 9–134.

Keohane, Robert, 'Reciprocity in International Relations', *International Organization*, 40 (1986), 1, 1–27.

—— 'Governance in a Partially Globalized World', *American Political Science Review*, 95 (2001), 1, 1–13.

Keohane, Robert, and Nye, Joseph, 'The Club Model of Multilateral Cooperation and the World Trade Organization: Problems of Democratic Legitimacy', in Roger Porter, Pierre Sauve, Arvind Subramanian, and Americo Beviglia Zampetti (eds.), *Efficiency, Equity, and, Legitimacy: The Multilateral Trading System at the Millennium* (Cambridge, MA: Brookings Institution Press, 2001).

Khor, Martin, 'Analysis of the Collapse of the Cancun Ministerial', *Third World Network Info Service*, 16 September 2003.

—— 'Lamy Still Insists that Singapore Issues are Part of Doha Single Undertaking; Report of Panel Discussion at the UN on WTO and Cancun', *Third World Network Info Service*, 7 November 2003.

—— 'US–EC Agriculture Paper Not Acceptable as Basis for Negotiations, Say Developing Countries', *Third World Network Info Reports*, 14 August 2003.

—— 'G33 Criticises Agriculture Process and US Proposal', *Third World Network Info Reports*, 18 October 2005.

—— 'Agriculture Talks at Boiling Point Over Special Products', *Third World Network Info Reports*, 9 May 2006.

—— 'Heated Fight on Policy Space Dominates UNCTAD Review', *Third World Network Info Service on WTO and Trade Issues*, 13 May 2006.

—— 'Pakistan's SP Paper Causes Stir as WTO Agriculture Talks Resume', *Third World Network Info Reports*, 26 April 2007.

—— 'Agriculture: Recent Developments in SPs', *Third World Network Info Reports*, 28 January 2008.

—— 'Reflections Begin on the WTO Failure and the Future Work', *South–North Development Monitor (SUNS) Report #6530*, 4 August 2008.

Kindleberger, Charles P., 'The Rise of Free Trade in Western Europe, 1820–1875', *Journal of Economic History*, 35 (1975), 1, 20–55.

Klandermans, Bert, de Weerd, Marga, and Costa, Jose-Manuel, 'Injustice and Adversarial Frames in a Supranational Political Context: Farmers' Protest in the Netherlands and Spain', in Donatella della Porta, Hanspeter Kriesi, and Dieter Rucht (eds.), *Social Movements in a Globalizing World* (Basingstoke: Macmillan, 1999).

Klotz, Audie, 'Case Selection', in Audie Klotz and Deepa Prakash (eds.), *Qualitative Methods in International Relations: A Pluralist Guide* (Basingstoke: Palgrave Macmillan, 2008).

Knei-Paz, Baruch, *The Social and Political Thought of Leon Trotsky* (Oxford: Oxford University Press, 1978).

Kornprobst, Markus, 'Argumentation and Compromise: Ireland's Selection of the Territorial Status Quo Norm', *International Organization*, 61 (2007), 1, 69–98.

Krasner, Stephen, 'State Power and the Structure of International Trade', *World Politics*, 28 (1976), 3, 317–47.

Kratochwil, Friedrich V., *Rules, Norms, and Decisions: On the Conditions of Practical and Legal Reasoning in International Relations and Domestic Affairs* (Cambridge: Cambridge University Press, 1989).

Kripke, Gawain, 'King Cotton: Abdicate or Subjugate? The Political Economy of US Cotton and Prospects for a Pro-development Policy Reform', in Eric Hazard (ed.), *International Trade Negotiations and Poverty Reduction: The White Paper on Cotton* (Dakar: Enda Prospectives Dialogues Politiques, 2005).

Krugman, Paul, 'What Should Trade Negotiators Negotiate About?', *Journal of Economic Literature*, 35 (1997), 1, 113–20.

Kwa, Aileen, 'Development Box: Can It Adequately Address the Agricultural Crisis in Developing Countries?', paper presented at Like Minded Group meeting, Geneva, 10 April 2002.

—— *Power Politics in the WTO* (Bangkok: Focus on the Global South, 2003).

Kwa, Aileen, and Bello, Walden, *Guide to the Agreement on Agriculture: Technicalities and Trade Tricks Explained* (Bangkok: Focus on the Global South, December 1998).

Laffey, Mark, and Weldes, Jutta, 'Beyond Belief: Ideas and Symbolic Technologies in the Study of International Relations', *European Journal of International Relations*, 3 (1997), 2, 193–237.

Lal, Deepak, *The Poverty of 'Development Economics'* (London: Institute of Economic Affairs, 1983).

Lamy, Pascal, 'Speech by Commissioner Lamy on the "Cotton Initiative" at the 5th WTO Ministerial Conference (Cancun)', 10 September 2003.

—— 'Result of the WTO Ministerial Conference in Cancún', Remarks to Plenary Session on the Ministerial Conference of the WTO in Cancún, Council of Europe, Strasbourg, 24 September 2003.

Lane, Jeremy, *Pierre Bourdieu: A Critical Introduction* (London: Pluto, 2000).

Lang, Andrew T. F., 'Reconstructing Embedded Liberalism: John Gerard Ruggie and Constructivist Approaches to the Study of the International Trade Regime', *Journal of International Economic Law*, 9 (2006), 1, 81–116.

—— 'Reflecting on Linkage: Cognitive and Institutional Change in the International Trading System', *Modern Law Review*, 70 (2007), 4, 523–50.

—— 'Legal Regimes and Regimes of Knowledge: Governing Global Services Trade', LSE Law, Society and Economy Working Paper Series, WPS 15-2009, July 2009.

—— *World Trade Law after Neoliberalism: Re-imagining the Global Economic Order* (Oxford: Oxford University Press, 2011).

Lawrence, Robert, 'China and the Multilateral Trading System', in Barry Eichengreen, Yung Chul Park, and Charles Wyplosz (eds.), *China, Asia, and the New World Economy* (Cambridge: Cambridge University Press, 2008).

Leander, Anna, 'Do We Really Need Reflexivity in IPE? Bourdieu's Two Reasons for Answering Affirmatively', *Review of International Political Economy*, 9 (2002), 4, 601–9.

Lebaron, Frédéric, 'Central Bankers in the Contemporary Global Field of Power: A "Social Space" Approach', in Mike Savage and Karel Williams (eds.), *Remembering Elites* (Oxford: Wiley-Blackwell, 2008).

Lee, Donna, 'The Cotton Club: The Africa Group in the Doha Development Agenda', in Donna Lee and Rorden Wilkinson (eds.), *The WTO After Hong Kong: Progress In, and Prospects For, the Doha Development Agenda* (London: Routledge, 2007).

Lee, Donna, and Smith, Nicola J., 'The Political Economy of Small African States in the WTO', *The Round Table*, 97 (2008), 395, 259–71.

Lee, Donna, and Wilkinson, Rorden (eds.), *The WTO After Hong Kong: Progress In, and Prospects For, the Doha Development Agenda* (Routledge: Abingdon, 2007).

Leebron, David, 'Linkage', *American Journal of International Law*, 96 (2002), 1, 5–27.

Ling, L. H. M., 'Cultural Chauvinism and the Liberal International Order: "West vs Rest" in Asia's Financial Crisis', in G. Chowdhry and S. Nair (eds.), *Power, Postcolonialism and International Relations: Reading Race, Gender and Class* (London: Routledge, 2002).

Little, Ian Malcolm David, Scitovsky, Tibor, and FitzGerald, Maurice, *Industry and Trade in Some Developing Countries: A Comparative Study* (Oxford: Oxford University Press for the OECD Development Centre, 1970).

Little, Richard, *The Balance of Power in International Relations: Metaphors, Myths and Models* (Cambridge: Cambridge University Press, 2007).

Love, Patrick, and Lattimore, Ralph G., *International Trade: Free, Fair, and Open?* (Paris: Organisation for Economic Co-operation and Development, 2009).

Lukes, Steven, *Power: A Radical View* (Basingstoke: Palgrave Macmillan, 2005).

—— 'Reply to Comments', *Political Studies Review*, 4 (2006), 2, 164–73.

Mably, Paul, 'The Role of Research on Trade Policy Changes Affecting the Developing World: Group of 33 Influence at the World Trade Organization', Working Paper 77 (Buenos Aires: Latin American Trade Network, May 2007).

—— 'Centralized Production: The Group of G33', in Diana Tussie (ed.), *The Politics of Trade: The Role of Research in Trade Policy and Negotiations* (Ottawa: International Development Research Centre, 2009).

McAdam, Doug, McCarthy, John, and Zald, Mayer, 'Introduction: Opportunities, Mobilizing Structures, and Framing Processes—Towards a Synthetic, Comparative Perspective on Social Movements', in Doug McAdam, John McCarthy, and Mayer Zald (eds.), *Comparative Perspectives on Social Movements: Political Opportunities, Mobilizing Structures, and Cultural Framings* (Cambridge: Cambridge University Press, 1996).

McGinnis, John, and Movsesian, Mark, 'World Trade Constitution', *Harvard Law Review*, 114 (2000), 2, 511–605.

Machiavelli, Niccolò, *The Prince* (Oxford: Oxford University Press, 2008 [1532]).

Magnusson, Lars, *The Tradition of Free Trade* (Abingdon: Routledge, 2004).

Mahona, Rianne, and McBridea, Stephen, 'Standardizing and Disseminating Knowledge: The Role of the OECD in Global Governance', *European Political Science Review*, 1 (2009), 1, 83–101.

Malaysia, 'Discussion Paper on Special Products; Contribution by Malaysia', 23 March 2006, unpublished private paper.

March, James G., and Olsen, Johan P., *Rediscovering Institutions: The Organizational Basis of Politics* (New York: Free Press, 1989).

Martin, Lisa, and Simmons, Beth, 'Theories and Empirical Studies of International Institutions', *International Organization*, 52 (1998), 4, 729–58.

Marx, Karl, *Capital: Volume 1: A Critique of Political Economy* (London: Penguin Books, 1990 [1867]).

Maskus, Keith, *Intellectual Property Rights in the Global Economy* (Washington, DC: Institute for International Economics, 2000).

Mattern, Janice Bially, 'The Concept of Power and the (Un)discipline of International Relations', in Christian Reus-Smit and Duncan Snidal (eds.), *The Oxford Handbook of International Relations* (Oxford: Oxford University Press, 2008).

Mauss, Marcel, *The Gift: The Form and Reason for Exchange in Archaic Societies* (Abingdon: Routledge, 2002 [1924]).

Maxwell, Simon, 'Food Security: A Post-modern Perspective', *Food Policy*, 21 (1996), 2, 155–70.

Mayer, Jörg, 'Policy Space: What, for What, and Where?', *Development Policy Review*, 27 (2009), 4, 373–95.

Meléndez-Ortiz, Ricardo, 'Foreword', in International Centre for Trade and Sustainable Development (ICTSD), *Special Products and the Special Safeguard Mechanism: Strategic Options for Developing Countries* (Geneva: ICTSD, December 2005).

Mérand, Frédéric, *European Defence Policy: Beyond the Nation State* (Oxford: Oxford University Press, 2008).

Messerlin, Patrick A., 'Enlarging the Vision for Trade Policy Space: Special and Differentiated and Infant Industry Issues', *World Economy*, 29 (2006), 10, 1395–407.

Mill, James, *Elements of Political Economy* (London: Baldwin, Cradock, & Joy, 1821).

Minot, Nicholas, and Daniels, Lisa, 'Impact of Global Cotton Markets on Rural Poverty in Benin', *Agricultural Economics*, 33 (2005), 3, 453–66.

Mishler, Elliot, *Research Interviewing: Context and Narrative* (Cambridge, MA: Harvard University Press, 1991).

Monke, Jim, 'Farm Commodity Programs in the 2008 Farm Bill', CRS Report for Congress (Washington, DC: Congressional Research Service, 23 July 2008).

Moore, Michael, *Ten Years of the WTO: A Success Story of Global Governance* (Bonn: Friedrich-Ebert-Stiftung, 2005).

Morgan, Peter, 'Technical Assistance: Correcting the Precedents', *Development Policy Journal* (UNDP), December 2002, 1–22.

Morgenthau, Hans, *Politics Among Nations: The Struggle for Power and Peace* (New York: Knopf, 1949).

Morriss, Peter, *Power: A Philosophical Analysis* (Manchester: Manchester University Press, 2002 [1987]).

Morton, Adam David, *Unravelling Gramsci: Hegemony and Passive Revolution in the Global Economy* (London: Pluto Press, 2007).

Mosoti, Victor, 'Africa in the First Decade of WTO Dispute Settlement', *Journal of International Economic Law*, 9 (2006), 2, 427–53.

Müller, Harald, 'Arguing, Bargaining and all that: Communicative Action, Rationalist Theory and the Logic of Appropriateness in International Relations', *European Journal of International Relations*, 10 (2004), 3, 395–435.

Murphy, Craig, 'Understanding IR: Understanding Gramsci', *Review of International Studies*, 24 (1998), 417–25.

—— *The United Nations Development Programme: A Better Way?* (Cambridge: Cambridge University Press, 2006).

Murphy, Sophia, and Suppan, Steve, *Introduction to the Development Box: Finding Space for Development Concerns in the WTO's Agriculture Negotiations* (Winnipeg: International Institute for Sustainable Development, 2003).

Myles, John, 'From Doxa to Experience: Issues in Bourdieu's Adoption of Husserlian Phenomenology', *Theory, Culture & Society*, 21 (2004), 2, 91–107.

—— 'Making Don't Knows Make Sense: Bourdieu, Phenomenology, and Opinion Polls', *The Sociological Review*, 56 (2008), 1, 102–16.

Mytelka, Lynn K., 'Knowledge and Structural Power in the International Political Economy', in Thomas Lawton, James Rosenau, and Amy C. Verdun (eds.), *Strange Power: Shaping the Parameters of International Relations and International Political Economy* (Aldershot: Ashgate Publishing Company, 2000).

Narlikar, Amrita, *International Trade and Developing Countries: Coalitions in the GATT and WTO* (London: Routledge, 2003).

—— *The World Trade Organization: A Very Short Introduction* (Oxford: Oxford University Press, 2005).

Narlikar, Amrita, and Odell, John S., 'The Strict Distributive Strategy for a Bargaining Coalition: The Like Minded Group in the World Trade Organization, 1998–2001', in John S. Odell (ed.), *Negotiating Trade: Developing Countries in the WTO and NAFTA* (Cambridge: Cambridge University Press, 2006).

Narlikar, Amrita, and Tussie, Diana, 'The G20 at the Cancun Ministerial: Developing Countries and their Evolving Coalitions in the WTO', *World Economy*, 27 (2004), 7, 947–66.

Narlikar, Amrita, and Wilkinson, Rorden, 'Collapse at the WTO: A Cancún Post Mortem', *Third World Quarterly*, 25 (2004), 3, 417–30.

National Cotton Council of America, 'NCC Lauds Cochran's Declaration on WTO Ag Trade Negotiations', Press release, 9 September 2003.

—— 'USTR Proposal on Trade Distortion Discussions Much Needed', Press release, 11 September 2003.

Nelen, Joost, 'Farmers' Organisations in West Africa: Emerging Stakeholders in Cotton Sector Reforms', in Giel Ton, Jos Bijman, and Joost Oorthuizen (eds.), *Producer Organisations and Market Chains: Facilitating Trajectories of Change in Developing Countries* (Wageningen: Wageningen Academic Publishers, 2007).

Neumann, Iver B., 'Returning Practice to the Linguistic Turn: The Case of Diplomacy', *Millennium: Journal of International Studies*, 31 (2002), 3, 627–51.

—— 'To Be a Diplomat', *International Studies Perspectives*, 6 (2005), 1, 72–93.

de Nigris, Maurizio, 'Defining and Quantifying the Extent of Import Surges: Data and Methodologies', Food and Agricultural Organization of the United Nations Import Surge Project, Working Paper 2 (Rome: FAO, May 2005).

Ocampo, José Antonio, and Parra, María Angela, 'The Terms Of Trade For Commodities In The Twentieth Century', *CEPAL Review*, 79 (2003), 7–35.

Odell, John S., 'Case Study Methods in International Political Economy', in Detlef F. Sprinz and Yael Wolinsky-Nahmias (eds.), *Models, Numbers and Cases: Methods for Studying International Relations* (Ann Arbor: University of Michigan Press, 2004).

Odell, John S., *Negotiating Trade: Developing Countries in the WTO and NAFTA* (Cambridge: Cambridge University Press, 2006).

—— 'Breaking Deadlocks in International Institutional Negotiations: The WTO, Seattle, and Doha', *International Studies Quarterly*, 53 (2009), 2, 273–99.

—— 'Negotiating from Weakness in International Trade Relations', *Journal of World Trade*, 44 (2010), 3, 545–66.

Odell, John, and Sell, Susan, 'Reframing the Issue: The WTO Coalition on Intellectual Property and Health, 2001', in John Odell (ed.), *Negotiating Trade: Developing Countries in the WTO and NAFTA* (Cambridge: Cambridge University Press, 2006).

Oduwole, Jumoke, 'Nothing Ventured, Nothing Gained? A Case Study of Africa's Participation in WTO Dispute Settlement', *International Journal of Private Law*, 2 (2009), 4, 358–70.

Omichessan, Arsene, 'Navigating the Dispute Settlement Understanding (DSU): How Benin Took on the Challenges in Cotton', International Centre for Trade and Sustainable Development Africa Dialogue on WTO Dispute Settlement and Sustainable Development, Mombasa, Kenya, 2–3 November 2006.

Organisation for Economic Co-operation and Development (OECD), *Agricultural Policies in OECD Countries: Monitoring and Evaluation 2005* (Paris: OECD, 2005).

Organisation for Economic Co-operation and Development (OECD) and Food and Agricultural Organization of the United Nations (FAO), *OECD–FAO Agricultural Outlook 2010–2019* (Paris: OECD–FAO, 2010).

Organisation for Economic Co-operation and Development (OECD), Sahel and West Africa Club, *Cotton in West Africa: The Development Dimension* (Paris: OECD, 2006).

Orwell, George, *Shooting an Elephant and Other Essays* (London: Penguin, 2009 [1950]).

Ostry, Sylvia, 'Cancun: Can Can't? Can Do?', paper presented at 'Building the Americas' Conference, Centre for International Studies and Globalization, Montreal, 5–7 November 2003.

Owen, David, 'The United Nations Program of Technical Assistance', *Annals of the American Academy of Political and Social Science*, 270 (1950), 109–17.

Oxfam International, *Cultivating Poverty: The Impact of US Cotton Subsidies on Africa*, Oxfam Briefing Paper 30 (Oxford: Oxfam International, September 2002).

—— *A Raw Deal for Rice Under DR-CAFTA: How the Free Trade Agreement Threatens the Livelihoods of Central American Farmers* (Oxford: Oxfam International, November 2004).

Page, Shelia, 'The Evolution of Special and Differential Treatment in the Multilateral Trading System', paper presented at International Centre for Trade and Sustainable Development (ICTSD) Workshop, Geneva, 6 December 2004.

Page, Shelia, and Kleen, Peter, *Special and Differential Treatment of Developing Countries in the World Trade Organization* (Stockholm: EGDI, Ministry for Foreign Affairs, Sweden, 2004).

Palen, Ronen, 'The Constructivist Underpinnings of the New International Political Economy', in Ronen Palen (ed.), *Global Political Economy: Contemporary Theories* (London: Routledge, 2000).

Parsons, Talcott, 'On the Concept of Political Power', *Proceedings of the American Philosophical Society*, 107 (1963), 3, 232–62.

Partridge, Eric, *Origins: A Short Etymological Dictionary of Modern English* (London: Routledge, 1977).

Paterson, Bill, 'Trasformismo at the World Trade Organization', in Mark McNally and John Schwarzmantel (eds.), *Gramsci and Global Politics: Hegemony and Resistance* (London: Routledge, 2009).

Pauwelyn, Joost, 'The Transformation of World Trade', *Michigan Law Review*, 104 (2005), 1, 1–66.

Payne, Rodger, 'Persuasion, Frames and Norm Construction', *European Journal of International Relations*, 7 (2001), 1, 37–61.

Pesche, Denis, and Nubukpo, Kato, 'The African Cotton Set in Cancún: A Look Back at the Beginning of Negotiations', in Eric Hazard (ed.), *International Trade Negotiations and Poverty Reduction: The White Paper on Cotton* (Dakar: Enda Prospectives Dialogues Politiques, 2005).

Petersmann, Ernst-Ulrich, *Constitutional Functions and Constitutional Problems of International Economic Law* (Fribourg: Fribourg University Press, 1991).

—— 'The WTO Constitution and Human Rights', *Journal of International Economic Law*, 3 (2000), 1, 19–25.

Piiparinen, Touko, 'The Rise and Fall of Bureaucratic Rationalization: Exploring the Possibilities and Limitations of the UN Secretariat in Conflict Prevention', *European Journal of International Relations*, 14 (2008), 4, 697–724.

Polanyi, Karl, *The Great Transformation: The Political and Economic Origins of Our Time* (Boston: Beacon Press, 2001 [1944]).

Polaski, Sandra, 'Agricultural Negotiations at the WTO: First, Do No Harm', Policy Outlook (Washington, DC: Carnegie Endowment for International Peace, June 2005).

—— *Winners and Losers: Impact of the Doha Round on Developing Countries* (Washington, DC: Carnegie Endowment for International Peace, March 2006).

Pollack, Mark, *Engines of European Integration: Delegation, Agency, and Agenda Setting in the EU* (Oxford: Oxford University Press, 2003).

Pop, Liliana, 'Time and Crisis: Framing Success and Failure in Romania's Post-communist Transformations', *Review of International Studies*, 33 (2007), 3, 395–413.

Poulantzas, Nicos, *Political Power and Social Classes* (London: Verso, 1987 [1968]).

Pouliot, Vincent, 'The Logic of Practicality: A Theory of Practice of Security Communities', *International Organization*, 62 (2008), 2, 257–88.

—— *International Security in Practice: The Politics of NATO–Russia Diplomacy* (Cambridge: Cambridge University Press, 2010).

Poupeau, Franck, 'Reasons for Domination, Bourdieu versus Habermas', in Bridget Fowler (ed.), *Reading Bourdieu on Society and Culture* (Oxford: Blackwell, 2000).

Poupeau, Franck, and Discepolo, Thierry, 'Scholarship with Commitment: On the Political Engagements of Pierre Bourdieu', *Constellations*, 11 (2004), 1, 76–96.

Priyadarshi, Shishir, 'Agriculture Text Poor on Core Development Concerns', *South Bulletin*, 24/25, 30 November 2001, 13–15.

Prowse, Susan, 'The Role of International and National Agencies in Trade-related Capacity Building', *World Economy*, 25 (2002), 9, 1235–61.

Qureshi, Asif, *The World Trade Organisation: Implementing International Trade Norms* (Manchester: Manchester University Press, 1996).

Ragin, Charles, and Becker, Howard, *What Is a Case? Exploring the Foundations of Social Inquiry* (Cambridge: Cambridge University Press, 1992).

Raja, Kanaga, 'Kamal Nath Sets Conditions for Success of WTO Talks', *South–North Development Monitor*, 23 July 2008, <http://www.sunsonline.org/index.php>.

—— '100 Developing Countries in Show of Strength on SP, SSM', *South–North Development Monitor*, 28 July 2008, <http://www.sunsonline.org/index.php>.

—— 'Kamal Nath Explains How the Geneva Talks Failed', *South–North Development Monitor*, 31 July 2008, <http://www.sunsonline.org/index.php>.

—— 'Schwab Still Blaming India and China at Press Briefing', *South–North Development Monitor*, 31 July 2008, <http://www.sunsonline.org/index.php>.

—— 'India, China, Brazil Leadership Key to Doha Success or Failure, says US', *Third World Network Info Service*, 27 May 2010, <http://www.sunsonline.org/index.php>.

Report by the Consultative Board to the Director-General Supachai Panitchpakdi, *The Future of the WTO: Addressing Institutional Challenges in the New Millennium* (Geneva: WTO, 2004).

Report of the Cotton Initiative, Heads of Delegations (HOD) Meeting, 12 September 2003, <http://www.wto.org/english/thewto_e/minist_e/min03_e/min03_12sept_e.htm>.

Ricardo, David, *On the Principles of Political Economy and Taxation* (New York: Dover Publications, 2004 [1817].

Risse, Thomas, '"Let's Argue!": Communicative Action in World Politics', *International Organization*, 54 (2000), 1, 1–39.

Rist, Gilbert, *The History of Development: From Western Origins to Global Faith* (London: Zed Books, 2008).

Rodríguez, Francisco, and Rodrik, Dani, 'Trade Policy and Economic Growth: A Skeptic's Guide to the Cross-National Evidence', *NBER Macroeconomics Annual*, 15 (2000), 261–325.

Rodrik, Dani, 'Goodbye Washington Consensus, Hello Washington Confusion? A Review of the World Bank's Economic Growth in the 1990s: Learning from a Decade of Reform', *Journal of Economic Literature*, 44 (2006), 4, 973–87.

Rosenow, Doerthe, 'Decentring Global Power: The Merits of a Foucauldian Approach to International Relations', *Global Society*, 23 (2009), 4, 497–517.

Ruggie, John Gerard, 'International Regimes, Transactions, and Change: Embedded Liberalism in the Postwar Economic Order', *International Organization*, 36 (1982), 2, 379–415.

Rupert, Mark, 'Globalising Common Sense: A Marxian-Gramscian (Re-)vision of the Politics of Governance/Resistance', *Review of International Studies*, 29 (2003), S1, 181–98.

Sachs, Jeffrey D., and Warner, Andrew M., 'Economic Reform and the Process of Global Integration', *Brookings Papers on Economic Activity* (1995), 1, 1–118.

Sahel and West Africa Club Secretariat/OECD, *Economic and Social Importance of Cotton in West Africa: Role of Cotton in Development, Trade and Livelihoods* (Paris: SWAC/OECD, 2005).

Sampson, Garry, and Chambers, W. Bradnee (eds.), *Developing Countries and the WTO: Policy Approaches* (Tokyo: United Nations University Press, 2008).

Sartori, Giovanni, 'Concept Misformation in Comparative Politics', *The American Political Science Review*, 64 (1970), 4, 1033–53.

Sartre, Jean-Paul, *L'idiot de la famille* (Paris: Gallimard, 1971).

Schattschneider, Elmer Eric, *The Semi-Sovereign People: A Realist's View of Democracy in America* (New York: Holt, Rinehart and Winston, 1960).

Schimmelfennig, Frank, 'The Community Trap: Liberal Norms, Rhetorical Action, and the Eastern Enlargement of the European Union', *International Organization*, 55 (2001), 1, 47–80.

—— *The EU, NATO and the Integration of Europe: Rules and Rhetoric* (Cambridge: Cambridge University Press, 2003).

Schwab, Ambassador Susan C., United States Trade Representative, 'Remarks on the Doha Development Agenda', National Press Club, Washington, DC, 7 July 2006, <http://2001-2009.state.gov/e/eeb/rls/rm/2006/68896.htm>.

Sell, Susan, *Private Power, Public Law: The Globalization of Intellectual Property Rights* (Cambridge: Cambridge University Press, 2003).

Sewell, William H., 'A Theory of Structure: Duality, Agency, and Transformation', *The American Journal of Sociology*, 98 (1992), 1, 1–29.

Shaffer, Gregory, *Defending Interests: Public–Private Partnerships in WTO Litigation* (Washington, DC: Brookings Institution Press, 2003).

—— 'Can WTO Technical Assistance and Capacity-Building Serve Developing Countries?' in Ernst-Ulrich Petersmann (ed.), *Reforming the World Trading System: Legitimacy, Efficiency, and Democratic Governance* (Oxford: Oxford University Press, 2005).

—— 'The Role of the WTO Director-General and Secretariat', *World Trade Review*, 4 (2005), 3, 429–38.

—— 'The Challenges of WTO Law: Strategies for Developing Country Adaptation', *World Trade Review*, 5 (2006), 2, 177–98.

Shahin, Magda, 'The Cotton Initiative', in Gary Sampson and W. Bradnee Chambers (eds.) *Developing Countries and the WTO: Policy Approaches* (Tokyo: United Nations University Press, 2008).

Shaw, D. John, *World Food Security: A History since 1945* (Basingstoke: Palgrave Macmillan, 2007).

Simon, Herbert A., 'Notes on the Observation and Measurement of Political Power', *Journal of Politics*, 15 (1953), 500–16.

Sinclair, Timothy J., *The New Masters of Capital: American Bond Rating Agencies and the Politics of Creditworthiness* (Ithaca: Cornell University Press, 2005).

Smith, Adam, *An Inquiry into the Nature and Causes of the Wealth of Nations* (Oxford: Oxford University Press, 1993 [1776]).

Smith, Fiona, 'Non-Trade Concerns and Agriculture in the Post-Doha Environment: Thinking Outside the Green Box', *Environmental Law Review*, 9 (2007), 2, 89–115.

Sneyd, Adam, *Governing Cotton: Globalization and Poverty in Africa* (Basingstoke: Palgrave Macmillan, 2011).

Snow, David, and Benford, Robert, 'Ideology, Frame Resonance, and Participant Mobilization', *International Social Movement Research*, 1 (1998), 197–217.

Snow, David, Rochford, E. Burke, Worden, Steven, and Benford, Robert, 'Frame Alignment Processes, Micromobilization and Movement Participation', *American Sociological Review*, 51 (1986), 464–81.

Sprout, Harold, and Sprout, Margaret, *Foundations of National Power* (Princeton: Princeton University Press, 1945).

Steinberg, Richard, 'In the Shadow of Law or Power? Consensus-Based Bargaining and Outcomes in the GATT/WTO', *International Organization*, 56 (2002), 2, 339–74.

—— 'United States: Subsidies on Upland Cotton, WTO Doc. WT/DS267/AB/R', *American Journal of International Law*, 99 (2005), 4, 852–61.

Stevens, Christopher, 'The Need for Special Products and Special Safeguard Mechanisms for Agriculture in the WTO: A Situational Analysis', paper presented at International Centre for Trade and Sustainable Development (ICTSD) Informal Consultation, 'Special Products and Special Safeguard Mechanism after the July Framework: How Do We Move Forward?', Geneva, 30 September 2004.

Stevens, Christopher, Kennan, Jane, and Meyn, Mareike, *South–South Trade in Special Products* (Geneva: International Centre for Trade and Sustainable Development, June 2007).

Stewart, Terence P. (ed.), *The GATT Uruguay Round: A Negotiating History (1986–1992); Volume 1: Commentary* (Deventer: Kluwer Law and Taxation Publishers, 1999).

Stirrat, R. L., and Henkel, Heiko, 'The Development Gift: The Problem of Reciprocity in the NGO World', *The Annals of the American Academy of Political and Social Science*, 554 (1997), 1, 66–80.

Strange, Susan, *States and Markets: An Introduction to International Political Economy* (London: Pinter, 1988).

Structural Adjustment Participatory Review International Network (SAPRIN), *Structural Adjustment: The SAPRI Report: The Policy Roots of Economic Crisis, Poverty and Inequality* (London: Zed Books, 2004).

Sumner, Daniel, 'A Quantitative Simulation Analysis of the Impacts of U.S. Cotton Subsidies on Cotton Prices and Quantities', mimeo, Department of Agricultural and Resource Economics, University of California: Davis, 2003.

—— 'Reducing Cotton Subsidies: The DDA Cotton Initiative', in Kym Anderson and Will Martin (eds.), *Agricultural Trade Reform and the Doha Development Agenda* (Washington, DC: World Bank, 2006).

Swartz, David, *Culture and Power: A Sociology of Pierre Bourdieu* (Chicago: University of Chicago Press, 1998).

Taylor, Ian, 'Hegemony, Neoliberal "Good Governance" and the International Monetary Fund: A Gramscian Perspective', in Morten Bøås and Desmond McNeill (eds.), *Global Institutions and Development: Framing the World?* (London: Routledge, 2004).

Therien, Jean-Philippe, 'Beyond the North–South Divide: The Two Tales of World Poverty', *Third World Quarterly*, 20 (1999), 4, 723–42.

Thompson, John B., *Studies in the Theory of Ideology* (Cambridge: Polity Press, 1984).

Thurow, Roger, and Kilman, Scott, 'Hanging by a Thread: In U.S., Cotton Farmers Thrive; in Africa, They Fight to Survive', *Wall Street Journal*, 26 June 2002.

Touré, Amadou Toumani, and Compaoré, Blaise, 'Your Farm Subsidies are Strangling Us', *New York Times*, 11 July 2003.

Townsend, Terry, 'World Cotton Situation', paper presented at WTO Director-General's Framework Mechanism on Cotton, 11th Round of Consultations, 24 April 2009, Geneva.

Toye, John, 'Poverty Reduction', *Development in Practice*, 17 (2007), 4–5, 505–10.

Tussie, Diana, *The Less Developed Countries and the World Trading System: A Challenge to the GATT* (London: Francis Pinter, 1985).

Uchatius, Wolfgang, 'Der Norden sät den Hunger', *Die Zeit*, 14 August 2003.

Ulbert, Cornelia, and Risse, Thomas, 'Deliberately Changing the Discourse: What Does Make Arguing Effective?', *Acta Politica*, 40 (2005), 351–67.

Ulbert, Cornelia, Risse, Thomas, and Müller, Harald, *Arguing and Bargaining in Multilateral Negotiations* (Berlin: Center for Transnational Relations, Foreign and Security Policy, May 2004).

United Nations Conference on Trade and Development (UNCTAD), *Trade and Development Report* (Geneva: UNCTAD, 2002).

—— *Trade and Development Report* (Geneva: UNCTAD, 2006).

—— *Green Box Subsidies: A Theoretical and Empirical Assessment* (Geneva: UNCTAD, May 2007).

United Nations Non-governmental Liaison Service (NGLS), 'Build-Up to the Third WTO Ministerial Conference', *NGLS Roundup*, 39, July 1999, <http://www.un-ngls.org/orf/documents/text/roundup/39wto.txt>.

United States House of Representatives, Hearing before the Subcommittee on Africa, Committee on International Relations, One Hundred Eighth Congress, First Session, 24 June 2003, Serial No: 108–130.

United States Trade Representative Press Release, 'U.S., Brazil Agree Upon Path Toward Negotiated Solution of Cotton Dispute', 4 June 2010.

Uruguay Round Agreements, Agreement on Agriculture (AoA).

Uruguay Round Agreements, 'Decision on Measures Concerning the Possible Negative Effects of the Reform Programme on Least-Developed and Net Food-Importing Developing Countries'.

Valdés, Alberto, and Foster, William, *The New SSM: A Price Floor Mechanism for Developing Countries* (Geneva: International Centre for Trade and Sustainable Development, July 2005).

Veiga, Pedro da Motta, 'Brazil and the G-20 Group of Developing Countries', in Peter Gallagher, Patrick Low, and Andrew L. Stoler (eds.), *Managing the Challenges of WTO Participation: 45 Case Studies* (Cambridge: Cambridge University Press, 2005).

Viner, Jacob, 'Power Versus Plenty as Objectives of Foreign Policy in the Seventeenth and Eighteenth Centuries', *World Politics*, 1 (1948), 1, 1–29.

—— *Essays on the Intellectual History of Economics*, ed. Douglas Irwin (Princeton: Princeton University Press, 1991).

Wacquant, Loïc, 'Reading Bourdieu's "Capital"', *International Journal of Contemporary Sociology*, 33 (1996), 2, 151–69.

—— 'Pierre Bourdieu', in R. Stones (ed.), *Key Sociological Thinkers* (Basingstoke: Palgrave Macmillan, 1998).

—— 'On Symbolic Power and Group-Making: Pierre Bourdieu's Reframing of Class', Preface to Pierre Bourdieu, *Et klassespørsmål* (Oslo: Forlaget Manifest, 2007).

Wacquant, Loïc, *Urban Outcasts: A Comparative Sociology of Advanced Marginality* (Cambridge: Polity Press, 2008).

—— *Punishing the Poor: The Neoliberal Government of Social Insecurity* (Durham, NC: Duke University Press, 2009).

Wade, Robert, *Governing the Market: Economic Theory and the Role of Government in East Asian Industrialization* (Princeton: Princeton University Press, 2002).

—— 'What Strategies are Viable for Developing Countries Today? The World Trade Organization and the Shrinking of "Development Space"', *Review of International Political Economy*, 10 (2003), 4, 621–44.

Wallach, Lori and Sforza, Michelle, *Whose Trade Organization?: Corporate Globalization and the Erosion of Democracy* (Washington, DC: Public Citizen, 1999).

Waltz, Kenneth, *Theory of International Politics* (London: McGraw-Hill, 1979).

Watkins, Kevin, and Mahmood, Akhtar, 'WTO Negotiations on Agriculture: What Can Be Achieved?', in Thomas Lines (ed.), *Agricultural Commodities, Trade and Sustainable Development* (Geneva: International Centre for Trade and Sustainable Development/ London: International Institute for Environment and Development, 2005).

Weber, Max, *Economy and Society, Volume 1* (Berkeley: University of California Press, 1978 [1922]).

—— 'The Meaning of Discipline', in H. Gerth and C. Wright Mills (eds.), *From Max Weber: Essays in Sociology* (London: Routledge, 1991).

Weiler, Joseph, 'The Rule of Lawyers and the Ethos of Diplomats: Reflection on the Internal and External Legitimacy of Dispute Settlement', in Roger B. Porter, Pierre Sauvé, Arvind Subramanian, and Americo Beviglia Zampetti (eds.), *Efficiency, Equity, and Legitimacy: The Multilateral Trading System at the Millennium* (Washington, DC: Brookings Institution Press, 2001).

Weintraub, Sidney, 'Theory and Practice in the Conduct of Trade Policy', in William Alexander Kerr and James D. Gaisford (eds.), *Handbook on International Trade Policy* (Cheltenham: Edward Elgar Publishing, 2007).

Wight, Martin, *Power Politics* (London: Royal Institute for International Affairs, 1946).

Wilkinson, Rorden, 'The Political Economy of International Economic Law: A Neo-Gramscian Perspective', in Asif Qureshi (ed.), *Perspectives in International Economic Law* (London: Kluwer Law International, 2002).

—— 'Crisis in Cancún', *Global Governance*, 10 (2004), 2, 149–55.

—— *The WTO: Crisis and the Governance of Global Trade* (Abingdon: Routledge, 2006).

—— 'Language, Power and Multilateral Trade Negotiations', *Review of International Political Economy*, 16 (2009), 4, 597–619.

Wilkinson, Rorden, and Scott, James, 'Developing Country Participation in the GATT: A Reassessment', *World Trade Review*, 7 (2008), 3, 473–510.

Williams, Michael, *Culture and Security: Symbolic Power and the Politics of International Security* (London: Routledge, 2007).

Wilson, Gorden 'Knowledge, Innovation and Re-inventing Technical Assistance for Development', *Progress in Development Studies*, 7 (2007), 3, 183–99.

Winters, Alan, 'Trade Liberalisation and Economic Performance: An Overview', *The Economic Journal*, 114 (2004), 493, F4–F21.

Winters, Alan, McCulloch, Neil, and McKay, Andrew, 'Trade Liberalization and Poverty: The Evidence So Far', *Journal of Economic Literature*, 42 (2004), 1, 72–115.

Wise, Timothy A., and Gallagher, Kevin P., 'The Doha Round's Development Impacts: Shrinking Gains and Real Costs', RIS Policy Brief 19, November 2005.

Wittgenstein, Ludwig, *Philosophical Investigations* (Oxford: Basil Blackwell, 1972 [1953]).

Wolfe, Robert, 'Informal Political Engagement in the WTO: Are Mini-Ministerials a Good Idea?', in John Curtis and Dan Ciuriak (eds.), *Trade Policy Research 2004* (Canada: Minister of Public Works and Government Services, 2004).

—— 'Decision-Making and Transparency in the "Medieval" WTO: Does the Sutherland Report have the Right Prescription?', *Journal of International Economic Law*, 8 (2005), 3, 631–45.

—— 'See You in Geneva? Legal (Mis)Representations of the Trading System', *European Journal of International Relations*, 11 (2005), 3, 339–65.

—— 'Sprinting During a Marathon: Why the WTO Ministerial Failed in July 2008', Groupe d'Économie Mondiale, Science Po Working Paper, April 2009.

—— 'The Special Safeguard Fiasco in the WTO: The Perils of Inadequate Analysis and Negotiation', *World Trade Review*, 8 (2009), 4, 517–44.

—— 'The WTO Single Undertaking as Negotiating Technique and Constitutive Metaphor', *Journal of International Economic Law*, 12 (2009), 4, 835–58.

Woll, Cornelia, *Firm Interests: How Governments Shape Business Lobbying on Global Trade* (Ithaca: Cornell University Press, 2008).

Womach, Jasper, 'Cotton Production and Support in the United States', CRS Report for Congress (Washington, DC: Congressional Research Service, 24 June 2004).

World Bank, *World Development Report 2008: Agriculture for Development* (Washington, DC: World Bank, 2007).

WTO, 'Annual Monitoring Exercise in Respect of the Follow-up to the Ministerial Decision on Measures Concerning the Possible Negative Effects of the Reform Programme on Least-Developed and Net Food-Importing Developing Countries; Statement by the Representative of the World Bank', 18 December 1997, not coded.

—— 'Preparations for the 1999 Ministerial Conference; Agriculture; Proposal under Paragraphs 9(a)(i) and 9(a)(ii) of the Geneva Ministerial Declaration', Communication from Cuba, Dominican Republic, Egypt, El Salvador, Honduras, Sri Lanka, Uganda, and Zimbabwe, 15 October 1999 (WT/GC/W/374).

—— 'Agreement on Agriculture: Special and Differential Treatment and a Development Box', Proposal to the June 2000 Special Session of the Committee on Agriculture by Cuba, Dominican Republic, Honduras, Pakistan, Haiti, Nicaragua, Kenya, Uganda, Zimbabwe, Ski Lanka, and El Salvador, 23 June 2000 (G/AG/NG/W/13).

—— 'EC Comprehensive Negotiating Proposal', 14 December 2000 (G/AG/NG/W/90).

—— 'Negotiating Proposal by Japan on WTO Agricultural Negotiations', 21 December 2000 (G/AG/NG/W/91).

—— 'Negotiations on WTO Agreement on Agriculture; Proposals by India in the Areas of: (i) Food Security, (ii) Market Access, (iii) Domestic Support, and (iv) Export Competition', 15 January 2001 (G/AG/NG/W/102).

—— 'Ministerial Declaration', Ministerial Conference, Fourth Session, Doha, 20 November 2001 (WT/MIN(01)/DEC/1).

WTO, 'Special Agricultural Safeguard; Background Paper by the Secretariat; Revision', 19 February 2002 (G/AG/NG/S/9/Rev.1).

—— 'Negotiations on Agriculture; Overview', 18 December 2002, (TN/AG/6).

—— 'Negotiations on Agriculture; First Draft of Modalities for Further Commitments', 17 February 2003 (TN/AG/W/1).

—— 'Negotiations on Agriculture; First Draft of Modalities for the Further Commitments; Revision', 18 March 2003 (TN/AG/W/1/Rev. 1).

—— 'Poverty Reduction: Sectoral Initiative in Favour of Cotton: Joint proposal by Benin, Burkina Faso, Chad, and Mali', 16 May 2003 (TN/AG/GEN/4).

—— 'Minutes of Meeting', Trade Negotiations Committee, 10–11 June 2003, (TN/C/M/10).

—— 'Summary Report on the Eighteenth Meeting of the Committee on Agriculture Special Session; Note by the Secretariat', 18 July 2003 (TN/AG/R/8).

—— 'Joint Text of the European Communities and the United States, Agriculture', 13 August 2003 (JOB(03)/157).

—— 'Preparations for the Fifth Session of the Ministerial Conference, Draft Cancún Ministerial Text; Revision', 24 August 2003 (JOB(03)/150/Rev.1).

—— 'Ministers' Communiqué; Alliance for Strategic Products and Special Safeguard Mechanism', 9 September 2003 (WT/MIN(03)/14).

—— 'Preparations for the Fifth Session of the Ministerial Conference; Draft Cancún Ministerial Text; Second Revision', 13 September 2003 (JOB(03)/150/Rev.2).

—— 'Poverty Reduction: Sectoral Initiative on Cotton; Wording of Paragraph 27 of the Revised Draft Cancún Ministerial Text', Communication from Benin, 7 October 2003 (WT/GC/W/516).

—— 'Statements by the Chairman of the General Council and the Director-General; Informal Heads of Delegation Meeting', Press release, 14 October 2003.

—— News Item, 'General Council: Follow-up to the Cancún Ministerial Conference; Key Issues Clearer, Possible Solutions Becoming Visible—General Council Chair', 15 December 2003, <http://www.wto.org/english/news_e/news03_e/stat_gc_chair_15dec03_e.htm>.

—— General Council, 'Minutes of Meeting', 15–16 December 2003 (WT/GC/M/84).

—— 'Doha Work Programme; Decision Adopted by the General Council on 1 August 2004', 2 August 2004 (WT/L/579).

—— 'United States—Subsidies on Upland Cotton; Report of the Panel', 8 September 2004 (WT/DS267/R).

—— 'WTO African Regional Workshop on Cotton; Cotonou, Republic of Benin; 23–24 March 2004', Note by the Secretariat, 17 November 2004 (WT/L/587).

—— 'Establishment of the Sub-Committee on Cotton; Decision Adopted by the Committee on Agriculture, Special Session on 19 November 2004', 26 November 2004 (TN/AG/13).

—— 'United States—Subsidies on Upland Cotton; Report of the Appellate Body', 3 March 2005 (WT/DS267/AB/R).

—— 'Ouagadougou Declaration on the Cotton Situation Since the Adoption of the July 2004 Package', Communication from Burkina Faso, 7 April 2005 (TN/AG/SCC/GEN/1).

—— 'G33 Proposal on Special Products; Communication from G33', 3 June 2005 (JOB (05)/91).

—— 'Summary Report on the Fourth Meeting of the Sub-Committee on Cotton Held on 22 June 2005', Note by the Secretariat, 13 July 2005 (TN/AG/SCC/R/4).

—— 'Technical Assistance and Training Plan 2006', 16 September 2005 (WT/COMTD/W/142).

—— 'Proposal on the Modalities for the Designation and Treatment of Any Agricultural Product as a Special Product (SP) by Any Developing Country Member; Circulated at the Request of Indonesia', 22 November 2005 (JOB(05)/304).

—— 'Doha Work Programme; Ministerial Declaration; Adopted on 18 December 2005', 22 December 2005 (WT/MIN(05)/DEC).

—— 'Proposed Modalities for Cotton Under the Mandate of the Hong Kong Ministerial Decision; Communication from the Co-Sponsors of the Sectoral Initiative in Favour of Cotton', 1 March 2006 (TN/AG/SCC/GEN/4).

—— 'United States Communication on Special Agricultural Safeguard (SSG) and the Special Safeguard Mechanism (SSM) Article 5 of the Agreement on Agriculture', 24 April 2006 (JOB(06)/120).

—— 'Thailand Paper on Special Products', 2 May 2006 (JOB (06)/135).

—— 'United States Communication on Special Products', 3 May 2006 (JOB(06)/137).

—— 'United States—Subsidies on Upland Cotton; Recourse to Article 21.5 of the DSU by Brazil; Report of the Panel', 18 December 2007 (WT/DS267/RW).

—— 'Revised Draft Modalities for Agriculture', 10 July 2008 (TN/AG/W/4/Rev.3).

—— 'Revised Draft Modalities for Agriculture', 6 December 2008 (TN/AG/W/4/Rev.4).

—— 'Biennial Technical Assistance and Training Plan 2010–2011; Revision', 21 October 2009 (WT/COMTD/W/170/Rev.1).

—— 'Negotiating Group on Agriculture; Report by the Chairman, H.E. Mr. David Walker, to the Trade Negotiations Committee for the Purpose of the TNC Stocktaking Exercise', 22 March 2010 (TN/AG/25).

Yafa, Stephen, *Big Cotton: How A Humble Fiber Created Fortunes, Wrecked Civilizations, and Put America on the Map* (London: Penguin, 2005).

Zartman, William, and Rubin, Jeffrey (eds.), *Power and Negotiation* (Ann Arbor: University of Michigan Press, 2000).

Zoellick, Robert, 'America Will Not Wait for the Won't-Do Countries', *Financial Times*, 22 September 2003.

Zunckel, Hilton E., 'The African Awakening in *United States–Upland Cotton*', *Journal of World Trade*, 39 (2005), 6, 1071–93.

Index